ABBIE HOFFMAN

★ ★ ★

AMERICAN REBEL

"There is only one word to celebrate this revealing contribution to counter-cultural history—Yippie!"—Paul Krassner, *The Realist*

"If Abbie Hoffman was a lost cause, America was a lost cause. In superior U.S. spirit he made mistakes and changed the nation, imprinting an image of revolutionary / libertarian idealist / hard worker / noble citizen / on minds of generations. . . . Jezer's biography traces an inside history officially disremembered, of activist lineage, ins and outs, secret police thuggery, political adventures and cultural gambles that this radical genius lost and won attempting to win back the planet for the human spirit."—Allen Ginsberg

"Fascinating and eminently readable . . . surprisingly witty, absorbing, and even significant."—*Library Journal*

"Jezer's book reminds us, not only of Abbie Hoffman's funny and outrageous antics, but of his serious, important, and unique contribution to the movement for social justice in our time."—Howard Zinn, author, *A People's History of the United States*

"A painstakingly chronicled, linear, detailed and largely sympathetic book. . . . a worthy and useful record."—*Boston Globe*

"[Jezer] has ideal credentials for this biography, and he brings an intimacy and depth of knowledge to the task."—*The Progressive*

"A critical and sympathetic portrait of one of the 60s' most compelling and persistent figures."—*Jewish Daily Forward*

"Engrossingly told. Marty Jezer has produced . . . the most thoroughly authoritative and carefully considered political assessment of Abbie in *all* his varied guises."—Paul Johnson, *Nonviolent Activist*

ABBIE HOFFMAN

★ ★ ★

MARTY JEZER

AMERICAN REBEL

Rutgers University Press, New Brunswick, New Jersey

First paperback printing, 1993

Library of Congress Cataloging-in-Publication Data

Jezer, Marty.
   Abbie Hoffman : American rebel / Marty Jezer,
      p.   cm.
   Includes bibliographical references and index.
   ISBN 0-8135-1850   0-8135-2017-7
   1. Hoffman, Abbie. 2. Radicals—United States—Biography.
3. Radicalism—United States. 4. United States—Civilization—1970–
5. United States—Popular culture. I. Title.
   HN90.R3H58   1992
   303.48′4—dc20
   [B]   92-7766
                                                                CIP
British Cataloging-in-Publication information available

This book is dedicated to the memory of Maris Cakars and to Paul Johnson, Susan Kent Cakars, and everyone who worked for *WIN* magazine on the front lines for justice and peace.

"Politics is like going to shul. It's what you have to do. But what I really want to be is an outlaw."
—Abbie Hoffman to Marty Kenner in the steam room of the Luxor Baths, New York City, ca. 1972

Contents

Acknowledgments

I began this book in October 1989 and finished it in September 1991.

Special thanks to Johanna Lawrenson for her cooperation during a difficult time. Grateful acknowledgment is also given Johanna Lawrenson, as executor of the estate of Abbie Hoffman, for permission to quote excerpts from Abbie Hoffman's letters to Joan Crawford Ashley, Father Bernard Gilgun, Allen Ginsberg, and Anita Hoffman.

Special thanks also to Anita Hoffman for her encouragement at every step of the way; to Mayer Vishner for answering all my questions; to Al Giordano and Christine Kelly for insisting, early on, that I pay attention to Abbie's work in the 1980s; and to Rick Spencer for showing me the beauty of the Thousand Islands.

I thank the following people for sharing their memories and insights: David Albert, Stew Albert, Joan Crawford Ashley, Carol Brightman, Benson Brown, Susan and Marty Carey, Hank Chaiklin, Lewis Cole, Jim Fouratt, Herb and Ruth Gamberg, Father Bernard Gilgun, Al Giordano, John Giorno, Bob Greenblatt, Jean Harris, Anita Hoffman, Jack Hoffman, Jeff Jones, Christine Kelly, Marty Kenner, Andy Kopkind, Paul Krassner, Sharon Krebs, Dr. Joel Kreps, Keith Lampe (a.k.a. Ponderosa Pine), Gerry Lefcourt, Julius Lester, Seena Levy, Wolfe Lowenthal, Dr. Todd Mandell, Ellen Maslow, Doug McAdam, Paul McIsaac, Ray Mungo, Nick Peck, Gus Reichbach, Leslie Richardson, Shoshana Rihn, Michael Rossman, Mark Rudd, Ed Sanders, John Scagliotti, Danny Schecter, Manny Schreiber, Jack Siemiatychi, Rick Spencer, Taylor Stoehr, Rich Torkelson, Alice Twombly, Mayer Vishner, Harvey Wasserman, Allen Young, and Tom Zerr.

Thanks also to Allen Ginsberg—and to Larry Smolen—for making available a taped copy of their interview.

Presentations by Fred Buck, Tracy Carluccio, Christine Kelly, William Kunstler, Rick Spencer, and Betty Tomlinson at the Learning Alliance in New York during a session called "What Abbie Taught Us" were especially helpful.

Stuart Hutchison of Ram's Horn Productions graciously allowed me to listen to tapes of the extended interview he did with Abbie during the last winter of Abbie's life.

Dave Dellinger generously sent me drafts of chapters from his autobiography in which Abbie was involved.

Equally generous were photographers Diana Davies, Maury Englander, and Allen Ginsberg, who gave me pictures of Abbie from their files.

Al Giordano, Frances Goldin, Anita Hoffman, Paul Johnson, Verandah Porche, and Mayer Vishner read the entire manuscript, sharpened my prose, and spared me from making embarrassing mistakes. Sean Adams, Maris and Susan Kent Cakars, Herb and Ruth Gamberg, Jack Hoffman, Seena Levy, Bobby Payne, Rick Spencer, Robert J. Stack, and Pam Thomas read sections of the book and gave me valuable criticism and encouragement. Aaron Krishtalka provided Yiddish translations. Bill Hively edited the manuscript with expertise, understanding, and an appreciation for political nuance.

The librarians and staff at the Worcester Public Library, the Special Collections at the UCLA Library, the Rare Book and Manuscript Collection at the Columbia University Library, the *Watertown Daily Times*, the Peace Collection at the Swarthmore College Library, the Tamiment Library at New York University, and the office staff at Del-AWARE and Save the River all offered valuable assistance, as did Jacqueline Gens, photo archivist for Allen Ginsberg. Jerry Carbone and the staff of the Brooks Memorial Library in Brattleboro, Vermont, proved once again how valuable a resource this small town library is.

Thanks to Naomi Glauberman and Russell Jacoby, the Cakars, and Danny and Sheila Teitelbaum for their hospitality when I was on research trips.

Thanks also to W. H. Ferry and Carol Bernstein Ferry, and to Harriet Barlow, for financial assistance.

My experience in the publishing world has been "let the writer beware." Hence, I am fortunate in having Frances Goldin as my agent.

I am doubly fortunate in having Kenneth Arnold of the Rutgers

University Press as my editor. He was enthusiastic about the book when it was an idea and remained enthusiastic even after two deadlines had passed.

Mimi Morton's confidence and enthusiasm were essential. As was Kathryn Jezer-Morton's understanding, good humor, and interest in the subject. Their love and support was a boon throughout.

All those listed above made writing this book an engrossing and stimulating experience. They won't all agree with my analyses and conclusions, and the responsibility for errors of fact is mine.

Introduction

In death, Abbie Hoffman has become a symbol of the activist sixties. He was there at the beginning, at the protests against the House Committee on Un-American Activities in San Francisco and as an organizer for the southern civil rights movement. His fame came as a result of his success at fusing the cultural radicalism of hippie youth with the anti–Vietnam War protest movement and the political agenda of the American left. It proved an explosive mix. In the late 1960s and early 1970s it seemed to many Americans that the country was at the brink of a revolution. What radicals like Hoffman believed (and what the authorities feared) turned out in the end to be an illusion. But the fallout from that period did change the course of American history. Some blame the demonstrations in Chicago during the Democratic national convention in 1968, which Abbie helped organize, for electing Richard Nixon president and igniting the right-wing backlash that infects American politics today.

But Abbie was not just a "sixties radical."* He did some of his most effective political work as an environmental activist in the 1980s. He was one of the best grassroots, seat-of-the-pants community organizers this country has likely ever known; certainly he was its most inventive. No one could raise a stink and attract attention to an issue with as few material resources—and with as much creative flair—as Abbie Hoffman. The organizing he did on the St. Lawrence River in the Thousand Islands region of New York and on the Delaware River in Bucks County, Pennsylvania, can stand

---

*By the 1960s, I refer to the activist period between the first Berkeley demonstrations and southern civil rights sit-ins of early 1960 and the defeat of George McGovern in the presidential election of 1972.

as models of how to galvanize a community to fight for its own interests. These were local battles fought during a difficult period, the Reagan era. Although he tried, Abbie never found a way of transforming his environmental efforts into a national movement.

Hoffman was the first political theorist on either the right or the left to master the use of television advertising techniques to create news. Lacking the money to buy time for television ads, he learned how to transform political protest into political theater and to cram powerful, attention-getting visual messages into the brief news bytes that the media allot protest stories.

He was a showman and an entertainer. He thought of himself not only as a community organizer but as a political artist. Without doubt he was the funniest activist in the history of the American left, if not in the history of American politics. He cared deeply about people, and his passion for justice inspired his creativity.

Abbie starred in his own political theater; he helped invent, in fact, what is now all too pretentiously called "performance art." His theater was for the street, however. Unlike today's artists, what he risked by inciting controversy was not a loss of federal funding but years in a federal jail.

In 1970 Eleanor Lester, a theater critic writing in the *New York Times*, called Hoffman "the boldest, most imaginative producer-director-performer of avant-garde theater" and compared him to Shakespeare in his "genius for reaching a multi-level audience." Abbie's masterpieces, she listed, were the throwing away of money at the New York Stock Exchange and the levitation of the Pentagon (1967), the Yip-in "massacre" at Grand Central Station and the Yippie demonstrations in Chicago (1968), and the conspiracy trial of the Chicago Seven (1969–1970), which, as described by Dwight Macdonald in another context, was Abbie's show, "a chance to act out in largest publicity his ideas about radical politics as theater, about 'putting on' the squares and goosing the media."

In this biography I describe these and other "theater pieces" as Abbie meant them, as deliberately conceived protest actions that were part of a seriously considered political strategy. My focus is on Abbie's life as an activist: the social, cultural, and political milieu in which he worked; the ideas that inspired his work; and what happened to America when he put his ideas into action. There is much still to be learned from Abbie about political theater and community organizing; he instinctively understood what it takes to motivate people into taking risks to better society. But we can also learn from his mistakes (which in most cases were also the movement's mistakes). They had profound effects on American life and on the ability of the radical movement (or the progressive movement, as it's called today) to improve that life.

I was not an intimate of Abbie's but was with him during the late 1960s at the stock exchange and the Pentagon, on the streets of New York's Lower East Side, and with the Yippies in Grand Central Station and in Mayor Daley's Chicago. During this period I was an editor of *WIN*, a radical pacifist "underground" magazine that was trying, even before Abbie came on the scene, to merge the hippie counterculture with the antiwar protest movement. In 1973, when Abbie was arrested for selling cocaine, I drafted a statement of support that was signed by many leading figures in the peace movement. I met him again in the 1980s after he emerged from seven years of living underground. He contributed to a symposium I organized on the state of the peace movement, and I interviewed him about the influence of the beat generation on his politics.

I loved Abbie for his courage and audacity, his humor, and his imagination. But I was always critical of the violence of some of his rhetoric and what I considered an irresponsible refusal to set limits in his conception of direct action. Abbie was three years older than I. His background (upwardly mobile, second-generation Jewish American), his enthusiasms (sports, hipsterism, American culture), and his ambitions (to make the world a better place) were similar to mine. I always felt that I knew where he was coming from. Nothing that he did surprised me; much that he did frightened me. Those of us, like Abbie and myself, who abandoned secure middle-class lives to become full-time activists against the Vietnam War were on the cutting edge of social change. Everything we did—from walking a picket line to committing civil disobedience and going to jail, from dropping out of respectable jobs to living catch-as-catch-can on subsistence wages, and from smoking marijuana to taking acid—was new and scary. Or at least I was scared. Nothing seemed to faze Abbie. We all drew lines, at actions and activities that went beyond what at any given time we were prepared to do. Abbie drew no lines. He obliterated all boundaries. He was a heroic figure who, by his example, inspired many of us to overcome our fears, take risks, and create new bounds with more distant lines.

After the 1968 demonstrations in Chicago I pulled back from direct action, not so much because I feared being injured by the police or going to jail (I remained active in the draft resistance movement) but because, as attracted as I was to the excitement of street confrontations, I could no longer see their political value. In the context of that time—in the political cul-de-sac that Abbie and many of us had entered—the options for political activity seemed to collapse into urban guerrilla warfare or retreating to the country in order, as we immodestly put it, to create a new society and live the revolution as if it had already happened. Too much of a pacifist to throw bombs and taunt or fight the police, I moved to Vermont as a founding member of Total Loss Farm, one of the first and most publicized of the back-to-the-land hippie communes. Thus, when I criticize the antiwar movement and the counterculture, as I often do, I do so as an insider, as one who lived at the core of that experience.

It is fashionable in certain circles to attack the activism of the 1960s in order to advance the right-wing agenda of the 1990s. This book is not an exercise in sixties bashing. I remain, as Abbie did, committed to the ideals of the sixties, to peace, environmentalism, civil liberties, racial and gender equality, the redistribution of wealth, and freedom and justice overall. For me, the civil rights struggle, in which Abbie learned his organizing skills, was one of the most heroic moments in American history. The war in Vietnam, as we in the antiwar movement claimed, was an immoral act of aggression by the United States against a country that represented no threat to our national security. The United States destroyed Vietnam (and much of Indochina) as an example to third-world countries who might consider making a revolution without taking direction from Uncle Sam. Had the Vietnamese been left to fight their own civil war, it would have been brief, with casualties in the thousands rather than the millions. Neither the antiwar movement nor the media were responsible for America's military defeat, as those who would rewrite the history of the period insist. Despite the massive U.S. invasion, America's South Vietnamese clients could not and did not deserve to win. Abbie, who organized his first antiwar demonstration in 1965, said this from the beginning. On the crucial issue of the war, he and the antiwar movement were right; the U.S. government, including the leaders of both the Democratic and the Republican parties, was wrong.

Nevertheless, as this book details, Abbie and most of us who were part of the radical wing of the antiwar movement* made serious mistakes in the way we protested the war. Although it was

---

* By radical wing, I mean that part of the antiwar movement that opposed electoral politics in favor of direct action in the streets and/or a strategy of alternative, countercultural politics. The liberal wing of the movement believed that the war could be ended by electoral activity, by supporting dovish liberals within the Democratic party.

characteristic of Abbie to look forward without apologies, his politics in the 1980s indicated second thoughts, if not actual regrets,
about some of his actions as a protester during the Vietnam period.
I certainly regret some of the political actions I advocated during
the 1960s, and this book reflects that perspective.

Abbie's life exemplified the difficulty of making radical politics a
lifetime career. There is money to be made in the think tanks and
political organizations of liberalism and the right, but radicals have
always traveled economy class. As an organizer in the 1980s, Abbie
had fame and the satisfaction of doing useful work. But he had
little money and no security. Many people admired him; others
considered him a dinosaur, a relic whose time had passed. But he
persisted.

In 1988 we ran into each other at an airport. We embraced, and
then Abbie started rapping at me. Everything was going great, he
said. The Sandinistas were going to win in Nicaragua, the Salva-
doran military was going to fall, and the facts about the October
Surprise—Reagan's stealing the presidency by bribing the Iranians
to hold the American hostages until after the 1980 election—were
going to come out and change the course of history. Then he left
with a group of admiring students who had come to take him to his
speaking date. I was heartened by his optimism. After all that had
happened in the 1970s and 1980s—the triumph of Reaganism, the
marginalization of the left—it was good to meet someone who had
kept the faith. But where did he get the energy to sustain that
optimism? I recalled that he was always upbeat and that his enthusiasms were contagious. But his optimism here seemed unrealistic,
and I sensed some kind of personal imbalance. A year later he
committed suicide. The circumstances of that suicide provided an
explanation for his behavior at our meeting.

Abbie was diagnosed in 1980 as having bipolar disorder, more
commonly known as manic depression, a metabolically caused
mental illness. In retrospect it is obvious that he was hypomanic
for most of his life. Hypomania is a less extreme and nonpsychotic
form of mania. According to Dr. Ronald R. Fieve, whose book
Moodswing is the basic layman's text for understanding bipolar
disorder, "Many of the milder high states will be beneficial and
appropriate to the individual, enabling him to achieve much of
value by means of his driven, manic energy."[1] And this was so with
Abbie. In his usual, hypomanic state he had exceptional energy,
was highly focused, and was always optimistic. He was a go-getter
in society—extravagant, reckless, talkative, articulate, creative,
perceptive, and relentless in his drive and his quest for achieve-

ment. He was also the life of any party, sexually promiscuous, and a risk taker who loved to gamble—on politics, on sports, and on life itself—and these too are classic symptoms of the hypomanic phase of manic depression. But as hypomania rises to a manic frenzy, the ability to harness one's energy is lost. When Abbie was in a full-blown manic state, he was unfocused and out of control; his frenetic behavior was often obnoxious, irrational, personally self-destructive, and politically self-defeating. In the manic phase Abbie was like a surfer riding the crest of a gigantic wave, soaring on top of the world until the wave crashed, taking him with it. Abbie's depressions, however, did not manifest themselves until he went underground; later, in the 1980s, he went through a number of severe manic-depressive cycles.

Certainly, Abbie's hypomania contributed to his charismatic personality and his creative and reckless brilliance. But it would be a mistake to interpret his life as the mere acting out of a mental disorder. Many great men and women in history—politicians and business people, as well as rebels and creative artists—have been diagnosed as manic-depressive. What is crucial to history is not that they suffered from a mental illness but that they touched people's lives. Manic depression likely killed Abbie Hoffman, but it is what he did in his life as a radical activist that inspires this biography.

ABBIE HOFFMAN

★ ★ ★

AMERICAN REBEL

CHAPTER

1

"I NEVER LEFT WORCESTER"

1936–1955

The Yippie who threw away money at the stock exchange, attempted to levitate the Pentagon, provoked mayors and judges, and helped to bring down a powerful president invented himself as a public personality "out of left-wing literature, sperm, licorice and a little chicken fat"—or so he gloated.[1] While there is nothing extraordinary about a public figure reconstructing a past in order to enhance an image (celebrities create self-serving autobiographies all the time), Abbie Hoffman turned the formula around. First he created himself as a one-of-a-kind American rebel; then he achieved his status as a "famous person." *Soon to Be a Major Motion Picture*, his immodest autobiography written while he was underground and published in 1980, recycled autobiographical snippets from his earlier books *Revolution for the Hell of It* (1968) and *Woodstock Nation* (1969).[2] These books in turn incorporated anecdotes about his youth from articles written for underground publications one and two years earlier and from stories about himself that he never ceased telling.

In his writings and speeches Abbie would constantly hark back to his youthful exploits in his hometown of Worcester, Massachusetts. Not skilled at (and lacking the patience for) richly detailed anecdotal stories, he honed his autobiographical reminiscences to punch home the point that he was a rebel from the "get-go": a cocky little street-smart wise guy, a *pisher* with a keenness for schoolyard justice and a willingness to fight for it.

Abbie's delight in romanticizing his past was, in part, egotism. "I'm such an egomaniac I figure if I'm an egomaniac then it's a good quality!!" he once wrote. But he also had a propensity for self-analysis, a fascination with the question of identity, and an ability to distance himself from and objectify his personality to see how he could put it to use in his work as a political activist. This, and an irrepressible wit (his saving grace), enabled him to ingratiate himself even with some of the people who were most put off by his egotism. Although there was a spiritual dimension to almost everything Abbie did (he wanted to be both a saint *and* a sinner), his self-identity was framed not by religious terminology but by the mythologies of American popular culture. "I'm just the guy who flies around in the cape and has the hots for Lois Lane" was typical of the way he characterized his radical calling.[3]

Abbie's experience growing up in Worcester—and what he made of it—was a key to his personality, his politics, and his self-conscious crafting of a public persona. He used his roots as a resource—as an anchor in the mainstream of American culture, and as ballast in the polemical swells of left-wing politics. "I don't really have a concept in my mind of ever having left anyplace," he said about his youth in Worcester. "I don't like the idea of leaving. I don't like the idea of conversion. I don't like the idea of being born again. I choose to try and find continuity from birth to death. I don't like to picture abrupt changes, so I don't feel that I ever left Worcester."[4]

Hoffman's ancestors were Russian Jews who immigrated to the United States around the beginning of the twentieth century. They came from "The Pale," an area near Kiev long disputed by Russia and Poland where Jews were allowed to settle. The Hoffmans were among more than a million Russian Jews who fled the region during this period to escape anti-Semitic pogroms.

Abbie's father, John, was one year old in 1906 when his family arrived at Ellis Island. The Hoffman family's Russian name was Shapoznikoff. According to Abbie, his grandfather's brother, the first of the Shapoznikoffs to emigrate to America, had somehow gotten hold of the identity papers of a German named Hoffman in order to come to the United States. The brother had settled in the Worcester area using the Hoffman name and encouraged the rest of his family to follow. When Abbie's grandfather and father passed through Ellis Island, immigration officials gave them the

Hoffman name of the brother who had sponsored them. That Abbie had the surname of a German Jew was an irony that would later delight him. German Jews who immigrated to the United States in the mid-1800s strove assiduously to assimilate into American society and looked down on the immigrant eastern European Jews as loud and unsophisticated greenhorns—a fact Abbie gleefully exploited when he came up against a real German Jew named Hoffman, federal judge Julius Hoffman, who presided at the 1969–1970 conspiracy trial.[5]

Abbie's mother, whose maiden name was Florence Schanberg, was born in 1906 in Clinton, Massachusetts, a small city of some 12,000 people a short distance northeast of Worcester. Until the Depression, Clinton was a textile town. Florence's mother worked in a sweatshop, and her father was a wrecker. A graceful and athletic woman, Florence toured the Northeast as a member of a gymnastics club. Her ambition was to become a physical therapist. In the 1920s and 1930s professional training was rarely open to Jewish daughters—or any daughters—of the working class, so Florence went to work as a payroll clerk at a local woolen mill. When its business office relocated to New York City, Florence went with it. Lonely in the big city (and unmoved by radicals she heard speak at the Y), she quit her job, moved to Worcester to be near her family again, and got a job as a secretary. She met John Hoffman at a Worcester bowling alley, and in 1935 they got married.

John Hoffman spent most of his youth working and studying. He helped his father sell fruit from a horse-drawn wagon, peddled newspapers, and for twenty-five years worked in his uncle's drugstore, commuting to night school in Boston for a degree in pharmacology. In 1944 John Hoffman started the Worcester Medical Supply Company, a wholesale distributor that served physicians and hospitals throughout central Massachusetts. Florence prided herself on her business skills and wanted to work for the firm, but John was conventional in his attitude toward women and work. He insisted that his wife keep house and raise their children according to the middle-class ideal. Florence Hoffman faithfully echoed her husband's conservative beliefs. Ten years after John's death she was still using the pronoun "we" to describe her own opinions.[6]

Abbie was born Abbott Howard Hoffman on November 30, 1936. His parents rented the top floor of a three-story frame house on Chandler Street, a major artery for Worcester's Jewish, Irish, and

Italian immigrant population. As the family prospered, they bought their own two-story house—neither big nor fancy—on Geneva Street, and then moved a few blocks away to a slightly larger house on Ruth Street, each of them a block off of Chandler. It was a warm and "happy-go-lucky household," according to Abbie's brother, Jack. Neighbors and relatives frequently came over to schmooze and play cards. The extended Schanberg and Hoffman/ Shapoznikoff clans gathered around the big dinner table to celebrate Jewish holidays. For most of the first thirty years of his life Abbie was part of this close extended family, living (except for his student years) as he did when he was a kid—in small private houses, all of them within walking distance of his parents in the neighborhood in which he grew up.[7]

Abbie was the oldest child. His brother, Jack, was born in 1939; his sister, Phyliss, in 1941. At three months, according to family legend, Abbie would lie on his back performing acrobatics—"like he was showing off," his mother remembers. More likely, his hyperactivity was a symptom of the manic depression that would afflict him in later life.

As the oldest child, Abbie was the center of attention. When he didn't get enough of it, he had an attack of asthma. But for the most part he was a healthy, active child—and mischievous, too. Florence Hoffman was protective of her trouble-seeking son. When the Worcester police accused thirteen-year-old Abbie of being the Halloween prankster who had switched the license plates on neighborhood cars, Florence provided an alibi. John Hoffman was the disciplinarian, spanking Abbie for his wise-guy attitude. But punishment did no good, John remembered. Abbie never changed. He was stubborn and always fought to get in the last word. "The whole world's wrong and you're right!" his father would admonish. "You're right! You got it!" Abbie would reply defiantly.[8]

There was a fierce rivalry between Abbie and his younger brother. "One time my father threw us both down the stairs when we came home from school," Jack recalls. "We were hell. We had fights. We beat each other up so badly we both had to go to the hospital." The parents got a respite from these battles when Abbie and Jack went for four weeks each summer to a farm in Clinton where their Uncle Schmully owned land. The boys collected eggs, hoed in the garden, and fed the cows. This was around 1945, the end of the Second World War. Abbie was eight when the war ended.

He and his friends played war games in the woods near his home and talked about "getting Hitler." It was a patriotic time with flags and bunting and parades, and a grateful people proud of its returning servicemen and women. John Hoffman was 4-F. Uncle Schmully was Abbie's hero because he had served in the army.

★   ★   ★

"The Heart of the Commonwealth," as Worcester was known, was an industrial city built on the inventiveness of local mechanics, who in the nineteenth century developed processes for the manufacture of textiles, grinders, and wire and steel specialty products. With a population that hovered around 200,000 between 1940 and 1950, Worcester, like all New England factory towns, had been on the decline since the Depression. The city once had a liberal tradition. Before the Civil War it was a hotbed of antislavery agitation, and in 1850 it was the site of the Women's Rights Convention that launched the women's suffrage movement. But after the war WASP industrialists governed the city with a paternalistic hand. They endowed it with impressive cultural institutions such as the Worcester Art Museum, founded in 1896, which holds paintings by Cézanne, Picasso, Matisse, and Monet. At the same time they were politically conservative and vehemently antiunion. With the large influx, especially after the First World War, of Catholic immigrants—Irish, Italian, and French Canadian—the city became politically Democratic yet culturally even more conservative.

The experience of Jews in small cities like Worcester was different from that of Jews in New York City, where most of the Jewish immigrants from eastern Europe settled. New York Jews arrived in large enough numbers not only to wield political influence but to create a separate and cohesive secular culture that influenced the thoughts and mores of the rest of society. Jews in New York lived with an illusion that they were a majority of the population. As lawyers, doctors, teachers, and businessmen, and as garment workers and other skilled tradespeople, they worked in sectors of the economy in which Jews were, at the very least, a conspicuous and influential minority. Jews were prominent in the entertainment field. And in the Catskill Mountains Jews had their own resorts, where many Jewish entertainers played in the summer—a "Borscht Belt" that reflected the brash and (among themselves) self-confident tastes of their secular culture.

In Worcester, by contrast, there was no Jewish culture outside the formal synagogue programs. The Hoffmans didn't know about the Catskills. They vacationed on Cape Cod and in the White Mountains of New Hampshire, never secure that the places they stayed would welcome Jews as guests. Although Abbie's sense of humor was very much influenced by Borscht Belt comics, he saw them on television and in nightclubs, not at Catskill resorts. It was not until 1984, when he stayed at Grossinger's for the fifteenth anniversary of the Woodstock rock festival, that he stayed at a Catskill hotel.

Among New York Jews during the 1930s and 1940s the political spectrum ran from Marxism on the left to New Deal liberalism on the right. Even in the 1950s, during the McCarthy era, New York Jews were conspicuous for their liberal positions. Jews in Worcester, however, did not want to be politically conspicuous, and their voting patterns reflected those of the broader community. Abbie's parents were not exceptions. His father voted like other Worcester businessmen. He was a Republican (a political species virtually unknown among New York Jews), supporting Thomas Dewey against Harry Truman, Eisenhower during the 1950s, and Barry Goldwater against Lyndon Johnson.

Thus Abbie, except for his college days at Brandeis, lived in a social environment where Jews were a tiny minority. Whereas New York Jews were often wary when they found themselves the minority in unfamiliar goyish territory, Abbie was sure of himself in that situation. He was confident in his ability to deal with people no matter what their background.

Assimilation was a crucial issue in the American Jewish community when Abbie was growing up. Jewish history had been shaped by the experience of Jews in hostile societies. The unprecedented tolerance of American society—as welcome as it was—threatened Jewish identity. Should Jews try to maintain their distinct culture? Would they fare better isolating themselves in their own cultural ghetto or integrating themselves into the broader society? It was tempting to abandon Jewish tradition in this land, as Abbie phrased it, "of milk, honey, the Red Sox, and lobster." But Jewish history suggested caution. How deep did American pluralism run? Anti-Semitism was still prevalent in Worcester, as it was throughout the United States. There were quotas limiting Jews as teachers and faculty members in most colleges and universities. Jews were also discriminated against in banking, in real estate, and in many corporations, where they could not obtain executive positions. Jews were also barred from many upscale neighborhoods, country clubs, and resort hotels. American society seemed open and welcoming, but Jews could never be sure whether the No Vacancy or Just Sold sign was an indication of anti-Semitism. In Worcester, as elsewhere, the Catholic church taught that the Jews had killed Jesus, and the young Irish-Catholic toughs in the city's parochial schools were determined to reap revenge. To avoid trouble, Abbie would sometimes take his hat off and cross himself when riding on the bus past Blessed Sacrament, a neighborhood parochial school. Other times he, Jack, and their friends would stand their ground and fight.

Conflicting emotions of hope and fear rippled through the Jewish community as its members tried to assess their position in American society. The Hoffman family adjusted to the melting pot in fits and starts. Abbie's grandparents spoke Yiddish and were religiously observant. But Abbie's parents joined the more modern and upscale reform temple (built in 1948 to look like a Unitarian church). Here the services were in English, the men and women sat together (in the orthodox shul the women sat separately, hidden from the men by a curtain), and there was an active social program to keep teenage boys and girls involved with one another as they reached dating age. But Abbie didn't stay involved. Although he liked the Bible stories he learned in Hebrew school and the discussions they inspired about good and evil, he had no patience for the orthodox rituals (which forbade, for example, his going to the movies or playing ball on the Sabbath) and no interest in the social conformity that the reform temple considered moral behavior. Food, more than anything, represented the Hoffmans' adjustment to the assimilationist climate. Gradually the Hoffmans went from a strictly kosher to a quasi-kosher home, from "benching" (saying the prayers before and after a meal) on Friday night to eating out on Friday night, from eating *traif* (nonkosher foods) in restaurants to bringing Chinese food and pizza into the house.[9]

Like many young Jews who grew up in the 1950s, Abbie was critical of his parents both for assimilating into the culture of the white, homogeneous, affluent society and for trying to maintain

vestiges of their old-country traditions. For Abbie, assimilation
wasn't the dilemma that it was for his parents. He considered himself an American and expected the country to live up to its principles. The defensive manner in which his parents often felt their
way into the mainstream society exasperated him. He never forgot
an incident, as a child, of his parents taking the family to a resort
in New Hampshire and turning around for home when they discovered, reading the resort's literature in the car, that it only accepted
Christians. His parents' passivity, their refusal to make a scene
and fight for their rights, galled Abbie. Assimilation, as Abbie perceived it, too often meant accepting Christian standards of refine-
ment and decorum. "Modesty," he once said, "was invented by the
gentiles to keep Jews out of real estate, banks, and country
clubs."[10] Abbie never drew back from making a scene; unlike his
parents he felt secure as an American, and so his Jewishness didn't
make him defensive. His feeling for his religion changed over the
years, but he never tempered the assertiveness that he considered
crucial to his Jewish identity. "I came into this world acutely aware
of being Jewish and am sure I'll go out that way," he wrote in his
autobiography.[11]

The order of his father's priorities, according to Abbie, was business first, then family, religion, sports, and politics. A sport who
smoked cigars (and flicked the butts everywhere), John Hoffman
liked the company of other men, reveling in the male talk in the
steam room of the Worcester Y, playing pinochle and poker, and
placing bets with a local bookie on all the big sporting events. Conservative in his politics and conventionally patriarchical in his
attitude toward his children and wife, he nevertheless had an expansive vision of his place in the Worcester community. His proud-
est achievement was his election as chapter, and later national,
president of the Probus (probusiness) club, a booster club of Jewish professionals and businessmen patterned on the Kiwanis and
Rotary clubs. In Worcester, Probus sponsored baseball and basketball leagues for grade school children, supported programs in
local orphanages, and financed scholarships at Clark and later
Brandeis universities. The determination to support nonsectarian
rather than purely Jewish activities was based, in part, on a survival instinct common then among American Jews: if we help them,
they'll leave us alone. But it also represented an authentic civic
pride. The immigrant Jews had come to the New World a despised

and persecuted people. America had not only allowed them to practice their religious traditions but also fostered an environment of economic opportunity that was unheard of in the experience of the Jewish diaspora. The postwar era was a boom time, and the Hoffman family rode the wave to a level of affluence which, while modest, was beyond all their imaginings. For good reason, Abbie's father was an unabashed civic booster. He believed in America and in the idea of the public-spirited citizen. Or, as Abbie put it, "He adopted America's values. He supported its wars, its courts, its charities, its police, its government."[12]

Abbie and his father fought throughout their lives. John Hoffman was a stickler for neatness and propriety. He demanded that Abbie eat everything on his plate, not make scenes, and do what was right according to the standards of Worcester's Jewish middle class. Yet, in a way, Abbie was a chip off the old block. He followed his father out into the wider Worcester community—and kept going. He was proud of his standing on the rebellious fringe, proud because of the distinction it drew between him and other kids his age who clung to what he felt were the overly safe (hence, to him, boring) confines of the insular Jewish community. John Hoffman probably had mixed feelings about his son's show of independence. He was ambitious that Abbie should shine in his own upwardly mobile Jewish circle. But he likely enjoyed Abbie's street-smart sass, his pool hall skills, and the other manifestations of "good old boy" badness. Despite their bitter conflicts over Abbie's political activities in the 1960s, they never broke off their relationship. Even during his Yippie period, when Abbie pushed generational conflict and advocated (for its shock value) that kids kill their parents, he maintained ties with his family, phoning them to tell them "not to worry," visiting them on holidays, and basking in the notoriety of the local rebel who had made good in New York City.

Abbie sometimes described his father to his friends as a Willy Loman character.[13] In Arthur Miller's play *Death of a Salesman*, Willy strives to maintain the illusion that he is a successful salesman, a good husband and father, respected by other salesmen, and beloved by his clients. For John Hoffman, however, success was no illusion. Though he lived in constant fear that the large pharmaceutical companies would begin to "sell direct" and thus drive out middlemen wholesalers like himself, the business prospered, as did John's standing in the Worcester community. After John Hoffman

died in 1974, from a heart attack a few weeks after Abbie went
underground, Abbie wrote a newspaper article in which he claimed
that Watergate had disillusioned his father and that he had "passed
away a loyal citizen but with a lingering doubt that maybe his *mi-
shuginah* son had some good points to make after all."[14] But this
attempt to turn his father into a tragic figure who felt betrayed by
the system he had always supported was self-serving. The major
disillusion of John Hoffman's life was Abbie. It was not the country,
it was his son who let him down.

As with so many fathers who have rebellious sons, sports was a
common ground. Friday nights, during the early 1950s, Abbie and
his father stayed up late to watch boxing from Madison Square
Garden on the "Gillette Calvacade of Sports." They went to Boston
Celtics games together and to Fenway Park to root for the Red Sox.
Holy Cross home football games were a Saturday ritual in autumn,
a reflection on how far the Hoffmans had strayed from observing
the Sabbath. When the Crusaders beat Boston College, their Catholic archrival, it was an occasion to celebrate, to go out and eat
lobster. Abbie was a typical young male in his passion for sports.
Whatever sport was in season, he played it: sandlot softball, basketball in the local schoolyard, and tackle football without any
helmets or pads. Years later he told his second wife, Anita, that
these football games toughened him for the beatings he received
from police in Mississippi, New York, and Chicago, and that his
athletic ability gave him a sense of physical self-confidence.

Abbie was also a champion at doing tricks with a Duncan yo-yo,
an accomplishment he boasted about in no less than two books
written ten years apart.[15] Tennis, however, was the game he liked
best and the sport in which he most excelled. This was a strange
choice for someone who preferred the pool hall to a swimming pool
at a country club, but understandable as an act of individualistic
rebellion. In the 1950s tennis was not a sport for minorities—
blacks or Jews. Barred from restricted local tennis clubs, Abbie
played on the public courts at Newton Square. According to
brother Jack, winning at tennis was Abbie's way of saying "fuck
you" to the upper-class WASPs of Worcester.

Abbie's embrace of American culture was unequivocal. On Saturday, instead of going to temple, he and his friends would go to the
Capitol Theatre in the morning to see Abbott and Costello, Laurel

and Hardy, and a raft of cartoons. In the afternoon they would go
to the Plymouth Theatre to see a double feature. Like most kids
growing up in the pretelevision era of the late 1940s and early
1950s, Abbie learned about American history by going to the movies. *Broken Arrow*, which he saw during the summer of 1950, was
the first film to break Abbie's stereotypical understanding of the
American pageant. With Jeff Chandler playing the Apache warrior
Cochise, it was one of the first Hollywood movies to present native
Americans in a sympathetic light. In the 1950s interracial marriage
was something to be condemned by all right-thinking people. (Even
those who accepted it on principle opposed it in actuality for fear
of upsetting family, friends, and neighbors.) In *Broken Arrow*,
however, the hero, a former Union army officer played by Jimmy
Stewart, marries Cochise's daughter, played by Debra Paget in rus-
set makeup. Abbie cheered for the Apaches as he would thereafter
always cheer for the underdog—both in the movies and in real life.
(The movie critic Pauline Kael, who saw *Broken Arrow* about the
same time as Abbie, was similarly moved. "Though the picture
never won any Academy Awards or brotherhood awards," she later
wrote, "it has probably done more to soften the hearts of racists
than most movies designed to instruct, indict, and inspire.")[16]

Radio was a family event in the Hoffman household. From quiz
programs like "Truth or Consequences" and "The $64 Question,"
Abbie absorbed American cultural trivia and learned verbal
repartee. The family was the first in the neighborhood to buy a
television—in 1951, when Abbie was fourteen—and this attracted
all the neighborhood kids. Although Abbie would later realize the
power that television wielded in enforcing social norms, he was basically a radio kid. The one-on-one intimacy of a voice in the night,
the way it stimulated his imagination, encouraging him to invent a
reality behind the sound, made an impression he remembered
throughout his life. He had a professional media maven's interest
in television and became an expert at exploiting the medium for
political purposes. But radio was the medium that he really liked,
both as a listener and later as a political performer.[17]

Abbie had a talent for comedy and a ready audience: the whole
family liked to laugh. Growing up, he loved the Marx Brothers,
Abbott and Costello, and all the other comedians he saw and heard
in the movies and on radio and television. As a teenager Abbie
discovered *Mad* when it was still a comic book. (It became a magazine in 1955 in order to circumvent the comic book code of

"decency.") For Abbie, as for many American kids in the 1950s, *Mad* was the first inkling that there was another way of looking at society, that there was a crass and hypocritical side to the American experience, that the country was not always—as was taught in school—motivated by righteousness.

Not that Abbie showed any interest in politics or social issues. Until he got to college, he never read a newspaper except for the sports and comic sections. During his early teens left-wingers were hounded out of school systems, labor unions, and the civil service; blacklisted from the movies, radio, and television; and persecuted by right-wing veterans' groups, "patriotic" societies, congressional committees, and the FBI. In the early 1950s the CIA overthrew democratic governments in Iran and Guatemala, and the United States began its intervention in Vietnam. Abbie was barely aware of any of this. But even had he been, there were no radicals among his friends or in his family; there was no one to point him toward a critical perspective of American society. There was, in fact, no visible radical movement in Worcester—or, for the most part, anyplace else in the United States—that Abbie could have joined. Senator Joseph McCarthy's witch-hunt for communists wasn't an issue in the Hoffman household because it was taken for granted that communism was the enemy and had to be stopped. As for Julius and Ethel Rosenberg, there was no question, as Abbie later recalled. Sure, they were the first civilians to suffer the death penalty for alleged espionage. But they were communists—weren't they?—and deserved to be fried.

In the absence of a political context, Abbie's rebellious nature could only take a cultural turn. As he grew into his teens, he began hanging out with his former Irish and Italian nemeses, gambling, shooting pool, pitching pennies, playing craps and poker. His parents were not happy. They wanted him to join the affluent temple crowd and date Jewish girls. But they trusted their son and did not try to crimp his social activities. Not that they could: even when they insisted he be home at night, he would climb out his bedroom window onto the roof of the front porch and from there shinny down to freedom.[18] Summers, during Abbie's teen years, the Hoffmans vacationed at a rented cottage in Onset on Cape Cod, a working- and middle-class resort community favored by Boston-area Irish, Italian, and Jewish families. Here, too, Abbie made friends with working-class kids.

Abbie was always unabashedly boastful about his success with girls. He had a flirtatious line and was an excellent dancer, able to toss his partner over his shoulder and between his legs to jitterbug tunes or do deep sexy dips when the music was slow and the saxophone moaned. For Jewish middle-class teenagers, the sexual double standard was the rule. The girls in the crowd that boys like Abbie were expected to date and marry were supposed to be virgins. Jewish males had more freedom. There was a certain unstated admiration for boys who successfully—but discreetly—cruised the goyish community and scored with the shiksas. Abbie exploited this loophole in the community's mores, dating the non-Jewish girls he met in Onset who lived near Boston, a convenient distance from Worcester. Jack Hoffman confirms Abbie's assertion of sexual precociousness, though this may represent nothing more than a younger brother's belief in an older brother's boasting. Abbie's male friends at Brandeis and Berkeley also recall the delight with which Abbie told tales about his sexual "conquests." The sexual revolution of the 1960s merely gave political legitimacy to sexual behavior that began for him a decade earlier.

In the early 1950s juvenile delinquency was a much publicized national issue, treated by politicians and the press as drugs are today. Like many teenage rebels, Abbie was attracted to the image of the juvenile delinquent. There were three overlapping stereotypes associated with juvenile delinquency during this period: greasers, rocks, and hoods. Greasers liked working on old cars. They wore tight jeans, motorcycle boots, and T-shirts with a pack of cigarettes rolled up in a sleeve. They were into hot rods more than they were into gang violence; most often they came from rural areas, small towns, or white, working-class suburban neighborhoods. Abbie liked the image of the rock, the greaser's more gang-oriented urban counterpart, but was too outgoing, trusting, and intellectually curious to fit the mold of these repressed and violence-prone male teenagers. The rock's stance was to be cool. His sense of personal space, the vibe he put out, was inviolable. Any threat, real or imagined, to his sense of masculinity could lead to explosive violence. The rock's uniform included pegged pants, metal taps on his shoes, and collars bent upward behind a D.A. (for "duck's ass") haircut.

Abbie's chosen style was that of a hood. He was into making

money shooting pool, playing cards, and gambling at sports and on
the horses, using his wit to stay out of the way of the police and the
more violent forms of juvenile delinquency. He liked flashy clothes,
zoot suits, pegged pants, and shirts with big, flamboyant "Mr. B"
(named for the black singer Billy Eckstine) collars. He liked fast
cars but sought out the greaser types when his cars needed work.

The difference between hoods, greasers, and rocks was one of
degree. Their common attitude was best exemplified by Marlon
Brando in one of Abbie's favorite movies, *The Wild One*. The movie
was based on an incident in 1949 when a gang of motorcyclists,
precursors to the Hell's Angels, took over and terrorized a small
California community. Released in 1953 with little critical acclaim,
the movie was produced to show the motorcyclists in the worst possible light. Yet Abbie, and many teenagers like him, identified with
their antisocial behavior. "Whaddayagot?" Brando replied when
asked what he was rebelling against. Incoherent as that answer
was, it expressed Abbie's mood precisely. Had Abbie lived in New
York, he likely would have discovered Greenwich Village and absorbed the creative and nonconformist ethos of the bohemian tradition. Had he been a "red-diaper baby," with parents who were
active—or had been active—in left-wing politics, he likely would
have known about the radical tradition in American politics and
perhaps expressed his rebelliousness as a young socialist or communist. But what could kids in Worcester know about Stalinists
and Trotskyists, or about beatniks and wild and crazy bohemian
artists? As in most places across America, being a hood, a rock, or
a greaser—being against anything that seemed normal, law-
abiding, decent, that is to say *square*—was the only model of rebellion available.

Fearless, quick-witted, ready to try anything, and absolutely
self-confident, Abbie fit easily into the street culture of his time.
The fact that he considered this a point of pride indicated his
awareness that he was infringing on a scene in which he didn't naturally belong. Working-class rebels, after all, had little to lose. The
upward mobility of postwar America—touted on television and in
the movies—didn't describe their prospects or experience. All they
had to look forward to was the military draft and then a lifetime of
low-paying, blue-collar jobs. Until it was necessary to pick up their
lunch pail, they might as well kick up some hell. Abbie, on the
other hand, knew he had a future. His was not a rebellion against
middle-class affluence; he and his family were just beginning to

enjoy it, and he, most of all, liked what money could buy. What he didn't like was the rigidity of middle-class social expectations, the idea that he would have to postpone gratification in order to work his way up the ladder of status and success. Abbie looked at what he liked and balanced it against what was expected of him. He believed that there was more to the future than a conventionally successful career, but he didn't know what that might be. Nevertheless, he wanted and expected more than what the pool hall and the street corner had to offer.

Abbie broke the mold of the ordinary street tough by his intellectual precociousness and his success in school. He was one of those kids who got all As and Bs with very little studying. He attended Seaver Prep, a public junior high school for gifted students, and then Classical High, Worcester's public high school for kids planning to attend college. The rote method of learning bored him, however, and he became a disciplinary problem not only because he wouldn't knuckle under to authority but because he was always asking questions and challenging his teachers. Florence Hoffman was often called to school to discuss Abbie's wise-guy attitude. "It's a wonder half of us aren't in the insane asylum because of you," one of Classical High's administrators chastised him in front of his mother. "What about the other half?" Abbie retorted.[19]

It is almost as if Abbie had a secret intellectual life in Worcester, secret in the sense that he edited it out of all his autobiographical writings. Both his brother and his mother recall Abbie bringing home books from the Worcester Public Library and spending days in his room engrossed in reading. Being a bookworm, however, was not an image he wished to project. Always intent on being seen as a street-tough rebel, he claimed to have taken up shoplifting because he was ashamed to purchase paperback books with sexy covers. The only books he ever admitted to reading as a youth were paperback novels like *The Hoods*, *A Stone for Danny Fisher*, and *The Amboy Dukes*. All these novels had an underground, cultlike reputation among literate teenagers in the 1950s; each told the story of Jewish sons of immigrant parents who made their way out of poverty by becoming involved in organized crime, one obvious opportunity for economic advancement. For Abbie, the books were a mirror of the Jewish immigrant experience. But instead of assimilating into the law-abiding middle class, as his own family did, the protagonists became outlaws, the kind of hoodlums that Abbie fantasized he could be.

Abbie also responded to the example of an older friend, Herb Gamberg, who, when home from Brandeis University, hung out with Abbie at the basketball court. Herb was a tough kid, at least in Abbie's imagination, and a scrappy ball player. But he was also a budding intellectual. He read serious authors like Kafka and Sartre, talked about existentialism, and expressed irreverent views about religion, politics, and the dull conformity of life in Worcester. In the 1950s many Americans looked down on intellectuals as weak, ineffectual, and somehow unmanly. By connecting the world of ideas to the more familiar street-corner reality, Herb Gamberg gave Abbie the notion that intellectuals could be rebels and that there were exciting ideas between the covers of books.[20]

Evidence of more serious reading came from a paper defending atheism that Abbie wrote for his sophomore English teacher, Mr. Brooks, titled "Reward, Punishment, and God." According to Abbie, the teacher took issue with his defense of atheism. When Abbie refused to back down, Brooks assailed him as a "little communist bastard," grabbed hold of his collar, and ripped it off his shirt. Abbie retaliated by overturning the teacher's desk and pummeling him. Whatever the facts (and it's true that defending atheism in the early 1950s could have been considered evidence of communist leanings), Abbie was suspended from school. If the suspension worried him at the time, he never admitted it. Indeed, the fact that he got kicked out of school became one of his favorite boasts, a feather in the cap, as he saw it, for a political organizer who wanted to be seen as an authentic spokesperson for rebellious youth.

Abbie played the dropout to the hilt, or so he said, spending days at the racetrack or in marathon poker games, or hanging out at the pool hall. Proud as he was of his jock skills and his success with women, he was prouder still of his pool-hustling ability. Even in his thirties, when confronted by the FBI about his role as a Yippie protest organizer during the 1968 Democratic convention in Chicago, he parried the agents' questions with stories of his teenage exploits:

NOTES FROM FBI INTERVIEW WITH ABBOTT HOFFMAN

By Special Agents John W. Robinson and Daniel H. Lucking

For a year thereafter HOFFMAN hung out in the
pool halls of Worcester. . . . HOFFMAN stated that

> he has always been able to make money as a pool
> hustler. HOFFMAN claimed to be a superior pool
> player.[21]

In *Revolution for the Hell of It*, Abbie described hustling pool as "a fine and delicate art." Its beauty, he explained, lay not in the skill of hitting a billiard ball into a pocket but in the ability to size up the opposition. A good pool hustler, Abbie said, knew whom he could beat, how much money to wager, and whether to string an opponent along by first losing a few games. A good hustler also knew, by the way the opponent looked and acted, whether to trust him to pay when he lost.[22]

Friends who watched Abbie shoot pool as an adult believed that they had discovered a key to Abbie's ingratiating political manner—his remarkable ability to charm potential converts and defuse hostile opponents. One friend, Mayer Vishner, followed Abbie into a pool hall in Ann Arbor, Michigan, where both were total strangers. Vishner, who knew nothing about pool, was not as impressed with Abbie's cue-handling skills as he was with his mastery of the hustler's art. "Abbie knew what you needed to see happen to stay interested," Vishner recalled. "That was his magic on the pool table for me. He just kept people exactly where he wanted them. If they needed to slaughter him, they did. If they needed to be awed by how good he was, they were. If they needed to feel it was an even game going, that's what they got. They came to him with the perfect pool game in their head and Abbie gave it to them. For fun. He was just as good as they needed him to be."[23]

As much time as Abbie spent in Worcester pool halls, he spent more time helping out at his father's store. Among friends, Abbie took a cynical attitude toward the family business, joking that the best thing he could say about the drugs his father sold was that "they wouldn't kill you." But he liked the challenge of selling and was good at it. Dealing with doctors and hospitals also brought its share of crises, and Abbie found that he enjoyed responding to emergencies. He was alone in the store on June 13, 1953, when tornadoes ripped through the Worcester area, killing 120 people and doing millions of dollars in damage. Abbie worked through the night ordering medical supplies and distributing them to the Red Cross and the local authorities. The next day he joined the search parties digging out bodies. "Disaster tested me," he wrote in his autobiography. "I liked the challenge."[24]

★   ★   ★

Next door to Worcester Medical Supply was a business that sup-
plied popular records to jukeboxes in the Worcester area, and
John Hoffman often brought home hit records after they had had
their run. Abbie wasn't interested in the hit parade of the 1940s
and early 1950s, however, and didn't become passionate about music until he was seventeen years old, when he discovered rock 'n'
roll. In 1954 a white disc jockey named Allen Freed began playing
black rhythm and blues records (which he called rock 'n' roll) on
WINS radio in New York. Likely because Abbie had his ears open
to whatever was different in popular culture (and in 1954 a white
deejay playing black music was startlingly different), he somehow
heard of the show and, by jerry-rigging an antenna out his window,
was able to pull in the signal. The first year that Freed was broadcasting, Abbie took Jack and two friends in his 1949 Ford to New
York's first rock 'n' roll concert. Big Joe Turner, Fats Domino, the
Drifters, and the Moonglows—all of them virtually unknown to
white audiences—were among the black acts performing at the St.
Nicholas Arena. This was the pre-Presley era of rock 'n' roll, before its breakthrough to a mass white audience. At a time when
blacks could not host their own television shows—or even appear
on television in the same act as white performers—Freed champi-
oned their music in the face of an outcry from religious leaders,
educators, and editorial writers who castigated rock 'n' roll for its
suggestive lyrics, its cannibalistic and tribal rhythms, and its
dangerous influence on American (for which read "white") youth.
Except for a cleaning woman who came into the Hoffman home
once a week, Abbie had had no contact with black people until he
started listening to rock 'n' roll. Not all the fans of the original
Allen Freed show responded to black music the way Abbie did. The
working-class hoods, for example, who adopted rock 'n' roll as part
of their teenage rebellion (as depicted in the movie *Blackboard
Jungle*) didn't translate their love of the music into a sympathy for
black Americans. But Abbie did. And as he would do ever after, he
turned his enthusiasm into a personal organizing project, trying to
get the rock 'n' roll records he heard on the Allen Freed show into
Worcester-area jukeboxes. As *Broken Arrow* inspired him to view
American history from the perspective of the American Indians,
rock 'n' roll encouraged him to look at the racial system in the

United States from the point of view of black Americans. Standing up for rock 'n' roll and speaking out for black culture in Worcester when no one else was doing it confirmed his status as a rebel, only now he had a cause.[25]

Abbie's dropout days did not last long. In September 1953 he enrolled at the Worcester Academy, a private boarding school that required students to wear preppy jackets and ties. Abbie was in the chess club and played tennis and junior varsity football. His grades were better than average, and he graduated in June 1955 without any disciplinary problem noted on his record. He wanted to go to Tufts in Medford, Massachusetts, and become a doctor, but was turned down. Instead he went to Brandeis University. Abbie later described his years at Brandeis as "the best education possible." John Hoffman, on the other hand, blamed Brandeis for influencing Abbie in the wrong direction.[26]

CHAPTER

2

BRANDEIS TO BERKELEY

A Radical Education
1955–1960

A bbie's first reaction to Brandeis was shock. Accustomed to being an academic star, he was awed by the better read, more sophisticated, and intellectually aggressive Jewish students from New York. Never before had he been in a scholastic environment where ideas were respected. In high school he had been taught that ideas were like dogma, to be accepted, not questioned. But at Brandeis he found that ideas were to be challenged, altered, and even rejected. To Abbie this confirmed that his instinct to challenge authority was not mere mischief-making. At Brandeis it had intellectual sanction. "Most of the other students . . . seemed used to this interchange of ideas," he wrote in his autobiography. "I was a comparative hick. Every new idea hit like a thunderclap."[1]

Brandeis in 1955 was seven years old and undergoing a period of rapid expansion. The school had been started in 1948 by a group of wealthy Jews who bought the campus of bankrupt Middlesex University in Waltham, Massachusetts. Their intention was to start a Jewish-supported but nonsectarian university that would hire for its faculty the cream of the Jewish intelligentsia, men (mostly) who could not get a job at other universities because of discriminatory faculty quotas or because they lacked academic credentials. (Discrimination in graduate programs prevented many Jewish intellectuals from studying for advanced degrees.) Most of the better colleges and universities in the United States had quotas against Jewish students similar to their quotas against Jewish teachers. Many Jewish youths, blocked from attending Ivy League and other prestigious colleges, thus ended up at Brandeis. Despite an effort to recruit students from all over the country, a majority, during the period that Abbie was there, were Jews from the Northeast, especially from the areas around New York and Boston.

Brandeis in the 1950s was an intense and intimate self-contained intellectual community. Through fortuitous circumstance the university escaped the McCarthyist scourge. In the early 1950s Senator Joseph McCarthy sent a team of investigators on a hunt for "subversives" in Boston-area universities. Because McCarthy feared he would be accused of anti-Semitism if he focused attention on the new Jewish-supported university, he targeted Harvard and MIT. (Their prominence as elite universities would not only guarantee the investigation publicity; it would fuel the class resentments that were the basis of so much of his working-class support.) As a result Brandeis was able to hire faculty members who would have been blacklisted at many other schools. Among them were Frank Manuel, a Harvard-educated historian who had fought with the communist-organized Abraham Lincoln Brigade in the Spanish Civil War and who taught Abbie's freshman History of Ideas course; literary critic Irving Howe and sociologist Lewis Coser, both veterans of Old Left sectarian squabbles; Max Lerner, a liberal newspaper columnist who, during the 1930s, had been considered a fellow traveler of the American Communist party; Philip Reiff and Stanley Diamond, a Marxist sociologist and anthropologist, respectively; Leo Bronstein, a nephew of Leon Trotsky; Philip Rahv, who had flirted with Trotskyism as an editor of *Partisan Review*; and Herbert Marcuse, a Marxist German émigré who, in 1954, had published *Eros and Civilization*, an attempt to reconcile the views of Marx and Freud. Intellectuals willing to buck orthodox opinion were rare in the 1950s, and the excitement of Brandeis classes spilled into the dormitories and student cafeterias.

Abbie's intention to become a doctor was an inevitable ambition given his background. In a family like the Hoffmans, becoming a doctor was the obvious step up in status for the number-one son. Abbie's sense of himself as a rebel did not negate his willingness to fulfill his family's expectation. Only when he found an interest strong enough to counter the push toward medicine did he assert his own will.

At Brandeis freshmen were required to take an introductory course in psychology taught by the chairman of the department, Abraham Maslow. In one of the first classes Maslow said it would

be all right to use words like *fuck* in his courses. Maslow's point
was that language in itself could not be obscene; it was the subjec-
tivity of the listener that made it so. At a time when words like *hell*
and *damn* were forbidden on the public airwaves and the *f* word
could not even be printed in novels, this was shocking stuff.[2] But
Maslow's attitude toward language was not the only quality that
endeared him to Abbie. Even more seductive was his belief that
social rebellion was not necessarily a manifestation of maladjust-
ment and that conformity did not necessarily represent healthy or
moral behavior. When society needed changing, or when the status
quo repressed an individual's need for self-expression, acts of rebellion might become a psychological necessity, Maslow taught.
Nonconformity could thus be a positive sign of mental health and
not a symptom of neurotic behavior.

This was music to Abbie's ears. John Hoffman had always fought
Abbie's rebelliousness and had baited him for his stubborn refusal
to give ground. "You think the whole world's wrong and you're
right?" he would demand of Abbie. Now Abbie could cite the authority of his Brandeis professor to bolster his rejoinder: "You got
it! I am right!"

At the end of his freshman year (and over John Hoffman's opposition), Abbie chose the psychology major.

"Most of all, I loved Professor Abe Maslow," Abbie wrote in *Major
Motion Picture*, a statement that is remarkable not only because
Abbie rarely, if ever, made so bold a declaration about another
man but because Maslow bitterly disapproved of Abbie and everything he stood for during the Vietnam War protest years. "There
was something about his humanistic psychology (considered radical
at the time) that I found exhilarating amidst the general pessimism
that pervaded Western thought. A hundred years of examining the
dark side of human experience, chiefly because of the influence of
Darwin and Freud, would be set in perspective by Maslow's insights regarding healthy motivation. . . . Maslovian theory laid a
solid foundation for launching the optimism of the sixties. Existential, altruistic, and up-beat, his teachings became my personal
code."[3]

The son of immigrant Russian Jews, Maslow had grown up in
Brooklyn, New York, was the approximate age of Abbie's father,

and likely represented an idealized father figure for Abbie. Although conventional in his way of life, Maslow was an intellectual rebel, an atheist from his youth, and a congenital optimist who admired the democratic socialism of Eugene Debs and Norman Thomas. The sectarian battles of the Old Left, which had raged at Brooklyn College when he taught there in the late 1930s, repelled him, however. Although he shared the idealism of the radical students and faculty, he was disturbed by what he considered to be the authoritarian personalities of many of the left's most assertive leaders. Rejecting the left, he remained determined to do good in the world, to help teach humans "how to be brotherly, cooperative, peaceful, courageous, and just," as he said in a speech to the American Psychological Association in 1955. "I sometimes think that the world will either be saved by psychologists—in the very broadest sense—or else it will not be saved at all."[4]

Do-gooder sentiments were heretical in the 1950s, and Maslow was going against the prevailing Freudian tide. As practiced in the United States, Freudianism was a tool for social adjustment. Dissident thought and nonconformist conduct were considered symptoms of neurotic behavior. The goal of Freudian psychotherapy was to help individuals adjust to the values of mainstream society.

Maslow's approach to psychology was the very opposite of Freud's. In *Motivation and Personality*, a collection of writings that Abbie used as a text at Brandeis, Maslow charged that psychology focused on the "darker, meaner" aspects of human personality—on "man's [sic] shortcomings, his illnesses, his sins"—while ignoring the more positive side, "his potentialities, his virtues, his achievable aspirations . . . his psychological height." Instead of studying mental illness, Maslow proposed to study mental health. By studying the characteristics of psychologically healthy people, Maslow hoped to uncover the inherent human qualities that made the best people tick.[5]

In his theory of human motivation, Maslow taught that humans are born with a hierarchy of needs. Once basic physiological needs like hunger and thirst are met, survival needs like having an income or a roof over one's head come to the fore, followed by the need for love or belongingness, and then the need for self-esteem. For many individuals who fulfill their need for self-esteem, an additional need becomes apparent, the need for self-actualization. This need "refers to man's desire for self-fulfillment, namely, to the tendency for him to become actualized in what he is potentially. This tendency might be phrased as the desire to become more and more what one is, to become everything that one is capable of becoming," Maslow wrote.[6]

Altruism was one of the traits that Maslow associated with self-actualized individuals. Abbie found this idea especially appealing when he became active in the civil rights movement. "Until Maslow, you challenged legal segregation because you hated your father or you wanted to sleep with your mother. You were deprived in early childhood and were fighting to overcome it," Abbie told an interviewer, explaining the orthodox Freudian position on individuals who asserted themselves to promote unconventional views. But Maslow "taught that you have a need to do good," Abbie explained. Maslow's hierarchy of needs was a "moral ladder," a challenge to motivate you to the point where you could give unselfishly, not out of guilt but from an inner need to do the right thing, to be altruistic. Protesting racial injustice was healthy human behavior.[7]

In Abbie's last years at Brandeis, Maslow began to take an interest in peak experiences. In his research Maslow found that self-actualized individuals all experienced transcendent moments of great joy, serenity, beauty, and wonder. Maslow speculated that the jolt of a peak experience might remove neurotic blocks and thus enable people to feel life as more worthwhile, even if life "is usually drab, pedestrian, painful, or ungratifying, since beauty, truth, and meaningfulness have been demonstrated [during the peak experience] to exist."[8]

Maslow's interest in peak experiences led him to an intellectual exploration of mysticism and Eastern religion. When Timothy Leary and Richard Alpert began their experiments with psychedelic drugs at Harvard in 1961, Maslow was an important supporter, although he did not try the drugs himself. (Maslow's daughter Ellen, who attended Brandeis with Abbie and would later work with him in the civil rights movement, was Leary's and Alpert's office administrator.) Abbie had already heard of the psychedelic experience from Dr. James Klee, Maslow's colleague at Brandeis who had researched magic mushrooms (psilocybin) in Mexico. Abbie's interest in hallucinatory drugs was strictly academic, however. There was some marijuana on the Brandeis campus, but Abbie, if he was aware of it, had no yen to smoke it.

The psychology department at Brandeis was small and informal. Classes often met in Maslow's Newton home, and students were invited over for dinner and weekend barbecues. Maslovian psychology was emerging as a controversial force in American psychology during the years Abbie was at Brandeis. In 1954 Maslow had initiated a committee of correspondence that linked psychologists and intellectuals of a sympathetic mind, including Gordon Allport, Eric Fromm, Kurt Goldstein, Paul Goodman, Rollo May, Ashley Montagu, Lewis Mumford, David Riesman, Carl Rogers, and Paul Tillich. This effort led in 1961 to the creation of *The Journal of Humanistic Psychology*, published at Brandeis, and to the acceptance by the psychology establishment of humanist psychology as a third and independent intellectual force, along with the Freudian and behavioristic approaches. Abbie attended a number of symposiums that Maslow organized and was thus able to meet Fromm, Karen Horney, Anna Freud, Harry Harlow, Erik Erickson, D. T. Suzuki, and Alan Watts. "Giants walked in the space of my intellectual world," he said of his Brandeis years.[9]

★   ★   ★

The big question that bugged Abbie and many of his Brandeis classmates was that of identity, the existential "Who am I?" As the children of first- and second-generation Americans, many Brandeis students, like Abbie, were the first in their family to be able to attend a university. The pressures—and the yearnings—to shed their ethnicity were powerful. But in rejecting their past, what were they to become? In their parents' time young people had been expected to work, not socialize. You studied, got a job, married, raised a family, and built a career. Identity was defined by race, class, religion, and what you did for a living. That a person might want to create a unique self-identity was considered self-indulgent, if not wicked—something actors did or eccentrics, bohemians, or neurotics. Yet the essential fact of growing up during the 1950s was that, despite the era's political conservatism, society was undergoing a revolutionary transformation, bending and breaking under the weight of new consumer products and new economic opportunities. As the United States crossed an economic threshold into affluence, the notion that one could choose one's identity suddenly became not only a new possibility but a problem. "The striking feature of present-day American life is precisely that there is no one over-all mode of conduct," wrote Allen Wheelis in *The Quest for Identity*, a book that made a profound impression on Abbie when he read it in the late 1950s.[10] For the first time, ordinary people were becoming aware that if they did not like the identity they had grown up with, they could invent one.

Abbie entered Brandeis playing the role of the hood from Worcester. His D.A. haircut, pegged pants, and black leather jacket with a slit down the back (which he claimed came from a knife fight) contrasted with the collegiate styles of the other students: white bucks or desert shoes, shirts with button-down collars, tan chinos or clean blue jeans. Other freshmen talked about concerts and books; Abbie talked about his tough friends and his exploits hustling pool, gambling, and picking up girls. At the first freshman mixer he stood out jitterbugging (while others did the lindy hop) in a shiny leopard-print jacket and blue suede shoes.[11]

A plethora of popular books gave names to those qualities in American society against which Abbie was rebelling. Book titles like *The Organization Man, The Man in the Gray Flannel Suit,* and *The Status Seekers* became, for Abbie and others, catchwords to describe the middle-class conformity they rejected. As working-class rebels expressed their rebelliousness by becoming hoods, intellectual rebels expressed their disenchantment by becoming bohemian. With its radical faculty and its strong program in the creative arts, Brandeis nurtured a bohemian scene to which Abbie was naturally drawn.

In the mid-1950s bohemianism was as much a functional way for creative people to arrange their lives as it was a defiant gesture at middle-class convention. Being a bohemian at Brandeis did not then imply being part of a movement for social change. For most Brandeis students in the bohemian set, being "bo" was simply a phase, a way of expressing an artistic inclination and making the university years socially adventurous. In the era before drugs were widely used and at a time when free love was a slogan more advocated than practiced, undergraduate bohemianism was more an attitude than a definable lifestyle.

When Abbie entered Brandeis, bohemianism was very much under the spell of European existentialism. The threat of nuclear holocaust was a constant reminder of the fragility and preciousness of life. The generation that came of age after the bomb was the first ever to face the possibility that human beings could destroy the world. The attitude on campus was serious and somber. There was little gaiety in the bohemian mood. The dark and intense Parisian dance hall "Apache" look (black leotards for women, dark glasses, and drab turtleneck sweaters) reflected the desperation that many people felt. (The Apache was a rigidly choreographed dance of violent male pursuit and female passivity, a creative expression of pent-up malevolence similar in pretense to the macho posturing and misogynist attitude of teenage rocks.)

There was also an American, more populist style of bohemianism. This was the bohemia where Abbie fit, and during his years at Brandeis it became an ascendant cultural force. Bohemian populism represented a quest for authenticity in the American experience. In black music—jazz, blues, and rock 'n' roll—and in folk music, bohemians found an aspect of American culture that they felt was honest and pure. Pete Seeger and the Weavers, Odetta, Big Bill Broonzy, Sonny Terry, and Brownie McGee were among the folk musicians Abbie heard live at Brandeis, along with the records of Leadbelly and Woody Guthrie. He also went to Club 47 in Cambridge to hear Joan Baez sing. Still a teenager, she was a cult figure around Harvard Square, known for her bare feet, long hair, and the pure soprano renderings of plaintive English and Appalachian ballads.

Folk music in the postwar era often seemed like left-wing politics in cultural disguise. Many folk musicians held left-wing views and were blacklisted from the popular media. They survived by performing in coffeehouses and on progressive college campuses like Brandeis. (Pete Seeger was banned even at Brandeis—a Brandeis women's fund-raising group in Iowa protested his appearance at the university after he was cited for contempt of Congress for refusing to answer questions about his politics at a House Committee on Un-American Activities hearing. The citation was ultimately overturned in the federal courts, but not before student and faculty protests led to Seeger's return to the campus.) Folk concerts often sounded like a cultural history of the "red decade," the 1930s. While Tin Pan Alley produced popular songs about romantic escapism, "folkies," in their songs about ordinary working people, presumed to represent a more politically radical America. It was an irony of 1950s popular culture that the music that celebrated the organizing struggles of the labor union movement during the 1930s found its most enthusiastic audience among bohemian rebels and that bohemians, through their interest in folk music, became more class-conscious than organized labor.

Few leftists saw any political potential in the populist bohemianism of the early 1950s. In 1954 Irving Howe published an essay in *Partisan Review* ruing that bohemianism—which he defined "as a strategy for bringing artists and writers together in their struggle with and for the world"—was fast disappearing. What passed in the 1950s for bohemianism, Howe charged, was a "disreputable . . . exhibitionism" that had only an "incidental relationship" with the real thing.[12] In actuality, bohemianism was on the brink of a revival that, for the first time, would transform it into a popular movement. The agent for this change was the beat generation, a group of writers who had come together in the 1940s and begun to get their works published in the mid-1950s. Allen Ginsberg made the breakthrough in 1955 with his poem *Howl*—a Whitmanesque assault on everything that was wrong with American life. Published a year later and banned as obscene by the San Francisco police, the poem and its author got national publicity after a successful trial overturned the ban. In 1957 Jack Kerouac's *On the Road* was published, as were poems by Lawrence Ferlinghetti, Gregory Corso, and a host of lesser-known writers. Suddenly the beats were controversial. The media massed for attack. Typically, *Life* magazine dismissed them with neo-Freudian rhetoric as neurotic, maladjusted losers whose childish rants would quickly be forgotten. *Mademoiselle* considered them "chic" but disparaged the substance of their protest. But among student bohemians, the beats found an attentive and understanding audience.

In Irving Howe's course on American literature Abbie read James T. Farrell, John Steinbeck, John Dos Passos, and other American writers with social concerns and learned, he said, to distinguish the American reality from the apple-pie mythology he had been taught, "so that was education as a subversive act which is the only proper education." But Howe had no sympathy for the beat rebellion and, according to Abbie, attacked beat writers as "guttersnipes" for their use of dirty language. By attacking the beats, Howe made them seem interesting. "For those of us who were in a rebellious mood, just to rebel against Irving Howe we went out and bought the beat literature," Abbie remembered.[13]* Abbie was immediately attracted to the beats because their description of life in the United States was true to his own experience. "They were talking about heavy shit in a language that was American," he said in a 1984 interview. "Any movement would have had to be American to reach us at that time. We could not be influenced by any foreign ideology; it would have been totally alien. So it would have had to have images of baseball and pool halls, Coney Island, Denver, and Paterson, New Jersey, the bomb, and supermarkets in California to make any sense. It would have had to use the rhythms of jazz, because those of us who had made the break with mainstream America were already listening to rhythm and blues, which was black and also sexy."[14]

Norman Mailer's 1957 defense of hipsterism, titled "The White Negro," brought out the beat movement's political dimension. Hipsterism, as Mailer defined the ideology of the beat generation, represented the merging sensibilities of Abbie's three favorite identity models: the bohemian, the juvenile delinquent, and the Negro. From the bohemian, the hipster drew a need for artistic creation, even in a materialistic culture that deadened sensitivity and compelled conformity. From the juvenile delinquent, the hipster drew a nihilistic spirit of defiance, a willingness to do anything to break the restraints of the dominant culture, even to commit acts of mindless violence. From the Negro, the hipster took the awareness that danger was everywhere, that one had to be alert and clever at all times in order to escape life-denying conformist pressures. Mailer argued that class conflict was no longer the motor that would drive revolution. A new dialectic was emerging, and, as with the class struggle, people would have to choose which side they were on. "One is hip or one is square. . . . one is a rebel or one conforms, one is a frontiersman in the Wild West of American night life, or else a Square cell, trapped in the totalitarian tissues of American society, doomed willy-nilly to conform if one is to

---

* Whether this story is true or not, Abbie's mocking attitude toward Howe had nothing to do with his relationship with Howe at Brandeis. Like many radicals of the 1960s, Abbie used Howe as a personal kicking board. His scorn was based on Howe's bitter and divisive attacks on the New Left and the radical antiwar movement during the 1960s.

succeed."[15] The dialectic of hip and square transcended geopolitical lines in favor of levels of consciousness. Squares sought security and, believing the lies of the politicians, conned themselves into political passivity. Hipsters, on the other hand, understood political reality, were hip to the power of the bomb, and knew that the Cold War, if allowed to fester, could end up destroying life on earth. Hipsters, staring into the face of death, demanded life. Here was the core idea for a countercultural political strategy, for if the existing political systems could not assure life, the hipsters and beats—or at least the hippies who followed in their footsteps— were going to create new, alternative ways of living outside the existing system.[16]

Abbie had read Mailer's novel *The Naked and the Dead* in high school. He admired Mailer, and when he read "The White Negro" at Brandeis, he identified with Mailer's hipster. "Mailer," Abbie said later, "took everything that was being said culturally—what the beat generation was saying in poetry and what was being said in jazz—and added a political perspective to it. As a result, I began taking a more active interest in American politics. I began reading Paul Goodman, C. Wright Mills, and other social critics."[17]

Abbie's personal hipster hero was Lenny Bruce, a stand-up comedian with a Borscht Belt delivery whose nightclub act was considered too controversial for network television. Bruce's satire defined the meaning of *hip*. He scoured politicians, organized religion, racial attitudes, and sexual stereotypes, but the butt of his jokes were not the obvious targets. Attributes that society considered deviant and worthy of scorn were, to Bruce, within the realm of the human norm. When he made jokes about "faggots" and "dykes"—as he often did—it was not homosexuality he was making fun of; it was the narrow-mindedness of the squares who thought homosexuality wrong. Bruce demanded of his audience that they accept his open-minded premises in order to get his jokes. Like Maslow, he analyzed "dirty" language in order to expose the hypocrisy of those who equated "clean" language with high moral standards. His jokes pointed out that words describing sex, love, and human procreation were considered obscene, but language describing hate and violence was not. As if to illustrate his point, police in San Francisco, Chicago, and New York who taped this shtick arrested him for using obscene language. These arrests eventually destroyed his career. Abbie didn't see Bruce in person while he was attending Brandeis, but he heard Bruce's records and read articles about his act. Abbie finally saw him perform in the early 1960s in New York. Abbie's brother Jack, who went with him, recalls that Abbie's "big desire" then was to be a stand-up comic. "I sensed that when we first saw Lenny Bruce at the Village Vanguard. I could see in his eyes, this was his guy."[18]

Abbie identified with the bohemian crowd at Brandeis, but he was not a hard-core bohemian. He continued to gamble at cards and on the horses. He remained a jock, playing pickup basketball and baseball, and varsity wrestling and tennis (he was captain of the Brandeis tennis team in his senior year). Years later he commented on how his love of sports compromised his standing as a bohemian. "I liked the role of being the jock who was a bohemian and the bohemian who was also the jock." A rebel among rebels, he exulted in the role of the outsider and "always wanted to be none of the above."[19]

There were other aspects of Abbie's life that made him suspect to hard-core bohemians. Although he gave up driving a Corvette for a more suitable Volkswagen bug, he also acquired a big-finned Cadillac in a poker game and insisted, the few times he got it running, on driving it around campus to the derision of the bohemian crowd. Worse, from the standpoint of bohemian orthodoxy, he reveled in what Ellen Maslow, Abe Maslow's daughter, called "his crazy business genius." Through his friendship with a racetrack tout who had an interest in a Waltham delicatessen, Abbie and his roommate, Manny Schreiber, began to sell submarine sandwiches late at night in the Brandeis dormitories. Funny, upbeat, and radiating "pure salesman energy," it was in the role of "the sub man" that Abbie was best known at Brandeis. Abbie earned eighty dollars a week selling subs—more than many blue-collar kids could make working full-time. He used the money to keep his cars on the road and take a summer trip through Europe after his junior year. Schreiber used the friendships he made selling subs to help him become president of the senior class.[20]

The year before Abbie entered Brandeis, Ngo Dinh Diem, an aristocratic Vietnamese who was virtually unknown to the Vietnamese people, was installed by the United States as the ruler of South Vietnam. The circumstances of Diem's coming to power attracted little attention in the United States. Indochina was, after all, a

French problem, or so it had seemed. The French had not been able to reassert their control over this remote corner of Asia—formerly called French Indochina—after having been driven out by the Japanese during World War II. In Vietnam a coalition of nationalists and communists called the Viet Minh had fought to evict the Japanese. The United States applauded the Viet Minh's war against Japan but then abandoned the cause of Vietnamese independence to support France in its attempt to reestablish colonial rule. Despite the United States' assuming up to 80 percent of the French war costs, the Viet Minh defeated the French in 1954. In the Geneva Accords of 1954 (which the United States refused to sign), Viet Minh leader Ho Chi Minh agreed to a temporary partition of Vietnam on the promise that elections in 1956 would unify the country once and for all. While the Viet Minh controlled North Vietnam, Bao Dai, a Vietnamese prince who had sided with the Japanese during World War II, was installed, by the Americans and the French, as ruler in the South. It was the unpopularity of this regime that led the United States to place Diem in power. With American approval, Diem canceled the 1956 elections. It was commonly acknowledged, even by U.S. President Dwight D. Eisenhower, that had the elections been held, Ho Chi Minh and the Viet Minh would have won in a landslide.

In order to consolidate his power, Diem began liquidating the veteran Viet Minh resistance fighters who had settled in their native South after the French defeat. In June 1955, when Abbie was graduating from high school, a team of CIA agents, under the cover of a Michigan State University police-training program, arrived in Saigon to train Diem's intelligence police in methods to "expose and root out Communists." With American backing, Diem's regime tortured and assassinated former resistance fighters or sent them to American-financed "reeducation" camps. Because many South Vietnamese supported the Viet Minh, Diem extended his campaign of repression to include peasants, Buddhists, and middle-class political opponents. In 1957 and 1958 civil war broke out in the South as the Viet Minh began to defend themselves and Diem's noncommunist opponents looked to them for protection. In 1959 the North Vietnamese began to send supplies to support their southern brethren. In June 1959, when Abbie graduated from Brandeis, there were only a few thousand Americans advising Diem's army. It's likely that Abbie never heard of Vietnam while he was a student at Brandeis—and in this he was typical of most Americans.

In the 1950s, according to the popular myth, everyone in America was happy; those who weren't satisfied must therefore be either maladjusted or—worse—communist. Cracks in the political consensus were beginning to appear, however. In 1954 the U.S. Supreme Court had unanimously outlawed public school segregation in the South. Television news coverage of the white South's violent resistance to integrated schooling forced the racial issue into the nation's consciousness. In December 1955 Rosa Parks, a black seamstress with a history of social activism, was arrested for refusing to sit in the back of a bus as required by law in Montgomery, Alabama. The subsequent Montgomery bus boycott brought the Reverend Martin Luther King, Jr., to the forefront of the civil rights movement and transformed the struggle for civil rights into a more aggressive, though still nonviolent, grassroots movement. During the Montgomery boycott King came to speak at Brandeis and drew the biggest crowd in the university's history. Abbie recalled the "reverential" feeling that everyone had for the young minister. Though "awestruck," Abbie was unsure of how he, or anyone at Brandeis, could support the civil rights struggle. The South was another world. And the students had no sense of themselves as a generation with a role to play outside the mainstream political structures.

By the tepid standards of 1950s politics Brandeis was a hotbed of left-wing radicalism. In 1954 Irving Howe and Lewis Coser had helped start *Dissent* magazine in order to combat the influence of Stalinism on leftist politics and sustain a vision of democratic socialism. The ideological battles of the Old Left often provoked heated debates among the university's left-leaning faculty, but these conflicts didn't interest Abbie. The American Revolution, on the other hand, fascinated him. For one history project he retraced the movements of the minutemen in the battles of Concord and Lexington. Tom Paine and Samuel Adams were his particular heroes. Like the radicals of the 1960s, he would later point out, they created their own underground press to fan the flames of rebellion. They didn't always stick to the facts but understood the necessity of publicizing themes that would ring true to the colonists' experience. And they understood, as he understood, that they didn't need a popular majority to start their revolution. ("You are never talking about a majority," Abbie explained in an interview in the mid-1980s. "You are talking about enough.")[21]

Among the many radicals who spoke at Brandeis, Dorothy Day

and Saul Alinsky interested Abbie the most. Both were committed
to action rather than theory. Day was the founder of the Catholic
Worker movement and had dedicated her life to service among the
poorest of the poor. Her religious-based radical pacifism also made
her an advocate of civil disobedience against nuclear weapons.
There was a purity to her politics that left no room for sectarian
squabbling. Alinsky was famous as a community organizer among
white working-class ethnic groups in Chicago. Abbie dug his down-
to-earth talk and the street-tough tactics with which he wrested
concessions from Chicago's rulers. In his own words, Abbie became
"somewhat of a groupie," going to hear Alinsky every time he spoke
in Boston and following him to his hotel to talk more about community organizing.[22]

But Abraham Maslow was Abbie's real hero, and becoming self-
actualized was his personal goal. The left-wingers on the Brandeis
faculty saw no political implications in Maslovian psychology.
While acknowledging Maslow's brilliance, they considered his ideas
impractical and utopian. Marcuse and Manuel, for example, although friendly enough with Maslow to go swimming and then have
Sunday brunch with him once a month, thought him a fuzzy-
minded idealist whose liberal Democratic politics indicated his political naiveté.[23] It was only after leaving Brandeis and becoming a
political activist himself that Abbie began to recast Maslovian psychology in a political light.*

As the 1950s came to a close there were no alternative lifestyles to
catch Abbie's attention, and there was no social crusade (except in

---

* Betty Friedan, in *The Feminine Mystique*, was the first social activist to
grasp the political implications of Maslovian psychology. In the early
1960s she set out to describe and analyze the discontents of American
women and discovered Maslow's writings. Drawing from her talks with
him, she challenged the Freudian orthodoxy that American women were
neurotic because they refused to accept their place in the patriarchal
society. "Our culture does not permit women to accept or gratify their
basic need to grow and fulfill their potentialities as human beings," Friedan wrote. To be everything that they wanted and, in Maslow's terms,
needed to be, women would have to rebel. Abbie knew about Friedan's
book because his first wife, Sheila, talked about it. Although he never
credited Friedan with influencing his political thinking, she was the only
person before him to use Maslow's ideas as a basis for a social movement.

the distant South) to inspire commitment. There was the draft, of course. And there was graduate school—a means of postponing the draft and the dreaded day when he would have to take on adult responsibilities and start a career. Abbie thought of doing graduate work at Duke, where there was a research program on extrasensory perception, but he knew he would need more practical courses in clinical psychology to establish professional credentials. At Maslow's suggestion he applied and was accepted to the master's degree program in psychology at the University of California at Berkeley. He got a position as a teaching assistant in the home economics department, helping to teach and grade papers for a class in child psychology.

Student activism was starting to heat up in September 1959, when Abbie arrived at Berkeley. A group of independent radicals, inspired by the resistance of faculty members to enforced loyalty oaths, had established a political organization in 1957 called Toward a More Active Student Community, which, after running a slate of candidates in the student election, became popularly known as SLATE. Disgusted with the attempts of the minuscule remnants of Old Left youth groups to dominate its meetings, SLATE adopted a nonideological policy that anticipated the open, nonsectarian politics of the New Left. Anyone could be active in SLATE, but only as an individual. Students who attended SLATE meetings were expected to leave their ideology and their organizational agenda at the door. Old Left squabbling about the fine points of Marxism was not tolerated.

The late 1950s was a period of structural change for the California public university system. Anticipating a demographic bubble when the baby-boom generation reached college age, administrators designated the Berkeley campus as a center for graduate studies. By 1960 graduate students represented a third of the student body, with more than 70 percent of them living, as Abbie did, in off-campus rooming houses and apartments. In the spring of 1959, while Abbie was in his last semester at Brandeis, SLATE won control of the Berkeley student government. The SLATE candidates were opposed to racial discrimination in fraternities and sororities, in the admission policy of the university, and in housing and job opportunities in the Berkeley area. They called for the abolition of capital punishment, of loyalty oaths, of nuclear testing, and of compulsory ROTC; and they supported California agricultural workers in their struggle to unionize. It was the first time

since the McCarthy era that the student government took such controversial and (for the time) radical stands. In the summer and fall
of 1959 Clark Kerr, the president of the university, unleashed a
counterattack against SLATE, disfranchising graduate students
from student elections and making student government beholden,
not to the students, but to the university administration. The Kerr
directives also forbade student organizations from promoting off-
campus political activities. Controversy over the Kerr directives
was raging in student political circles when Abbie began his graduate studies at Berkeley.[24]*

Abbie took no part in SLATE's deliberations and was not close
to the radical graduate students who were most involved. His one
political friend was Marty Kenner, a freshman from New York who
started a lifelong friendship with Abbie at Berkeley. Kenner, who
was active with SLATE, remembers Abbie there as "an outsider
with a great reservoir within himself for enjoyment and seeing. He
was not being an actor in the world but an observer and commen-
tator. He knew who he was. Abbie would visit me at my rooming
house, and we'd go out and eat and talk. . . . Abbie always wanted
to teach me how to shoplift. He'd recount tales of picking up girls
at the movie theater. He loved these stories. It was genuine. It really
was Abbie. At Berkeley his irreverence was so deep that he didn't
have to assume any poses. New York Jews at Berkeley were trying
to become Californians. But Abbie was the Jew from Worcester
who did not try to adapt."

Abbie's enthusiasms at Berkeley were Abe Maslow, Lenny Bruce,
and the beat scene. He heard Ginsberg read *Howl* at a Berkeley
theater and felt "a call to action" as he joined Ginsberg in shouting
denunciations at the materialistic god "Moloch." He made frequent
trips across the Bay Bridge to Lawrence Ferlinghetti's City Lights
bookstore. "His weltanschauung," according to Kenner, "was the
hipster scene, an attitude towards life, isolated, not communal-
oriented." But Abbie was not close to the beat circles. He was still
the outsider, observing, learning, absorbing, integrating into his
life selected aspects of the beat sensibility that fit his own experience. As always, he found tennis partners and a group of jocks with

* In 1964 the Free Speech Movement waged a successful student strike to
overturn the Kerr directives and regain the right for students to publicize
and raise money on campus for such issues as civil rights.

whom he played ball. He found poker games, shot pool, and kept an eye out for business opportunities. Needing money, he organized the Bo-Rah Travel Club and chartered a plane to fly East Coast students home for Christmas. The "Bo" stood for bohemian, the "Rah" for the rah-rah, Joe College, fraternity and sorority types. Sympathetic to the Bos, he saw no reason to break sharply with the Rahs. He'd take what he needed from both. His identity was securely his own.[25]

When Abbie returned to Berkeley after Christmas break, the activist 1960s were about to begin. On February 1 four black college students sat down at a Woolworth lunch counter in Greensboro, North Carolina, and inaugurated the southern sit-in movement to integrate public facilities. The movement stirred the idealism of many white students on campuses in the North and inspired a spirit of direct action that was in stark contrast to the political apathy of the 1950s.

In the spring of 1960, as the southern sit-in movement was gathering steam, three events took place in Berkeley that further defined the political radicalism of the 1960s.

First, a seventeen-year-old freshman, the son of an Air Force colonel, was expelled from the university for conducting a seven-day fast against compulsory ROTC. The fast drew the attention of Abbie and other students to the existence of a small radical pacifist movement that was using Gandhian tactics to protest nuclear weapons and to the university's complicity with the military system through its support of ROTC and its connection to the Livermore Radiation Laboratory, where nuclear weapons research was taking place.

Second, on May 3, 1960, a convicted rapist named Caryl Chessman was scheduled to be executed at San Quentin prison on an island in San Francisco Bay, the eighth time his execution had been scheduled over a period of twelve years. While the proof of his guilt, supporters claimed, was ambiguous, the fact of his rehabilitation was not. In prison Chessman had educated himself and then begun to teach others. He had written books, become a jailhouse lawyer for other prisoners, and composed the legal briefs that resulted in stays of his own execution. Over the years, as each new execution date was postponed, Chessman's case had become a cause for opponents of capital punishment all over the world. In the Bay Area small groups of Quakers vigiled at the prison every time Chessman's execution was scheduled. In 1960 hundreds of Berkeley students joined them.

The night before Chessman's date came due, about seven hundred people gathered for an all-night deathwatch at the gate to San Quentin. The next morning, after an announcement that the state supreme court had voted four to three against clemency for Chessman, about thirty demonstrators spontaneously sat down in front of the entrance to the prison. When the police tried to clear the road by dragging them away, they brushed themselves off and returned to the blockade. Finally, the police had to use force to clear a passage.

Chessman's life was now in the hands of Governor Pat Brown, a liberal Democrat who claimed to be opposed to capital punishment. But Brown refused to stay the execution, arguing that he could not impose his personal view on the law. At ten o'clock that morning Chessman was executed, and everyone went home. The execution left a bitter aftertaste among the vigilers. Politics, they felt, had taken precedence over morality, and the governor, though a liberal, had not had the courage to stand on his moral principles. At the same time they were exhilarated by their protest, surprised at their own audacity. Walking a picket line was a new experience for most members of Abbie's generation. Michael Rossman, a Berkeley student active in SLATE who had sat down in the road, was not alone in feeling that he was participating in the birth of some new, and as yet unnamed, spirit of dissidence. "The long march went on, slowly, and just as slowly the feeling grew that we were marching not for Chessman alone, but for something much more important, something transcending politics and laws," Rossman wrote the day after Chessman's execution.[26]

Nine days later HUAC came to town.

Earlier in the year the House Committee on Un-American Activities had announced plans to hold hearings in San Francisco's City Hall to investigate subversive activity in the Bay Area. HUAC hearings were an essential weapon in the right wing's arsenal to destroy liberal and left-wing initiatives. The committee's method was to assemble raw data collected by right-wing vigilante groups, the FBI, and police "red squad" units, and then confront subpoenaed witnesses in public hearings with allegations of communist activity. The public hearings were theater pieces in which witnesses were not allowed to question informants or challenge the data being used against them. In the political climate of the 1950s merely being subpoenaed by HUAC was sufficient cause to get one fired from a job or blacklisted from a profession. What was more insidious about HUAC's tactics was the damper they put on all political activity. If in 1960 a person's life could be destroyed for a political position taken in 1950 or even during the "red decade" of the 1930s, then a person risked being destroyed in 1970 or 1990 for a political position taken in 1960. Because of the power of HUAC— along with local and state versions of the committee—people were afraid of taking political stands. Signing a petition for peace, giving money to a liberal cause, or walking a picket line against racial injustice would be recorded by informants for future use by the House committee.

The courage to challenge HUAC's authority was building slowly in the Bay Area. The area had a strong grassroots left-wing community centered on the longshoremen's union headed by Harry Bridges, long a target of HUAC investigations. And the 1960 hearings caught student activism at a rising tide. It seemed especially outrageous to the anti-HUAC forces that the chairman of the committee was a Louisiana congressman, Edwin Willis, who represented a district in which blacks could not vote.

Although the hearings were supposed to be open to the public on a first-come basis, HUAC provided its right-wing friends with special passes that enabled them to pack the hearing room. As a result, in the opening session on May 12, only a small number of HUAC opponents were able to get in. In the afternoon the students who were on line waiting for seats began chanting, "Let us in!" and singing "The Star Spangled Banner." When the students already seated in the chamber heard the chants, they began their own chant, "Let them in! Let them in!" forcing Willis to call in police to remove them. Inspired by this show of support from the students, the witnesses were emboldened to challenge the legitimacy of the committee and to question Willis's right to a seat in Congress. Never before had the committee faced losing control of its hearings; never before had witnesses and spectators been so openly defiant.

The resulting publicity brought thousands of HUAC's opponents to picket City Hall for the next day's hearings. Abbie was one of them. Again, several hundred protesters, most of them students, lined up to get seats. Only twenty were allowed in for the morning session, and a few more in the afternoon despite the availability of empty seats. About two hundred students who had not been able to get into the hearings stayed in the rotunda of City Hall singing loudly enough to interfere with the proceedings. Without warning, the police turned high-pressure fire hoses on them, expecting, no doubt, that they would flee the building. But the students refused to budge and began to sing "We Shall Not Be Moved" (a left-wing labor song that many had probably learned from the *Talking Union* record album of 1930s labor songs sung by Pete Seeger and the Almanac Singers). The police then attacked with billy clubs and tossed and dragged the students down the second-floor stairs. Sixty-three students were arrested for disorderly conduct.

That night the Berkeley students held a meeting on campus. The turnout was "unbelievable," according to Rossman. "On this campus where you can't raise fifty people for a poetry reading, when only 1,000 students will sign an anti-ROTC petition in two weeks of circulation, where attempts to organize peace programs, discussion groups, and similar things have met repeated failure, 800 people came to an informal, unpublicized meeting."[27] The next day more than four thousand people gathered in protest outside City Hall.

Throughout his life Abbie claimed to have participated in the Berkeley events he properly described in *Major Motion Picture* as "the birth of the sixties." Likely, he was one of the hundreds of anonymous vigilers for Caryl Chessman and the thousands of picketers protesting the HUAC hearings. Although he had been accidentally caught in a police sweep against student demonstrators in Paris during his summer trip to Europe, he had never seen police attacking American students, and their brutality shocked him. Still, Abbie played only a supporting role, at most, in the nascent New Left at Berkeley. But he chose to identify with its birthing and to define his politics as an extension of this experience. As Michael Rossman remarks about Abbie at Berkeley, "These concentrated events made a deep, reverberant impression on any young person of hip/progressive/alienated disposition even so peripherally involved. . . . Though his stay here was short, it came at a formative time of his life, and intersected a peak, seminal instant of public activity. I imagine that many themes of his later career were oriented and/or energized in part by his Berkeley experience."[28]

The HUAC and Chessman demonstrations were a heady conclusion to Abbie's year at Berkeley. He went there as a hipster, critical of society but reluctant to commit himself to collective action; he left identifying with the moral concerns of a budding activist movement. His exposure to activism led him at least to consider a career as a radical organizer. Fired up by the spirit of the protests, he went to see Harry Bridges, the leader of the West Coast longshoremen. As Abbie told this story, he said to Bridges, "I want to change society. I want to be a union organizer."

Bridges, however, told him to forget it. "Unions are finished. Automation. The FBI. There is no future in changing society with the union movement."

"So what am I supposed to do?" asked Abbie.

"You're a smart Jewish boy," Bridges responded. "You'll figure out something."[29]

3 CIVIL RIGHTS WORKER

Worcester and the
South
1960–1966

During spring break in 1960, just before the Chessman vigil and the HUAC protest, Abbie's girlfriend from Brandeis flew out to visit him at Berkeley. Sheila Karklin was a year behind Abbie, and the two had been dating on and off for two years. "A petite, olive-skinned 'bo' with mysterious green eyes," as Abbie described her, she was studious and intense, interested in classical music and fine art, outspoken in her opinions, and, according to Abbie, "a feminist before her time." They did the California tour: Marin County and the redwoods, then south to Big Sur. In a cabin by the sea Sheila got pregnant, and in the summer of 1960 the couple got married. With Sheila, Abbie eventually had two children, Andrew and Amy.[1]

Abbie was thinking of returning to Worcester even before he got married and had already been offered a job as a staff psychologist at Worcester State Hospital. Married life in his old hometown was not a foreclosure on more exciting plans. There was as yet no counterculture or alternative society to drop into; he had no sense of himself as part of a generation with a mission to change the world.

At Worcester State Hospital, Abbie worked mostly in the admitting office, interviewing and administering Rorschach and other psychological tests to incoming patients. It was a dead-end job for someone without a master's degree, and despite his autobiographical claims he never got one. Family responsibility, he later said, prevented him from studying for an advanced degree. As likely, it was his disenchantment with being a psychologist, his distaste for academic discipline, and his growing commitment to movement organizing. Working in a state mental institution gave Abbie a hard-headed view of mental health. Unlike the radical psychologists who would come to prominence in the late 1960s and debunk the idea of madness itself, Abbie was ready to concede that many of the people he saw were, in fact, "whacked out of their skulls." But he also saw that many of his patients were institutionalized because they were too much trouble to be cared for by their families and that their symptoms were often related to their being institutionalized against their will. Verifying Maslow's teachings, Abbie saw psychological disorder as a social problem; it was not enough to try to make things better for individuals one at a time. "After listening to hundreds of patients, I was convinced the problem lay out there," he wrote. "Beyond the walls."[2]

In the autumn of 1960 Abbie attended a screening at Clark University of *Operation Abolition*, a documentary produced by right-wing filmmakers with the assistance of the House Committee on Un-American Activities and the FBI in order to show how a handful of disciplined communists had supposedly "duped" thousands of innocent students into protesting the San Francisco HUAC hearings and had then deliberately incited them to riot. According to the movie, the demonstrations were part of a larger communist plan to sully the reputation of HUAC and thus undermine American democracy.

In fact, *Operation Abolition* was a hodgepodge of network news clips, some of which had nothing to do with the San Francisco hearings. In the discussion period after the film Abbie rose to point out the film's distortions. His assertion that he had been at the hearings touched off a shouting match between conservative students calling him "pinko" and liberal students demanding, "Let him speak!" It was the first time Abbie had ever spoken publicly about politics. He was proud of how he handled himself, and he liked the excitement his speaking caused.

Operation Abolition was then being shown to student, community, and patriotic groups around the country. On progressive campuses, where it was met with jeers, it helped to solidify student opposition to the crude anticommunism of the House committee. But elsewhere it was received as proof that the demonstrations, as Gordon H. Scherer, a Republican member of the committee, asserted, "were clearly planned at the highest Communist levels."[3] As a result of speaking out at Clark, Abbie was hired by the Worcester chapter of the American Civil Liberties Union (ACLU) to travel with the film around central Massachusetts and defend the anti-HUAC position.

The small, rural hill communities of central Massachusetts were still very much affected by the antiradicalism of the McCarthy period. Liberals kept their views to themselves, and speakers representing progressive positions were rarely seen or heard. In the town of Orange the screening of the film was followed by questions that were brutal, frank, and typical of the period. Was Abbie a communist? Did he believe in God? Was the ACLU a communist organization? What did Abbie think about Negroes? Would he want one to marry his daughter? Finally, one old farmer standing in the back said that he agreed with Abbie's criticism of the movie. Suddenly it was as if a dam of fear had been broken. One man's dissent inspired others to honestly say what they thought of the film and of HUAC. The tenor of the meeting quickly turned. Almost twenty years later Abbie recalled the thrill he felt at that moment: it was as if he was in a time capsule hurtling back to the country's radical past and witnessing a farmer-labor movement rising out of the dust. "I fell in love with America that night," he wrote in *Major Motion Picture*. "Cornfields. Town meetings. Niagara Falls. Hot dogs. Parades. Red Sox double headers. America was built by people who wanted to change things. It was founded on strong principles. I saw myself as a Son of Liberty, riding through the night, sounding the alarm."[4]

In the autumn of 1960 political epiphanies such as this were precious and rare. But the spirit of the southern sit-in movement and the student radicalism that had so moved Abbie at Berkeley was slowly making itself felt. Within the year his peers would begin organizing among black sharecroppers in the Deep South and among white coal miners in Appalachia. They would meet ordinary people with extraordinary courage who were willing to risk everything for a better world. Some of these people, like Fannie Lou Hamer of Mississippi, would become national heroes. Others, like the farmer who had sided with Abbie, would remain anonymous to history, important only for how they inspired this or that solitary organizer to carry on. For activists like Abbie, these experiences were profoundly patriotic. In their aggregate they engendered a transcendent faith in the human capacity to grow and change, as well as a belief that ordinary Americans would respond to the organizers' efforts. For Abbie, the ability to recall that farmer in Orange would always be a key to his political effectiveness. When he stopped believing that people were listening, as he did at times in the late 1960s and early 1970s, he lost his grounding in the American culture, and his politics took a reckless, churlish, and self-defeating turn.

During Abbie's first few years living as an adult in Worcester, the New Left was as yet unformed. His tour for the ACLU took place in a political vacuum. A person who wanted to be active in the ban-the-bomb or civil rights movements would have no meetings to attend, no organizations to join, and no local leader to call. McCarthyism had completely destroyed even the vestiges of a left-of-center political culture. But Abbie would never be content to be just a family man. Much like his father, he found fulfillment outside the house, as a man about Worcester. In January 1961 he enrolled in a film course at Brandeis and the following October, with backing from a local Cadillac dealer, reopened the Park Arts Theatre, an old movie house, with a plan to show old movies, foreign movies, and those noncommercial movies too offbeat to play the commercial circuits. Abbie's theater was the first of its kind in Worcester and one of only a few foreign film/revival houses outside major cities and university communities. Though he was still holding a full-time job at Worcester State Hospital and had a newborn baby at home, he spent most of his free time getting the theater off the ground. He selected the films, chose the music to play before and after each screening ("to create an atmosphere suitable for the film," he told a local reporter), wrote and mailed a monthly schedule describing the forthcoming films, selected and sold art posters and books about movies in the lobby, and encouraged local artists to hang their works there. Much of his time was spent tracking down films he wanted to see. One such project was the German propaganda film *Triumph of the Will* ("To me, this film represents the best way to see what life was like under the Nazi regime and the effects of propaganda on the human mind," he told the reporter); another was the complete works of Charlie Chaplin. His taste in movies was more populist than avant-garde, however. He once previewed *Guns of the Trees*, an experimental film by Jonas and Adolphus Mekas (underground filmmakers who had a following in bohemian circles in New York), and decided it was too obscure to inflict on a Worcester audience.

There was an elitist, college-boy's sense of bringing culture to the locals in this endeavor. In his autobiography Abbie recalled selling popcorn and "classy" books on film in the lobby, but in fact he was too much a snob to sell popcorn. "The crackling of popcorn makes concentration difficult," he told the Worcester reporter, and he was determined to attract a serious audience. "I may be idealistic," he proclaimed, "but I believe there's entertainment in a thought-provoking adult theme." A Worcester newsman recalls Abbie from this period as "a polite young man with a nice smile and laughing brown eyes who would ask for just a tiny notice about some art exhibit he was planning for the theatre lobby."[5] Abbie's enthusiasm for film was not matched in Worcester. The theater closed after seven months at a loss, Abbie claimed, of ten thousand dollars to the Cadillac dealer.

Still, Abbie saw movie theater management as a possible career. The next year, separated from Sheila and the children, he quit his job as a psychologist and went to New York to manage the soon-to-open Coronet and Baronet theaters, one of the original intimate, dual first-run theater complexes under construction in New York. He was fired on opening night. In constructing the theater, the workers had forgotten to clean the hot air ducts under the lobby floor. When Abbie gave the signal to turn on the warm air, soot and plaster dust blew up into the lobby, where the invited guests were sipping champagne in formal clothes.[6]

With nothing to hold him in New York, Abbie returned to Sheila, who was then living in Cambridge, and got a job as a sales representative for the Westwood Pharmaceutical Company, a Buffalo-based manufacturer of dermatological salves and ointments. Because Abbie's sales territory was central and western Massachusetts, the Hoffmans moved back to Worcester.

Before going to New York and while still working as a psychologist, Abbie had signed on as a volunteer in H. Stuart Hughes's independent campaign for U.S. senator from Massachusetts. The grandson of Supreme Court Justice Charles Evans Hughes, Stuart Hughes was a political science professor at Harvard and cochairman of SANE (The Committee for a Sane Nuclear Policy), which was organized in 1957 by pacifists, liberals, and noncommunist left-wingers as a mass-membership organization to work for disarmament and the cessation of nuclear bomb testing. Running against the sons of two other prominent Massachusetts (and Harvard) political families, Hughes had no chance in the November election. Edward Kennedy had the support of his brother, President John F. Kennedy, while the Republican contender, George Cabot Lodge, was the son of Henry Cabot Lodge, President Kennedy's ambassador in South Vietnam. Hughes's race was considered a trial run for third-party peace candidates, and it attracted support from idealistic college students in the Boston area. (The war in Vietnam was not discussed in the campaign, however. Hughes's issue was nuclear disarmament.) Abbie helped with fundraising and organized a signature-gathering campaign in central and western Massachusetts to get Hughes on the ballot.

Not since the 1948 presidential campaign of Henry Wallace had a serious attempt been made to run a progressive third-party campaign in the United States. In Massachusetts the peace movement's supporters were concentrated in and around university campuses. It was therefore discouraging to stand in front of supermarkets in small towns and ask strangers to sign a ballot petition for a candidate who did not belong to a major party. Abbie tried to make signature gathering fun, arranging for students from the Boston area to work in rural parts of the state and thus get a day in the country. Despite the tough going, he found the petition drive exhilarating; it was a test for his gregarious, pool hustler's personality to see whether he could break through the public apathy. The Hughes campaigners collected more than the 17,000 signatures (not, as Abbie claimed in *Major Motion Picture*, 146,000) to get him on the ballot.

Hughes's goal was to draw votes from Ted Kennedy and convince the Democratic party to take its left-of-center peace wing seriously. But the Cuban missile crisis in the autumn of 1962 destroyed his campaign. When aerial photographs showed that medium-range Soviet ballistic missiles were on the island, President Kennedy placed an economic embargo on Cuba. Hughes protested Kennedy's brinkmanship: if the U.S. Navy insisted on searching Soviet vessels en route to Cuba, any incident could escalate to a nuclear war. Hughes proposed that a delegation from neutral countries go to Cuba to investigate the presence of the Soviet missiles, and that the United Nations encourage negotiations between the United States and the Soviet Union to defuse the confrontation. (As it turned out, both Kennedy and Soviet premier Nikita Khrushchev realized the danger of the situation and privately negotiated a peaceful settlement.) Behind Hughes's position were two assumptions. First, if the Soviets did have missiles in Cuba, it was only to counterbalance American missiles in Turkey and Western Europe, which made the Soviet Union an easy target for American nuclear weapons. Second, if there were missiles in Cuba, they were there to protect the island against a second American invasion designed, like the attempt at the Bay of Pigs, to overthrow the Castro government. Both assumptions, which Abbie shared, were well outside the prevailing consensus. The Kennedy administration, though embarrassed by the Bay of Pigs fiasco, continued to believe, as did most Americans, that the overthrow of Castro was a legitimate goal. The American people also believed that while the United States had a right to deploy nuclear weapons anywhere in the world, a similar move by the Soviets was an act of aggression. To the American public, Hughes's proposal was certainly naive and possibly pro-communist. Although Hughes outpolled Ted Kennedy in a straw vote of the Harvard faculty, his support outside Cambridge was invisible. Kennedy won the election with more than 1.1 million votes. Hughes got 49,102 votes, 2.4 percent of the total.

Although the campaign was an electoral debacle, it brought new people into the peace movement and, in the process, introduced them to the nascent New Left. In the summer of 1962, while Abbie was getting signatures for Hughes, fifty or so members of the Students for a Democratic Society (SDS) were meeting in Michigan to draft their founding principles, which became known as the Port Huron Statement.* A number of Hughes's staffers, like Todd Gitlin and Rob Burlage of Harvard, would soon play important roles in SDS. But as an older, married, and job-holding field organizer, Abbie was an outsider in Hughes's Cambridge office; he formed no close relationship with the radical students. The importance of the campaign for Abbie turned out to be the people it brought together in the Worcester area.

Abbie began drumming up support for Hughes in Worcester by writing a letter to the editor of the local paper. One person who responded was Father Bernard Gilgun, an Irish-American par-

---

*Founded in 1960, SDS had, in the summer of 1962, about 800 members and a mailing list of 2,000. The Student Peace Union (SPU) and Campus Americans for Democratic Action (ADA) had about 3,000 members each. The youth groups of the Communist party and the Socialist party were barely functioning. Not counting the Student Nonviolent Coordinating Committee (SNCC), which was not campus-based, that was the extent of the student left at the time of the Hughes campaign.

ish priest ten years older than Abbie. The two formed a friendship ("you Catholic priest and me Jewish atheist," Abbie once described it in a letter to Gilgun) that lasted until Abbie's death. "Every minute together was undiluted joy," Father Gilgun recalled. That Abbie was able to set aside, without forgetting, the anti-Semitism he had experienced from Catholics in his youth impressed Gilgun as the measure of Abbie's trust and openness to change.

Gilgun was inspired by Dorothy Day, the leader of the Catholic Worker movement whose talk at Brandeis had so impressed Abbie. Father Gilgun took the Catholic Worker message seriously: one affirms Christ by helping the poor and by confronting injustice with active nonviolence. Whatever feelings of guilt brought people to the Catholic Worker movement were submerged in the spiritual joy of community that arose from their belief that they were doing God's work.[7] The teachings of Pope John XXIII (1958–1963) seemed to imbibe much of the same spirit that animated the Catholic Worker movement. His ecumenism, his populist determination to recast the Latin liturgy into the vernacular languages of ordinary worshipers, and his stand for peace, articulated in his 1963 encyclical *Pacem in Terris*, had a profound effect on Catholics like Gilgun. The priests and nuns who met at conferences to reform the liturgy met again at civil rights and ban-the-bomb demonstrations and, later, formed an activist network of radical clergy in the movement against the Vietnam War. Gilgun brought this ardor to his work in Worcester and, in the ecumenical spirit encouraged by Pope John, welcomed non-Catholics to share in this spirit. In 1962 Gilgun and two art students from Holy Cross opened the Phoenix, an ecumenical meeting place in the front of an abandoned fish store on Main Street. The Phoenix became the energy center for Worcester's new activist community. Through the Phoenix, Abbie and Sheila became close to the small radical Catholic activist community, sharing in its communal meals and holiday celebrations and even attending an occasional mass.

As program director for the Phoenix, Abbie used his Brandeis connections and, later, his contacts in the southern civil rights and the New York peace movements to plan Friday night discussion programs. A hundred or more people would often pack the tiny storefront and stay into the early morning hours. The excited talk about social change led many to question their own lives, encouraging some to become activists. Among those who led Phoenix

discussions were David McReynolds, an editor of *Liberation* and
the field organizer for the War Resisters League, and Howard
Zinn, a left-wing historian who made the connection between racism and Vietnam in a program titled "Governor Wallace in Saigon."
Dorothy Day also spoke at the Phoenix, as did Ammon Hennacy, a
former Wobbly who promoted the idea of "one-man revolution"—
the responsibility of every citizen to withdraw his or her support
from the state. Robert Drinan, a liberal Jesuit from Boston College
who would soon win election to Congress, also spoke, as did other
dissident Catholic activists and theologians. Abbie cast a
wide net for Phoenix speakers. One person who didn't respond to
an invitation was Allen Ginsberg. Abbie wrote him a letter the day
before Christmas in 1965 and offered to pay his expenses and
"share some pot" if he would read his poetry at the Phoenix. The
letter was addressed to Ginsberg c/o the City Lights bookstore in
San Francisco and signed "Abbott Hoffman."[8]

Both Hoffmans took part in Phoenix programs. In November
1965 Abbie discussed Abraham Maslow's self-actualization theory
under the heading "Morality for the Non-Religious." Sheila Hoffman was part of a panel discussion about Betty Friedan's *The Feminine Mystique*, defending it before an audience that felt threatened by feminist ideas. As part of her presentation Sheila read an
earthy selection from Henry Miller, illustrating the sexist way that
females were treated in literature. Miller's writings were banned by
the Catholic Church in Massachusetts, and it was the first time that
many of the middle-class Phoenixers had ever heard the subject of
sex discussed in public. There was "extreme discomfort" in the
audience, one participant recalls, but Abbie "beamed with pleasure."[9]

Abbie and Sheila shared a growing interest in radical politics and
became, as a couple, central figures in the Worcester movement.
Indeed, Sheila helped organize the first peace demonstrations in
Worcester and was as involved as her husband in local civil rights
activity. The Hoffmans' home on Hadwen Road was an unofficial
movement center. Lawn signs with movement slogans filled their
front yard. They were proud to show their collection of movement
buttons to visitors. Plans for political activities were hatched over
dinner and late into the night. Father Gilgun recalls many "beautiful, memorable" nights when Abbie would cook lobster and he
and Sheila would play host to visiting radicals and socially con-

cerned people from the area. "Abbie and Sheila were great hosts. It was like a storybook, not anarchist radicals but two young kids."

In 1963 the civil rights movement in Worcester consisted of one organization: the local chapter of the National Association for the Advancement of Colored People (NAACP). Unlike the more radical Congress on Racial Equality (CORE) and the Student Non-violent Coordinating Committee (SNCC), the NAACP was a conservative and, at least in Worcester, a "Do-Nothing" organization, as Abbie described it in *The Drum*, the activist newsletter he helped start and edit. The officers of the NAACP were middle-aged and middle-class blacks. Not unlike the Worcester Jews of John Hoffman's generation, they were reluctant to rock the boat by challenging the political and industrial leaders who ran the city. The NAACP leaders preferred back room negotiations to public demonstrations, and they almost always deferred to the opinions of the white authorities. The hunger for justice and impatience for change that drove the movement in other cities was suppressed in Worcester. In *The Drum*, Abbie wrote, "If discrimination in Worcester seems minimal in comparison to the more publicized racial problems of the South, that is because local attempts to solve the problems have themselves been minimal."

Under Abbie's editorial direction *The Drum* was earnest, humorless, and comprehensive in its coverage of the civil rights movement, reporting news from the southern struggle, listing movement activities in Worcester, Boston, and Springfield (a speech by CORE's James Farmer in Boston, for example), reviewing pending state and federal civil rights legislation, recommending books on the Negro* experience, publishing the words of freedom songs, and advertising movement buttons, bumper stickers, and other fundraising paraphernalia from SNCC and CORE as well as from the NAACP.

Abbie wanted the newsletter to be a catalyst for action and was relentless in urging greater commitment from local activists. Many in the NAACP agreed with Abbie in wanting the chapter to become more assertive but lacked the initiative to challenge the old guard. Abbie, Father Gilgun, and D'Army Bailey, a Negro student from

---

* Up through 1966 and until the rise of the black power movement, *Negro* was common usage. That is the word Abbie and others in the civil rights movement would have used, and I use it here for historical accuracy.

Clark University who had been active in the Louisiana freedom
struggle, led the battle to radicalize the chapter. Using Father Gilgun's clerical authority as a cloak of respectability, they formed a
Direct Action Committee in order to bypass the established leadership. Abbie became the publicity director of this committee and
used his position to recruit new members, especially young people,
in the white and Negro communities. Father Gilgun's fiery speeches
and the introduction of protest songs from the southern movement
brought a new urgency to the membership. Bailey started the
Worcester Student Association, encouraging students from Clark
and Holy Cross to work with the NAACP. The students did research into the hiring practices of the major Worcester employers
and pushed for picket lines (and civil disobedience) to put clout
behind their demands that those practices be changed. The national office of the NAACP, and of course the local leaders, opposed direct action tactics. But with Abbie and Father Gilgun
among those speaking on behalf of the students, the chapter endorsed direct action and, as a result, forced the established leaders
to resign.

Abbie was like a political whirlwind in the Worcester movement,
involving himself in everything. "I am first and foremost as you
know a guy who loves action who hates the dullness of regular
life—the boredom of this fat system," he wrote Father Gilgun in a
letter castigating the priest for his reluctance to "wheel and deal"
in movement infights. Abbie considered running for city council as
an insurgent candidate but dropped the idea when he sensed that
his comrades, especially Father Gilgun, lacked his enthusiasm. Impatient with the NAACP, he helped start a local CORE chapter,
but he then so bothered the elected CORE leadership with his incessant demands for action that they complained to the national
office that he was a communist trying to take control. James
Farmer, CORE's national chairman, had to come to Worcester to
see what was happening. Father Gilgun accompanied Abbie to a
meeting with Farmer, but the allegation never was discussed.
Whatever trouble Abbie was causing in Worcester CORE was not
a result of Abbie's ideology, Farmer realized.

The rap against Abbie was that he often thought of himself as a
one-man movement and refused to submit to organizational structures. He was completely goal-oriented and impatient with group
processes, but he had so many ideas and so many projects that he

had to leave them to others to complete, and it only made him more impatient when other people did not bring them to fruition his way. It was not that he aspired to leadership in order to give directions to others. On the contrary, he would lick stamps and sweep the floor if no one else was doing it. "He was a gadfly, a change agent. He never stayed with anything," one Worcester activist recalls. "But his goal wasn't to become the power. He didn't want to take over. He wanted to move them to action."[10]

Abbie's disregard for group discipline was evident in the attempt to force the Wyman-Gordon Company, a manufacturer of machine tools and one of Worcester's largest employers, to institute an affirmative action program and hire Negroes. The Worcester Student Association had researched the employment records of the company and found that of the thirty-three Negroes it employed, thirty-two were janitors and one was their supervisor. Although some of them had the education to do better-paying skilled jobs, their requests for promotion were continually passed over. The president of the company, Robert W. Stoddard, was chairman of the board of Worcester's morning and evening newspaper and a supporter of the John Birch Society. Negotiations with Stoddard, in which Abbie participated, brought no progress, so the decision was made to picket. Abbie published a special edition of *The Drum* attacking Wyman-Gordon with embellishments that went beyond the students' accusations. Abbie later acknowledged that he had invented the additional charges but argued that the important fact was that Wyman-Gordon discriminated against Negroes and the actual details did not matter.[11]

Abbie was still working for Westwood Pharmaceutical during this time. He always boasted that he could complete his weekly tasks in a day or two and spend most of his time working on his political projects using the company car. He was making about twenty thousand dollars a year, including money earned by selling "freebies" (the promotional drugs he was supposed to give out to doctors) to large drugstores in the Boston area.[12] Although often cynical about selling cures for acne, he took pride in his skills as a salesman. His employer held frequent workshops on salesmanship, and Abbie liked the positive, can-do approach that the company impressed on its sales force. Movement activists, Abbie would later complain, lacked the one-dimensional drive that makes salespeople successful. Although often disorganized himself, he was critical of the nonbusinesslike approach many activists brought to their organizing efforts. "People come to corporate workshops prepared, wanting to make things happen. They learn how to present problems and solve them," Abbie said, recalling his selling career. By contrast, Abbie charged, the left knows only how to "complain"; they actually like feeling victimized and would rather talk about how they *can't* "sell" their issues, because corporations control the media, than how they "can make it change."[13]

★   ★   ★

On his trips to Boston to sell his sample drugs, Abbie often stopped at the SNCC (or as he sometimes spelled it, SNICK) office in Cambridge. There, early in 1964, he met Bob and Dottie Zellner. (Bob was the first white southerner to be an organizer in SNCC.) The Zellners told him about Freedom Summer, the plan to recruit hundreds of white college students to go to Mississippi to register voters and organize Head Start programs, Freedom Schools, and Freedom Centers. The political focus would be the organization of a biracial Mississippi Freedom Democratic Party (MFDP), which would come to the 1964 Democratic national convention in Atlantic City to challenge the legitimacy of the all-white, regular Democratic delegation from that state.* Among northern activists Abbie's age, SNCC was the stuff of legend. It was the only civil rights organization started and staffed by Abbie's generation, and its members were lionized for their courage. SNCC organizers went into the areas of Mississippi, Alabama, and southwestern Georgia that were the most dangerously racist in the country. They did so without weapons but with an assertiveness that made their nonviolence bold and audacious. Their success in motivating poor Negroes to overcome their fears and, at the risk of their lives, demand their right to participate in American democracy gave them a self-confident élan, a belief that they could create a "beloved community" of interracial justice and harmony in America.[14]

SNCC was committed to "participatory democracy." The people rather than the organizers would make the political decisions. The

* The MFDP was actually a project of the Council of Federated Organizations, a coalition of civil rights groups that coordinated Freedom Summer. But SNCC was the driving force behind both Freedom Summer and the MFDP and provided most of the staff.

good organizer thus worked quietly in the background; the process—empowering people—was as important as the organizing goal. A correct decision made by an organizer in the name of the people was of less value than the wrong decision made by the people themselves. In the long run, the goal of a SNCC organizer was to transform politically passive individuals into a politically assertive community.

Encouraging southern Negroes to vote was the crucial part of a long-range liberal strategy. Ending white supremacy, many liberals felt, would lead to a national political realignment. A brutal system of state-supported terrorism against Negroes enabled southern Democrats to rule the South without opposition. But in national politics southern Democrats often voted with the most reactionary members of the Republican party. Using their seniority to control congressional committees, southern Democrats and their Republican allies were able to stifle liberal legislation. Because of the power of the one-party South, the national political consensus—the arena of practical politics where public policy is determined—was skewed to the right throughout most of the twentieth century.

The Kennedy administration provided SNCC access to liberal foundation money but reneged on its promise to protect the organizers from white violence. FBI director J. Edgar Hoover held racist views and believed that the civil rights movement was part of a communist plot, and in the South FBI agents worked hand in glove with white supremacists in and out of local government. FBI agents spied on and kept files on the Kennedy brothers (as well as on every American whose political views were not to Hoover's liking). Attorney General Robert F. Kennedy, ostensibly Hoover's boss, was afraid to order Hoover to protect civil rights workers. Likely, he feared the scandals Hoover might expose concerning the Kennedy brothers' womanizing.[15]

Without federal protection, the voter registration drive in Mississippi stalled. Between 1962 and 1964 fewer than four thousand Negroes were added to the voting lists. Despite the violence mobilized against them, SNCC volunteers continued to organize. In the summer of 1963 more than eighty thousand Negroes voted in an unofficial freedom election (held as an alternative to the all-white Democratic primary) for an integrationist "freedom slate." Mississippi Negroes were determined to participate in American democracy—if only they had the physical protection that would enable

them to vote. The idea of flooding Mississippi with white students
was a measure of SNCC's desperation. If the murders and beatings
of Negroes did not stir the nation's conscience and bring in federal
forces to protect Negro voters, then perhaps violence against white
students would compel the government to act. Nothing less than a
frontal assault on racism would crack the power of white supremacy, and Abbie felt he had to be part of that effort.

Because of his family responsibilities, Abbie did not go south for
Freedom Summer. But in addition to his job and his work with the
NAACP he became a volunteer organizer for Friends of SNCC, the
northern support group that raised money and publicized the efforts of the southern movement. This group became the focal point
of his life in Worcester. Its achievements included sending 425 car-
tons of books, clothes, canned goods, and toys to Holly Springs,
Mississippi; financing "freedomships" that paid the expenses of at
least five Worcester residents to work in Mississippi; contributing
to the bail fund for Freedom Summer; holding fund-raisers to send
delegations from Worcester to take part in civil rights marches and
congressional lobbying campaigns in the South and in Washington;
forming a teenage singing group called the Worcester Freedom
Singers, modeled after a SNCC group of that name; and organizing
a speakers bureau, a photographic exhibit in the Worcester Library about the movement in Mississippi, teenage dances and picnics, freedom parties ("you invite your friends and supply food,
refreshments and booze, and we supply records, buttons, literature, posters, and singers"), and a "SNICK Halloween Party."
Abbie was also involved in the programs but not in the founding
(as he claimed and for which he is often credited) of Prospect
House, a community center in Worcester modeled after the Freedom Houses of Mississippi.

In August 1964 Abbie joined hundreds of other civil rights activists in Atlantic City who were vigiling on the Boardwalk and
lobbying in support of the MFDP's challenge at the Democratic
national convention. All the SNCC organizers he had read and
heard about were present at Atlantic City, and Abbie felt his own
experience in Worcester merging with their efforts in the South.
Atlantic City, he later recalled, "was the largest gathering of heroes
since the signing of the Declaration of Independence."[16] Few of the
veteran SNCC organizers expected the challenge to succeed. Their
goal was to put the Democratic party on the spot and radicalize the

movement by showing that the system would not respond to their demands. The MFDP delegates themselves, elected at the grass-roots, were more hopeful. They had come more than a thousand miles in old cars and rickety buses, and they intended to reap their rights as a reward for their courage.

For President Lyndon Johnson, the MFDP challenge was nothing more than a procedural nuisance. His goal at the convention was to keep a tight rein on the delegates and unite the party for his reelection. He knew that if the MFDP delegates were seated, most white southerners would bolt the party, and this would destroy the Democrats' control of the one-party South. The MFDP's challenge was the only internal dispute on the convention's agenda, and Johnson was determined to squelch it before it caused him trouble. With Robert Kennedy's acquiescence, Johnson ordered J. Edgar Hoover to tap the phones of the MFDP and its supporters. Although the white Mississippi regulars refused to comply with convention regulations by taking a loyalty oath to support the Johnson ticket, Johnson assured them that they would not be abandoned. To work out a deal that would satisfy both the MFDP and the Mississippi regulars, he called in Hubert Humphrey. Humphrey wanted the vice presidency. Johnson hinted he could have the nomination if he would use his liberal credentials to temper the demands of the MFDP.

The MFDP's case before the credentials committee was legally and morally unimpeachable. The MFDP was David to white Mississippi's Goliath. All that the MFDP was demanding was that the Democratic delegates take a moral position upholding the right of all citizens to vote, the most basic principle of democracy. At the hearings of the credentials committee the descriptions of white brutality and the betrayal of democracy in the South shocked the delegates and the national television audience. The testimony of Fannie Lou Hamer was especially dramatic. She lived in the county in which U.S. Senator James Eastland had his plantation, but she could not vote. When she tried to register, she lost her job. When she tried again, she was taken to jail and brutally beaten. Still determined to exercise her democratic rights, she became an organizer for SNCC and an MFDP candidate for U.S. Congress. "All of this is on account we want to register, to become first-class citizens," she told the credentials committee, "and if the Freedom Democratic Party is not seated now, I question America."

Support for the MFDP was growing within the convention. The singing and the spirit of the MFDP delegates and of their friends vigiling outside the convention center captivated liberal delegates. Many wanted the opportunity to vote their conscience and support the MFDP. The administration offered a concession to stem the ground swell: Aaron Henry and Edwin King, the biracial MFDP leaders, would be seated as at-large delegates to the convention, and the other MFDP delegates would be admitted to the proceedings as guests of the convention. Regular delegates who took the loyalty oath would retain their official seats. Further, Humphrey promised, the party would bar any state delegation that practiced racial discrimination from the 1968 national convention.

The MFDP produced a counterproposal, introduced in the credentials committee by Edith Green, a liberal congresswoman from Oregon. It offered a voting seat in the convention to any member of either Mississippi delegation who signed a loyalty pledge to support the party ticket, with the total Mississippi vote apportioned among those who were seated. As the regulars would walk out of the convention rather than accept any Negro in their midst, the MFDP would, by default, become the official Democratic party in Mississippi.

The Green proposal had enough support in the credentials committee to force a debate by the delegates on the convention floor and an open vote by the entire convention. There was no telling what might happen then. In the emotion of the moment the convention might endorse the Green proposal, and the southern delegations would bolt the party. Johnson and Humphrey began putting pressure on members of the credentials committee, threatening, in essence, to destroy the political career of anyone who voted for the Green proposal. Support for the MFDP vanished, and the challenge was defeated.

Humphrey's earlier offer to give the MFDP two at-large seats was still on the table, however. Humphrey and his liberal allies demanded that the MFDP accept this compromise. Bayard Rustin, an influential civil rights strategist, pleaded with the MFDP delegates to put "politics over protest" and accept the compromise. It represented a gain for the movement, he argued, more than most organizers had expected and as much as was now possible. Protest movements can afford to take absolutist stands on moral principles, but it was time to move beyond protest and enter the political fray, where compromise is necessary. The struggle would not get any easier, and it was imperative that the movement maintain its links to its liberal supporters within the Democratic party.[17]

Martin Luther King also argued for accepting the two-seat compromise as the best that could be achieved and, overall, a gain for the civil rights movement. Yet, as he acknowledged in a speech to the MFDP delegates, it also represented a triumph of backroom politics, the kind of wheeling and dealing the movement had always opposed. His endorsement of the compromise was lukewarm. If he were in the delegates' shoes, he reflected in private, he likely would have felt compelled to reject it. In the end that is what the MFDP delegation voted to do—overwhelmingly.[18]*

The 1964 MFDP challenge represented the point at which many members of SNCC gave up on the Democratic party. SNCC organizers had given their all for democracy. Instead of reflecting on how much progress they had made, many chose to view the defeat as a symbol of liberal hypocrisy, a measure of the refusal of white liberals to back their own principles. As SNCC veteran Julian Bond later put it, "Many people felt that the FDP had all the right—legal, moral, etc.—on its side. . . . It seemed you couldn't do anything if you couldn't get through such a clearly *right* challenge."[19] Abbie, too, saw Atlantic City as a turning point. "If that one event had gone the other way," he wrote two years later, "the history of America would have been changed."[20] In *Major Motion Picture* he reiterated this sense of betrayal. "I never forgave Humphrey for the spineless role he played. . . . The press and party politicians complimented us on a historic victory but we wanted more. Much more."

In light of the decline of the civil rights movement after the 1964 convention and of Abbie's (and the radical antiwar movement's) refusal to accommodate Democratic liberals at the 1968 convention in Chicago, the compromise rejected at Atlantic City deserves

---

* The Johnson/Humphrey-backed compromise was also too much for the Mississippi regulars. Only three took the loyalty oath; the rest left the convention. Delegates from Michigan and Massachusetts (with Abbie lobbying for this arrangement) gave their passes to the MFDP delegates, who attempted to take the vacant seats of the regulars. But security guards removed the seats, and the delegates were left to stand, lost in the celebration as Johnson and Humphrey were nominated by acclamation.

closer scrutiny. Yes, morality and constitutional law were on the side of the MFDP, and in hindsight it seems clear that the Democrats would have had nothing to lose in taking a stand for principle: Lyndon Johnson would have defeated Barry Goldwater even without the support of the white South, and *any* commitment to civil rights, even of the most compromising kind, would have cost the Democrats the support of racist whites, North and South. But political change—and the social changes that underlie it—comes slowly. Abbie, like many movement activists of the period, was unwilling to acknowledge the necessity of tactical compromise. In consistently taking absolutist positions and in viewing politics as a moral drama between good and evil, Abbie and his comrades would, time and again, define as definitive defeats those modest— and hard won—victories that might have served as stepping-stones to further gains.

Despite his disillusion, Abbie returned to Worcester fired up by the experience. The MFDP planned to extend its challenge with an attempt to unseat the Mississippi congressional delegation. Because Mississippi Negroes were discriminated against in the voting, the 1964 election was fraudulent, the MFDP argued. Worcester Friends of SNCC raised money for this challenge and sent delegations to Washington to lobby in Congress. In September 1965 the MFDP went down to its final defeat, by a vote in the House of Representatives of 228 to 143.

Earlier, however, in January 1965, SNCC and Martin Luther King's Southern Christian Leadership Conference (SCLC) had begun demonstrating for the right to vote in Alabama. When their efforts were met by tear gas, cattle prods, bull whips, and billy clubs, the call went out nationwide for a march from Selma to Montgomery. At least four civil rights workers were killed during this period, including the Reverend James Reeb, an Episcopalian minister from a Boston suburb. James Lee Jackson, a black SNCC organizer (and Vietnam veteran) from Alabama, was also murdered. Abbie helped coordinate a memorial service on the Worcester Common near City Hall, and more than a thousand people showed up. Abbie also helped raise money to send a delegation, including Father Gilgun, to join the march to Montgomery. Significantly, the rally raised four hundred dollars as a donation for Jackson's mother. In the national media the shooting of James Lee Jackson got lost in the coverage of Reverend Reeb's murder.

Yet because of Friends of SNCC, the shooting of a southern black man in Alabama did not go unnoticed, at least in Worcester.

It was as a result of the blood shed in Alabama that President Johnson introduced and Congress quickly passed the Voting Rights Act, which secured, on paper at least, the voting rights for which the southern civil rights movement had been fighting. But SNCC was too bloodied to celebrate. Besides, when civil rights activists looked at racism in the North and the economic barriers confronting Negroes all over the country, they saw such massive and complex problems that it seemed nothing short of revolution would provide a solution.

Abbie had yet to spend time in the South, but he was determined to go. "I need the movement," he wrote Father Gilgun. "I need it as much as I need the oxygen to breathe. I want to be with people who want to change things, really change things." On a vacation during the summer of 1965 he and Sheila used their own money to go to McComb, Mississippi, and Americus, Georgia, in order, as Abbie later put it, to show the southern freedom fighters that they had northern support. What Abbie learned on this trip was how important culture was to political change. A high point was taking part in a voter registration rally in a Negro Baptist church and being introduced by the preacher: "Mr. Hoffman has come from Massachusetts to teach us about voter registration." In McComb, Abbie joined in the picketing of the Holiday Inn, where maids, who were making thirty-nine cents an hour, had formed a Freedom Labor Union and walked out on strike. The picket line was harassed by the Ku Klux Klan, and Abbie was stopped in his car by Mississippi police for running a traffic light in a town that, according to Abbie, had no traffic light. In the South of this period the police operated outside the framework of law. Civil rights workers, white and Negro, were totally at their mercy. They might be ticketed, as Abbie was, for traffic offenses they didn't commit, or jailed, or beaten, or, as in the case of James Chaney, Andrew Goodman, and Mickey Schwerner during Freedom Summer, kidnapped by the police and murdered. This was a side of America that was not taught in the civics texts; it gave civil rights workers a perspective that the vast majority, who never risked their lives for civil rights, did not understand.

When Abbie arrived in Americus, an uneasy coalition of SNCC and SCLC was locked in a confrontation with the white power structure over the issue of voter registration. The mere enactment of federal voting rights legislation did not bring automatic southern compliance. In southwestern Georgia local officials were still using violent tactics to keep Negroes from voting, and the onus remained on the civil rights movement to force confrontations in order to create publicity that would attract the federal government's attention. Here Abbie accompanied other civil rights workers going door to door through the Negro districts, encouraging people to join their neighbors who were at the local courthouse demanding the vote.[21]

While in Mississippi during this summer sojourn, Abbie met Jesse Morris, a SNCC organizer who was setting up a Poor People's Corporation (PPC) as a bootstrap economic development program for Mississippi Negroes. Since blacks who were active in the civil rights movement were often fired by their white employers, it was necessary to develop an economic base that was invulnerable to white retaliation. The introduction of the black power slogan was still months away, but as Morris explained, it was a paradox of the movement that in order to integrate Mississippi, Negroes would have to develop a separate economy. The idea of the PPC was to raise capital by selling Freedom Bonds to movement supporters. The capital would be used in a revolving loan fund as seed money for worker-owned cooperative enterprises. The fund would be controlled by the co-op members themselves, each of whom would pay twenty-five cents a year in dues.

Unable to get any federal assistance, the PPC organizers had to begin small. But their hope was to serve as a model for other southern states. Typical of the appropriations was four hundred dollars to an eight-employee co-op in McComb that manufactured handbags. In Adams County ten men set up a co-op to manufacture "Papa's Brand New Bag," white leather handbags that the co-op hoped to market with the cooperation of James Brown, who then had a rhythm and blues hit called "Papa's Got a Brand New Bag." In Ruleville, Fannie Lou Hamer's hometown, eighty-seven women worked part-time manufacturing tote bags. One of the most successful operations, this co-op gave the women an opportunity to earn two hundred dollars a year from their own business. That small income was, for most of them, one-third of what they used to earn working full-time as white people's maids.

The PPC hired Abbie's friend from Brandeis, Ellen Maslow, to open a New York office to raise money and solicit donations of

leather, cloth, sewing machines, and other manufacturing necessi-
ties. She also recruited craftspeople to go to Mississippi and train
co-op workers. Maslow, who had worked as a secretary to radical
pacifist leaders A. J. Muste and Dave Dellinger, set up her office at
the "Peace Pentagon" on the top floor of 5 Beekman Street, where
Muste and Dellinger were then organizing the first demonstrations
against the Vietnam War. Abbie volunteered to find retail outlets
for PPC goods throughout New England. One of the few movement
people trained as a salesman, he was ideal for this job.

Abbie spent much of his time from late 1965 through the summer
of 1966 promoting the products of the Poor People's Corporation
throughout New England, visiting potential retail outlets as he
made his rounds selling dermatological drugs. In March 1966 he
transformed the Phoenix in Worcester into a "SNICK shop," selling Humphrey Bogart and other movie star posters, Batman comic
books, movement buttons and bumper stickers, and quilts, handbags, tote bags, and Greta Garbo hats made by the Mississippi
co-ops.

Occasionally Abbie delivered raw materials to Mississippi and
drove north with the finished products. Ellen Maslow often accompanied him, as did SNCC workers traveling to and from the South.
Often the blacks had to be hidden; young blacks and whites riding
together through the South in out-of-state cars were in "death
traps," Maslow recalls. "We were in Mississippi and it was raining
hard and we ran out of gas or got a flat—the car just stopped. The
sheriff drove up and looked like Sheriff Rainey [the Mississippi
sheriff implicated in the 1964 murder of Chaney, Goodman, and
Schwerner]. He had a huge gut hanging down, and we thought that
we were dead. For some reason, I have no idea, this guy was cour-
teous, helpful, and we went on our way."

Rarely reluctant to talk back to police, Abbie, in this situation,
kept quiet. In fact, while working for the PPC, he was considered
responsible and a hard worker, "very democratic." Cultural mis-
understandings often caused tension when educated northern
whites worked with poor rural southern blacks, but Abbie was always welcome, Maslow remembers. "He was profoundly sure of
himself and relaxed, so he wouldn't offend people."[22] Todd Gitlin,
in his book *The Sixties*, characterizes Abbie as "a floater" in
SNCC, the kind of civil rights worker who moved from project to
project always looking for excitement and action.[23] Yet, aside from
the fact that Abbie wasn't in the South long enough to acquire any

movement reputation, he was totally committed to the work of the
Poor People's Corporation; the time he spent working for the co-
ops was one of the few periods in his activist career that he willingly
accepted an organization's discipline.

By 1966 Abbie was devoting more time to the PPC and his other
movement activities than he was to selling Westwood products, and
early in 1966 he was fired. His marriage was also breaking up. In
February 1966 Abbie applied to Saul Alinsky, the Chicago activist,
for a job as a community organizer. Alinsky was impressed with
Abbie's credentials and asked him to meet with him after a speaking date in Boston. Father Gilgun went with Abbie to meet Alinsky.
Alinsky told Abbie that he would love to hire him, but Abbie was
of the wrong skin color. Alinsky's organizing projects now centered
on black ghettos, and with the rise of the black power movement
only blacks were effective in organizing black people. If Abbie had
approached Alinsky earlier, he might have gotten a job organizing
in white working-class communities in Chicago. Abbie likely would
have done well as an Alinsky-style organizer. Unlike SNCC, which
put so much emphasis on process, Alinsky had a goal-oriented approach. His organizers were trained to identify local leaders and
to act as their advisers in battles with the ruling establishment. But
practical as they were, their style was not bland. Alinsky had a
combative personality and a flair for theatrical confrontation. Had
Abbie worked for him as a community organizer in Chicago, there
likely would have been no group like the Yippies demonstrating
against the Democratic party in 1968, and the history of the antiwar movement might have been different.

Abbie's work for the PPC corresponded to that period in SNCC's
evolution when it adopted the black power slogan, purged all its
white organizers, abandoned its commitment to nonviolence, and
gave up on moral suasion and patient grassroots organizing. Because the PPC was independent of SNCC, Abbie had no role in the
internal debates that led to SNCC's transformation, but he followed them closely.

From his work in the ban-the-bomb and civil rights movements
and his empathy for the Catholic Workers, Abbie understood how
nonviolence could be a powerful political force. By refusing to fight
back when physically attacked, civil rights workers negated any

possible justification for their opponents' use of violence and, at the same time, secured for themselves the moral high ground, so that when racists did use violence against them the unprovoked viciousness of their brutality was starkly exposed. But Abbie was impatient with ideology, and he also identified with the street-smart hoods of his youth, tough guys who always gave the impression they would fight back when attacked, even if it was only a bluff. Understanding the tactical need for nonviolence, Abbie never identified himself as a pacifist—a true believer in the principle. Writing in *The Drum* in the spring of 1964, he noted that many in the southern civil rights movement were expressing impatience with "the familiar passive demonstrations. . . . It must be remembered that non-violence is employed as a method for achieving a desired goal, in the South desegregation. If the method appears to be failing, advocates of other methods will be given greater attention." In these comments, Abbie was struggling with his attraction toward two rival ideals: the nonviolent discipline and the all-American style of macho heroism. He knew that southern blacks, like rural people everywhere, kept guns in their homes. He also knew that blacks, for the first time, were talking of using these weapons to defend themselves against the terrorism that had been mounted against them. Abbie surmised that white "bomb tossers and snipers" might think twice if they feared that blacks would fire back.[24]

Generally, however, Abbie defended SNCC's original goal of a biracial and nonviolent movement. Although never interested in Marxist ideology, he consistently argued that economic issues were more important than racial ones. At a spring 1964 Phoenix symposium on civil rights Abbie spoke on the need to create a coalition of blacks, Puerto Ricans, and even "poor white trash" to fight for economic rights. "Even if there is integration in schools and housing and the civil rights bill is passed," he told the more than 150 people who filled the Phoenix storefront, "the economic gap between whites and nonwhites will be greater in ten years. The time has come to say it's not because you're black that you're getting a raw deal, it's because you're poor." A year later, at a Worcester symposium on the future of the civil rights movement, he reiterated that the struggle was foremost one of social and economic rights.

Abbie always identified himself with the original SNCC style of organizing. Even in Worcester, where the political culture was different than it was in the South, he wanted to be known for his

SNCC affiliation. But quiet, grassroots organizing was not what he liked to do. Staying in the background, trying to empower others to become leaders and then boosting their ego by placing them in the spotlight, was not something he did easily. His natural ability lay in *mobilizing* people who were already motivated toward political action (but didn't know what to do) rather than in patiently *organizing* individuals in the sense that SNCC used the word. The distinction between organizing and mobilizing is an important one: Abbie often used the terminology of SNCC-style organizing—patiently empowering individuals to work collectively toward a defined objective—to give credibility (and historic continuity) to his ideas for mobilizing people to participate in massive dramatic action for the purpose of communicating a political statement.

Abbie expressed his feelings about SNCC's new direction in a two-part essay written in the autumn of 1966 and published in the *Village Voice* in December, shortly after he moved to New York to open a retail outlet for the Poor People's Corporation and a few weeks after SNCC had purged its white staff members and turned decisively from the goal of integration to the goal of black power.[25]

Within SNCC, opinions about these changes did not divide strictly along racial lines: some whites supported black power, some blacks still supported integration. Most activists, black or white, with experience in the southern movement recognized that the presence of white organizers in the black South did not help southern blacks gain the assertiveness and racial pride they would need to effectively challenge entrenched white authority. While some of the proponents of black power within SNCC advocated black nationalism—that is, black separatism—as an ultimate goal, Abbie accepted it only as a transitional phase; once blacks established a strong political identity, he hoped that they would rejoin the biracial coalition. Abbie would never waver in his opposition to cultural nationalism whatever its form.

Abbie's polemic attracted attention because it articulated, in a scattershot manner, a critique of the movement that many white insiders felt but were reluctant to state publicly. Correctly, Abbie guessed that SNCC leaders would find it easier to guilt-trip whites about white racism than to do the patient work of organizing among blacks. He was also correct in guessing that many guilt-ridden whites would accept SNCC's charge. But Abbie wasn't buying into white guilt. Nor did he accept the idea that suffering for the cause was proof of one's commitment. Activists had to remove the "dichotomies between intellect and emotion, between love of self and love of one's cause." They should be motivated by positive thoughts, not guilt or feelings of pain. "I believe that when one actualizes his inner potential, he is rewarded. He feels better, he enjoys life, he is, in every sense of the word, FREE," Abbie wrote. The ideas were from Abraham Maslow, but Abbie attributed them to what he had learned as an organizer for SNCC.

The articles in the *Voice* catapulted Abbie from an unknown activist to a potential spokesman against SNCC's new direction. Abbie wrote in *Major Motion Picture* that as a result of threatening remarks by one member of SNCC, he went briefly into hiding. It was the only time, recalls the historian Howard Zinn, an advisor to SNCC, that "I had seen Abbie truly frightened." Nevertheless, there were liberal whites in New York who hoped that Abbie would take a leading role in opposing black power. But Abbie wanted no part of a negative, oppositional, ideological, and rearguard action. Having made his critique, Abbie accepted what SNCC leaders were telling their white friends to do: organize whites in their own communities and focus their attention on the Vietnam War.[26]

Abbie had already helped organize, in October 1965, Worcester's first anti–Vietnam War demonstration. About fifty protesters walked from Clark University to the federal courthouse downtown. A second antiwar demonstration, in March 1966, brought out more than five hundred protesters, but they were outnumbered and drowned out by counterdemonstrators, including a group from Holy Cross who, after the demonstration was over, attacked the marchers. Most Americans responded with hostility to the first, small protests against the Vietnam War. It wasn't so much that people supported the war (in 1965 very few knew anything about it). But protesting American foreign policy still provoked suspicion of communist sympathy and was seen, by many, as betraying the soldiers who were fighting and dying. The activists who in 1965 began the Vietnam protest movement had their work cut out for them.

In the summer of 1966 Abbie signed on as an organizer for Thomas Boyleston Adams's primary campaign to be the Massachusetts Democratic nominee for the U.S. Senate. Adams, 56, was a direct descendant of presidents John and John Quincy Adams. He was running as a peace candidate against two liberal Democrats, Boston mayor John Collins and former Massachusetts governor Endicott "Chub" Peabody, both of whom backed President Johnson's Vietnam policy. "The issue is not between me and two other candidates," Adams said. "The issue is between the people of Massachusetts and the government of the United States." Adams was giving voters a rare chance to say no to America's Vietnam policy. While he offered no proposal for extracting the country from Vietnam, his opposition to the war was uncompromising. Like H. Stuart Hughes before him, he hoped to build a liberal/left coalition by joining the civil rights and peace movements. But with little money to finance his campaign and with a position on the war that many people thought treasonable, his efforts received little coverage.

In joining the campaign Abbie realized how uphill the battle was. Giving a pep talk to fifteen volunteers on a canvassing crew sent to western Massachusetts, he told them not to be discouraged when people became hostile. "We must keep at it," he urged; "we must give people the chance to save themselves from the Vietnam War." Among Adams's campaign workers, Abbie had a reputation for unstoppable energy. One worker recalls seeing him tear apart, by hand, Department of Public Works sawhorses to make frames for Adams for Senate lawn posters.[27]

In the primary, won by Peabody (who was defeated in the general election by Edward Brooke, a moderate Republican), Adams got 21,828 votes. In the four years of political organizing since the Hughes campaign, the peace vote in Massachusetts had grown from 2.4 percent to 7.7 percent.

While he was helping to organize the first antiwar protests, Abbie began to spend time with Marty and Susan Carey, two artists who, virtually by themselves, constituted the avant-garde in Worcester. Abbie was excited by a mixed-media happening that Marty Carey had produced at Clark University ("disruptive art," Susan Carey described it). He also liked the artistic perspective that the Careys brought to the world around them. "I saw Abbie's creative side—that's what brought us together," Marty Carey recalls of their meeting. "I conceptualized things as art, and Abbie understood this." The Careys shared Abbie's disdain for the suburban, middle-class lifestyle. They were all attracted to what was new and experimental. "Abbie was into creating change," Susan Carey says. "He had to experience something in order to make it part of him. His words and actions always meshed. He liked people who were creative and had a sense of humor. That is where he made his stand. He was not one-dimensional. Politics alone bored him."[28]

Abbie had not yet smoked marijuana when Manny Schreiber, Abbie's roommate from Brandeis, introduced him to LSD in the autumn of 1965. Schreiber had been drafted into the army as a psychologist and was working on a secret military project testing the effects of LSD on soldiers.[29]* Abbie had invited him to speak at the Phoenix about the psychedelic experience, and Schreiber had brought some acid to give to Abbie before the meeting. Because Sheila disapproved of drugs, Abbie and Manny (who would act as his "guide") borrowed the use of the Careys' loft. A young Catholic priest (not Father Gilgun) took the drug with Abbie. Set and setting—meaning the mental set one brings to an acid trip and the physical and social environment one takes the acid in—are crucial factors in determining the nature of the LSD experience, and Abbie's first trip was thus filled with Catholic symbolism. In the

---

*LSD was introduced to the American people by Timothy Leary and Richard Alpert and also by the U.S. government. In 1951 the CIA began experimenting with LSD for use as a chemical weapon. As the drug was tasteless, odorless, and invisible, the CIA hoped that it could be slipped to enemy agents or government leaders as a truth serum or to disorient or embarrass them in public. The CIA also investigated the use of LSD as a weapon against civilian populations. (Contaminating a city's water supply was theoretically impossible, the CIA found; too much would be needed for it to have an effect, and besides, chlorine neutralized LSD's active ingredients.) Unable to find a practical use for the drug, the CIA worried that the communists might devise a way to use LSD against them. Thus began a project in which CIA agents began taking the drug in order to prepare themselves should the Soviets spike American drinks with acid. While high-level officials considered the drug a dangerous, psychosis-inducing weapon, the researchers who were taking it wanted only to share it with friends and colleagues. (An internal CIA security memo, dated ten days before Christmas in 1954, warned against spiking the punch bowls with LSD at CIA office parties.) Taking their cue from the CIA, army intelligence officers conducted experiments to monitor how soldiers would react to an LSD attack by enemy forces. That is how Schreiber got the drug and was able to give it to Abbie.

evening, still tripping, he attended a civil rights gathering. The songs and spirit of the freedom movement were always inspiring. On acid everything Abbie saw, heard, and felt was intensified. The vision of racial harmony was transcendent.[30]

Abbie now began to smoke marijuana whenever it was available and to drop acid. No doubt this contributed to his breakup with Sheila. They were both deeply committed to radical politics and ambitious to be leaders in the Worcester movement. But, as Susan Carey recalls, Abbie "had a direction in which he was going, and he was always thinking of himself in those terms." He wanted free rein for his politics and his imagination; Sheila was the one who raised the two children. In 1966 she divorced him. Without a job and estranged from his family, Abbie had nothing left to hold him in Worcester. "Like a kid shortstop being called up to the majors," he felt ready for New York, the world of "big-time protest," as he called it.[31]

CHAPTER 4

THE EAST VILLAGE

Organizing Hippies
1967

In the autumn of 1966, when Abbie moved to New York City to open Liberty House, he lived first in a tenement flat on Avenue C and Eleventh Street. One could live cheaply in the slums of New York during the affluent 1960s, and Abbie's was a typical Lower East Side pad of that time: forty-five dollars a month for three small rooms, a bathtub in the kitchen, and a toilet in the hall. When he came home at night and turned on the light, thousands of cockroaches, which had the run of the apartment in the dark, scurried to their bunkers under the floorboards and into cracks between the molding and the walls. But the dinginess was not depressing. "New York is naturally fantastic—especially where I live—just one gigantic happening. It's like everyone is on a never-ending TRIP," Abbie wrote Father Gilgun, who had helped him move to New York.

Abbie's divorce was final, and whatever ambivalence he had about leaving his children was neutralized by the possibilities he was discovering on the Lower East Side. He felt himself free of all the possessions and responsibilities that had riveted him to Worcester. In the divorce settlement he had promised—or so he confided to Father Gilgun—to pay Sheila seventy to seventy-five dollars a week, but he wasn't expecting ever again to be making that kind of money. His work at Liberty House provided him with a subsistence income: the going weekly wage for movement jobs during this period was between fifty and seventy-five dollars. But he had no intention of reentering the job market and embarking upon a new career. Never again would he split his life into movement and non-movement compartments. He was fired with an ambition to change the world. "I really want to teach and not just the young but everybody. . . . I want to talk to the spirit that's within each soul. . . . The real problem I face is how can I turn on the people who are ready. . . . I want only to try to live in accord with the promptings which come from my true self—is that so much?" he wrote in a series of ecstatically scrawled letters to Father Gilgun in Worcester.

Flush with the prominence he had gained from his *Village Voice* articles, Abbie thought of becoming a writer. He sent poems to *WIN*, a radical pacifist magazine published out of the same warren of movement offices where the Poor People's Corporation was located. He also prepared an article about Liberty House for *Liberation*, one of the movement's most respected magazines, published down the hall and edited by Dave Dellinger, Barbara Deming, Sidney Lens, Staughton Lynd, and Paul Goodman. Hanging out in the movement offices, Abbie heard talk of sending a nonviolent peace brigade to Vietnam to protest the sending of American combat forces in 1965 and to assist the victims of the war. Although the project never got further than the talking stage, Abbie was excited by the idea. "A move on to get 2000 people to go to Vietnam to rebuild the country—Probably will go—The fuckin War poisons everything. I can't work right," he wrote Father Gilgun.

Paul Goodman was Abbie's role model. He was influenced by Goodman's book, *Growing up Absurd*, which justified the rebellion of American teenage males by showing how little society offered to inspire their commitment. Abbie heard Goodman speak at a Catholic Worker meeting and got him to participate in a Liberty House conference on economics and equality with Jesse Morris, Cesar Chavez, and Oscar Lewis. Abbie admired Goodman because he was an activist as well as an intellectual. Goodman was prominent in his support of draft resisters, and when invited to speak at think tank or university symposiums, he invariably used his position to promote opposition to the Vietnam War. Abbie was impressed that Goodman had stuck to his radical principles. Even though he had become a famous author, Goodman had not sold out.[1]

Abraham Maslow sometimes visited Liberty House to see his daughter Ellen. He disapproved of her work in the movement. Intent on making an impact on mainstream American life, Abe Maslow considered the Poor People's Corporation to be squan-

dered idealism, a marginal enterprise. His visits with Ellen often
deteriorated into arguments about politics, economics, and the
state of American society in which Abbie took Ellen's side.[2] But
Abbie still admired Maslow and used his ideas about self-
actualization to justify the gleeful way in which he embraced his
new life. In Abbie's new, hip, bohemian milieu, family life was considered secondary to the quest for creative fulfillment. In theory
this quest was open to any man or woman of courage. In actuality
it was the man who appropriated the right. Hip bohemians repli-
cated the sexism of the straight world. The woman's role was to
support the man as he embarked on the noble quest of holy art.[3]

Despite his need for personal independence, Abbie did not feel
his life complete without a woman, so his optimism about his life's
direction was confirmed when, shortly after his *Village Voice* articles came out, he met Anita Kushner, a volunteer at Liberty
House. Abbie met her on the first day she worked there. The Beatles were playing in the background, and Abbie tossed her a tab of
purple acid. Later Abbie talked to Ellen about the new volunteer.
"Her father manufactures fabrics. Maybe we can get some fabric
out of him."

Abbie and Anita dated and at Anita's apartment danced to the
Beatles' *Revolver*. Abbie told her about Mao Tse-tung—how Mao
wrote poetry and how, under his leadership, the people in China
were no longer starving. What impressed her was his passionate
belief that hunger was not God-given, that people could change the
world, and that political leaders could write poetry.

Anita Kushner was an intense and energetic woman who, by her
own account, "was moving in a direction that naturally crossed
Abbie's path." She had grown up in a Jewish middle-class family in
Queens, graduated with honors in English from Goucher College in
Towson, Maryland, and gotten a Danforth Fellowship to study
English literature at Columbia University, where her adviser had
been Jeffrey Hart, a young conservative and a darling of William
Buckley's *National Review*. But Anita felt stifled in the academic
atmosphere. She dropped out of Columbia after a year, worked as
a secretary in the publishing field, and quit in frustration at the
lack of opportunity for women to advance beyond secretarial
work. She then entered Yeshiva University and got an M.A. in psychology. Working for the New York Civil Liberties Union to document police brutality in order to win public support for a Civilian

Review Board, she was again relegated to secretarial work. "Completely fed up with white-collar hypocrisy," as she put it, she quit her job.

At Goucher when Abbie was in Berkeley, Anita Kushner had taken part in civil rights demonstrations in Baltimore to support the first lunch counter sit-ins in the South. Years later, working as a Pinkerton security guard at the 1964 World's Fair in Queens, she was angered by the brutality of the police in breaking up a civil rights demonstration at the Florida pavilion and sent her week's paycheck to SNCC. "If I had been born a woman I would have been Anita," Abbie wrote, a description that rings true to people who knew them. "Sometimes couples take fifty years of living together to get to look and act alike: we began right off."[4]

About two weeks after they met, Abbie and Anita rented a basement apartment—their "nest," they called it—on St. Marks Place between Second and Third avenues, at the center of hip activity in the East Village. In the winter of 1966–1967 the neighborhood was going through a cultural transformation. The traditional immigrant quarter for eastern Europeans, especially Jews, the Lower East Side had become, by the early 1960s, a neighborhood of poor black and Hispanic families and aging Ukrainians and Poles whose children, like the Jewish population as a whole, had moved to the Bronx, Brooklyn, Queens, or the suburbs beyond. The influx of white bohemians completed the mix.

The Lower East Side had always been a low-rent ghetto for creative people who could not afford to live in Greenwich Village, the more affluent bohemian quarter to the west. In the late 1950s and early 1960s, in the wake of the beat generation, a new wave of bohemians began to settle there. Artists, craftspeople, teachers, social workers, journalists, and hip entrepreneurs were part of this emigration. They adopted the beats' lifestyle of voluntary poverty, sexual freedom, a belief in personal expression, and the idea that the quest for heightened consciousness and new experience is more important than the conventional goals of marriage, career, and affluence. The newcomers (abetted by real estate developers who saw in their arrival possibilities for gentrification) began to call the neighborhood the East Village. Like Abbie, most of these East Villagers were in their late twenties or older. They were highly motivated self-starters. And with a booster spirit (endemic to bohemia as it is to cities like Worcester), they touted the East Village as the *real* hip underground, the successor to Greenwich Village as the heartland of bohemianism. Already, the more socially conscious East Village denizens were beginning to proselytize in behalf of bohemian values. Abbie and Anita felt a part of this generational ferment. They would sit in their loft bed—covered with an American flag bedspread—and listen to Bob Fass's late night talk show on WBAI, New York's listener-sponsored FM radio station. "We'd have the phone near the bed and call in," Anita recalls. "It was an incredible feeling of a small, intimate community."

Because it was an integrated community and proud of that fact, and because black artists, especially jazz musicians, were its secular saints, the hip underground considered the civil rights movement to be an extension of itself. Most everyone in the East Village knew someone who had gone South for civil rights, and WBAI treated the civil rights movement with the same partisan thoroughness that the mainstream media treated the United States at war. The hip underground also had an affinity for the existential, action-based politics of the radical pacifists who organized the first demonstrations against the Vietnam War. Although there were bohemian leftists who opposed pacifism and advanced various Marxist positions, the principle of nonviolence was widely accepted. In the antiwar movement as in the civil rights movement, nonviolent direct action was a starting point from which discussions of political tactics and strategy flowed.

In 1966 a new generation of bohemians began settling in the East Village. These first hippies—meaning "baby hipsters"—were mostly young high school and college dropouts. This surge was more pronounced than previous bohemian waves. The baby boomers were coming of age; anything conspicuous that they did would be noticeable simply because of their numbers. In addition the economy was riding the crest of postwar prosperity. Young people willing to rough it could live, without working, on the crumbs of the affluent society. The styles of teenage rebellion had been evolving since the early 1950s, when Abbie first fancied himself a hood. Youthful rebels now had a choice of identities; in addition to being hoods they could model themselves after beatniks, New Left activists, Hell's Angels motorcyclists, long-haired poets, avant-garde artists, or any combination of the above. There were also more

exciting destinations than the local pool hall. The media publicized
the attractions of the East Village and San Francisco's Haight-
Ashbury, and most cities and college towns also had bohemian
areas. Then there was the war. Youths waiting to be drafted had
time to kill; those who intended to avoid the draft flocked to the
East Village, where they were given protection and treated as heroes. Finally, there was the attraction of drugs, sexual freedom,
and a total escape from parental authority. But hedonism had
always been a lure that attracted young people to the bohemian
lifestyle.

Abbie was initially dismissive of the young hippies who panhan-
dled him on St. Marks Place in order to get money for the mescaline, hashish, marijuana, and LSD that were openly peddled in
front of his apartment building. Abbie's generation of bohemian
dropouts defended their rejection of middle-class America with a
social and political critique that they articulated through artistic
and political expression. They were serious in their use of psychedelic drugs and in their espousal of utopian politics. The hippies of
this new generation were a different breed entirely. To Abbie they
seemed vacuous, without any intellectual drive or curiosity. They
were raised on television and hence, from his standpoint, illiterate.
They were also inexperienced. Abbie's generation identified with
the civil rights movement and, through their love of blues, jazz, or
rock, had black heroes. The newcomers had not gone through the
civil rights struggles. Their lack of social concern bothered Abbie,
and he was repelled by the commercialism that all too often rushed
into the vacuum. The white musicians of Abbie's generation—folkies like Baez, Bob Dylan, Tom Paxton, and Peter, Paul, and
Mary—sang for the civil rights movement. The Jefferson Airplane,
to take the example of one of the new San Francisco psychedelic
rock bands, did advertisements for Levi jeans.

Because the hippies were young, they had no experience in going
to work. Abbie's efforts at Liberty House made him acutely aware
of the hippies' innocence in this regard. To the degree that hippies,
or their adult mentors, voiced an economic theory, it was to the
effect that the cybernetic revolution would free people from the
necessity of work. Automated machines would produce the goods,
and people would share the wealth. Everyone would have a guaranteed income and would choose whether or not to work. For the
hippies, work represented a barrier between themselves and au-

thenticity. In his *Liberation* article, published in April 1967, Abbie
debunked the radicals' idea of a guaranteed annual income as "another extension of a bankrupt welfare program." Working for the
Poor People's Corporation put Abbie in a social milieu where work
had meaning. "People want to work, that is to say, they want to
live an authentic existence," Abbie wrote of the blacks in the Mississippi co-op movement.[5] He rejected careerism but, like his
peers, craved useful work and was sufficiently self-motivated to
create it for himself.

Aspects of the hippie movement attracted Abbie, however. He
liked the long hair on the men and the expressive and practical
clothing styles. St. Marks Place was a theater of the street, a continuous costume show. Kids wore clothes to express who they
wanted to be. Imagination ruled. The most authentic hippies created their costumes out of secondhand clothes. As the fashion
industry tried to copy hippie vestments, the hippies grew more outrageous in their gaudy inventions. The hippies had broken with
their past, Abbie saw, and because of their use of drugs had become criminals in the face of the law. This appealed to Abbie's
sense of himself as an outlaw and to his instincts as a political organizer. The challenge, as he saw it, was to turn their rebellion in
a political direction.

Few leftists saw anything redeemable in the hippie rebellion. To
Marxists, the youth revolt was symptomatic of a crisis in capitalism, the failure of the system to attract a commitment from its
youth. But Abbie's perspective was Maslovian rather than Marxist.
Hippies didn't have to fit the left's neat ideological scheme; what
made them interesting to Abbie was their potential. Drawing upon
Maslow's pyramid of needs, Abbie figured that while young people
had their basic physical security assured, their higher needs were
going unfulfilled. American society elevated the false needs of status, wealth, and power, but repressed the drive for authentic
needs: friendship, community, and self-expression. The hippie rebellion pointed toward these life-affirming qualities that American
society quashed. More than any other group in the country, Abbie
thought, hippies were moving toward the apex of Maslow's pyramid, toward a vision of society that encouraged self-actualization,
the right to be everything one is capable of being.

In exploring the meaning of the hippie rebellion Abbie was influenced by Danny Schechter, a white activist who had worked in

Harlem and was studying political sociology at the London School
of Economics. Schechter had read Abbie's critique of black power
in the *Village Voice* and, impressed by its emotional honesty, had
written Abbie a long letter urging him to be more sympathetic to
the black power movement. Abbie wrote back, apparently thrilled to
be taken seriously by another activist. The American Revolution had
begun with committees of correspondence, Abbie said, and in that
spirit suggested that he and Schechter open a dialogue. In London, Schechter was writing a sociological paper on how cultural
ferment can produce political change. In a characteristically American fashion he was turned off by the dogmatic Marxism of the
English left. Drawing on his own love of black rhythm and blues,
he was suggesting that the New Left take a cultural turn. By fusing
popular culture with politics and by using the media as a megahorn
for their message, Schechter thought that radical organizers could
forge the hippie's raw alienation into a mass youth movement.

These ideas meshed with Abbie's observations in the East Vil-
lage. Abbie wrote back describing his own experiences (and to
Father Gilgun asserted that he was "writing a book with a guy in
England who I've never met"). When Danny Schechter returned to
New York on his spring vacation, he met Abbie at Liberty House.
They attended a big antiwar demonstration together and visited
SDS activists organizing blacks in the Newark ghetto, where Danny
introduced Abbie to Tom Hayden, the leader of the project. The
Newark Community Union Project was one of the last community-
organizing efforts led by white SDS activists in black ghettos. Visiting Hayden sharpened Abbie's doubts about the effectiveness of
whites organizing among blacks. As for Schechter, he viewed Abbie
as still living with a foot in the 1950s, as an activist who still identified with the beat generation rather than with the counterculture
that was blossoming around him. But he was impressed that Abbie
saw himself as an organizer in the tradition of the civil rights movement. In the South organizers had used gospel-inspired freedom
songs to mobilize blacks. In the North, Abbie understood, rock 'n'
roll could be used to mobilize young whites.

It was the use of psychedelic drugs, however, especially LSD,
that made the radical bohemianism of the sixties so different from
earlier bohemian experiences. Alcohol was the drug of favor in pre-
sixties bohemia. Various forms of amphetamines were also abused.
Marijuana was considered a treat. Harsh laws and government-
propagated horror stories (smoking marijuana, said the authori-

ties, was the first step to heroin addiction and a life of crime) made paranoia endemic behind the drawn shades and locked doors where, typically, pot was smoked. When pot smokers found that the scare stories were untrue, this revelation created a breach in government credibility. The officials were lying about dope. Might they also be lying about LSD, communism, and the war in Vietnam?

By the time of Abbie's arrival in the East Village the paranoia about marijuana had been broken, and people were smoking it openly. LSD was plentiful. It was cheap and pure. The purple acid that Abbie had tossed Anita came from California, where Augustus Owsley Stanley III was manufacturing it in order, he hoped, to transform the consciousness of the world. It was certainly transforming the consciousness of the East Village. Its aggregate effect was to exaggerate the hip bohemians' apocalyptic sense of their revolutionary destiny. Many felt that they were living on the cusp of history and that their creativity and their peaceful, communal spirit were solutions to the problems of humankind. (That rock groups like the Beatles shared this consciousness—and were critically acclaimed by intellectuals as well as idolized by young people everywhere—contributed greatly to this euphoria.) For many acid trippers, the promise of the new consciousness shone so bright that it melded illusion into reality. Abbie, however, was at first more cautious. In June 1967 he wrote a letter to *Punch*, the new underground paper published in Worcester, describing the East Village's psychedelic culture and the six acid trips he had taken since Manny Schreiber had turned him on in Worcester. "I feel it's worthwhile," he said, "but no illusions. It's what you do between trips that counts, and life is still a greater high than acid."[6] Walking through the Lower East Side while tripping with Anita, Abbie saw a tenement burning down. "This is part of it, too," Anita recalls Abbie saying as they watched firemen putting out the fire. "Acid doesn't take you out of reality. Poverty and social injustice are part of the reality." For Abbie, Anita says, LSD was not an escape; it just made everything much more intense.*

* In 1972 or 1973 Abbie told Allen Young, an underground journalist, that he had taken acid about three hundred times. Probably an exaggeration (it would have meant tripping on an average of once a week for five or six years), it does reflect a level of use that was not uncommon in hip circles.

Abbie began hanging out on St. Marks Place with the young hippies and became familiar with the drug dealers, the crash pads, the whole sociological context in which they lived. His and Anita's apartment became a safe place for troubled kids. From his brother Jack, who was now running the Worcester Medical Supply, he obtained quantities of niacinamide, which he used to help kids come down from bad acid trips. The unique role that drug dealers played in the hippie culture intrigued him. "Righteous dealers" specialized in the "soft," psychedelic drugs: marijuana, hashish, mescaline, psilocybin, and LSD. They sold these drugs as if they were a holy sacrament, and they often treated their business as a priestly calling. Just as prohibition-era bootleggers exaggerated the materialist values of the Roaring Twenties (and so spent their profits on public ostentation, as well as on bribes to public officials for the sake of protecting and expanding their illicit business), righteous dealers exaggerated the egalitarian values of the hippie community. They shunned public displays of personal prosperity and gained status through the quality of their drugs, their fair prices, and the money that they poured back into community projects.

Righteous dealers sold drugs not to get rich but to buy time in order to pursue their own projects: arts, crafts, politics, or just to hang out stoned listening to rock music. The era of the righteous dealer was not long-lived, however, even though the myth persisted. As the potential for profit increased, drug dealing became infected by underworld values and, some claimed, the underworld itself. Rip-offs involving the sale of impure drugs and violence between dealers became commonplace. But the sordid underworld of the drug culture was easy for hip leaders like Abbie to ignore, because they lived in an elite world above it—a world animated by social theories and creative endeavors. Refusing to give up the self-image of a hood that he had created for himself in Worcester, Abbie was prone to romanticize the criminal underworld and to interpret any antisocial behavior as a positive, liberating force in the context of the antibourgeois, counterculture rebellion.

True to his street-smart, tough-guy persona, Abbie continued to publicly proclaim experience over book learning. But in private, as always, he was a voracious reader, speed-reading books on social psychology and communications theory, taking what he needed out of the texts to fit his own evolving social theory. He read history and biography in a similar subjective manner, seeing himself in the historical figures that he read about, analyzing how he would have responded to their political challenges and how they would have responded to his.[7] Two writers, in addition to Paul Goodman, especially influenced Abbie during this period. Marshall McLuhan's notion that the medium is the message had not yet become a cliché. It inspired Abbie to pay more attention to television and to think critically about the ineffective ways that the movement was getting its message out. He was also reading the French avant-garde writer Antonin Artaud. A contemporary of Freud, Artaud saw theater as a way of expunging humankind's repressed instincts. Whereas Freud offered analysis and, ultimately, adjustment as a cure for neurosis, Artaud offered the idea of the theater of cruelty, "a poetry of festivals and crowds" that would mirror the unconscious and induce, by drawing the audience into the spectacle, a cathartic release of emotions and desires.[8] "We as a movement must become concerned with communication and that involves emotional visual presentations more than factual analysis," Abbie wrote in *WIN*, describing the importance of these books. "I think we should watch more TV than read, listen to music more than lectures, and devise a style which will convey our message beyond an intellectual acceptance."[9]

On Easter Sunday 1967 Abbie and Anita joined about ten thousand other New Yorkers at the East Coast's first be-in, held in the Sheep Meadow, a large open field in Central Park. The idea of a be-in came from the Bay Area. (Everything the East Village hippies did happened three to twelve months earlier in California.) In January 1967 the Haight-Ashbury community held the first be-in, a so-called "gathering of the tribes" in Golden Gate Park in San Francisco. That be-in emphasized the role of leaders in the hippie movement, with a stage full of youthful rock bands (the Jefferson Airplane, the Grateful Dead, Country Joe and the Fish), with older bohemian mentors (Ginsberg, Ferlinghetti, Gary Snyder, Tim Leary, and Ken Kesey), and with Jerry Rubin, the one speaker representing a political perspective—and he was mildly booed. The speakers' function was to lay out the hippie ethos for the stoned youngsters in the audience, to give the hippies a sense of themselves as part of an assertive "counterculture" (here the term started being used), and to describe a lifestyle that would attract, and ultimately transform, the bored and disillusioned dropouts from the middle-class world.

The New York be-in was planned to show that the new generation did not need leaders, that young people understood the new ethos—that with the proper cues hippies would know how to act. They did. From sunrise into the night the participants, many with painted faces and in weird and colorful psychedelic costumes, swarmed through the meadow, sharing food and hugs, and even marijuana, with strangers, pelting each other and the bemused police (who stayed on the perimeter) with daffodils. Without any prompting the celebrants formed huge circles and then ran toward the middle to collapse on one another. In letting their guard down, many people experienced a rush of new feelings: openness, tenderness, and trust. Everyone was astonished at the diversity of the crowd. In addition to the hippies there were families and straight people from all parts of the city. If participants at first didn't understand what the be-in was about, they quickly caught the spirit. Whatever cynicism and uptight standoffishness individuals brought to the park was washed over by a contagious sense of solidarity, an almost spiritual empathy that all these strangers suddenly felt for one another.

"The Be-In seems almost a sacred event, harking back to medieval pageants, gypsy gatherings, or the great pow-wows of the American Indians," wrote Don McNeill, a young journalist who had the East Village beat for the *Village Voice*. The spectacle seemed to act, in Artaud's terms, as a psychological catharsis. The spirituality that the nonviolent civil rights movement had suggested was suddenly apparent to all; a transcendent wave of emotion carried people out of the negative, uptight posturing of the rebellious fifties into an unexplored social and emotional experience. What was its meaning? Could it be transferred into the matrix of everyday living? "The hippies have brought something beautiful into our middle-class lives, and opened up new possibilities for all of us," wrote a young left-wing intellectual named Marshall Berman a few months later in a letter to the *Village Voice*. "They've shown us how it's possible to be open, sweet, joyous, friendly, spontaneous, trusting, loving, even in the United States of America, even in the city of New York, even in the year of Our Lyndon, 1967."[10]

The be-in was organized and promoted on a budget of $250. Anonymous posters, in Spanish and English and hung throughout the city, told people to bring picnics, flowers, and Easter eggs to share. The event was publicized on WBAI and, most effectively, by word of mouth. There was no structure, no stage, no program; there were no speakers, no musicians, no leaders, no prominent people who, conventional wisdom had it, were necessary to draw a crowd. The organizers identified themselves to the media to assure a proper interpretation of what was happening but otherwise remained anonymous.

When Abbie first heard about the plan for the be-in, he tracked down one its organizers, Jim Fouratt, and volunteered to help spread the word. In age, experience, and sensibility Fouratt was typical of the hip East Village bohemians trying to forge a community out of the hippie invasion. He had come from a Rhode Island Catholic working-class family and had given up a Harvard scholarship to become an actor in New York. As a student at the Actors' Studio in the early 1960s, he was introduced to radical politics and began going to ban-the-bomb demonstrations with his actor friends. Organized by radical pacifist groups and the Catholic Workers, these demonstrations usually attracted no more than a few hundred people, many of whom were hip bohemians from the Lower East Side or Greenwich Village. Fouratt became known in avant-garde circles as a person with a sharp and critical mind, a social conscience, original ideas, and the ability to organize events. He was in San Francisco for the first be-in. Returning to New York, he brought together a group that included Paul Williams, a young Swarthmore dropout and editor of *Crawdaddy*, the first hip rock 'n' roll magazine; Susan Harnett, an artist who headed a group called Experiments in Art and Technology; and Claudio Badel, a poet from Chile who worked with the Bread and Puppet Theater and other avant-garde theater and mixed-media groups.[11]

Through Fouratt and his friends, Abbie began working with other East Villagers to provide a social support network for the young hippies. A number of groups were established: the Community Breast, to raise seed money for neighborhood projects; a Communications Company (based on an idea Fouratt had brought back from Haight-Ashbury), to mimeograph and distribute pithy leaflets advising the community about rumors, arrests, bad drugs, social services, and public events; and the Jade Companion Bail Fund, to provide bail and legal aid to hippies (including drug dealers) who were in trouble with the law. In the summer of 1967 many of these activities were brought together under ESSO, the East Side Service Organization, with funds from a New York City antipoverty agency (and thus with Fouratt and Hoffman indirectly on the city payroll).

Among the competing male egos assuming leadership positions in this emerging hip community, Abbie's stood out. At community meetings, where everyone would sit quietly (sometimes in a circle on the floor as if at an Indian powwow), Abbie would jiggle and pace or teeter in his chair; whenever the mood was solemnly earnest, Abbie would crack jokes. As usual he was impatient with process; and in hip circles the agonizing process of decision making by consensus often seemed more important than coming to a decision. When the group process got too muddled, Abbie would go off and make decisions on his own. As treasurer of one of the bail funds, he once went off without authorization to bail out a local drug dealer. His explanation was that the man was part of the community, and getting people out of jail was what the bail fund was for.

Drawing on his SNCC experience, Abbie was, at first, determined to involve the young hippies in community projects. He was wary of outsiders with good intentions who wanted to do things for hippies that the hippies ought to be doing for themselves. At one meeting of hip professionals in the West Village, Abbie tried to discourage the group from setting up a defense committee for hippies in the East Village. The youngsters had to learn how to fend for themselves, he insisted. "We had a good thing going on the East Side. The groups were stumbling along. I think that this committee could do a real service to the community by disbanding." Typically, he softened his opposition with a humorous twist. "Think of it," he added. "A committee disbanding after two days. It'd be a whole new turn in American political life."[12]

As in Mississippi, the vagueness of participatory democracy invited manipulation and self-delusion. Abbie and the other more experienced hip organizers constantly mistook themselves for the young people they intended to organize. And this circle of older organizers expanded as more and more veteran white activists, searching for a means of remaining politically committed and unwilling to reenter the straight white world most of them had dropped out of, entered the hip community instead. If Abbie's efforts to organize hippies seemed to be working, it was primarily because more and more socially conscious members of his own generation were dropping out and becoming hippies themselves.

Inspired by the be-in, Abbie and Anita got married on June 8 behind the Metropolitan Museum of Art in Central Park, in a public event with the press invited. Linn House, the self-styled Chief Boo Hoo of the Neo-American Church, a satirical (and psychedelic) religion, performed the ceremony, after which the guests gave flowers to the police, who draped them over their squad car. (Later, to appease Anita's parents, the couple got "properly" married at a temple service.) This was probably the first public hippie wedding, and it initiated a fad. A month later thirteen couples got married in Brooklyn's Prospect Park in an event staged by the Parks Department, and thereafter couples began marrying in whatever setting had personal meaning.[13] It was the "summer of love," as the underground media dubbed it. "All these drugs, and being in love gave a rosy glow to our political thinking," Anita recalls. "The world was glorious. You could do anything. Magic was possible."

★ ★ ★

As Abbie began to carve out a role for himself as a community organizer in the East Village, he began to do less and less work at Liberty House. He was never purged from the civil rights movement, as he sometimes alleged. He merely shifted his attention to the East Village and, without ever declaring his intentions, left Liberty House—debts and all—in the hands of Ellen Maslow. By the summer of 1967 Abbie was identifying himself as a "Digger," on the model of a San Francisco group organizing white hippies in Haight-Ashbury. The leaders of the Diggers came out of the San Francisco Mime Troupe. They were theater people rather than political organizers, and they used "guerrilla" or street theater as a means for organizing the hippie community. To protest the city's unwillingness to deal with an infestation of rats in the Haight-Ashbury district, they went to City Hall carrying pennywhistles and dressed in the costume of pied pipers. Had they gone through the usual political channels, telephoning authorities or even getting people to sign petitions, they would not have grabbed the attention of City Hall as they succeeded in doing with guerrilla theater.

The Diggers also worked up a plan for a moneyless economy based on recycling surplus goods. They began by making the rounds of supermarkets and restaurants, collecting food that would otherwise be thrown out and cooking it in a soup that they would give to the hippies in Golden Gate Park. Of course, this was nothing more than a soup kitchen, like those run by the Salvation Army. But the Diggers played to the flamboyant theatrics inherent in the hippie movement; the soup they dished out became a communal affirmation that the hip community could sustain itself on the scraps of the affluent economy; soup time in the park became a social gathering, a mini be-in, with music, dancing, and food and dope to share.

From the idea of free food came the idea of free clothes, free housing, free garages, and an entire network of enterprises based on bartering and sharing. Utopian in theory, the scheme was undermined by the hippies' nonexistent work habits. The work got done by hip social activists (the majority of whom were women) who drew their reward from their sense of nurturing a new community. But these organizers continuously got burned-out, while the majority of hippies, too stoned to work, remained passive consumers—just as they were in the world of their parents.

Part of the Digger mystique derived from their public anonymity. Digger activists used made-up names in order to encourage the idea that hippies were new people who, in adapting new identities, were ridding themselves of their past. Being anonymous also did away with problems of responsibility and accountability. Insisting that they were not leaders (because hippies didn't have leaders) gave the Diggers the protection of ready-made denial. Responsibility was a choice that they assumed with their social work and disavowed when their scene turned sour. Digger theatrics were no substitute for a real social movement. A small core of activists, pretending that they were the community, could not transform the Haight-Ashbury reality: bad drugs, no money, a growing population of teenage runaways, and a growing hoodlum population preying on the innocence and desperation of the hippie youngsters. The Diggers responded by staying one step ahead of reality, continually manipulating symbols and writing new scripts to sustain their vision. When the hippie movement in San Francisco became too sordid to defend, they simply created a ceremony in which they buried the hippie and declared themselves "free men"—a sleight of hand that was quickly picked up in the East Village. ("Freemen," Abbie wrote Father Gilgun at the end of 1967: "that is the term we dreamed up—better than Diggers.")

Abbie met Emmett Grogan and Peter Berg, the leaders (despite their disclaimer) of the San Francisco Diggers, when they visited the East Village in the spring of 1967. He also kept up with their activities by reading about them in the underground press. The San Francisco group would later say that Abbie stole their ideas. But an organizer, Abbie believed, takes ideas as he or she finds them and alters them when necessary to make them politically effective. "I get a million ideas a minute," Abbie once exclaimed to Anita. "How do you steal ideas? Ideas are free."[14]

Digger theater became almost a weekly event in the East Village after the visit by the San Francisco Diggers. "We'd get an idea and we'd go ahead and do it," Marty Carey says of the circle of friends that included Abbie, Jim Fouratt, WBAI's Bob Fass, and others. "We didn't need permission. We'd go on WBAI and talk about it. People would donate. We didn't have overhead. No staff or structure. Whoever was involved in doing it did it. If you got a few bucks you paid the rent."[15] One of their first efforts was a sweep-in on Third Street that brought people together in a festive, be-in, partylike atmosphere to clean up a street in the East Village during a sanitation worker strike. The point was to show what people could accomplish if they took civic responsibility for their neighborhood. (The idea was later adopted by the environmental movement, which sponsored volunteer cleanup or "greenup" days in many states.) Leftists, however, accused Abbie and his friends of being scabs for doing the work of the sanitation workers. Abbie accepted the criticism but did not give up on the idea of using guerrilla theater to demonstrate the possibilities of an alternative society.

To protest the automobile traffic on St. Marks Place, Abbie and his friends called for a "do your own thing" demonstration one Saturday night during the summer and, until the police came to clear the street, transformed it into a dance stage and a pedestrian mall. The next week, protesting the lack of green space on the Lower East Side, they returned to St. Marks Place and mock-planted a tree in the middle of the street while a neighborhood rock band played music on a flatbed truck and people danced in the street until, again, the cops came and broke up the party. When tourist buses began cruising St. Marks Place to view the hippie scene, Abbie and his friends announced plans to stick up the bus and rob the tourists of their socks. Abbie and Marty Carey brought a live duck to David Susskind's television talk show, doing a takeoff of Groucho Marx's "You Bet Your Life" quiz show. ("Say the secret word and win a hundred dollars" Groucho would tell the contestants; when one of them said the designated word, a duck—looking like Groucho—would drop into view with the money stuck to its webbed foot.) Abbie released the duck the first time Susskind mentioned the word "hippie." These pranks made Hoffman and Fouratt media favorites. The *New York Post*, the newspaper read by Jewish New Yorkers, adopted Abbie as its favorite hippie, dubbing him a "happy," not a hippie.[16]

Hoffman and Fouratt, as well as Susan and Marty Carey, were key organizers of the Free Store, which, in Digger fashion, recycled (before that ecological concept was in popular use) secondhand clothes and other household goods by giving them away free in the store. Paul Goodman, who came down to fold clothes and stock the shelves, pronounced the Free Store an interesting experiment; "it sets your mind going." As usual, Abbie's sense of zaniness attracted media attention. (There was an opening-day "sale," and neighborhood kids were encouraged to come in and play dress-up). Unfortunately, the publicity also attracted other secondhand clothing dealers, who emptied the shelves to stock their own profit-making used-clothes emporiums.

Abbie got a lot of political mileage out of the *idea* of a Free Store. "We saw ourselves as visionaries in the Mean Streets. A utopia would rise out of the garbage. BE REALISTS—DEMAND THE IMPOSSIBLE," he wrote in *Major Motion Picture*.[17] But Abbie was confusing the theater of the Free Store with the reality of its daily existence. To the organizers, the store was part put-on, a parody of capitalistic ethics. But it also existed as an actual establishment. Those who had the original vision had other projects they wanted to nurture and left the store's operation in the hands of hippie volunteers. This, of course, went with the idea of empowering young people to take responsibility for their movement. But in the deliberate structurelessness that was part of the hippie philosophy and that Abbie actively believed in, there was no way for the organizers to insist that the store be properly run; indeed, there was no standard of propriety to define responsibility. To insist on proper management was to buy into bourgeois values and totally defeat the hippie ethos. It was a fact of life in the hippie subculture that bad energy drove out good energy. People would start projects that, because of the excitement, would attract, like moths to light, hangers-on with nothing to contribute. Their passivity, which drew on other people's energy, would eventually drive away the motivated people (who would go off to start a new project), and the cycle would be repeated.

Responsibility for the Free Store was passed from hippies to bikers to transients to anyone who wanted to oversee the operation for a day, a week, an hour. The store became a focus for trouble. Abbie was called in to deal with the street toughs who would storm through the store intimidating and sometimes beating up the hippies. He was good at dealing with hoodlums. He was able to call up his past at will and deal with them in the macho manner they respected. But the problems, in the end, were overwhelming. In a rare moment of candor Abbie told a visiting writer, "One week it was assaulted by everyone. First, a group of Negroes threw a garbage can through the window. Then another one came in with a hammer. . . . Then some Puerto Ricans came in and grabbed a girl, took her out, and raped her. The whole place is one big amphetamine trip. There's no community. No one can make it here." More often, Abbie turned his back on the problems and continued to talk about the Free Store as if it was a utopia in the making.

"People got beat up, women were raped at the Free Store," Jim Fouratt, with his more critical eye, remembers. "But Abbie wouldn't admit it. He didn't let anything break into his optimism. The reality of the Free Store didn't dampen his enthusiasm, because he refused to see the ugliness beneath the surface."[18]

It was Abbie's idea to take clothes from the Free Store and give them away in Macy's, New York's largest department store. The press would be tipped off, and as a media event it would contrast the hippies' emphasis on sharing with the straight world's focus on money and profit. Abbie was a radical in a hurry. "His approach was not slow and steady reeducation," Fouratt recalls. "It was his genius to see the big picture, to turn alternative social work into a symbolic showdown with the consumer society." But, at Macy's, as with the Free Store, Abbie was so taken with the ideological overview of his theater that he ignored the detail—the facts of what happened that, in the end, determined the message. According to Fouratt, most of the shoppers at Macy's were put on the defensive by the hippies' assertiveness and refused to take the free clothes the hippies offered. To Fouratt the demonstration, like the

Free Store, was a lesson in how difficult it was for people to change their thinking. According to Abbie, however, the demonstration worked, because it effectively contrasted the generous values of the hippie world with the uptight attitudes of the straight shoppers, who "performed" exactly as Abbie expected they would.

Meanwhile the East Village scene drew another sort of audience. The growing numbers of young runaways, the widespread use of drugs in public, and the increasingly provocative social activism attracted the attention of the police. Some of the political activists welcomed this; they thought that hippies could be more easily radicalized by conflict with the police and were always looking to build minor incidents into larger confrontations. But Abbie, in 1967 at least, accepted that the revolution was not going to be touched off by events in the East Village. He was looking at a bigger picture; he wanted to attract the national media in order to publicize the hippie subculture and identify it with the broader radical movement. He was therefore willing to keep a line of communication open with Inspector Joe Fink, the commanding officer of the Ninth Precinct.

Fink, a New York Jew, was more liberal and tolerant than the stereotyped cop, and he understood that the cultural revolution taking place in his precinct was a result of larger social forces than the police could contain. He and Abbie had a genuine liking for each other and occasionally met to see how they might cooperate to keep the social peace. For Fink, keeping the peace was an end in itself; Abbie wanted to keep a lid on the violence in order that the hippie culture could become better established and, hence, politically stronger. Many of the more militant radicals in the East Village accused Abbie of collaborating with Fink and the local police. Abbie, after all, liked to play pool with the cops and kid with them on the street. He defended himself against the radicals' accusations by explaining that this was a way of coming to know the enemy, but he also enjoyed the encounters. Unlike many radicals who vented their hatred of injustice on the police, Abbie was determined to see cops as human beings. "I always dealt one-to-one with those lined up behind the law," he wrote in *Major Motion Picture*. "Fink, like a few police I've met, became one because of some deep social concern and it showed."[19] Abbie tried to stake out a middle ground in the hip community between the nonviolent believers in flower power and the militant street anarchists who wanted to create confrontations with the police. "Personally, I always held my flower in a clenched fist," Abbie wrote in his autobiography. "A semi-structure freak among the love children, I was determined to bring the hippie movement into a broader protest." [20]

The spring and summer of 1967 brought the hippie movement on the Lower East Side out into the open. Suddenly there were hippies everywhere. Tompkins Square Park, the neighborhood's one green area, became a battleground. The park had always had a delicate ethnic mix; the eastern Europeans, the older bohemians, and the black and Puerto Rican youth coexisted peacefully because they all understood the unwritten rules of the turf. The hippies upset that balance. On weekends, especially, their numbers were augmented by "day trippers," young people drawn to the hippie scene from the suburbs and outer boroughs. When the hippie community took the initiative to organize free rock concerts in the park's bandstand, it was as if the newcomers had completely taken control of the park. The neighborhood kids, black and Puerto Rican, fought to reclaim their territory. There were fights and stabbings. The potential existed for an all-out war against the white longhairs.

It was a test for Abbie and other community leaders: How could they teach the white hippies to be sensitive to the cultural diversity of the area, and how could they deal with the hostility of the local kids? As tensions increased, a young Puerto Rican woman named Linda Cusamano got the idea of appointing all the kids in the park—Puerto Rican, black, and hippie alike—as peacekeepers. One night she, Abbie, and other community people handed out cloth bands with the Spanish word *sereno*, for peacekeeper, painted on them. The gambit appealed to the machismo of the neighborhood kids, for now they had the authority to keep the peace, while the hippies saw *sereno* as an affirmation of their own nonviolent ideals. The park was suddenly transformed; it had the spirit of a be-in, with everyone trying to outdo one another in taking responsibility for keeping the peace. Abbie never forgot this incident. At a protest demonstration in Bucks County, Pennsylvania, some fifteen years later, he organized local working-class men into the movement by dubbing the bar in which they all hung out "security headquarters," giving them walkie-talkies, and assigning them to patrol the area in their pickup trucks. In both instances the idea was the same: to keep potential troublemakers from spoiling an event, invite them to participate by appealing to their self-esteem. [21]

★   ★   ★

Abbie's focus on the big picture induced him to ally white hippies
with the black movement. In July 1967, when riots in the black
ghetto of Newark broke out, he and Fouratt, calling themselves
Diggers but working out of Liberty House, arranged with Tom Hayden to bring baby food, canned goods, fresh bread, and even meat
to the besieged neighborhood. At first they did it anonymously;
their emphasis was on getting in supplies. After a week, with the
uprising at an end, they brought flowers, candy, and even an oven
to bake bread for a be-in for the children at a Newark housing
project. Abbie solicited publicity for this event. Again, he was
trying to impose the politics of the older organizers—the commitment that he and Fouratt had to civil rights—on the younger hippies. He wanted them to see in the media that yes, supporting the
black struggle is what being a hippie is about.[22]

Abbie went to great lengths to forge a black-white alliance in the
East Village. One night he, Anita, Paul Krassner, and another
friend were on an acid trip in the Hoffmans' apartment. They were
interrupted by hippies knocking at the door. Some black kids had
gotten arrested in Tompkins Square Park for smoking dope, and
they wanted Abbie to know. Still tripping, the four of them went to
the station house, where Inspector Fink was on duty. Abbie at once
began remonstrating with Fink, demanding that he release the
black kids.

"Hippies smoke pot in the park all the time," Abbie argued,
"and the cops rarely bother them."

"If we catch them smoking, we'll arrest them. If you break the
law, I'll arrest you," Fink replied.

With that Abbie gave a quick kick and shattered the glass of
the precinct's trophy case. Fink arrested him and put him in the
lockup with the black youths. Krassner and Anita Hoffman went
back to the apartment to get a lawyer and raise bail to get Abbie
and the kids out of jail.

For Abbie, politics took priority over tripping on acid. By getting
himself thrown in jail, he again created an image of hippie-black
solidarity.[23] "Diggery Is Niggery," he wrote in an article for the
underground press. "On the Lower East Side pot is an effective
prop, it is the least common denominator. It makes us all outlaws,
brothers, niggers."[24]

CHAPTER

5 | PROTESTING THE WAR

1967

Americans had been protesting the war in Vietnam for two years when Abbie arrived in New York. In communities like Worcester, where activists were few in number, ideological differences were not considered important. Thus, as a civil rights activist (his difficulty with CORE aside), Abbie could move back and forth between the NAACP and SNCC and work for a peace candidate in a Democratic primary even while holding far more radical views. In New York, where the citywide peace movement overlapped into the leadership of the national peace movement, ideology was everything. There were always enough people to form a political group, no matter how small its numbers or arcane its politics. Most antiwar protesters were like Abbie, however: nonideological, freelance activists with no interest in becoming part of any formal organization.

In the beginning of 1967 the antiwar movement had two competing strategic perspectives. Liberals in organizations like SANE and Americans for Democratic Action (ADA) wanted to work within the Democratic party. Civil rights and the war on poverty were still high on their agenda, and they feared that a radical attack on the Johnson administration would jeopardize their ability to push those programs. Only a coalition of liberal, labor, civil rights, and peace activists, working inside the Democratic party, would have the numbers and influence to change Johnson's war policy, they thought. Liberals argued not that the war was morally wrong or that it was a result of the country's imperialist drive but that it was a result of good intentions gone bad—mistaken policy rather than expansionist ideology. Their call for a negotiated settlement to the war put them in an untenable situation. The Johnson administration consistently claimed to be putting out "peace feelers," which, it insisted, the Vietnamese communists ignored. Trying to maintain influence with the administration, the liberals could not openly denounce the president as a liar. The Vietnamese, for their part, were always willing to negotiate the terms of an American withdrawal—and nothing less. Johnson, however, was determined to "bring the coonskin home." Misled by senior military advisers into thinking that "victory was just around the corner," he believed the war to be winnable. He would need only to escalate American firepower until the Vietnamese cried uncle.

The liberal strategy offered only two means to affect the war: elections and lobbying. Abbie was willing to try either route. But after working for Thomas Boyleston Adams, he began to question the fairness of American democracy. As he found out through Adams's poor showing, peace candidates lacked the financial resources to mount effective campaigns. Liberal "fat cats" and labor groups who financed the regular Democratic candidates would not give money to insurgents for fear of losing access to the politicians in power. In 1966 a number of peace candidates ran for Congress, but most did as poorly as Adams. The movement's best showing, not surprisingly, was in Berkeley, where Robert Scheer got 45 percent of the vote in the Democratic primary against hawkish liberal Jeffrey Cohelan, who had the active support of the Johnson administration and the Kennedy family. As with the defeat of the Mississippi Freedom Party in 1964, radicals around the country interpreted Scheer's defeat as one more proof that political change could not come through electoral politics.

More than anything else, however, it was the cowardice of liberal Democratic incumbents that undercut the liberal position. Many Democrats—and Republicans, too—had doubts about the war policy but were afraid of publicly breaking with President Johnson. What the antiwar movement was up against was a political culture that didn't allow for popular opposition. In 1965 a delegation of intellectuals tried to persuade UN ambassador Adlai Stevenson to quit the administration and lead the antiwar movement. Acknowledging his doubts about the war, he demurred, saying, "I would never take advantage of my political position to resign for political reasons. That's not the way we play the game."[1]

Within the Johnson administration were a number of liberals who
opposed the war but also insisted on playing the game. Under Secretary of State George Ball remained as an in-house critic on the
condition that he would not make his opposition to the war public.
Secretary of Defense Robert McNamara went from an enthusiastic
hawk to an anguished dove without ever publicly expressing his
changed perspective. There was no point in lobbying in Washington, radicals argued, because even those liberals who opposed the
war were reluctant to say so publicly.

Robert Kennedy was the one political figure who, many pundits
believed, could effectively challenge President Johnson. Kennedy
made his first public criticisms of the war in February 1966, protesting Johnson's decision to resume the bombing of North Vietnam
and calling for negotiations with the National Liberation Front
(NLF)—the South Vietnamese who were fighting against the United
States. When administration officials fired back, Kennedy back-
tracked and then maintained a low profile on the war for almost a
year.[2] In late 1967, when he finally broke with the administration,
the antiwar movement, organized largely by radicals, no longer felt
it needed the leadership of established liberals.

Then there was Hubert Humphrey. Liberals had thought enough
of his credentials in 1964 to abandon the cause of the Mississippi
Freedom Democratic party in order to secure him the vice presidency. Their hope was that he would articulate liberal positions
within the White House. But Humphrey turned out to be the
administration's loudest cheerleader. Returning from a tour of
Vietnam in 1966, he gushed with enthusiasm, calling the war an
opportunity "for realizing the dream of the Great Society in the
great area of Asia."[3] Humphrey's betrayal confirmed the radicals'
belief that liberal Democrats could not be trusted.

Instead of seeking influence within the Democratic party, the
radicals put their energy behind an effort to build grassroots opposition. Their demands were simple: stop the war, bring the boys
home. They saw no need for complicated negotiations—only for
unilateral American withdrawal. If the movement could raise a
popular outcry against the war, the American government would
figure out a way to end it.

The void in liberal leadership created a vacuum for the radicals
to exploit. But they were in no position to lead a mass movement.
With the exception of Martin Luther King, who didn't publicly

come out against the war until the spring of 1967, and perhaps Dr. Benjamin Spock, the country's best-known pediatrician, the antiwar movement had no leader of national stature. The organizations that made up the radical antiwar coalition were virtually all fringe groups with no direct influence on American politics. Dave Dellinger, the radical pacifist who edited *Liberation* magazine, was the major spokesperson for the Mobe after 1966.* He had been imprisoned twice during World War II for refusing to accept the conscientious objector status to which he was entitled. Between 1945 and 1966 he was active in small pacifist groups that, while important to the development of the New Left, the ban-the-bomb, and the Vietnam War protest movements, were unknown to the public. *Liberation*, one of the most influential of the antiwar publications, had a press run of under ten thousand. Dellinger himself doubted his ability to lead a mass movement, but as a pacifist he was one of the few people that the ideological groups within the coalition all trusted; hence he was indispensable for keeping the Mobe together.

Preserving the radical coalition was Dellinger's priority, for without the Mobe there would be no antiwar movement. For this reason the Mobe focused more on its internal dynamics than on appealing to the general public. The ideological diversity of the member groups meant that the coalition could not espouse a political program or participate in electoral politics. This enhanced the influence of the pacifists, for their métier was direct action: nonviolent marches, rallies, and civil disobedience. The Mobe thus existed only to organize demonstrations. Its leaders, like Dellinger, were not accountable to the unaffiliated rank and file, and had no way of controlling the conduct of the people who attended its demonstrations.

With little money and no access to the media (except for listener-

* The radical antiwar coalition went through a number of name changes, usually with *mobilization* as the key word. I refer to it simply as the Mobe, which was what Abbie and most activists called it. The Mobe was composed of numerous and often competing pacifist, socialist, communist (including Trotskyist) parties, grouplets, organizations, and sects; civil rights, peace, and student organizations; and a smattering of left-leaning liberal groups and labor unions. As the movement grew, new organizations composed of business executives, returned Peace Corps volunteers, and even Vietnam veterans came on board.

supported FM radio), the only way for the antiwar movement to attract public attention was to make news by taking to the streets. The mainstream media acknowledged these demonstrations only to criticize them, but at least that was publicity. The only positive coverage came from student newspapers and the underground press. By 1967 there were hundreds of such papers around the country with a readership in the millions.[4] Thus two realities were emerging in the country. In the mainstream media the war was patriotic; victory was, as the administration promised, just around the corner; and the antiwar movement was irresponsible, unpatriotic, and of no political consequence. In the underground press the war was evil; the government was lying; the NLF was winning; and the hippie counterculture and the antiwar movement were not only the wave of the future but the hope for civilization.

The first New York demonstration that Abbie took part in was a march, on November 5, 1966, from Tompkins Square Park to Bryant Park in midtown, where the East Village contingent joined feeder marches from other neighborhoods. It was the first time that East Village hippies and bohemians participated in the New York movement as a distinct, self-organized antiwar constituency. Abbie himself captured the uniqueness of the occasion: "Our Lower East Side contingent assembled at Tompkins Square Park and marched north, gathering more people along the way. The artists all turned out, so naturally our form of presentation was pretty colorful: Ginsberg's bells and chants, The Bread and Puppet Theater group, gaily dressed and stoned, a Yellow Submarine, and a lot of people who looked like they had posed for the Sergeant Pepper album cover."[5]

Bearded, long-haired, guitar-strumming beatniks were a fixture at movement demonstrations, but many in the peace movement and on the left were embarrassed by their presence. The media often fixated on the "beatniks" at demonstrations. By picking out bearded protestors to symbolize antiwar demonstrators, the media helped marginalize the movement, at least in the eyes of the straight middle class. But even student New Leftists were sensitive about the movement's beatnik image. Many members of SDS were outraged, for instance, when the *New York Times* Sunday Magazine published a feature about them in November 1965 illustrated with

a picture of a long-haired youth standing next to a poster of a napalmed child. The *Times*'s photographer had taken numerous pictures of SDS leaders, all of whom were clean-cut, but the editors
had chosen a picture of SDS's printer, the only male in the office
who had long hair.

Until 1967 most New Leftists felt about drugs and the hippies'
sexual openness as they did about long hair. In early 1966, when
members of an SDS chapter in Oklahoma were busted for smoking
marijuana, most of the leaders of SDS wanted to disassociate the
organization from its wayward chapter.[6] In 1966 older pacifists con-
nected with the Committee for Nonviolent Action tried to suspend
publication of its youth-oriented *WIN* magazine because the editors
had published a play by Tuli Kupferberg with the word *fuck* in it.
But the times were rapidly changing. By 1967 many activists—in
SDS and pacifist circles—were looking and acting like hippies,
smoking marijuana and experimenting with psychedelic drugs.

The Bay Area, as usual, was well ahead of the East Village when
it came to mixing hippie culture with antiwar politics, but the differences between the hippies in Haight-Ashbury and the radicals
in Berkeley were as wide as the bay that separated Berkeley from
San Francisco. In the autumn of 1965 Jerry Rubin, who was then
a leader of the Berkeley Vietnam Day Committee (VDC), invited
the novelist Ken Kesey to address an antiwar rally in Berkeley.
Kesey, the leading figure of the Merry Pranksters—the Johnny
Acidseeds of the psychedelic revolution—played an off-key version
of "Home on the Range" on a harmonica and then told the audience, "There's only one thing to do. There's only one thing's gonna
do any good at all. . . . And that's everybody just look at it, look
at the war, and turn your backs and say . . . fuck it." The message,
aimed at the hippies, confounded the radicals.

Later in the day the demonstrators attempted to march on the
Oakland Army Terminal, a central depot for shipping troops and
supplies to Vietnam. At the border between Berkeley and Oakland
they were stopped by Oakland police and assaulted by a gang of
Hell's Angels. Afterward Kesey, Allen Ginsberg, and a delegation
of Merry Pranksters went to meet the Hell's Angels carrying LSD
as a peace offering. As a result of tripping together, the bikers allied themselves with the hippie movement and promised not to interfere with the next peace march scheduled for November. The
treaty was sealed by male bonding, a mutual appreciation for hip

and outlaw machismo. The Angels celebrated at a party thrown by Kesey by gang-raping biker women. The hip leaders advocated a tolerant "do your own thing" attitude toward life; if rape was the Angels' "thing," who were they to pass judgment? This was before the women's liberation movement, and besides, condemning bikers would have ended the alliance.

It was at the November VDC demonstration that Ginsberg, asked by Rubin to be a speaker, read his poem "Berkeley Vietnam Days," which, published in *Liberation*, greatly influenced antiwar activists in the East Village. Drawing lessons from the confrontation with the Oakland police and his efforts at mediation with the Hell's Angels, Ginsberg suggested ideas for a new kind of hip pacifism that would blend the older activists' nonviolent principles with the new hippie culture: Gandhian flower power or psychedelic nonviolence. Ginsberg's idea was to transform antiwar protests into visual spectacles, with peace marchers in the front lines carrying gentle props like flowers, children's toys, religious symbols, musical instruments, and American flags to undercut the public's fear of demonstrations and to put forward "imaginative, pragmatic, fun, gay, happy, *secure* Propaganda" in order to "change war psychology and surpass, go over, the habit-image-reaction of fear/violence."[7]

Ginsberg's poem inspired "peace happenings" in New York. By late 1966 the Bread and Puppet Theater was staging antiwar pageants in city streets and parks. During the 1966 Christmas season a group of artists carrying large boxes inconspicuously entered Grand Central Station during rush hour. A tape recorder hidden on the balcony filled the station with the amplified sounds of war. That was the signal for the artists to open their boxes and then disappear into the commuter crowd as huge helium-inflated balloons rose upward out of the boxes to the station's ceiling, trailing colorful streamers proclaiming Peace, Vietnam, Napalm, War. Radical pacifists who had previously protested nuclear submarines by paddling out in canoes to disrupt their launchings were now inspired by the Beatles' music to build a "yellow submarine" and, accompanied by musicians and leafleteers distributing flowers and balloons along with antiwar propaganda, carry it around the neighborhoods of the city.

WIN (for Workshop in Nonviolence) magazine, published by a group of nonviolent activists, most of whom lived in the East Village, was the principal proponent of psychedelic pacifism. The

WIN people saw flower power as a theatrical means of encouraging nonviolence. Instead of issuing a "discipline" to inform participants in a demonstration what they could and could not do, they wanted to orchestrate the nonviolent spirit of the hippies into the guiding spirit of their demonstrations. They were impatient with being perceived as being *against*, as in *non*violent and *anti*war. By using positive, upbeat symbols they wanted to convey the idea of peace activism as an affirmative lifestyle. Like Abbie, the *WIN* activists were older than the hippies who were moving in amongst them. They, too, were intrigued by the hippie rebellion and saw the young flower children as potential supporters for a large nonviolent movement.

The pacifists' attempt to bring the hippies into the antiwar movement was opposed, in the East Village, by what Abbie would later call "hippie nationalists." These were the advocates of nonpolitical, psychedelic revolution. Timothy Leary and Richard Alpert (soon to rename himself Baba Ram Dass) had an office of their League for Spiritual Discovery in Greenwich Village near Liberty House, and Abbie sometimes attended their gatherings. "Turn on, tune in, drop out," Leary urged: change your consciousness and you change the world. Abbie was enthusiastic about acid; he valued the new insights and perceptions it engendered about himself and the world. But he grounded those psychedelic insights in a materialistic framework for revolution—shared by, among others, Maslow and Marx. With Abbie it was always politics first. Create free institutions and satisfy material needs. Then and only then will people have the wherewithal to free their minds.

Leary and Alpert were hostile to the antiwar movement and tried to steer young hippies away from peace marches and demonstrations. At one meeting, called by the Jade Companions, Alpert rebuked a draft resister who asked him what he would suggest doing to end the war. Alpert replied that the war was an illusion, that the real problem the draft resister had to deal with was the anger in his own heart. Abbie had no use for such psychedelic solipsism; nor was he comfortable with Leary's aphorism about dropping out. It was one thing for Alpert, with a Ph.D. in psychology and a father who was chairman of the board of the New Haven Railroad, or Leary, a charismatic psychologist who had the ability to charm millionaires, to quit their jobs and concoct a new life as psychedelic gurus. But the hippie kids who were flooding the East

Village had no resources. It was up to the more socially concerned political organizers, like Abbie, to do the social work that would assure their survival. What Abbie meant by dropping out was different from the Leary-Alpert definition (although he did not always emphasize the distinction). Abbie wanted people to drop out of their white-collar lives and use their skills as doctors, scientists, teachers, technicians, as he was using his: to create an alternative society that would lead to revolution.[8]

As much as Abbie distrusted Leary's message, he appreciated his showmanship. It was the appreciation of one hustler for another. Leary was the P. T. Barnum of the psychedelic movement. He had a gift for using the media that Abbie greatly admired. Leary would say anything to get publicity, knowing that it was supercharged statements—such as, "In a carefully prepared, loving LSD session, a woman will inevitably have several hundred orgasms" (which he proclaimed in a *Playboy* interview)—that people would remember, while the contextual verbiage, necessary to attract the media, would be quickly forgotten. Abbie was also impressed by Leary's sense of theater—his use of costume, props (bells and gongs), and nonlinear, hyperinflated exaggerations to promote his idea of a psychedelic revolution. And Leary had courage. He gave up a successful career as a research psychologist in order to promote his utopian ideas, and he continuously flouted the law in order to live as if the revolution had already happened.

The first antiwar demonstrations in 1964 in New York attracted no more than a couple of hundred people, the veteran activists who were on existing mailing lists. In 1965 and 1966 the largest demonstrations, in the hotbeds of New York and Berkeley, attracted as many as forty thousand. In late 1966, however, President Johnson's supportive consensus began to crumble. On Christmas Day 1966 the *New York Times* began an extraordinary fourteen-part series by Harrison Salisbury written from inside North Vietnam. These articles confirmed what leaders of the antiwar movement had long been saying: the United States was bombing civilian targets in North Vietnam, and the bombings, far from breaking civilian morale, seemed only to be stiffening Vietnamese resistance. In subsequent weeks the *Washington Post*, the *New York Times*, and other major newspapers began casting doubts on the merits of the war. On April 7, 1967, *Life* ran twelve pages of pictures documenting the destruction that American bombing was causing in Vietnam. Television news footage of American forces using napalm and burning peasant villages contributed to the public's revulsion. Yet, even as the media were reporting events in Vietnam that confirmed what the antiwar movement had been saying, their news coverage continued to depict the movement itself as a marginal irritant that was undercutting American resolve. And congressional doves still refused to take up the cudgels. Demonstrations organized by the radicals still represented the only way for ordinary people to express their political disquiet.

In the beginning of 1967 antiwar leaders began planning for a Spring Mobilization—two mass rallies against the war, one in New York, a second in San Francisco. The movement hoped that a mass display of popular support would encourage Democratic doves to break with Johnson. Martin Luther King was to be the featured speaker at the New York demonstration. Antiwar organizers in New York were hoping for a turnout of 50,000 people. Anything less, they thought, would be a setback; a turnout of 70,000 would be a victory. Many liberals in the peace movement refused to endorse the mobilization on the ground that it didn't exclude communists. (One exception was Dr. Benjamin Spock, who broke with the leadership of SANE and agreed to join King as a featured speaker at the rally.) Predictably, HUAC issued documents alleging that the antiwar movement was controlled by communists, and even the *New York Times* tried to red-bait the leadership. Despite these efforts, the April 15 demonstration was a success far beyond the movement's imagining. New York City police estimated the turnout as between 100,000 and 125,000; the *Times* said 100,000; the movement claimed 250,000 at a minimum. Whatever the number, it was the largest demonstration in American history. Abbie and Anita went to the demonstration with Ellen Maslow and Danny Schechter. The first New York be-in had taken place two weeks earlier, and its gaiety infused the antiwar marchers, many of whom carried flowers and balloons along with antiwar banners and posters depicting the war's brutality. But what was most noticeable about the turnout was the number of white, respectable, middle-class adults.

In the activists' view, this demonstration proved that the antiwar movement was no longer a fringe protest; it was now gaining broad popular support. But neither the administration nor the congressional doves seemed impressed. On "Meet the Press," Secretary of State Dean Rusk said he was "concerned . . . that the authorities in Hanoi may misunderstand this sort of thing." General William Westmoreland, the commander of American forces in Vietnam, was flown home to drum up support for the war effort. American troops in Vietnam, he told a luncheon of cheering newspaper publishers, "are dismayed, and so am I, by recent unpatriotic acts here at home." The antiwar movement, he warned, offered "the enemy" an opportunity to "win politically what he cannot accomplish militarily." A few dovish senators, including Frank Church, J. William Fulbright, George McGovern, and Robert Kennedy, spoke out against the escalating conflict, but none of them was willing to break with the president or accept a leadership role in a movement that, by their silence, had grown beyond their control.[9]

This, then, was the situation in mid-1967, when Abbie began to take an active role in the antiwar movement. Two arenas were open for his participation. One was to become a leader in Vietnam Summer. Organized in Cambridge, Massachusetts, by community activists associated with SDS (and supported avidly by *Dissent* magazine), the idea, based on Mississippi's Freedom Summer, was to flood targeted communities with student antiwar organizers in the hope of fomenting neighborhood-based opposition to the war. Abbie, of course, had the credentials from his civil rights experience for this kind of work. But it would have been too much like going home to Worcester. Far more intriguing and fun, too, was the potential for organizing hippies into the movement against the war. Abbie was not alone in choosing to do his political work in the haven of bohemia. Many other white activists, disillusioned with white America (hence unwilling to return to the neighborhoods in which they had grown up) and no longer welcome by blacks in the civil rights movement, joined Abbie there.

In response to the success of the Spring Mobilization, the Veterans of Foreign Wars organized a Loyalty Parade in New York City for April 29 and predicted that 100,000 would turn out. Only 7,500 actually marched. Stunned by the small turnout, a broader coalition, this time with strong craft-union support, tried again two weeks later. This march had a less controversial and more positive slogan: Support Our Boys. Many activists in the peace movement felt that the only way to support the boys would be to bring them home, but they also felt that this was a right-wing parade that, by its definition, was closed to them. Abbie and Jim Fouratt had been thinking, independent of each other, that the movement should convey a positive message and not be viewed as being against patriotic sentiments. Looking for an image that would convey something positive, they decided to organize a Flower Brigade and, under the banner of supporting the boys, join the parade.

Fouratt called the parade organizers and got permission to march as an official contingent. The press was secretly contacted so that the media would give coverage to the brigade. Jim and Abbie felt that once their intentions were discovered, they would be tossed out of the parade. In any case, violence was a likely prospect. For this reason it was not easy to recruit participants within the hippie community. Abbie justified his decision to lead others into danger by articulating the SNCC ethos: if right-wingers attacked, he, as an organizer, had the moral responsibility to be in the front line to absorb the violence. Jim was with him. "I wasn't going to ask people to do something that I wasn't going to do," he later recalled.

The day of the march, Abbie gave the participants lessons in nonviolent protection: Don't wear pins, earrings, anything that can stick into you or be grabbed. If attacked, try to relax and roll up into a fetal position. Protect your groin and the back of your head from kicks or punches. Then the brigade took its assigned place in the procession, behind the Flatbush Conservative Club and a troop of Boy Scouts. Abbie wore a colorful cape with the word *Freedom* emblazoned on it. Anita Hoffman was dressed in red, white, and blue. Everyone was carrying something: flowers, American flags, Support Our Boys signs, and pink posters with the word *love* on them.

Concerned about the hippies' safety, a police sergeant asked that they withdraw from the parade. "This was the most dangerous crowd I have ever seen in nineteen years on the job," the policeman told Joe Flaherty, who was covering the event for the *Village Voice*. When the brigade refused to leave, the Boy Scouts began to march double time in an attempt to pass around the Flatbush Conservatives and get away from the hippies. As the Flower Brigade moved out trying to follow the scouts, it was set upon by angry zealots. "Shouts of 'murder the bastards' split the air," Flaherty reported.

Grown men lustily punched and kicked girls no older than their daughters. American flags were ripped from their hands and torn into bits seemingly because they were contaminated. "The men in the group were bashed into cement walls. . . . Housewives cheered their hubbies on to destruction," Flaherty wrote. Anita Hoffman recalls being pelted by eggs, while Fouratt remembers the assault as "more frightening and scary than I had ever expected it to be." "Zonk, fists, red paint, kicks, beer cans, spitting—the whole American Welcome Wagon treatment," was Abbie's description.

He thought it was worth it. The attack on the Flower Brigade got as much attention in the media as the prowar demonstrators; the graphic television spot of right-wingers pummeling the flag- and flower-holding hippies could not have come off better if it had been staged. In fact, the messages that Jim and Abbie wanted to get across came across powerfully on both television and in the newspapers: that peace people supported the boys in Vietnam and that hippies were willing to take risks to express their opposition to the war. "The Flower Brigade lost its first battle, but watch out America," Abbie summed up in an article in *WIN*. "We were poorly equipped with flowers from uptown florists. Already there is talk of growing our own. Plans are being made to mine the East River with daffodils. Dandelion chains are being wrapped around induction centers. Holes are being dug in street pavements and seeds dropped and covered. The cry of 'Flower Power' echoes through the land. We shall not wilt. Let a thousand flowers bloom."[10]

The Saturday after the support-our-boys parade was Armed Forces Day. The *WIN* pacifists had a tradition of blocking the annual military parade on Fifth Avenue with a nonviolent sit-down. The media routinely covered the event, and anything out of the ordinary would dominate the coverage. The previous year the pacifists had blocked the parade by sitting down in the middle of the avenue carrying bouquets of flowers. The sit-down had had a lighthearted feel to it, different from the tension-filled self-righteousness that often marked civil disobedience actions. The image of formations of soldiers tramping over garlands of flowers had made a winning visual, the kind of photograph that news photographers could not ignore.

In 1967 the pacifists planned to build on the idea of the be-in by dubbing Armed Forces Day "Flower Power Day" and attracting hippies to protest, if not disrupt, the parade. After the beating of the Flower Brigade, however, leaders in the hippie community pressured the pacifists to call off the confrontation. Abbie, Jim, and be-in organizers Linn House and Paul Williams, who represented the more cultural, "hippie nationalist" position, attended a meeting at 5 Beekman Street to discuss the plan. House and Williams urged the pacifists to drop the whole idea. Politicos, they charged, were manipulating innocent hippies into a potentially violent situation. Further, they argued, the very idea of confrontation was counterrevolutionary. Real change could come only from a new consciousness. The Armed Forces Day parade was a manifestation of a dying culture, and in a clash between cultures psychedelic drugs and rock music were far more potent than nonviolent action.

In backing the idea of a Flower Power Day confrontation, Abbie and Jim made a decisive break with hippie nationalism. Abbie again spoke from his SNCC experience. The violence of the war could not be ignored, he said. One had to accept risks to effectively protest the war. Everyone attending Flower Power Day would be warned of the possibility of violence and given the opportunity to withdraw without being made to feel ashamed or defensive. The organizers should respect the idealism of the young people who came out to demonstrate. "Flower power is love plus courage," he concluded.

Although impressed by Abbie and Jim's presentation, the pacifist organizers of Flower Power Day, recognizing that there was no consensus within the hippie community for a confrontation, decided to begin the demonstration in Central Park and let the participants themselves decide whether or not to confront the parade on Fifth Avenue. The hundred or so hippies who gathered in the park were at a loss to decide whether they wanted to be-in in the park or sit down in the middle of Fifth Avenue to block the parade. Experienced in planning disciplined civil disobedience, the pacifists were at a loss when improvising unscripted street theater. Abbie, dressed in white and wearing a bedspread as a cape pinned together with an antiwar button, stepped into the void. "We're huddled here in a fuckin' ghetto instead of being at the parade," he said. Very few people knew who he was at that time; Abbie Hoffman was not yet a movement name. But the demonstrators followed him out to Fifth Avenue, where, lacking a plan to do anything better, they heckled the troops marching past in ranks.

Abbie's leadership impressed Paul Krassner, the editor of *The*

Realist, who was present at the demonstration, and afterward the two of them went out for dinner. Abbie was a subscriber to *The Realist,* so he knew who Krassner was. Indeed, one of Abbie's most memorable escapades in Worcester had been taking a Fuck Communism poster, which he had ordered by mail from *The Realist,* to a symposium on communism at the Worcester Public Library. Krassner sold the posters at some risk to his publication, because it was then illegal to send literature with words like *fuck* through the mail. But it was a highly calculated risk. Had the Post Office attempted to prosecute him, Krassner was prepared to turn the event into political theater by accusing the Post Office of being "soft on communism."

Krassner was immediately taken by Abbie's sense of himself as a street-smart activist. Organizing was "a way of life with him. It was what he did. It was as natural as breathing," he recalls. The two men shared a sense of the absurd and a belief that boredom was an issue that they could organize against. Abbie, like Paul, could understand "the dehumanization implicit in pay toilets all the way up to napalm bombing." The two men became friends and political buddies.[11]

As for the *WIN* pacifists, Abbie always kept them informed of his plans and could count on them to publish his articles, publicize his projects, and participate in his demonstrations. But the chemistry was absent. Abbie wanted to work with more freewheeling, creative types. Although Krassner was a pacifist and Fouratt was very close to that position, they shared Abbie's gift for theater, as well as his belief that demonstrations need not be didactic. On the contrary, demonstrations could be fun. Political messages, seemingly, could be irrational in structure and nonpolitical in substance. The movement's traditional earnestness and self-righteousness, Abbie thought, undercut effective communication. Understanding and getting inside the American psyche was more important than working out the nuances of a political position.

As he experimented with guerrilla theater, Abbie began to develop a critique of nonviolence. Doctrinaire nonviolence, he felt, went against the grain of American culture. As he later wrote in his autobiography, nonviolence "jarred my American heartland upbringing," which, for him, included the macho tough-guy image he held on to from Worcester. Spontaneity, enthusiasm, and optimism were American qualities to be admired, he felt. Asking people to join a disciplined, nonviolent sit-down inhibited spontaneity and creativity. When policemen clubbed people on the head, it was natural to become angry and want to strike back. To deny one's anger was unnatural, he felt. The anger would have to find expression in some way. Abbie believed that pacifists often turned their anger against themselves and then transformed it into what he called a politics of masochism. Pacifists were courageous, he acknowledged, but too often their bravery was a result of guilt. They were always reacting *against* injustice, protesting in the negative, unwilling to create a vision of the positive. Helping others was good in itself; people needed to express their altruistic drive in order to lead a healthy emotional life.[12]

Abbie liked to batter pacifists with what was essentially an outdated stereotype. Yet, despite his disdain for the nonviolence, he understood its tactical value. His political theater was almost always directed to encourage nonviolent conduct. That is why many pacifists admired him and considered him a nonviolent fellow traveler. Julius Lester, the writer and Abbie's friend from SNCC, once told him that he was "the most original practitioner of nonviolence" in the movement, but Abbie feigned surprise. He refused to be put into what he considered a self-limiting context.[13]

The issue of violence was one of the important questions the movement faced. Should radicals be nonviolent? Should nonviolence be a tactic—a way of acting at demonstrations? Or a strategy? That is, should pacifism be a way of life? There were related questions to answer as well. Should the movement distinguish between violence against property (destruction) and violence to human life? Do individuals, movements, and countries have a right to self-defense when under attack? Is it morally right to initiate violence against a known evil, the existence of which is itself an act of violence? The vast majority of activists in the antiwar movement were not pacifists. But they adhered to the discipline of tactical nonviolence, because the alternative seemed self-defeating and dangerous. The government had a monopoly on the weapons of violence and a legal framework to use them against the movement. Violence played to the government's strength. Nonviolence, at the least, confronted the government on a playing field on which it had no experience. Pitting its life-affirming faith in people's basic goodness against the authorities' cynical reliance on weapons gave the movement an advantage it lost when politics became a contest of physical force.

Weapons might coerce bodies, but symbols could win hearts and minds.

Abbie's break with doctrinaire nonviolence set him on a slippery slide toward power confrontations—yet he avoided the hard questions. It wasn't that he was ever proviolence. It was just that he refused to rule out violence as a tactical option. The essential questions of violence versus nonviolence didn't engage him. In the context of spontaneous guerilla theater they seemed irrelevant. "Revolutions like water seek their own level in terms of tactics," he wrote on one of the rare occasions when he grappled with the subject.[14]

Abbie's changing political orientation came into focus in June 1967, when he attended the Back to the Drawing Board conference at a camp in Denton, Michigan, organized by veteran New Leftists associated with SDS. Black power had forced them to redefine their ties to the black movement. Community organizers like Tom Hayden were uncertain about what to do with their lives now that they could not organize in black ghettos. Although never personally close to the SDS leaders, Abbie knew many of them from the Hughes campaign in Massachusetts and from his work with SNCC and Liberty House and, up until now, felt himself a part of their history. But he went to the conference with an ambiguous allegiance. Emmett Grogan and Peter Berg were leading a delegation of Diggers to the conference from San Francisco, and Abbie was eager to renew their friendship. The West Coast Diggers had no movement background. They looked down on the politics of SDS as an impediment to their cultural revolution. They were coming to the conference to "blow the minds" of the straight New Left, to expose and mock its squareness and to convince those who were open to their message that they, the Diggers, were the movement of the future.

Tom Hayden was concluding a presentation on the future of his organizing project in Newark when the Diggers walked into the conference. Peter Berg immediately took the floor, upstaging Hayden and short-circuiting the discussion. Berg looked like "a young angry Sitting Bull, only different . . . unique, a white Snick nigger," as Abbie described the scene in *Revolution for the Hell of It*. Berg began to talk, and Abbie was transported: "Property is the

enemy—burn it, destroy it, give it away. Don't let them make a
machine out of you, get out of the system, do your thing. Don't
organize students, teachers, Negroes, organize your head. Find out
where you are, what you want to do and go out and do it. Johnson's
a commie. The Kremlin is more fucked up than Alabama. Get out!
Don't organize the schools, burn them. Leave them, they will rot."

When Berg finished, Grogan climbed onto a table and comman-
deered the meeting. "All of a sudden he erupts and kicks the
fuckin' table over," Abbie wrote. "He knocks down a girl, slapping
SDS'ers right and left. 'Faggots! Fags! Take off your ties, they are
chains around your necks. You haven't the balls to go mad. You're
gonna make a revolution?—you'll piss in your pants when the violence erupts." Having succeeded in disrupting the meeting and
forcing their ideas onto the agenda, the Diggers left. Abbie stayed,
however, disdainful, he says, of the earnest SDSers and feeling
smug that he and Jim Fouratt were on the Diggers' road to revolution. "The seminars drag on . . . a total bore. . . . Jim and I are
avoided, except by a small group. They do socialism, we blow pot
in the grass, they do imperialism, we go swimming, they do racism,
we do flowers for everybody and clean up the rooms."

Ignored in Abbie's account is that he and Jim also participated
in a well-attended workshop on the New Left and the hippies. In it
Abbie argued that the young people using drugs were motivated to
question authority and that drugs, because they were against the
law, turned people into opponents of the status quo. Drugs could
transform people into activists, Abbie insisted. As an example, he
told of riding a crosstown bus caught in traffic; he had caused a
commotion by standing up and shouting that the riders should take
over the bus, because public transport belonged to the people.
"They threw me off the bus," Abbie acknowledged, "but there I
was stoned out of my mind, and organizing."[15]

But Abbie was not organizing, not in any sense that the New Left
or he himself understood that term. Organizing meant empowering
people, giving them information and the courage, by example, to
take political action. Abbie's outburst on the bus, whatever its effect, was not organizing but agitation. From here on Abbie and
others in the movement would use the word *organize* to describe
all kinds of political activity. Yet after 1967 there was a whole lot
of agitating going on, but very little organizing. Instead of relating
to individuals one on one, "organizers" like Abbie began dealing

only with what they called "the people." This phrase was as much
an abstraction as was "the masses," the term favored by leftists
during the 1930s to describe the faceless and thoughtless entity on
whose behalf the left presumed to be speaking and acting. Under-
standably, activists like Abbie were impatient. There was a war
going on, and increasingly they felt a need for a political shortcut
to end American involvement. As well, for Abbie, there was the
temptation of the media: he was confident that he could use it to
reach great numbers of people. But the New Left had originally
rejected Old Left notions of organizing precisely because of the way
they dehumanized individuals. Whereas the Old Left sought to
organize "the masses" as faceless recruits, the New Left, at its in-
ception, wanted individuals to participate in all the decisions of the
movement.

Abbie returned from the SDS conference with a new sense that the
hippie movement was more significant than the political left and
that the values it represented were more profound than orthodox
revolutionary goals. It was at this time that he withdrew from Liberty House, plunged into social service work among the hippies,
and began, with Jim Fouratt, to stage guerrilla theater acts, which
reached a creative climax in August with the hippie "assault" on
the New York Stock Exchange. Abbie was initially skeptical of targeting Wall Street because of his uninterest in Marxist economics,
but once he saw the theatrical potential of throwing away money,
he made the idea his own. The challenge was a simple one: how to
show the greed of the capitalist system and counterpose the values
of the hippie culture. Entire forests had been felled to print Marxist manifestos by the Old Left, but few people in the United States
ever read them. Marxist ideas were never presented in the American media except as caricatures to be criticized. Maybe the hippies
could do better.

Using the East Side Service Organization as a cover, Abbie
phoned the stock exchange to arrange a guided tour. He and Fouratt then tipped off their contacts in the media and invited members
of the underground press to be part of the ESSO delegation. I was
one of the underground writers Abbie invited. Although committed
to organizing young people in behalf of the antiwar movement, especially draft resistance, it had not yet occurred to me that the

youth culture, in and of itself, might represent an alternative to the mainstream society. I saw Abbie's idea as simply a funny Marxist zap to expose the greed of capitalism. Because I associated Marxism with conspiratorial politics and assumed we would have to look respectable in order to get into the stock exchange, I got a haircut and put on a suit and tie. Of course, Abbie and Jim had come dressed in their most hippie-like outfits. My first reaction was, what fools—they'll never get past the guards. A second later, as Abbie began jiving the guards and leading us all up to the visitors' gallery, it became obvious that the contrast between the creatively dressed hippies and the well-tailored Wall Street stockbrokers was an essential message of the demonstration.

Abbie and Jim had given out wads of one-dollar bills to the demonstrators, and from the gallery overlooking the trading floor we began throwing the money. There was a pause in business as brokers and stock clerks looked up at the balcony to see who was making the commotion and then a stunned silence as they saw the dollar bills floating toward them. Some booed, but others dove to the floor to pick up the free money. This was the precise image that Abbie wanted. Hippies throwing away money while capitalists groveled. Quickly, the guards hustled everyone out of the gallery. (Months later the stock exchange enclosed it in glass.) On the street Abbie and Jerry Rubin burned dollar bills for the benefit of the press.[16]

Rubin had just arrived in New York from Berkeley. Dave Dellinger had hired him as project director for a demonstration being planned for Washington, D.C., in October. Like Abbie, Rubin was intrigued by the hippie phenomenon. He wanted to bring hippies into the antiwar movement but didn't have any idea of how to go about it. He had heard about Abbie and looked forward to meeting him.

A year younger than Abbie, Jerry Rubin was born and grew up in Cincinnati, Ohio. His father dropped out of high school and drove a bread truck. But he was also a Boy Scout leader and a civic activist, winning election, with the backing of Jimmy Hoffa, as the business agent of his Teamster local. Jerry's mother came from an affluent family, and Jerry grew up envious of his more middle-class cousins. Unlike Abbie, who was secure and self-confident, Jerry was tormented by what he perceived as the middle-class snobbery of his relatives and their disdain for his working-class father. Whereas Abbie, even as a youth, rebelled against middle-class values, Jerry was a striver who was desperate to prove himself to middle-class society. He began working for the *Cincinnati Post and Times Star* while still in high school and rose to become a feature writer and editor of the paper's youth section even while a full-time American history major at the University of Cincinnati. Unlike Abbie, he took politics seriously. As a teenager he volunteered in both of Adlai Stevenson's presidential campaigns.[17]

Jerry went to Berkeley to do graduate work in sociology and was there in 1964 when the Free Speech Movement shut the campus down. He helped organize the first teach-ins against the war and became a leader of the Vietnam Day Committee. In May 1965 he invited Norman Mailer to speak at a Berkeley Vietnam Day Committee rally. Others in the committee argued against Mailer because he didn't represent a recognizable political position, but Jerry understood that Mailer could speak to a broad audience. Mailer's presentation at the rally was a mocking and satirical attack on Lyndon Johnson. Many of the protesters were shocked by Mailer's language and the personal tenor of his attack. Up until then the movement had stated its opposition to the war in moral and political terms. Here was Mailer now suggesting that the movement make LBJ a personal target. Abbie, still in Worcester, read the text of the speech in *The Realist* and understood what Mailer was doing. "Mailer showed how you can focus protest sentiment effectively by aiming not at the decisions but at the gut of those who make them," he would later say.[18]

Although not as naturally funny as Abbie, Jerry had a flair for theater. Like Abbie he had a huge ego, but unlike Abbie he did not have a firm sense of his own identity; thus, as a performer, he had a chameleon-like willingness to assume any role that he thought would further the cause. Subpoenaed with other VDC activists to testify before HUAC in 1966, he took the suggestion of Ronnie Davis of the San Francisco Mime Troupe and appeared in the costume of an American Revolutionary War soldier. Abbie heard about this while he was still in Worcester and appreciated the way Jerry had appropriated a patriotic symbol to attack the superpatriotic right-wing committee.[19]

For Abbie, the hippie movement was one stage in a lifelong rebellion. For Jerry, it was also therapy, a way to stop pushing himself to succeed, a way to relax and enjoy his life. Yet even as a
dropout he was determined to make his mark. At the Spring Mobilization in San Francisco in April 1967 he noted the number of
"freeks, longhairs, beatniks, students, kids, [and] the unwashed"
who had come out to protest the war. He was outraged when the
rock group Country Joe and the Fish was cut off in order to make
time for more political speeches. The peace movement was too
straight, he thought. Rather than directing its message to young
people, it was trying to appeal to middle-class guilt, "still using
pictures of napalmed babies to shame the public, despite the fact
that CBS-TV was already doing it better—in color!—on Cronkite." Jerry had a propensity for curt speech. "The Speech Movement was too fucking polite," he concluded.[20] It was Jerry's
reputation for pushing the movement beyond its existing bounds
that recommended him to Dellinger. Rubin would be controversial,
yes—and might even cause ruptures in the Mobe. But the experience of the Spring Mobilization had convinced Dellinger that sheer
numbers of protesters would not impress the Johnson administration. Since Democratic doves seemed unwilling to make the war an
election issue, the movement would have to move "from protest to
resistance." It was time to use the tactics of nonviolent confrontation to disrupt society and *force* the war onto the political agenda.

The Mobe announced plans for its October protests the day before the action at the stock exchange. There would be a week of
demonstrations in Washington and in the Bay Area. It would begin
with a day of resistance, on which male members of The Resistance
and their supporters would turn in their draft cards to Justice
Department officials, risking substantial fines and prison terms.
The next day there would be a mass rally at the Lincoln Memorial
designed, like the Spring Mobilization, to attract the largest possible turnout. This would be followed by a march to the Pentagon
for a smaller rally and then, for those willing, a further march to
the steps of the Pentagon for nonviolent civil disobedience.

As part of the action at the Pentagon Abbie and his friends from
the East Village were planning to surround the building for a religious ceremony to exorcise its evil. In many religions a pentagon is
a symbol of evil, and to the antiwar movement the Pentagon was
the personification of evil. Abbie got the idea for a political exor-

cism from Keith Lampe and the poet Ed Sanders, both of whom were friends of Gary Snyder, who had probably originated it. Lampe, who was Abbie's age, was a pacifist and an army veteran. He had helped to organize Flower Power Day and did public relations work for the Mobe. Sanders was two years younger than Abbie. He was the proprietor of the Peace Eye bookstore and, between police raids, publisher of *Fuck You: A Magazine of the Arts*, "dedicated to pacifist, unilateral disarmament, national defense through nonviolent resistance, multilateral indiscriminate apertural conjugation, anarchism, world federalism, civil disobedience, obstructors and submarine boarders, and all those groped by J. Edgar Hoover in the silent halls of Congress."[21] Not content merely to spew forth provocative manifestos, Sanders was once arrested for paddling out in a canoe and attempting to disrupt the launching of a nuclear submarine as part of a ban-the-bomb demonstration. He had also, with Allen Ginsberg, visited Joe McCarthy's grave and performed a ceremony of exorcism "to purify his spirit," as Ginsberg described it. Sanders was also, with fellow poet Tuli Kupferberg, a founder of the Fugs, a rock band dedicated, like the magazine, to peace, sexual freedom, and psychedelic revolution. To complete the connection between Abbie's Pentagon plans and the history of the beat generation, Kupferberg was the twenty-one-year-old poet celebrated in Ginsberg's poem *Howl* who jumped off the Brooklyn Bridge (actually it was the Manhattan Bridge) and, as Ginsberg put it, "walked away unknown and forgotten."[22]

In short, there was no lack of creative talent for Abbie to draw from. He saw an exorcism ritual as a perfect way of attracting hippies to Washington and transforming the religious mysticism that was an essential part of acid consciousness into the political goal of ending the war. Delighted by the idea, Rubin invited Abbie to participate in the Mobe's initial press conference.[23]

In typical Mobe fashion, the speakers at the press conference represented every point of view in the radical antiwar coalition. The Reverend Thomas Lee Hayes of the Episcopal Peace Fellowship emphasized the peaceful nature of the massive "peace-in." Dave Dellinger promised a nonviolent confrontation that would leave "no government building left unattacked." H. Rap Brown, the new chairman of SNCC who had just been arrested for carrying a gun aboard a plane, allowed as he couldn't bring a gun, "because you all took my gun last time," but "I may bring a bomb,

sucker." And Abbie, introduced by Jerry, described plans for an
exorcism of the Pentagon, vowing to levitate the building three
hundred feet in the air.[24] Aligning himself with Abbie's exorcism
was a major decision for Jerry. He had been hired as project
director for the entire demonstration; now he was formally identifying himself with the hippie contingent, giving what was tantamount to an official Mobilization endorsement to Abbie's idea
of monkey theater, a play on the phrase guerrilla (gorilla) theater
emphasizing, instead of dramatic confrontation, silliness and
farce.

Abbie and Marty Carey went to Washington to measure the Pentagon. They wanted to figure out how many people it would take to
encircle it. They were counting off steps along one side of the building when MPs apprehended them. Brought inside the Pentagon for
questioning, Abbie joked that though there were only two of them
now, they were coming back with fifty thousand people to raise it
off the ground. Answering questions with wisecracks, Abbie tried
(unsuccessfully) to provoke the authorities. He wanted the publicity that an arrest would bring. In the coming months he jousted
with the Pentagon's public relations officials, using them as straight
men to create good media copy. If the military wouldn't grant a
permit to levitate the building three hundred feet, he said, he
would compromise and settle for ten feet.[25]

In New York, Abbie involved the creative community in planning
the ritual. Costume designers made witch costumes and scavenged
through rummage sales, secondhand stores, and the Diggers' own
Free Store for the two vanloads of costumes that Abbie would take
to Washington. Paul Krassner, scheduled to speak at a literary conference at the University of Iowa, was assigned the task of buying
cornmeal from an Iowa farmer to spread around the Pentagon as
a prelevitation rite. East Village craftspeople built a plywood
model of the Pentagon, attached it to piano wire, and at a benefit
concert for the Mobilization raised it high into the air as smoke
bombs went off and the Fugs chanted and played music. When
Washington authorities threatened to use Mace to control the demonstrators at the Capitol, Abbie claimed that hippies had come up
with a new chemical aphrodisiac called Lace, consisting of LSD and
a secret skin-penetrating agent. When sprayed on the skin or on
clothes, Abbie said, it penetrated into the bloodstream, causing the
victims to become uncontrollably horny. Abbie called a press con-

ference at his apartment in which four hippie couples sprayed each other with a water pistol supposedly filled with Lace, tore off one another's clothes, and began making love as the members of the press took notes. All of this was good copy and free publicity for the Pentagon demonstration.[26]

This was Abbie at his peak. According to Ed Sanders, Abbie "could go up to artists like himself, people who were already skilled and self-organized, and empower them to act." To Marty Carey, who designed the poster for the exorcism, Abbie's ability to involve other artists in his projects was the mark of his organizing genius: "Abbie knew how to get people involved politically by getting them to contribute something that they were very good at, or getting them to do something that they would feel very flattered in doing, even if they didn't know much about politics."

Jerry Rubin's attempt to instill a youthful, psychedelic spirit into the antiwar coalition caused huge battles within the Mobe. Abbie, however, kept out of the political squabbles. In *Major Motion Picture* he portrayed himself as cognizant that the Mobe "could reach into age, class, educational, and union groups which might have turned off to our particular style. Never the hippie nationalist, I had always considered myself a secret member of the Mobe steering committee." Many of the older leftists were nevertheless thankful that Abbie kept away from Mobe meetings. Fred Halstead of the Socialist Workers party, one of the few Old Left leaders to have a leading role in the antiwar movement, recalls Abbie's "unerring ability to get under the skin of those who took seriously whatever he chose to make the butt of a joke."[27]

In *Major Motion Picture* Abbie presented the exorcism ceremony as the starting point for the more spectacular weekend confrontation on the Pentagon steps. In actuality it was a sideshow involving only a tiny percentage of the 50,000 people who marched across the Potomac River from the Lincoln Memorial (where more than 150,000 had attended a rally) to the Pentagon. The closest a flatbed truck—necessary as both a stage and a mobile amplification system—could drive to the building was a lower parking lot that the demonstrators passed through as they rushed toward the Pentagon steps. The Fugs stood there on the flatbed, intoning an incantation: "In the name of the generative power of Priapus, in the name of the totality, we call upon the demons of the Pentagon to rid themselves of the cancerous tumors of the war generals." All around them people were banging on bells, cymbals, beer cans, and drums, chanting Hindu mantras, and imploring to sundry deities for divine intervention: "Out demons out, out demons out!"

In less than an hour the exorcism was over; there was no way the authorities would let the hippies ring the Pentagon, and there was no real plan to do so. Many of the hippies stayed to picnic. But Abbie, dressed as an American Indian with an Uncle Sam hat, grabbed Anita by the hand—she was wearing a Sergeant Pepper costume—and led her toward the barricades. They climbed over a toppled fence and were stopped by MPs. "We're Mr. and Mrs. America and we declare this liberated territory," Abbie exclaimed. It was Anita's first confrontation with the military, as it was for most everyone else. Already the acrid smell of tear gas was wafting through the air. To herself, she wondered why they could not have stayed with the hippies frolicking on the grass. They were not arrested, however, and so made it up the Pentagon steps, where the main drama of the weekend was unfolding.

The demonstrators, thousands of them, had charged up the steps to a higher parking lot directly in front of the Pentagon's main entrance and had sat down at the feet of soldiers from the Eighty-second Airborne Division who had been flown in to protect the building. From Saturday evening to Sunday night the protesters stayed there, conducting a spontaneous teach-in with the troops on the steps of the Pentagon. Late Saturday night, after the television crews turned off their lights and the reporters left the scene, the paratroopers, carrying unloaded weapons and sheathed bayonets, formed a wedge and moved into the sit-in, trying to split it in half and break it up. Federal marshals pulled people through the advancing line of troops, arrested them, and in many cases beat them up. Movement veterans had not confronted such brutality since the South, but this time it was the U.S. marshals playing the role of southern cops.

In the face of this attack, leaders of SDS, speaking through a bullhorn on one side of the wedge, urged people to leave. Getting arrested and possibly beaten up was "bourgeois politics," these militants claimed, a "selfish and indulgent personal catharsis irrelevant to the real war abroad." But most people, including Abbie and Anita, stayed. As night fell, people from Washington brought food—and joints!—which were passed up and down the line. Protesters cuddled up next to one another and sang songs. They took turns at the bullhorn, explaining to the soldiers who they were, why they were at the Pentagon, why they opposed the war. Gradually an almost mystical feeling of warmth and solidarity spread among the seated demonstrators and seemed, many felt, to envelop the troops as well. There was a shock of recognition that the soldiers were the same age as the protesters. "Join us! Join us! We love you! We love you!" demonstrators began chanting. There was no way of knowing what the troops were thinking or feeling, though the consensus was that the soldiers, with a few exceptions, were trying not to hurt people and that it was the middle-aged marshals who had committed most of the violence. In any case the demonstrators felt that they were communicating to the troops. "It was Valley Forge revisited," Abbie wrote. "We were scared and singing songs," Anita recalls, "and there was a feeling of great unity; we were not alone. That demonstration had a spiritual feeling that you rarely get in life." Anita, like many veterans of the Pentagon steps, calls that protest her "favorite demo."

Abbie and Anita were not among the five hundred who were arrested during the wedge, and so spent all Sunday at the Pentagon talking to the troops. They were arrested on Sunday night, when the steps of the building were finally cleared. In the armory that served as a jail Abbie put a sheet over his head and ran to the front of the dorm, screaming at the cops, "I'm in here with Jews and Commies. Let me out!"[28]

The impact of this demonstration within the movement was as great as if the Pentagon had actually been levitated. First-person reports by participants were carried not only in the underground press but were the major stories in the campus press. And these versions differed drastically from what the major media reported. Pentagon officials at first claimed no tear gas had been used, but when reporters insisted they themselves had been gassed, Pentagon public relations officers countered—and the press reported—that the demonstrators had thrown the canisters. James Reston, the dean of Washington journalists and a columnist for the *New York Times*, accused the demonstrators of pushing innocents into the line of soldiers and acting like "Saturday night drunks." "It is difficult to report publicly the ugly and vulgar provocation of many of the militants," he reported. "They spat on some of the soldiers in the front line at the Pentagon and goaded them with the most vicious personal slanders." In a follow-up story the *Times* reported that many of the youths arrested at the Pentagon were "teenage runaways from home."[29]

Many activists, by contrast, considered the teach-in with the troops to be the movement's finest hour. The protesters at the Pentagon were overwhelmed by the feeling of generational solidarity and their new sense that the young men in the military could be reached.* Whether the paratroopers were in fact reached on that October night is beside the point. Within a few years the hippie idea of peace, love, and enlightenment by the use of psychedelic drugs would reach Vietnam and undermine the willingness of many American soldiers to fight. But meanwhile the lack of a positive reaction from the Democrats and the distorted reporting in the mainstream media only raised the activists' level of frustration and their feeling of isolation.

What would it take to turn the country around? In the minds of the radicals it was morally incomprehensible that the leading opinion makers in the country could be outraged by a few four-letter words when their country was destroying a peasant society on the other side of the world. Events in Berkeley that same weekend suggested what activists might do to ease their frustration even if they could not change the war policy. In Berkeley demonstrators tried to shut down the army induction center by filling the streets and blocking off access. When the police tried to clear the streets, the activists returned to the sidewalks or, when that proved impossible, ran down adjacent streets, clogging intersections and disrupting traffic in a wider and wider area. Many radicals, including Abbie, saw these new "mobile tactics" as a way of bringing the war home to the American people. The government, they hoped, would have to end the war as the price for maintaining the social peace.

---

* Shortly after this demonstration movement activists began opening GI coffeehouses near U.S. military bases.

CHAPTER

6 | THE ROAD TO CHICAGO

1968

The success of the confrontation at the Pentagon and the idea of mobile tactics rejuvenated the movement. Many activists began looking ahead to the Democratic and Republican national conventions scheduled for the next summer. The movement lacked the resources to mount demonstrations at both conventions and, at any rate, lacked leverage on the Republican party. The Democrats were the obvious target. Not only were they the war party, but they needed the support of the antiwar movement, which the Republicans, on the right, could more safely ignore. It was an apparent certainty that President Johnson would be nominated for a second term at the Democratic national convention in Chicago the coming August. It was also a certainty that despite the efforts of the antiwar movement, his Vietnam policy would be dutifully endorsed. "A group of us are already working on Chicago next August," Abbie wrote with premature enthusiasm in a Christmas Day letter to Father Gilgun. "We plan to bring 250,000 people there to the Democratic Convention. We expect about 100,000 of them to be committed to disruption or sabotage. Both are worthwhile persuits [sic]."

Abbie sent that letter from Ramrod Key in the Florida Keys, where he was vacationing over the Christmas holidays. He had secured a small advance from Dial Press to write a book about political organizing and guerrilla theater. (His letters to Danny Schecter had formed the basis of his proposal.) He and Anita used the advance to finance the trip. Paul Krassner and Ellen Sander, a rock critic for the *Saturday Review of Literature*, accompanied them.

Abbie and Paul spent much of the vacation talking about the issue of revolutionary violence. On a visit to Key West they saw the movie *The Bible*. The scene in which Abraham prepares to slay Isaac, his first son, stirred an intense discussion. Krassner criticized Abraham for his "blind obedience" in following the orders of God. Abbie argued that Abraham was acting out of "revolutionary" trust—his faith that there would be a better world if he followed God's dictates. For Krassner, the pacifist, killing was killing even if sanctioned by holy authority in the name of a revolutionary vision. Ends don't justify means, and individuals have to take moral responsibility for their own actions. For Abbie, furthering the goal of revolution took precedence over an individual's moral scruples.

One day, while the vacationers were tripping on acid, a tropical storm blew in from the Gulf, and it seemed as if the house might blow away. Cuba was just ninety miles south, and Abbie ran out on the sun deck howling, "We're coming, Fidel!" Like many radicals of his generation Abbie admired Fidel Castro, not because he agreed with the Marxist-Leninist ideology of the Cuban Revolution, but because Castro had defied the United States and survived American attacks. Old Leftists scrutinized events in Cuba as evidence of Cuba's adherence to or betrayal of socialist principles. Since Abbie had no clearly defined socialist ideology, there was nothing for Cuba to either uphold or betray. He viewed Castro as he did all third-world revolutionaries, as a righteous David holding off the American Goliath. Even better, Castro was a baseball fan. The Cubans were like his beloved Red Sox, Abbie joked. In Cuba, as in the bleachers at Fenway, everyone hated the Yankees.[1]

Bored with the incessant talk of revolution, Sander decided to return to New York. Driving her to the Miami airport, the group passed a chain gang fixing the road. Abbie pulled off to the side and beckoned a black prisoner to get in the car. The man smiled and shook his head no. A guard turned to see what was happening, and Abbie screeched off laughing. Abbie was full of revolutionary derring-do. But as a veteran of the southern civil rights movement he should have known better than to put a black man in jeopardy simply as a goof to impress his friends.

Before she left the Keys, Sander had talked of her experience at the Monterey Pop Festival the previous June. Rock bands in the Bay Area had organized a free, three-day concert to bring California's hip community together. The music had been wonderful, the dope plentiful; and the police, many of them wearing flowers in their caps, had done nothing to interfere. Building on the success of the East and West Coast be-ins, Monterey intensified the hippies' belief in themselves as a movement of destiny, a countercultural model for a peaceful, cooperative world. Hearing Sander talk about Monterey got Abbie thinking about rock festivals as arenas for political organizing. Next summer's action in Chicago could be a giant festival, a countercultural alternative to the Democratic convention. Full of enthusiasm for the idea, Abbie, Anita, and Paul cut their vacation short and returned to New York.[2]

On New Year's Day 1968, Abbie, Jerry Rubin, and Paul Krassner, along with Anita Hoffman and Jerry's girlfriend, Nancy Kurshan, met in the Hoffmans' apartment. They were lying on pillows on the floor, smoking dope, and, with gales of laughter, talking about their accomplishments the past year and their plans for the coming summer. They believed that they were inventing a new form of protest art and that there was no limit to what they could achieve with their audacity and creativity. In a burst of communal inspiration they came up with the idea of Yippie! (The exclamation point was essential, Abbie insisted, in order to convey the excitement of the word's meaning.) Hippies would become Yippies. Yippies were politicized hippies. Yippies would be members of YIP, the Youth International Party. The media would take it seriously as an organized political party representing international youth. The kids would get the joke, however, and understand that there was no organization. Yippie meant political action as excitement and fun. Everyone a revolutionary.[3]

The word *Yippie!* would describe what they were about, but they would also need a satirical symbol to describe what they were against. Cartoonists often used a pig to portray corrupt politicians. The Democrats had their pig, Lyndon Johnson; the Republicans would also have a pig, probably Richard Nixon. But the Yippies would nominate a real pig, and no matter who won the election a pig would be in the White House. The idea of using a pig as a symbol began as an innocent joke with precedents in the history of American political satire. But its timing coincided with the rise of the Oakland-based Black Panther party. Reflecting the perception that black ghetto youths had of white policemen, the Black

Panthers began using the word *pig* as a synonym for policeman.*
White radicals, may of whom were in awe of the Panthers' tough,
urban machismo, picked the expression up. What began as political satire became an ugly way of baiting the police.

Contrast was essential to the idea of Yippie. As the Yippies envisioned it, their "Festival of Life" would be a living, palpitating alternative to the straight and square Democratic convention, which
Krassner now named the "Convention of Death." Never mind the
political risks—the possibility that attacking the square Democrats
might weaken the party, bring down a liberal government, and help
the Republican right. Abbie was a gambler. The war had to be
stopped. He believed that the country's social fabric was coming
apart. More and more people—and not just the young—were
using, and enjoying, illegal drugs. The outlaw mentality was catch-
ing on. From the perspective of the East Village (where nothing
existed west of the Hudson except a few progressive college campuses and then Berkeley and San Francisco), America seemed
headed in a revolutionary direction. "The country is up for grabs,"
Abbie told his friends.[4]

Abbie and Jerry's ability to attract media attention was essential
to the Yippie plan. Instead of having to raise money through advertising and mailings, they would get national publicity by playing
to the media. Yippie was an idea rather than an organization.
People would come to Chicago not because the Yippies organized
them to come but because Abbie and Jerry would hype Chicago as
the place to be during the week of the Democratic convention.

Abbie talked about his idea of structured nonleadership, of creating a "blank space" in the media for people to fill in as their
imagination allowed. There would be no official definition or authoritative explanation of what Yippie meant. People would be free
to invent their own meaning of Yippie and so come to Chicago as
performers in their own spectacle. Anyone could declare him- or
herself a Yippie. There was no charter; there were no by-laws,
membership cards, or dues. "We had to create a kind of situation
in which people would become their own leaders," Abbie would

---

* Calling police pigs goes back to the mid-1800s, but according to Stuart
Berg Flexner in *I Hear America Talking*, a dictionary of slang, the gibe
had become obsolete in the twentieth century until the Black Panthers
revived it.

later testify. "This would go along with our philosophy that people were basically good, they had innate potential for creativity and for life if we just created the kind of situation in which these potentials could come to the fore." The idea, Abbie continued, was to "create a society in which everyone was an artist."[5]

The then-popular expression "do your own thing" was not a cliché to Abbie. He took the idea of nonleadership seriously. He saw his role as that of a revolutionary artist creating a political theater in which people could invent their own roles. "We're cheerleaders. We encourage everything," he said of the Yippie leadership style. "A cheerleader doesn't say no. We say that . . . people got a bitch against the government, . . . or want to see a better system, they know what they're doing, . . . and they'll figure out a way of doing it, in a style that feels good to them. So if their style is to print up a leaflet, if their style is to carry a picket sign, if their style is going to stand in a vigil or fast or burn themselves or burn the president, or whatever it is, that's their thing."[6]

Gradually there emerged two visions of what the Festival of Life should be. Jerry, committed to the idea of creative disruption, saw it principally in confrontational terms. Like many of the more militant radicals in the movement, he had given up on both the electoral process and on organizing the straight middle class. "We say to hell with middle-class 'security' and phony status games, we are going to screw up this society. And we can do it," he proclaimed in the *Village Voice*. Instead of a broad-based movement trying to pressure Congress into ending the war, Rubin envisioned "a massive white revolutionary youth movement" that would work "in parallel cooperation with the rebellions in the black communities." Together, they "could seriously disrupt this country, and thus be an internal catalyst for a breakdown of the American ability and will to fight guerrillas overseas." Rational persuasion and moral arguments no longer worked, Jerry was convinced. Violence was a necessity, not because he had any illusion that the movement could overthrow the government, but because "power and violence" were the only things that blacks and working-class whites would respond to and that politicians would understand.

This was Jerry Rubin's view before Chicago. Violence, he believed, was an effective form of communication, the best means for the movement to grab public attention. He perceived the American people as Hollywood and television caricatures, telescoping human dynamics into a shoot-out or a brawl. Abbie, however, still had faith in monkey theater, in tickling the nation's funny bone, grabbing its attention with humor and satire.

Although Jerry was talking about organizing the young, he was still, early in 1968, focused not on organizing a counterculture but on ending the Vietnam War. Even before the idea of Yippie was born, he was thinking of an "American Youth Festival" that would bring "500,000 people to Chicago to camp out, smoke pot, dance to wild music, burn draft cards and roar like wild bands through the streets, forcing the President to bring troops back from Vietnam to keep order in the city while he is nominated under the protection of tear gas and bayonets!" Jerry's scenario did not offer the hope of reversing the Democrats' war policy. All it aimed to do was polarize the country by exposing government violence.

Like many antiwar militants, Jerry claimed not to be afraid of political repression. Far from fearing it, he saw it as a creative challenge. He knew the impact of McCarthyism on the Old Left, but as he had shown at his own HUAC appearance, a counteroffensive of aggressive guerrilla theater could put the forces of repression on the defensive. "Repression turns demonstration/protests into wars; actors into heroes; masses of individuals into a community," Jerry said. "Repression eliminates the bystander, the neutral observer, the theorist; it forces everyone to pick a side. A movement cannot grow without repression."[7]

Abbie, for his part, conceptualized a festival that would contrast the "death and decay symbolized by the Democrats" with a "free explosion" of youthful energy, 500,000 Yippies partying in the streets. "Theirs will be a political circus," he said of the Democratic convention, "ours will be the real thing complete with sawdust and laughing bears." The Democrats will have "sterile roll calls, we will dance in the streets to Country Joe and the Fish." The delegates will "debate meaningless resolutions, we will listen to the poems of Allen Ginsberg. While the platform is formulated we will make love in Grant Park. When the Vice President gives his acceptance speech, we will sing the glories of the Second American Revolution. When Johnson mounts the rostrum, we will run naked through the streets."[8]

Yet it would be an oversimplification to assess these two visions as parallel tracks and to portray Abbie and Jerry in disagreement over their ultimate goal. Jerry understood that without a youth festival and rock bands, the Yippies could not attract enough kids for a viable demonstration. Abbie's vision did not rule out confrontation and disruption. "We have two alternatives in Chicago, both of them OK," he told Sally Kempton of the *Village Voice* early in March. "The opposition determines what will happen, they're living actors in our theater. Suppose they choose to tolerate us. Then we'll get a chance to deal with the problems of relating to people in a community, feeding them, sleeping them, living collectively. We'll present a vision of a new life-style that will be projected across the country. Suppose they don't tolerate us? Then they'll face a bloody scene. We'll have to adopt guerrilla techniques for dealing with them. And we'll take home their message of a brutal society and deal with it in the local communities."[9]

Leadership in Yippie would be open to everyone as a manifestation of "participatory democracy," Abbie said, but the manipulation was undisguised. There was never any secret about who wielded power. Abbie and Jerry personified Yippie in the public eye and were the strategic masterminds. Paul Krassner, Ed Sanders, Stew Albert, and Keith Lampe were the trusted advisers who had enough influence with Abbie and Jerry to shape the Yippie image. Anita Hoffman also had influence through Abbie, as did Jerry's girlfriend, Nancy Kurshan, who had been a political activist before she met Jerry. This inner circle was accountable to no one. To be sure, Jerry was constantly networking, asking people for advice and observations. Jerry had followers because—like a candidate who kisses babies and knows the names of all the voters—he worked hard at being a politician. But movement activists distrusted politicians. Hence many considered Jerry to be egotistical and ambitious. People were more tolerant of Abbie's egotism. He was so upbeat and funny that they accepted it as an authentic part of his charisma. When they disagreed with Abbie, they would shake their head, shrug, laugh, and say, "That's Abbie." Moreover, Abbie was considered a catalyst rather than a politician. Yippies who were sufficiently creative and self-motivated to work without detailed direction enjoyed working with Abbie. "He energized people," one Yippie recalls. "He created an idea, provided direction, raised money for you to use, gave you the names of people to contact, and then left you alone. He gave you the go-ahead to be an organizer."[10]

In the early days the Yippies made an attempt to involve people in open meetings. They held these every Saturday at the Free University on Fourteenth Street. As with all open political meetings on the Lower East Side, the result was anarchist theater. With no formal agenda, with balloons being batted about, and with Jerry or Abbie presiding without the benefit of Robert's Rules of Order, chaos ruled. The Motherfuckers, a group of hip East Village anarchists, would invariably attack Abbie and Jerry for hogging the media spotlight and being unaccountable as leaders.* Jim Fouratt, reasonable even in the midst of mayhem, would try to raise serious questions. He wanted to deemphasize Chicago and turn Yippie into more of a community organizing project that would politicize the growing hippie movement in the many cities and campus communities to which it was spreading. But Fouratt had already lost this argument in Yippie's inner circle, and raising the issue in an open meeting was impossible in the general disorder.

Before long, Fouratt's criticism of the Chicago project led to a falling out with Abbie. According to Fouratt, Abbie refused to respond to his political critique of Yippie. Instead, Abbie attributed the split to Fouratt's homosexuality and said that Fouratt was making passes at him. (This was before the Stonewall riot and gay liberation.) Fouratt couldn't fight back and, as a result, felt that Abbie had disempowered him in the movement. (Much later, Abbie criticized himself for his homophobic attitude.) Abbie also led a raid (one of the raiders was future feminist Robin Morgan) to Fouratt's Bond Street loft and stole (or "liberated," as Abbie would

* There were three main branches of anarchism in the movement. One was the individualist, "one-man revolution" anarcho-pacifism of Ammon Hennacy. A second, personified by Paul Goodman and emphasizing civic responsibility, was pragmatic and nonviolent. The third was inspired by East Villager Murray Bookchin. An ex-communist who sometimes wrote under the name of Lewis Herber, Bookchin was the first leftist to recognize the dangers of pollution to the environment and to call for a radical, left-wing solution. (His first writings on the subject predated Rachel Carson's *Silent Spring*.) Groups of his followers began moving from the East Village to Vermont, New Mexico, and California in the mid-1960s and represented the first wave of the back-to-the-land movement. Those who stayed on in the East Village formed Up against the Wall Motherfuckers. In order to widen their influence they affiliated as the East Village chapter of SDS.

have described it) the mimeograph machine on which Fouratt printed Communication Company leaflets—one of his East Village organizing projects. Such raids were becoming typical of the way movement factions dealt with political disagreements. "Abbie and I don't approve of what you're doing," Morgan informed Fouratt when Fouratt went to reclaim the machine at the Yippie office.

In short, despite the show of openness, there was no mechanism for airing political disputes or personal issues within Yippie. Decisions were made by the inner circle, and if you couldn't abide by the decisions you dropped out of Yippie, as Fouratt eventually did.

Abbie conceived of the Festival of Life as a joint effort involving artists, writers, theater people, rock musicians, intellectuals, and psychedelic gurus. Chicago would become a giant theater stage for a rock concert, an arts festival, a be-in, a university without walls, an alternative constitutional convention. He spoke of inviting futurists like Buckminster Fuller and Marshall McLuhan, as well as more practical visionaries like Paul Goodman, to create a new blueprint for America. The vision was grandiose but enticing. If only half of what he promised actually happened, it would be a historic event, worth attending and promoting.

Judy Collins, Arlo Guthrie, Janis Joplin, Country Joe and the Fish, Steve Miller, the Fugs, and Allen Ginsberg were among those who supported this idea of Yippie at the beginning. But there was still a concern about the possibility of violence. Ginsberg told Abbie that he was worried "whether the government would let us do something that was funnier or prettier or more charming than what was going to be going on in the convention hall."[11] The performers and their managers all insisted that the Yippies secure permits from the city and that everything be legal. Believing that it was in Mayor Daley's own best interest to allow a legal festival, the Yippies went about generating support and publicity, confident that the city would ultimately come through with the necessary permits.

Despite the growing enthusiasm for the Yippie vision, some movement activists were critical of the irresponsible way the Yippie leaders were organizing support for their festival. Most serious was Michael Rossman's charge, carried by many underground newspapers, that the explosion of Yippie publicity, "however spectacular, is neither moral nor . . . effective." The respected Berkeley radical accused the Yippies of luring kids to Chicago, just as they came to Haight-Ashbury, without any political grounding and without any preparation for the probability of "official violence." The Yippies had given up on the serious work of political organizing; their promotion of the event lacked moral and ethical content. Participants would be passive spectators, just as they were at rock concerts. To be an organizer, in the movement tradition, meant reaching out, educating and empowering others. "The brilliant formless Yippie publicity, on waving the magical beckoning symbol of our Muse, projects grooving and warmth, and does not warn that joy . . . must be won from within—not absorbed from others," Rossman wrote. "If there's any ethical principle we can fix for our actions in this fractured time, it's that we must keep straight with our own, with those we speak for, lead and invite."[12]

While Abbie and Jerry were focusing on Chicago, other Yippies in New York were planning a celebration of the spring equinox, a midnight Yip-in on the night of March 21–22 in the cavernous main waiting room of New York's Grand Central railroad terminal. The publicity was vintage Yippie, playful and with lots of blank space for people to fill with their imagination:

> It's a spring mating service celebrating the equinox,
> a back-scratching party, a roller skating rink, a
> theater . . . with you as performer and audience.
> Get acquainted with other Yippies now, for other
> Yiptivities and Chicago Y.I.P. Festival this summer.
> Bring: Flowers, Beads, Music, Radios, Pillows,
> Eats, Love and Peace. Meet later on at Sheep
> Meadow to Yip Up the Sun.[13]

As was the custom in New York when planning a demonstration, the Yippies discussed the plan with the mayor's office. Mayor John V. Lindsay, who opposed the war and was intent on preserving New York's "Fun City" image, was keen on maintaining ties with the East Village activists. No one wanted or expected violence; hence little thought was given to the problem of entering and exiting the terminal. This was going to be all peace and love, an indoor be-in to take the chill off winter, and Grand Central seemed a grand place to hold a party. There was tension between the police and the hippies, however. The police had been raiding hippie crash pads and busting the inhabitants on drug charges. A demonstration the previous night at the Ninth Precinct had degenerated into a battle between egg-throwing hippies and club-swinging tactical patrolmen. The Yippies (and other East Village activists) were intent on drawing a parallel between the police repression of drug users and the military's repression in Vietnam. In making this analogy, they found themselves being drawn into confrontations with the police strictly over lifestyle issues. Although they assumed that the hippies' anger at the local police could be channeled into protest against the war, targeting the police as "the enemy" detracted from the focus on the Johnson administration.

The police made no initial attempt to stop the Yip-in. Hippies, movement activists, and curious kids from all over the metropolitan area flooded into Grand Central to check out and be part of the scene. Many of them had painted faces and wore colorful costumes. Abbie himself came dressed as an American Indian. "Costumes work wonders," one movement journalist wrote later. "People get out of their angry paranoid winter roles into the gentle, playful roles of their fantasies. (The revolution is living the life you dream of living.)" [14] People batted around balloons, formed and reformed conga lines, and shared popcorn with commuters.

By describing the Yip-in in the spirit of a be-in, the Yippies hoped to create a theatrical context that would discourage acts of violence. But the very nature of a do-your-own-thing demonstration invites free-lance performers to introduce their own theatrical agenda. The East Village anarchist group Up against the Wall Motherfucker believed that people are radicalized by being beaten by cops. (This is not a farfetched notion, as history is filled with incidents of police wading into peaceful protesters and, instead of subduing them, transforming them into angry, revolutionary mobs. But being part of an angry mob is not the same thing as being a dedicated revolutionary.) Abbie admired the Motherfuckers for their talent in making trouble. It was almost as if the Motherfuckers represented his alter ego. They were the outlaws of the movement; they would fight any attempt to impose discipline on a demonstration. Although the Motherfuckers never cooperated with him or anybody and often attacked him for being an egotistical leader, Abbie never criticized them. They were the "middle-class night-

mare," Abbie called them, "an antimedia media phenomenon
simply because their name couldn't be printed."[15] They were the
blank space that everybody feared.

At the Yip-in the Motherfuckers tried to organize a provocative
snake dance, but their militancy went against the crowd's mood.
Taunting the police worked better, and when a small group of provocateurs climbed on top of the information booth and began
breaking apart the station clock, the police charged out of an adjacent waiting room and began clubbing everyone within range,
including late night commuters waiting for trains. The Yippies ran
for the exits, and when the attack subsided returned chanting,
"Hell no! We won't go," the slogan of the draft resistance movement, which took on a double meaning as the police attacked and
the protesters retreated and then returned to the station. In a distant corridor, safe from the police, Jerry Rubin paced back and
forth, stopping breathless Yippies fleeing the assault and asking
them how they thought the violence would affect plans for Chicago.

If Jerry was like a staff general, planning strategy behind the
lines, Abbie was the field commander leading his troops while
under fire. In the main concourse and in the middle of the action,
Abbie and Anita Hoffman were trying, without success, to negotiate with the police. Although the Yippies had tried to portray themselves as being without leaders, Abbie realized someone had to
assume responsibility and bring the situation under control. He
went to Barry Gottherer, Mayor Lindsay's youth aide, and offered
to calm the Yippies if Gottherer would get the police to withdraw.
But Gottherer couldn't help. The police were out of control, he
claimed. Drawing on their civil rights experience, the Hoffmans
then tried to get the Yippies to sit down. It was a gutsy move in the
late sixties: Abbie would get no credit from the militants for advocating nonviolence, but it was the only way to stabilize the situation
so that the police would withdraw. Still the police kept attacking.
When police saw from Don McNeill's press credentials that he represented the *Village Voice*, they threw him through a plate glass
door, as they also did a youth from Baltimore. Alan Levine, a lawyer from the New York Civil Liberties Union who was at the station
as a legal observer, described the scene as "the worst example of
police brutality I've ever seen outside of Mississippi." Abbie himself
was seized and made to run a gauntlet of policemen's clubs. He
went into the fetal position he had learned in the South as Anita

tried to throw herself on him to protect his body from the blows. From Grand Central he went to Bellevue Hospital to get bandaged up, and then to WBAI to talk on the Bob Fass show about what had happened. At three in the morning there were still a thousand Yippies at the station. With calm finally restored, the Yippies filed out, as planned, to watch the sun come up in Central Park. They left in a solemn procession, holding up the two-finger V sign for peace that the movement had appropriated from Winston Churchill and humming "om," the chant that Allen Ginsberg had suggested would reduce anxiety and calm everyone's fears.

Abbie's blank space had been filled. The Yippie "invasion" of Grand Central Terminal "may have signalled a new turn in the hippie movement towards political activism in politics and the arts," began a front-page article in the *New York Times*. Keith Lampe provided a Yippie spin. Young people "have a feeling that the next six or eight months can make a real difference in the United States in stopping the war in Vietnam," he was quoted as saying by the *Times*.[16] Abbie and Jerry also tried to put the police attack in a positive light. The baptismal bloodletting had served a purpose, they argued. No longer could the Yippies be accused of leading innocents to slaughter. As Abbie wrote in *Revolution for the Hell of It*, "The Grand Central Station Massacre knocked out the hippie image of Chicago and let the whole world know there would be blood on the streets in Chicago."[17]

The morning after the Bob Fass show, Abbie flew to a Mobe conference at Lake Villa, a YMCA camp near Chicago. With him were Jerry Rubin, Paul Krassner, Bob Fass, Jim Fouratt, Ed Sanders, and Marshall Bloom and Ray Mungo of Liberation News Service.[18] Dave Dellinger, Tom Hayden, and Rennie Davis had invited two hundred activists to the conference to discuss plans for the Democratic convention. The principal order of business was a proposal titled "Election Campaign Offensive," drafted by Hayden and Davis. Ambitious in scope but vague in detail, it called for a grassroots challenge to the Democratic party that harked back to the days when the movement was focused on community organizing. Local antiwar organizations might contest the selection of delegates for the convention, the paper suggested, or hold teach-ins to debunk the party, or hold local hearings to formulate a people's platform

for the convention. These local activities would build support for
three days of protest in Chicago during the August convention. The
demonstrations "should be non-violent and legal," the proposal
continued; the movement "should not plan violence and disruption
against the Democratic Party." Nonviolence was a tactical necessity, Hayden and Davis insisted. "The right of rebellion is hardly
exercised by assembling 300,000 people to charge into 30,000 paratroopers." Moreover, "any plan of deliberate disruption will drive
people away" and play into the hands of prowar politicians.[19]

The Yippies were invited to Lake Villa to present their own proposal for Chicago. The delegates had already received a synopsis
of the Yippie plan, written by Rubin and Sanders. But the Yippies
came to the conference with a hip chip on their shoulder. Stoned
most of the time (Ray Mungo recalls them tripping on acid), they
were intent on blowing the minds, Digger-fashion, of the Mobe.
Rather than take part in the discussions about the value of demonstrating in Chicago, they acted as cheerleaders for their own
proposal, handing out Yippie buttons and posters and disrupting
the proceedings with shouts of "Abandon the creeping meatball!
Come to Chicago!" Many of the leftists were hostile to the emerging
youth culture and unsympathetic to what the Yippies were attempting. According to David Farber, author of *Chicago '68*, a
richly detailed book on the August demonstrations, "Many of the
Mobe delegates were young but they were hardly hippie types interested in the sex, drugs, and rock 'n' roll revolution Yippie was
promoting."[20] Although the Yippies were treated respectfully by
Dellinger, Hayden, and Davis, they were dismissed as nuisances
and pranksters by many of the other delegates.

It was typical of the movement to break conferences down into
small workshops. Perhaps because he was looking to provoke sectarian leftists, Abbie attended the Anticapitalist Workshop. Most
of the other participants were Marxists determined to push one or
another version of socialism. Few took seriously Abbie's proposal
that the movement endorse free public toilets. Some thought he was
being disruptive. Others gave him credit for at least being funny,
which he was. But he was also serious. To Abbie, it was a sign of
decaying civility, as well as capitalist greed, that it was becoming
difficult to find a free public toilet when one was in need. Stop these
endless debates about theoretical conceptions of socialism, Abbie

was saying. Liberating public toilets was the kind of real-life issue around which the movement could attract attention and organize.[21]

The Mobe's rejection of the Yippies at Lake Villa embittered Abbie. "We were treated like niggers, you know, like we were irrelevant," he wrote, still angry, four months later.[22] The charge that the Yippies represented no real constituency was especially galling. To Abbie, organizing young people was the most important work on the left. Hippies were no longer a bicoastal phenomenon of alienated acid-heads, dropouts, and runaways. With the backing of the underground press the Yippies were reaching millions of people across America. Abbie had always insisted that he was organizing youth within the antiwar coalition. Now he began to feel alienated from that coalition. The underground culture was exploding everywhere. The subject of books, articles, television reports, it was gaining adherents even within the professional white-collar class. All kinds of straight middle-class people were experimenting with psychedelic drugs and thinking about dropping out of the "rat race." Young reporters were smoking dope with the hippies they were supposed to be reporting on and becoming secret allies, hip infiltrators in the world of the straights. Looking at these changes, Abbie began to see the youth culture not just as an important constituency in a broader radical movement but as a revolutionary force in and of itself.

After Lake Villa and along the road to Chicago, the Yippie *tactic* of organizing the youth culture to end the war was transformed into a countercultural *strategy* to revolutionize society. This was not a conscious change of direction on the part of Abbie, Jerry, and the other Yippie organizers. But it was reflected in their rhetoric about revolution and in their plans for the festival in Chicago. If hip youth were the motor force of change, then straight people were the enemy no matter what their position on the war. *Épater les bourgeois* was something bohemians had always done to show their hip superiority. Now the Yippies began to see "sticking it to the straights" as a serious political strategy.

To add to Abbie's alienation from the antiwar coalition, the Mobe was unable to come to a consensus on what to do at the Democratic convention. Abbie saw this as symptomatic of the left's penchant for talk rather than action. "The Left masturbates continuously because it is essentially rooted in an academic tradition. It is the rhetoric of the Left, its insistence on ideological exactness rather than action, that has held the revolution back in this country as much as the actions of the people in power," he wrote of the Mobe's indecision at Lake Villa.[23]

The Mobe had reason to be indecisive. In the weeks leading up to the conference political earthquakes had upset the electoral equation. In the wake of the Tet offensive in Vietnam, NBC, ABC, the *Wall Street Journal*, the *New York Times*, and the *Washington Post* all reversed their hawkish positions and came out against further escalation. CBS News's Walter Cronkite, the most popular television newsman in America, did a special report from Vietnam and declared the war a stalemate. "The only way out will be to negotiate, not as victors, but as an honorable people who lived up to their pledge to defend democracy, and did the best they could," he told the nation. Then, on March 12, Senator Eugene McCarthy, running as a peace candidate against President Johnson, got 42 percent of the vote in the New Hampshire Democratic primary. New Hampshire was one of the most hawkish states in the nation, and his showing was considered a victory for the antiwar movement. Although McCarthy had offered to challenge the president as early as October 1967, the antiwar movement had never viewed him as a viable candidate. Those who supported him did so only because they felt they had no alternative. "He seems to lack heart and guts," wrote I. F. Stone, an early albeit reluctant McCarthy supporter. "A certain cynicism and defeatism seem basic to the man."[24] Doubting McCarthy's ability to beat Johnson, many radicals feared that he would co-opt the movement by luring people out of the streets and into the Democratic party. Abbie compared McCarthy to the New York Mets, then a hapless baseball team a year away from their miracle season. Supporting McCarthy was like rooting for an underdog, he suggested. The rules of the Democratic convention were proof of his campaign's hopelessness. Party regulars, controlled by Johnson, held 60 percent of the delegate votes no matter what McCarthy did in the primaries. Even if he won every primary by a landslide, he would still enter the convention in a minority position.

Four days after McCarthy's New Hampshire victory Robert F. Kennedy declared his intention to run for the presidency. A Gallup poll released the weekend of the Lake Villa conference showed Johnson defeating McCarthy 59 percent to 29 percent but Kennedy leading Johnson 44 percent to 41 percent. With Kennedy in the race it was a new election. Kennedy had the ability to build momentum in the primaries and storm the convention at the head of a grassroots movement. Many delegates committed to Johnson would switch to Kennedy if only out of yearning for a return of Camelot. Some radicals felt that Kennedy was sincere in wanting to end the war and do something about racism and poverty at home. Unlike Eugene McCarthy, he was actively soliciting ideas from movement radicals. Tom Hayden had been invited to Kennedy's home to discuss the issues with Kennedy and his advisers and had come away convinced that Kennedy could unite the white working class, the black community, and the middle-class antiwar movement into a progressive coalition that could win the White House.

Abbie didn't share Hayden's enthusiasm for Kennedy. He had committed himself to the Yippie strategy of opposing electoral politics. Writing in March about the 1968 elections, he stated, "In this country change can never come through the present electoral process. It will come only through action in the streets."[25] Nevertheless, Abbie understood that Kennedy was a "challenge to the charisma of the Yippies." He believed that a battle between Kennedy and Johnson at the Chicago convention would be an epic struggle of two political titans for the soul of the nation. Anything the Yippies might do in the streets would be inconsequential. And most of the people who would come to Chicago with the Yippies would end up emotionally involved on the Kennedy bandwagon. With his youth and charisma—and his promise to end the war—Kennedy could easily co-opt the youth rebellion.*

Kennedy's candidacy was not the last of the political surprises, however. The same week as Lake Villa, President Johnson assembled the most respected members of the liberal foreign policy establishment to review the war's prospects. Among them were

---

* Many radicals, including Abbie, distrusted Robert Kennedy because of his dismal record as attorney general and because he had supported, as a young Senate aide, Senator Joseph McCarthy. To oppose people simply because of their past is a strange argument coming from radicals, much less a radical Maslovian like Abbie. For if people lack the capacity to change, as the argument against Kennedy implied, then the very idea of reform or revolution is called into question.

Dean Acheson, Clark Clifford, Henry Cabot Lodge, Abe Fortas, Maxwell Taylor, Arthur Dean, Douglas Dillon, George Ball, and Averell Harriman—all of them, except for Ball, hawks on Vietnam and architects of the Cold War. The "Wise Men," as they were called, had met four months earlier and endorsed Johnson's war policy. This time they concluded that there was nothing the United States could do, short of destroying the Vietnamese people, to save the corrupt regime in South Vietnam; the American public would not tolerate the level of escalation necessary to make that kind of military "victory" possible. As Clark Clifford, Johnson's once-hawkish secretary of defense, told Dean Rusk and others after the meeting concluded, "What seems not to be understood is that major elements of the national constituency—the business community, the press, the churches, professional groups, college presidents, students and most of the intellectual community—have turned against the war."[26] But this meeting was held in secret, and the Mobe did not know that the most influential voices in government had accepted the movement's critique of the war's futility. Nor could the Mobe know that such leading congressional hawks as Senators Richard Russell and Henry "Scoop" Jackson had come to the same conclusion.[27] Thus the antiwar activists, like everyone else, were startled when, on March 31, President Johnson announced a halt to the bombing of North Vietnam and a willingness to begin peace negotiations. They were further astonished by Johnson's declaration that he would not seek a second term as president.

The Vietnam protest movement had won the battle within the Democratic party. But few radicals grasped the scope of the triumph. Even after Johnson's resignation and Kennedy's move to make peace and racial justice an electoral issue, Dave Dellinger was reiterating the Mobe's position that the "fight against the war cannot be won in the ballot box."[28] As for the Yippies, they would look to youth, not to Bobby Kennedy, to change American politics. And in this they were not entirely off the mark. It was, after all, the children of hawks like Robert McNamara who had educated them into becoming doves, and it was the children of doves like Robert Kennedy and Eugene McCarthy who had finally convinced them to break with Lyndon Johnson.[29] Even in the White House it was Lynda Johnson Robb, whose husband had just been shipped off to Vietnam, who tearfully implored her father to seek a negotiated end to the war. Moreover, for many young people, the McCarthy and Kennedy campaigns were their final test of the system: if becoming "clean for Gene" didn't stop the war, they were ready to follow the radicals into the streets. "I felt that this was the last gasp within the process, and you couldn't live with yourself if you didn't do everything you could to make a try of it," said one of the youthful organizers who coordinated McCarthy's New Hampshire primary campaign.[30]

★   ★   ★

After the Lake Villa conference the Yippies went to Chicago to meet with local freaks, most of whom were involved with the *Seed*, Chicago's underground paper. Sensitive to being viewed as outside agitators, the New Yorkers persuaded the Chicago group to cosign their application for a permit requesting the use of Grant Park, the city's major downtown open space, for the "nation's biggest music festival" the week of the Democratic convention. They also requested permission to sleep in the park and the city's cooperation in providing sanitation facilities and mobile kitchen units for the concertgoers.

The next day the Yippies staged their first Chicago press conference. After quietly presenting their permit application to Chicago Park Department officials as required, they invited the media to witness some guerrilla theater at Mayor Daley's office. But the mayor, nobody's fall guy, made himself unavailable, offering up in his stead his deputy, David Stahl. With television cameras whirring and reporters taking notes, a Yippie from the New York delegation presented the permit application rolled up in a *Playboy* Playmate of the Month centerfold inscribed "To Dick with love, the Yippies." She then kissed the deputy mayor and pinned a Yippie button to his suit. Stahl retreated to his office, and Abbie and the other Yippies cavorted before the media, answering questions and passing out Yippie fliers. The event, from the Yippie standpoint, was a great success. The Chicago Yippies were delighted. They were impressed by the New Yorkers' audacity in publicly twitting the mayor's deputy. In Chicago, where Daley was The Boss, nobody poked fun at the mayor or his men.

Richard J. Daley was more than a match for Yippie theater. His stance toward the Yippies, as toward all peace demonstrators, was to stonewall their applications for permits and frighten protesters from coming to his town. It was not that Mayor Daley was a hawk on the war. On the contrary, he had privately told leading Democrats that he did not like what the war was doing to American society. Uneasiness about Johnson's war policy was spreading from liberals to centrists like Daley. Yet the public had no way of knowing this.[31]

Daley's national standing stemmed from his total control of Chicago politics and his fabled ability to steal elections. No one knows if Daley rigged the vote count to deliver the state of Illinois and the presidency to John F. Kennedy in the 1960 election. But the notion that he could have thrown a national election contributed to his image as a power broker that no Democratic presidential aspirant dared to cross. Given the authoritarian nature of his rule, Daley was bound to fight any insurgency. Just as he had frustrated Martin Luther King's effort to mobilize the black community, he was determined to stop the peace movement from setting up camp in Chicago. The assassination of King had touched off riots in the Chicago ghetto, as it had in many other major American cities. Daley criticized the Chicago police for handling the rioters with kid gloves. Next time they would "shoot to kill," he promised. Like Abbie, Daley knew how to get a message across through the media: his "shoot to kill" statement played on national television. Although public outrage forced him to soften that language, his get-tough policy got through to the peace movement as well as the black militants—which was the purpose of his threat to "shoot to kill." Shortly thereafter, at a peace rally at the Chicago Civic Plaza in late April, five hundred police inexplicably attacked seven thousand peace marchers, most of whom were respectably white and middle class. According to David Farber in *Chicago '68*, the police surrounded the protest, ordered the protesters to disperse, and then attacked any demonstrator who tried to comply with that order and leave through their line. Not satisfied with beating these strays, the police "attacked the entire, absolutely peaceful, absolutely nonprovoking, non-stone-throwing, nontaunting crowd. Dozens and dozens of people were clubbed, slugged, kicked, and Maced," Farber wrote. Hippies were especially targeted. "A few police chased long-haired demonstrators several blocks in order to club them."[32] A civic commission that studied the incident concluded that the "policemen who committed acts of violence" were "doing what the Mayor and the Superintendent had clearly indicated was expected of them." But never mind. Daley's message was clear. He would brook no protests, even from nonviolent peace demonstrators.

When Abe Peck, the editor of the *Seed*, wrote an "Open Letter to Mayor Daley" requesting that the city sit down and talk with the local Yippies in the shared "desire to avoid bloodshed and needless hardship," the mayor began a campaign of harassment against the underground newspaper's hippie vendors, arresting them, releasing them on bond, and then dropping charges when the cases came to court. At the same time the police began to round up hippies hanging out on Wells Street, Chicago's bohemian district. Two days before the attack on the peace marchers, the police disrupted a Yippie meeting, roughly questioned the seventy young people present, and arrested ten on charges of disorderly conduct. In May they barged into a benefit dance for the Yippies and arrested all the underage teens for curfew violation. Meanwhile April and May passed, and the Yippies hadn't received any reply to their request for a permit.[33]

Abbie and Ed Sanders had gotten many of the country's best-known rock bands to agree to play at a free festival on the assurance that they would have permits from the city and the police would not interfere. Just as the Yippies excelled in generating publicity about a festival in Chicago, Daley had no problem conveying his message that the Yippies were not welcome. After the police attack on the peace demonstrators, Country Joe McDonald told Abbie that the vibrations coming out of Chicago were bad and that the musicians were getting scared. In June the situation seemed to improve. Stahl indicated that the Yippies might have Lincoln Park, two miles north of the downtown hotel area and ten miles from the site of the convention. He warned them, though, that the police would close the park if they caught even one person smoking a joint.

The Yippies continued to believe that it was in Daley's best interest to issue a permit and that the city would stall as long as it could but issue a permit just in time for the convention. A legal rock festival in far-off Lincoln Park presented less of a threat to the Democratic convention than a political demonstration in the streets right outside, and Daley would lose standing if he couldn't stop a demonstration he considered illegal. Besides, with Kennedy in the race the Yippies realized that political militancy would serve no purpose. A peaceful rock concert, modeled on Monterey, as part of a week-long be-in was the best countercultural demonstration they could offer, and this led to second thoughts about even going to Chicago.

Jerry Rubin, despite his professed opposition to electoral politics, was thinking of running for vice president on Eldridge Cleaver's Peace and Freedom party ticket being organized in California. Abbie was also distracted: he spent much of April and May involved with the student strike at Columbia. It had begun on April 23 with a rally in front of the office of university president Grayson Kirk to protest the placing of six SDS leaders on probation for previous demonstrations. The leader of Columbia's SDS chapter was Mark Rudd, whose "action faction" believed that the student body could best be radicalized through confrontation: education would follow action. SDS demanded that the university end its support of war research and cancel its plans to expand into the adjacent black ghetto. But the issues were not as important to the action faction as action itself. By refusing ever to give ground and by upping the demands as they went along, Rudd and his comrades escalated the April 23 rally into an occupation of five of Columbia's buildings. In the seized files of Grayson Kirk the students found justification for their protests, documents proving the university's complicity with war research and the CIA.

Activists from all over the city poured onto the campus to support the students. Abbie, Anita, Jim Fouratt, and a group of Motherfuckers, as well as Tom Hayden and other out-of-town and off-campus activists, joined 150 students occupying Mathematics Hall. Hayden was elected to chair "the commune." The doors were barricaded in expectation of a police attack. Inside, as Abbie recalled, "We talked endlessly of issues and strategies, fought boredom, fought fear, got hung up on how decisions were to be made, worked out evacuation routes, laughed, made love, smoked dope, sang, argued, and waited." (Tom Hayden, in his memoir, is certain that the occupiers voted to prohibit all use of drugs.)[34] Abbie's role in the strike was to build off-campus support. The activists inside the buildings were free to come and go, and Abbie was returning to the campus from the Bob Fass show early on the morning of April 30 when the city police struck. They cleared the occupied buildings with the permission of the university administration, beating people with their clubs and arresting more than seven hundred, including Abbie, who was caught in a sweep of the campus. The students accepted arrest nonviolently, despite their militant rhetoric. The violence of the police, however, polarized the faculty and student body against the police and the administration and set off a strike that lasted for the duration of the semester. As a milepost on the road to Chicago, Columbia confirmed Abbie's belief that young people were on the brink of an explosion and that police violence would radicalize them. He still differed with SDS veterans like Hayden, however, believing that the young could be politicized more easily by cultural and lifestyle issues than by the political rhetoric of the left.

Many influential commentators shared this perception. "These youngsters," wrote a frightened editorial writer in *Fortune*, "are acting out a revolution—not a protest, and not a rebellion, but an honest-to-God revolution. They see themselves as the Che Guevaras of our society, and their intention is to seize control of the university . . . and establish . . . the redoubt from which to storm and overthrow 'bourgeois' America. This is what they say they are doing—they are the least conspiratorial and most candid of revolutionists—and this is what they *are* doing."[35] Students—it was true—were seething with anger on many college campuses. Between January and May 1968 there were ten reported burnings and bombings related to student protests against the war, five of them in Berkeley and at Stanford University, and the majority of them aimed at ROTC offices. These were the first incidents of violence against property in the history of the student left.

On June 5 Robert Kennedy was assassinated. He had just won a big victory in the California primary, and the stage was set for a convention showdown with Hubert Humphrey. Had Kennedy lived, the Yippies would likely have canceled their festival. The Mobe would have continued to be split on the issue of whether they should get involved with the dovish Democrats. Dave Dellinger would have pushed for an independent, nonviolent presence in order to keep the pressure on the politicians. Tom Hayden, Rennie Davis, and other antiwar leaders, however, would have gone to Chicago very sympathetic to Kennedy's case. As it was, with Kennedy dead, the Mobe was still undecided about its plan of action. Dellinger, Hayden, and Davis continued to plan for a demonstration without the official approval of the antiwar coalition.

Abbie took Kennedy's death as further evidence that the old order was crumbling and that the future was up for grabs if only the movement would act decisively. Emboldened by the possibilities, he was also worried about the future. It was during this period that he began to talk about building an ark on Hoving Hill, the highest mound of dirt in Tompkins Square Park. In it, Abbie said, would live two blacks, two Puerto Ricans, two orthodox Jews, two Chinese, two Ukrainians, two Poles, two hippies—two humans representing every ethnic, religious, racial, and cultural group struggling to live in the crowded tenements of the Lower East Side. There is no way of knowing whether this was just a funny rap or a serious project that Abbie didn't have time to start. For with Kennedy dead and, in the eyes of the Yippies, McCarthy no match against Hubert Humphrey, all his energy was focused on Chicago less than three months away.

In mid-July the Yippies submitted a new permit application requesting the use of Lincoln Park for a five-day "youth convocation to be known as the Festival of Life." They also asked for use of Soldiers Field on August 30. A concluding rally, they argued, would enable them to get people out of Lincoln Park and out of Chicago. The Chicago authorities, however, continued to stall, even rejecting the mediation services of Attorney General Ramsey Clark, who sent an aide, Roger Wilkins, to persuade the mayor to issue permits. Clark's sympathy for the antiwar movement (and his isolation within the Johnson administration) was another sign of a split within the Democratic party that the antiwar movement was unable to perceive, hence could not exploit.

A third group, the Coalition for an Open Convention, now announced plans to come to Chicago. Allard Lowenstein, the liberal Democrat who had first promoted the idea of running a peace candidate against Johnson, wanted to bring 100,000 McCarthy supporters to Chicago in a last-ditch effort to create a popular ground swell against the Democratic party bosses. But Daley stonewalled him, as he did the Mobe and the Yippies. Indicating an unwillingness to take his fight to the convention, McCarthy spoke of the possibility of violence in Chicago and urged his rank and file supporters to stay at home.

Within the movement, opposition to the Festival of Life also continued. The Chicago group was especially uneasy. In an open letter published in the underground press, *Seed* editor Peck took the Yippies to task for their do-your-own-thing attitude and their refusal to exercise leadership responsibility. "The New York feeling is that Yippie is a golden opportunity to shit all over the Old Men, while the Chicago ethos . . . is that a festival . . . can be carried off despite the choice of convention week, as the time for fun and frolic." City officials, Peck said, were freaked out about Yippie talk of confrontation, drugs, and fornication, and about what black youth gangs might do if encouraged by white radicals. "If you're coming to Chicago," Peck warned, "be sure to wear some armor in your hair."[36]

On August 7 Abbie, Jerry, Ed Sanders, Paul Krassner, and Richard Goldstein, a rock critic for the *New York Times* who was sympathetic to the Yippies, flew to Chicago to meet with Deputy Mayor Stahl once again. Abbie did most of the talking for the Yippies. When it became obvious that he was getting nowhere, he joked that for $200,000 he would leave town. Chicago officials didn't understand irony. They took Abbie's offer as a demand for a bribe, just as they took the Yippie vow to put LSD in the water system as a serious threat. (Although the FBI advised them that this was technologically impossible—as CIA research had shown—the police still placed guards at city pumping and filter stations to make sure that nobody dropped LSD into the water supply.) To the New Yorkers, Mayor Daley and his men were easy foils. But what was funny to them was interpreted as provocation by Daley and his staff.

After the unsuccessful meeting with Stahl, Peck and other local Yippies met with the New Yorkers and tried to persuade them to call the festival off. Acknowledging the likelihood of violence but citing his experience in the civil rights movement, Abbie argued that whatever the threat of violence, it was essential that young people take a stand against the war. He was still convinced that the city would come through with a permit. The two sides argued into the night and then got Tom Hayden out of bed to act as a mediator. Hayden agreed with Abbie that Daley would not want violence. There might be mass arrests, he allowed, but no "massacre." Dismissing Peck's fears as one hippie's "drug paranoia," he then turned against the Yippies and disparaged the idea of a festival, calling it mere entertainment, a sideshow to the Mobe's more politically focused demonstrations. Ultimately the New Yorkers agreed to cool their rhetoric and treat violence as a serious possibility.

As all this was going on, the Republicans were in Miami nominating Richard Nixon for president. As Democratic convention time neared, the Yippies, as well as the leaders of the Mobe, paid little attention to the rightward shift in the Republican party; nor did they pay much attention to George Wallace's strong showing in the opinion polls as a white supremacist third party candidate. The possibility that Wallace might attract enough white, working-class votes to elect Nixon didn't faze the radical movement. Instead of an analysis, the radicals struck an attitude. They had reluctantly supported Johnson in 1964 as the peace candidate against the warmonger Barry Goldwater, and Johnson had given them Goldwater's Vietnam policy. Never again would they vote for the "lesser of two evils."

Abbie stayed on in Chicago to prepare for the festival. Fortunately he found Rennie Davis, the Mobe's detail man, willing to share resources. Davis had opened an office, secured local housing for thirty thousand out-of-town demonstrators, and established movement centers in sympathetic churches for the different constituencies that he hoped would be coming. It was the first time that Yippies and Mobe leaders had talked seriously together since Lake Villa. With Davis's help Abbie arranged for medical and legal assistance. Mobe marshals would be stationed at Lincoln Park, where the Yippies intended to gather, as well as Grant Park, which the Mobe, still without a permit, had decided to use as its staging ground. Both groups agreed to a joint rally at the Chicago Coliseum on the night of August 27, and the Yippies would join the Mobe on its march to the convention the next day, when Humphrey was expected to be nominated.

Abbie also spent time in the streets trying to get support from black gangs and white greasers. The blacks knew that if they joined forces with the Yippies they would be vulnerable to retaliation after the Yippies (and the media) left Chicago. They knew the prejudices of the Chicago police and were content to let the white radicals absorb the punishment for a change. Abbie had more success with a local motorcycle gang called the Headhunters. They agreed to support the Yippies in Lincoln Park. The Chicago hippies, in the meanwhile, braced for trouble. "Chicago may host a Festival of Blood," warned the *Seed*. "The cops will riot."

In Chicago, Abbie wrote the first and only Yippie schedule ever published and distributed it to the press under the heading "Daring Exposé: Top Secret Plans for Lincoln Park." Mixing the serious with the absurd, it was a last-ditch attempt to put a light, nonconfrontational spin on the Yippie concept. August 26, for example, would include workshops on drug problems, underground communication, guerrilla theater, self-defense, communes, and draft resistance. In the afternoon there would be a beach party at the lake with singing, barbecues, swimming, and lovemaking. On the morning of August 28 there would be Yippie olympics with a Miss Yippie contest and "normal and healthy games" such as catch the candidate, pin the tail on the donkey, and pin the rubber on the pope, followed in the afternoon by a Mobe rally at Grant Park and a march to the convention. Abbie drew a map of Lincoln Park divided into three sections: Free City, where people would camp and eat; Future City, the site of the festival itself; and Drop City, with a special site set aside for bikers. The schedule was pure fantasy. Except for the Mobe's march on the convention, nothing had been organized.

By August 20 the Yippie leaders were all in Chicago. There was still no permit, and most of the bands and theater groups had pulled out. Abbie and Jerry were also feuding. Many activists who supported Yippie had taken sides in their feud as the rhetoric evolved and the lack of planning became apparent. Abbie was still viewed as the softy who wanted a counterculture festival, while Jerry was perceived as wanting to use the festival to lure kids to a confrontation. In the broadest sense those images were true. Abbie did have a more creative vision of Chicago and was willing to embrace other scenarios besides confrontation. On the other hand, he was not one to shy away from a battle with the police, if that was what Mayor Daley wanted. With protesters gathering in Chicago, the two Yippies argued about what their responsibility was to be as leaders. Jerry argued that having gotten the demonstration off the ground, the leaders should obey their own rhetoric and disappear into the crowd. Despite all he had said about the virtues of leaderlessness, Abbie now argued that leadership was needed. Whatever happened in the coming week would be a form of guerrilla theater, and they had to take responsibility for doing it right.

The Mobe was in a similar state of uncertainty. Dellinger and Hayden, the most visible leaders, were presenting conflicting visions of what the demonstrations in Chicago would be. To liberal audiences, Hayden was calling for a reconciliation with rank and file Democratic doves. He wanted to bring experienced organizers to Chicago to recruit the disillusioned McCarthy forces into the radical fold. To the radicals, however, Hayden was pushing for a confrontation with the Daley forces as a way of exposing the bankruptcy of the Democratic party. Dellinger was caught in the middle of the contradictory positions. He, too, was determined to reach out to the doves and wanted peaceful demonstrations to attract liberal participation. On the other hand, with the Pentagon action as his model, he was equally determined to pursue—separate and apart from the peaceful legal rallies—a more confrontational strategy based on disciplined nonviolence. Dellinger's problem was that he still saw militant action as nonviolent action, whereas most of the young people involved in both the Mobe and the Yippies had given up on nonviolence. In actuality the Mobe leaders, like the Yippies, could try to set a tactical tone, but they had no real way of controlling their followers.

On August 22 the Yippies joined the Mobe and the Lowenstein group in going to court to get a permit on the basis of First Amendment rights. The presiding federal judge was William Lynch, a crony and former law partner of Mayor Daley. When the judge rejected the permit application of Lowenstein's Coalition for an Open Convention, the Yippies withdrew their suit. They then held a press conference in which Abbie stated that they had no more faith in orderly, legal procedures: "We saw Lynch and we got lynched. We saw Stahl and we got Stahled." Abbie then issued a list of eighteen Yippie demands, written the night before, which constituted the only Yippie platform ever drafted. His frequent interjection of the word *fuck* to spice up the reading ruined the session for television use, however. Abbie had blown the media opportunity. But by this time the Yippies, as well as the Mobe, were so caught up in the drama with Mayor Daley that they had lost sight of the national audience and the noble purpose to which their plans had been directed.

Two days later, with the convention about to begin, a Gallup poll reported that 53 percent of the American public thought that sending troops to Vietnam had been a mistake. In 1966 opposition to the war had never exceeded 25 percent of the population. In two short years the antiwar movement had split the Democratic party and was winning the battle for public opinion.

CHAPTER

7 | CHICAGO

August 1968

In his own stolid, unflinching way Mayor Richard Daley proved himself as adept a director of political theater as Abbie Hoffman and Jerry Rubin. His promise that the police would shoot to kill, the police assaults on peaceful demonstrators, the harassment of local hippies, and his refusal to negotiate permits with either the liberal Committee for an Open Convention or the Yippies and the Mobe effectively conveyed the message that (the Bill of Rights be damned!) demonstrations would not be tolerated in Chicago during the Democratic convention. The Yippies' manipulation of the media and the Mobe's extensive contacts with antiwar organizations could not counter the ominous message coming out of Chicago. "There is no doubt," a team of journalists who reported on the 1968 election concluded, "that a hundred thousand marchers could have been assembled in Chicago had it not been for one factor: the increasingly belligerent and obstructive temper exhibited by Mayor Daley's administration."[1] Because of that one factor, only about five thousand activists turned out for Chicago.

The decisive fact of Chicago was that the mayor frightened followers of both the Mobe and the Yippies away. It was a measure of the Yippies' failure that very few young people showed up in Chicago. No more than one or two thousand ever gathered at Lincoln Park for the Festival of Life, and many of these were local youths who were curious about the Yippies. The movement's main effort, a rally at Grant Park the day Hubert Humphrey was nominated, brought out the largest number of protesters, ten thousand at most. But aside from the locals, many of these were McCarthy supporters; others were undercover police. According to the *Chicago*

Tribune, there were a thousand federal agents on the scene when the convention began. The Chicago police department's intelligence unit, or "red squad," even had an agent in the inner circles of the Mobe, and CBS News later reported a military intelligence claim that one out of every six demonstrators was working for the government.[2] With fifty-six hundred national guardsmen backed by six thousand regular army troops armed with M1s, carbines, shotguns, tear gas, and gas masks, in support of twelve thousand Chicago police, and the thousand or so undercover agents, Daley had the city firmly under his control.

Both the Yippie and Mobe leaders were tailed by plainclothes police twenty-four hours a day. Abbie got to know his tails and even hitched rides with them to and from Lincoln Park. A hulking undercover investigator on the staff of the state attorney's office named Robert Pierson, posing as a member of the Headhunter motorcycle gang, volunteered to act as Jerry Rubin's bodyguard. Jerry considered this to be evidence that the white working class was sympathetic to Yippie aims and was thrilled. Recalling the efforts of Ken Kesey, Allen Ginsberg, and his own Berkeley Vietnam Day Committee to recruit the Hell's Angels, Jerry considered Pierson a coup. Pierson also tried to gain Abbie's confidence, but Abbie, who liked to operate at demonstrations on his own, didn't give Pierson any time.

From government intelligence, including FBI monitoring of bus, plane, and train bookings to Chicago, Mayor Daley knew that his strategy had worked even before the convention began. Daley could have given the protesters the use of Lincoln Park for the entire week of the convention and easily contained them far from the downtown hotel district and the convention center. But the mayor, his police, and indeed many Chicagoans despised and feared everything that they imagined the demonstrators represented. To many Chicagoans, the followers of the Yippies and the Mobe were indistinguishable. They were hippies, beatniks, dope fiends, commies, perverts: the long-haired men and boys an insult to everything manly and patriotic; the women and girls both threatening and alluring in their violation of what Chicagoans considered feminine and therefore good. To Daley and his followers, the demonstrators were the barbarians at the gate. He was not going to allow them to encamp in his city.

The Yippies, for their part, were quite willing to polarize the

1. Abbie's mother, Florence, thought he was pretending to be Elvis Presley. More likely he was posing as either Pete Seeger or Woody Guthrie, the left-wing folksingers he first heard during his Brandeis years. Courtesy of Anita Hoffman.

2. Pitching softball during the early 1960s when Abbie was a staff psychologist at the state-run mental institution in Worcester. Courtesy of Anita Hoffman.

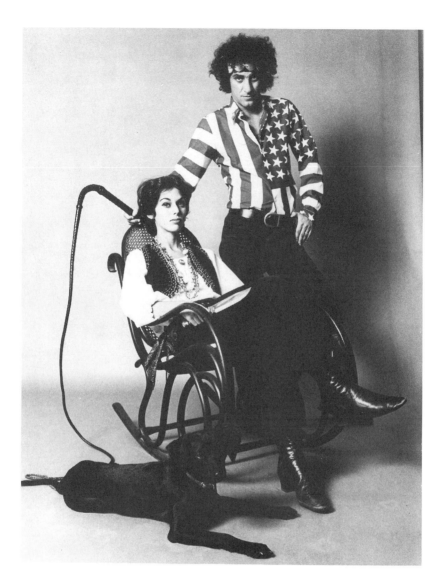

3. Anita and Abbie Hoffman pose for a 1969 issue of *Eye* magazine, a now-defunct Hearst publication aimed at the youth market. Photo by George Rosenblatt, courtesy of Anita Hoffman.

4. Anita and Abbie reach out to each other during the Yip-in, Grand Central Station, New York, March 1968. The Hoffmans tried to act as peacemakers with the police, but Abbie was later clubbed to the ground. Photo copyright by Fred W. McDarrah.

5. Abbie, Dave Dellinger, and Jerry Rubin in front of the Federal Courthouse in New York, March 22, 1969, the day of their conspiracy indictment for the Chicago demonstrations. Lawyers William Kunstler (left)

and Gerry Lefcourt (right) are with them as, in the background, are members of the Black Panther party protesting the indictment of Bobby Seale. Photo copyright by Maury Englander.

6. Abbie, Jerry Rubin, and friends in the Hoffmans' St. Marks Place apartment watch TV news of their conspiracy indictments. Photo copyright by Fred W. McDarrah.

7. Abbie and Jerry Rubin were forbidden by the rally organizers to speak at the huge Washington, D.C., Moratorium against the Vietnam War, November 15, 1969. Here they flank Dave Dellinger who is announcing a march on the Justice Department to protest the Conspiracy Trial. John Froines, another Chicago Eight defendant, stands between Dellinger and Hoffman. Photo copyright by Diana Davies/Insight.

8. Abbie speaks at a Black Panther rally at Yale University, May 1, 1970. The United States had just invaded Cambodia and Bobby Seale and other Panther leaders were on trial for murder in a New Haven court. They were ultimately acquitted. Photo copyright by Fred W. McDarrah.

9. Abbie in Central Park, 1980, with Joanna Lawrenson, his "running mate" and co-founder of "Save the River." Photo copyright by Harry Benson.

10. Abbie and his son america at a Naropa Institute conference on peace-
making in Boulder, Colorado, summer 1986. Photo copyright by Allen
Ginsberg.

11. Abbie sporting an Oliver North "American Zero" button at an April 1987 demonstration in Washington, D.C., protesting American intervention in Central America. Photo copyright by Allen Ginsberg.

12. Johanna Lawrenson and Abbie at the courthouse in Northampton, Massachusetts, in April 1987 when Abbie, Amy Carter, and a group of University of Massachusetts students put the CIA on trial and won. Photo copyright by Diana Davies/Insight.

public over cultural contrasts; the distinction between hip and straight was, after all, the basis of their politics. They wanted to contrast the hip culture with the American way of life, but they didn't fully appreciate that in challenging the way people lived—in making culture the cutting issue—they were attacking people's identity and deeply wounding them. The Yippies' frame of reference was national and global. "'Vietnam'" as Farber wrote, "*was, by and large, more real to them than the lives of their neighbors.*"[3] In confusing their own national agenda with Chicago's local response, they saw Mayor Daley as simply a stand-in for the Johnson administration, and the ferocity of the police as symbolic of American policy in Vietnam.

There were few innocents in the movement's muster. The cultural radicals who gathered at Lincoln Park (like the straighter Mobe supporters meeting at Grant Park) represented the movement's hard core. Veterans of the Pentagon march, of campus strikes and sit-ins, and of the mobile street tactics used in New York and Berkeley, they came to Chicago prepared for the worst. A small minority, including the Motherfuckers and some of the more militant SDS action-factions, had formed affinity groups and come prepared to deliberately provoke the police and harass the delegates (although the worst weapons in their arsenal were stink bombs). The majority of the demonstrators, while expecting violence and prepared to withstand it, were not predisposed to provoke it. Many activists were critical of both the Mobe and the Yippies for the way Chicago had been organized, but came as a kind of existential witness. They sensed that history was going to be made. Although they disagreed with what the movement leaders were doing, they still felt the need to be a part of it; their identities were wrapped up in the movement's past as well as its future, and they had to stand by their comrades in what promised to be a decisive test.

The movement was no longer united on the question of tactical nonviolence. Dellinger could call for nonviolence, but he lacked the authority to compel it. The Mobe had recruited a volunteer group of marshals to keep a semblance of discipline, but many of the demonstrators, especially among the Yippies, were hostile to the idea of marshals and would refuse, almost on principle, to heed their advice. In addition the marshals were poorly trained and had a contradictory mandate. On the one hand they were supposed to keep the demonstrators orderly and minimize the possibility of confrontations with the police; on the other hand they were being taught, in public workshops, provocative tactics like snake dancing and karate. At one training session Abbie himself led them through a workshop in karate. Abbie knew no karate and treated the workshop as a theatrical farce, but the undercover agents and the reporters who were watching assumed that the marshals were serious, however inept.

While the Mobe, with its marshals, created an illusion of organizational authority, the Yippies were committed to their concept of a do-your-own-thing demonstration. Despite the agenda that Abbie had printed, the Yippies had very little actually scheduled for Lincoln Park. In such a power vacuum the initiative for action easily passed to those groups—like the Motherfuckers and the various SDS action-factions—who came to Chicago determined to create their own theater. They were intent, as usual, on provoking the police, on the assumption that police brutality would radicalize the demonstrators and propel the movement in a more leftward and revolutionary direction.

★   ★   ★

In the early morning hours of Thursday, August 22, three days before the convention opened, the police stopped two teenage hippies near Lincoln Park. One of them, a seventeen-year-old native American from South Dakota named Dean Johnson, allegedly pulled a gun. Police said that he attempted to shoot them but his gun misfired and, in a defensive reaction, the police opened fire and killed him with three shots. Abbie was at the *Seed* office, talking to some CBS reporters, when word of the killing reached him. "He flung himself around the *Seed* office banging tables and smashing his fist into walls and pillars," wrote David Stein, a young newsman covering the Yippies for a Canadian newspaper. "Abbie looked stunned. . . . 'Don't let them kill no more people. We've got to stop them killing our people,'" Stein reported him saying.[4] Whether Dean Johnson had come to Chicago for the demonstrations or was even a supporter of the Yippies was not known, but the Yippies adopted him as one of their own.

The killing momentarily sobered the Yippies. At a planning meeting that night they came to a consensus, as Stew Albert put it, to "keep it light, lots of laughs." Ed Sanders was the most vehement in warning against provocative behavior. "There's going to be thousands of people there during the day, all grooving and listening to rock bands, but at eleven o'clock, the cop blows his whistle and there's only a couple of hundred left. They all go into karate stances and they all get snorkeled. What's the sense in that?" Abbie, who earlier had vowed "to die for my right to sleep in the park," now seemed willing to drop sleeping in the park as a confrontational issue. But in the back of his mind was the idea that if the Yippies could create a permanent presence by sleeping in the park, the festival, no matter how haphazardly it was put together, would take shape and draw more people to Chicago so that by Wednesday, the day that Humphrey was to be nominated and the Mobe planned to march to the convention center, the Yippies would have a stronger presence.

At the same meeting the Yippies decided to conduct a memorial service for Dean Johnson in Lincoln Park and to link it to the Soviet invasion of Czechoslovakia, which had begun a week earlier. Keith Lampe made the memorial service his project and went to Tom Neuman, a leader of the Motherfuckers, for assistance. None of the key Yippies appeared as speakers at the service, and Neuman, a convincing speaker, downplayed the distant Soviet invasion in order to focus the crowd's anger on the immediate issue of the Chicago police. Johnson's death, he concluded, was a result of "pig poisoning."[5]*

As we have seen, the metaphor of the pig figured prominently in Yippie plans. Recalling how political cartoonists often used a pig to portray political greed and corruption, the Yippies decided to nominate a pig, named Pigasus, for president. The Hog Farm, a New Mexico hippie commune, was asked to supply the pig and also to provide security, medical services, and food for the campers at Lincoln Park. The leader of the Hog Farm was a former beat poet named Hugh Romney, who in the late 1950s and early 1960s had been known in Greenwich Village for his coffeehouse poetry readings that bordered on stand-up comedy. When the hippie movement gathered steam, Romney transformed himself into a zany,

* To be sure, a great majority of the demonstrators were sympathetic to Czechoslovakia. The Yippies considered the "Prague spring" that had preceded the Soviet invasion as another manifestation of an international youth rebellion, and they interpreted the Soviet reaction in generational terms, as the authoritarian Old Left cracking down on youth.

Red Skelton-like hippie character named Wavy Gravy, moved to New Mexico, and started the commune. Under his benign direction the Hog Farm began to perform Digger-like support services for hippie gatherings throughout the country. The Hog Farmers were competent organizers, as well as pranksters. Their presence in Chicago would have provided the Festival of Life with a positive model of countercultural communal values. But without permits, fearing violence, and getting mixed messages about the goals of the festival from Abbie and Jerry, the Hog Farmers refused to come. In their absence the symbol of the pig took on the Black Panthers' more sinister connotation.

The Black Panther party began as a self-defense organization in the Oakland ghetto in order to protect black residents from the local police. Controlled by the right-wing political leader and newspaper publisher William Knowland, Oakland was notorious as a racist city, with a police force recruited from the white South. The Panthers patrolled the Oakland streets carrying, as they were legally entitled to carry, unconcealed weapons. When police arrested or harassed a black person, the Panthers came on the scene to assure that the police respected the person's legal rights. Depending on one's politics, the Panthers were an impressive or a fearful sight. With the decline of SNCC, white radicals of Abbie's generation had no black organization to which they could relate. The Panthers filled that vacuum. White radicals expressed their support for the Panthers, not only by supporting those arrested and put on trial after spectacular shoot-outs with police, but by copying Panther rhetoric, especially their vilification of the police as "pigs."

The Yippies, of course, felt that they had reason to make an issue of the police. San Francisco police had had a heavy hand in destroying the psychedelic community of Haight-Ashbury, and even in the East Village (where Inspector Fink was a moderating influence) the police invaded hippie communal crash pads and harassed longhairs on the streets. Elsewhere in the country, where hippies were more isolated, police were often more brutal. Hippies traveling almost anywhere could expect to be stopped and searched by state and local police simply because of the way they looked. Hippies, at first, gave flowers to the police in an attempt to neutralize their hostility and perhaps win some over. But flower power wilted under the weight of police assaults and the heavy movement rhetoric. The more political activists were the first to pick up the

Panthers' parlance and start calling cops "pigs." The politically oriented underground papers followed, and the hippies adopted the usage. But calling police officers pigs eroded the moral high ground that was vital for the movement's success. It made a mockery of the humanistic values that both the hippies and the New Left radicals professed to believe. And in making local police the target, it distracted the focus from more important issues of war and peace, enmeshing the antiwar movement in the explosively complex issues of neighborhood, culture, class, and race in which the clarity of the original goal was lost.

Abbie understood that the movement communicated to the public in symbolic flashes, and he knew that a crowd of demonstrators calling policemen pigs carried an emotional charge that would offend many Americans. Offensive language was part of his repertoire, however. Concerned more about reaching young people than he was about communicating with their mothers and fathers, he was always willing to exploit profanity. As a product of the 1950s he tended to see profanity as a liberating experience. Yet he was clearly uneasy about the use of the word *pig* and other rhetorical forms of cop baiting. It's significant that many of the people who knew Abbie during this period do not recall his calling cops pigs. "It was not original, it was not creative, it was not the kind of thing that Abbie would say," Anita Hoffman remembers. And Abbie himself often tried to distance himself from its use. During the conspiracy trial, when Abbie took the stand to defend the Yippies in Chicago, he insisted that he called policemen "cheese" (the "big cheese" is what authority figures were sometimes called in grade B Hollywood movies) rather than pigs.

> PROSECUTING ATTORNEY SCHULTZ: Isn't it a fact that you announced publicly a plan to kidnap the head pig?
>
> HOFFMAN: Cheese, wasn't it?
>
> SCHULTZ:—and then snuff him—
>
> HOFFMAN: I thought it was cheese.
>
> SCHULTZ:—and then snuff him if other policemen touched you? Isn't that a fact, sir?
>
> HOFFMAN: I do not believe that I used the reference of "pig" to any policemen in Chicago including some of the top cheeses. I did not use it during that week.[6]

Up until the period of Chicago, Anita Hoffman's recollection is a true one. But in Chicago, and more so in its aftermath, as Abbie's anger at the system overwhelmed the faith in humanity that was at the source of his creativity, his rhetoric descended to the level of demagogic cop baiting that, at Chicago, became standard for the movement.

★   ★   ★

The Yippies planned to kick off the festival on the Friday before convention week by introducing their presidential candidate at a rally at the Chicago Civic Center. Abbie and Anita had gone outside Chicago with a young Yippie from the surrounding rural area and bought a small pig at a farm auction—one that, Abbie felt, would be easy to handle. Symptomatic of their conflict, Jerry Rubin decided that Abbie's pig was too cute. The politically correct pig, he argued, had to be big and ugly; so he and his allies within Yippie drove out to a pig farm and bought one that was appropriately more fearsome-looking. The media were gathering in Chicago waiting for the convention to open, and the Yippies knew that their nominating a pig for president would make a good, visual television news story. Jerry was holding his pig and delivering its nominating speech for president when a squadron of police cars and paddy wagons roared up to the Civic Center. "Grab Rubin," a plainclothesman shouted, and then Jerry, the folkinger Phil Ochs, and five other Yippies were arrested while Pigasus was taken to an animal shelter. The whole event lasted five minutes, but the Yippies could not have scripted it any better. From that point on the media tended to describe all demonstrators as Yippies, while casting the Yippies as pranksters and the police as the humorless heavies.

That night Abbie went to the Electric Circus hoping to persuade Country Joe McDonald, who had a gig at the nightclub, to stay in Chicago and play at Lincoln Park on Sunday. Along with the Fugs, Country Joe and the Fish was the acid rock band most identified with antiwar politics. Testifying for the defense at the conspiracy trial, Country Joe recalled that "I said to Abbie, no, I was not going to be in the Festival because the vibrations in the town were so incredibly vicious that I felt it was impossible to avoid violence on the part of the police and authorities in Chicago." Country Joe also requested that the band's "symbolic support of the Festival . . . be withdrawn" out of concern that fans would "be clubbed and Maced and tear gassed by the police and that the possibility of anything positive or loving or good coming out of that city at that time was impossible." Returning to their hotel after playing their gig and talking with Abbie, McDonald, and David Cohen, the band's organist, were assaulted in the elevator by three men with crew cuts. The next day the band left Chicago.

On Saturday the Yippies opened their headquarters in Lincoln Park. About two thousand people hung out on what was a warm summer day, playing guitars, singing, smoking marijuana, and lounging about. It was, in the language of the time, a mellow scene. When a chemistry student from San Francisco volunteered to bake cookies laced with honey and hashish, Abbie found him an apartment to work in, and the next day many Yippies were too stoned to do anything but lie on the grass and enjoy their reveries. Surprisingly, the police made no attempt to arrest people for openly smoking marijuana. And the popularity of the honey cookies was evidence that given a choice, most Yippies would rather get stoned than fight.

The Yippies held their last formal meeting at the Free Theater across from Lincoln Park late Saturday afternoon. The day in the park had put Abbie in a more defiant mood, and again he argued that they should hold the park. Even if there were no permits and thus no rock bands, "there's going to be bands of people," Abbie vowed—"fifty or sixty people in a band going out from the park to loot and pillage if they close it up at eleven." Ed Sanders was furious at this outburst. "I'm getting sick and tired of hearing people talk like that. I don't want some kid who hasn't been through it all and doesn't know what it's all about going to get his head busted. You're urging people to go out and get killed for nothing. Man, that's like murdering people."

Allen Ginsberg had arrived at the park Saturday afternoon. He had flown to Chicago to act as a calming influence. He had publicly endorsed the Festival of Life and felt a responsibility to offer non-violent leadership.[7] Ginsberg supported Sanders, and so did Paul Krassner. Ginsberg pulled weight with the Yippies; he was the elder statesman, and they needed his support to give their idea of a politicized counterculture credibility. Abbie and Jerry thus agreed to a Yippie statement accepting the eleven o'clock curfew and the ban on sleeping in the park. But they would not give up their militant rhetoric. "The cops want to turn our parks into graveyards," they wrote in a joint statement drafted independently of the more moderate statements of Ginsberg, Sanders, and Krassner. "But we, not them, will decide when the battle begins. . . . Leave the park as small groups and do what is necessary," they advised. "Make them pay for kicking us out of the park."[8]

There was one stranger at the Yippie meeting. He was straight-looking, and everyone assumed that he was a cop. Abbie pointed him out and said, "We are all cops here. The cops know all our plans. We're going to put LSD in the water supply. Right?" Everyone laughed, and the meeting broke up.

In the weekend edition of the *Chicago American*, the tabloid's featured columnist Jack Mabley published what he claimed were the Yippies' actual plans for Chicago. They included spreading "guerrilla nails"—boards full of three-inch spikes—on the expressway to tie up traffic; seizing gas stations, opening the pumps, and flooding sewers with gasoline in order to torch the city; blowing up natural gas lines serving the city; posing as restaurant workers and poisoning or putting drugs into the food of the delegates; forging convention credentials to infiltrate saboteurs into the convention hall; painting cars to look like taxis and kidnapping delegates; posing as hookers who would spike delegates' drinks with LSD; jamming police and all media communications, as well as blowing up the control tower at O'Hare Airport; and hijacking gasoline trucks and aiming them, motors running and in gear, at police stations and hotels. Threats to the convention site itself, Mabley wrote, included putting gas into the air conditioning system, shelling the site with mortars from several miles away, storming it with a mob, cutting the power and phone lines. . . . "These are just some of the threats," Mabley concluded. "Every one of these has been printed or mimeographed and has been circulated among militants. How many other sophisticated schemes of sabotage exist may only be imagined." In actuality, only the LSD and taxi stories were the products of the Yippies' tongue-in-cheek imagination. Likely, Mabley got his "facts" from an article in *Saga*, a blood and guts men's magazine that had published an article allegedly exposing Yippie plans. The article was written under the byline "Malcolm W," whom *Saga* identified as a member of the black power underground. This anonymous author cited, as his source for the Yippie plans, Rennie Davis, identifying Davis as "a native of Panama" and a leading black militant. At the time, Mabley was paying a young student to infiltrate the Mobe (and so should have known what everyone else who watched the news on television knew: Davis was white). Dwayne Oklepek, Mabley's plant, understood Yippie humor and knew that the demonstrators' preparations were nonexistent. But the joke got out of hand. Mabley's column was farther off the mark than most, but it typified the slanted way some local journalists covered the demonstrations. In slavishly attempting to justify Daley's military buildup, he bought into a myth that, in its preposterous but menacing detail, truly frightened the city.[9]

There were fewer than one thousand people in Lincoln Park Saturday night when police moved in to clear it. Ginsberg, with Sanders by his side, led the Yippies out. They were chanting "om," and it seemed to be having a calming effect. Forced out of the park and into the streets, however, the activists quickly saw an alternative. No movement leader had to encourage or explain it. Since Berkeley's Stop the Draft Week in October 1967, mobile tactics had become the radicals' tactics of choice—written about, analyzed, and practiced in at least a dozen demonstrations in New York and the Bay Area. The Chicago police were apparently unaware of this, however. Prepared to protect the water system from LSD, they were not prepared to control the demonstrators once they were driven out of the park. By refusing to let a few hundred hippies sleep in the park, where they could easily have been contained, the police opened the entire downtown area of the city to the one kind of disruptive tactics the activists knew how to use effectively. For a few hours demonstrators ran through the streets, and the police chased them. With sirens blasting, the police created a spectacle of a full-blown riot. But there was little property damage, and the only injuries were to the demonstrators and bystanders whom policemen caught and clubbed.

Two thousand people gathered at the park on Sunday afternoon for what was supposed to be the official opening of the Yippie festival. Police were everywhere, as were journalists and photographers. The presence of so many reporters robbed the gathering of its spontaneity. Although Abbie, Jerry, and the other Yippie leaders delighted in jousting with the press, the rank and file demonstrators were totally unprepared for such intense public scrutiny. The primary interest of the media was the potential for trouble.

With the situation itself so explosive the media made it even more volatile by interpreting everything that the Yippies did in terms of how provocative it might be to the police.

Despite the tension, Abbie and Ed Sanders were determined to stage the festival. On Sunday morning they went to Lincoln Park and organized a first aid area, opened a rudimentary free store, hung balloons from the trees, and set up a stage for the few theater groups and rock bands that were still willing to play. In addition to local bands these included MC5, hard rockers from Detroit associated with the White Panthers (a Yippie-like group organized in the Motor City by poet/radical John Sinclair); Jim and Jean, a folk duo who were longtime friends of Phil Ochs and popular in Greenwich Village; the Fugs; and the Pageant Players, a guerrilla theater group from the East Village. The police, however, continued to set up obstacles. Abbie had rented a flatbed truck for a stage, but the police refused to allow it into the park. When MC5 began playing on the grass, the police cut off their power supply. In the ensuing confusion Abbie tried to get the truck into the park. The police blocked it, and the Yippies surrounded the police. While Abbie was negotiating with officials about the truck, police began to make arrests. Some in the crowd began taunting, "Pigs eat shit!" Others shouted "Prague! Prague!" a reference to the suppression in Czechoslovakia. Still others sat in the grass and began to sing "My Country, 'Tis of Thee." The police lashed back, calling the Yippies "fags" and telling them to go back where they came from. A few people—possibly but not necessarily police agents—threw bottles and stones, and the police then waded into the crowd using their batons to push and hit people. (As in every confrontation during this week in Chicago, there is no way of knowing whether the instigators of violence were protesters or government agents; even if undercover agents did instigate violence, they never lacked for followers from the demonstrators' ranks.) Stew Albert, evidently targeted as a Yippie leader, was clubbed by blackjack-wielding undercover police, and the Yippies' supply of bullhorns and walkie-talkies was destroyed. Abbie continued talking with the police, arguing that the Yippies had a legal right to be in the park until eleven o'clock and demanding, sarcastically, that the police wait at least until the curfew before they attacked. To reduce the possibility of further violence, he then led a couple of hundred people, followed by a crowd of reporters, to a nearby baseball diamond for what he called "a workshop in dispersal tactics." Meanwhile Allen

Ginsberg sat down in the park and began chanting "om." People gathered around him and the chanting continued, with Ginsberg leading, for seven hours. That night, as Ginsberg and his group chanted, other Yippies gathered around campfires. Abbie went around to each campfire urging people to create affinity groups and stick together when the police expelled them from the park. A lot of people, especially the male teenagers, wanted to fight for the park, but Abbie discouraged them. Mobe marshals were also urging people to leave the park, but others were countering their advice and shouting, "Fuck the marshals!"

Shortly before the curfew the police attack began. It was led by a special jeep fitted with barbed wire in front. Behind it marched the police, throwing tear gas and clubbing those who were slow in getting away. Ginsberg, still chanting, tried to keep people calm. Again, the demonstrators retreated into adjacent streets. This time the police, prepared for mobile tactics, closed off the streets outside the park to traffic and forced the people leaving the park to stay behind barricades lining the sidewalk. It was an eerie sight lit up by police searchlights. Blue-and-white squad cars raced up and down, their wailing sirens setting off a cacophonous chorus of angry and contradictory chants: "Pigs! Pigs!" "Peace Now!" "End the War." "Zieg Heil!" Meanwhile battalions of helmeted policemen, most of whom had removed their name tags, were pushing and swearing at the crowds, seizing individuals and beating them with their clubs as they pulled them past the barricades and into the street. The demonstrators broke out of this trap by splitting into two groups and running in the only directions open to them: south toward the hotel district (the Loop) and west through Old Town. The police gave chase, clubbing anyone they could catch, including residents of the area, members of the press, and white-coated medics who had volunteered to help the demonstrators. The group heading toward the Loop was scattered by police reinforcements, who blocked off a drawbridge over the Chicago River. The group running through Old Town broke up as individuals ducked into buildings, down alleys, and into side streets to escape the rampaging police.

Thus the battle was joined. Jerry Rubin was ecstatic at the sight of a few thousand young people provoking the police into a reaction that the situation did not warrant. Many of the veteran demonstrators understood immediately that the police in their zeal had made a strategic error that could easily be exploited. The activists had lost the park but gained the city! If they could create enough of a disruption within the city proper, they could provoke Mayor Daley into declaring martial law, so that the Democratic convention would have to be held under totalitarian conditions. And that, they considered, would be a great Yippie victory.

Abbie shared this perspective. He figured that the city would realize its mistake and give the Yippies a permit if only to get them back into the park. Late that night, after the streets had quieted, he phoned David Stahl, pleading with him to allow the Yippies to sleep in the park. He was astonished that the city still refused. "The decision to drive people out of the park in order to protect the City was about the dumbest military tactic since the Trojans let the Trojan horse inside the gate, and there was nothing to be compared with that stupidity," he recalled saying to Stahl.[10]

On Monday morning the Yippies, and many demonstrators who had come to Chicago with the Mobe, again gathered in Lincoln Park. The police arrested Tom Hayden and Wolfe Lowenthal for letting air out of a squad car's tires, and Abbie went to the Central Police Station to check on their status. Rennie Davis, with the help of Mobe marshals, organized a march to the police station as well. The march was peaceful, and Davis negotiated with city leaders every step of the way. After the march he led demonstrators to Grant Park across from the Hilton Hotel, where many delegates were staying and the television networks had put their cameras. There he established a picket line. As night fell and it seemed as if the police were mobilizing to chase the picketers out of Grant Park, Davis told people to break up into small groups and return to Lincoln Park. There, about three thousand demonstrators were already assembled, waiting to see what move the police would make at the curfew hour. Present also was a group of eighty clergy and laymen from local churches who were holding a prayer service behind a makeshift eight-foot cross in support of the demonstrators' right to be in the park. Abbie, along with other veteran organizers, again walked through the crowd urging everyone to leave peacefully, but again many wanted to stay. One group built a barricade of trash cans and park benches. At eleven o'clock, the police moved two thousand of the demonstrators out of the park and into the streets without disorder, but another thousand stayed to defend the barricade. The police attacked this barricade behind a barrage of tear gas and smoke grenades. Two fire trucks, stationed in their rear, lit the demonstrator's positions. Again, the demonstrators retreated from the park and ran through the streets. That night the Democratic convention opened. Greeting the delegates, Mayor Daley proclaimed that the Democratic party welcomed protest and dissent but not people who "seek to destroy instead of build . . . who would make a mockery of our institutions and values." [11]

★   ★   ★

On Tuesday Abbie set out for the park early, hitching a ride with his police tails. Allen Ginsberg was leading a sunrise service on the beach in Lincoln Park. Abbie joined them for an hour of prayer, chanting, and meditation, after which the participants took turns expressing their feelings about the meaning of the festival and the violence of the police. Abbie said that their ceremony was very beautiful but it wouldn't be shown on the television news because the mass media were a glutton for violence, which was the only thing that would be reported. "America can't be changed by people sitting and praying, and this is an unfortunate reality that we have to face," he said. He went on to blame the police for destroying the festival and vowed that he would "never again tell people to sit quietly and pray for change."

After the service Abbie went down to Mobe headquarters to talk with Davis. A press conference was underway, and Abbie expressed amazement at the "stupidity" of the police in driving "city yippies out into the streets . . . when if they were allowed to sleep in the rural area, you know, the park, the way we want to, and establish our community . . . everything would be cool." [12]

Abbie next went to the Free Theater, which had a courtyard where many Yippies had taken refuge. The scene reminded him of an American Revolutionary War encampment. Some demonstrators had bandages on their heads. Some were cooking hot dogs over little fires or were stretched out in their clothes sleeping; others sat with groups in circles, talking quietly and singing folk songs. A group of police entered the courtyard, and Abbie challenged them to produce a warrant, insisting that this was private property. Then he addressed the encampment, telling them that this was like Valley Forge, that what they were engaged in was a second American revolution, and that the battle for Lincoln Park was their Lexington and Concord.

Later in the day Abbie sat under a tree in Lincoln Park and conducted a workshop on the media and politics. He talked about using the advertising principles of Madison Avenue to change political consciousness, and about conning reporters, manipulating the media, staging monkey theater, and outwitting the cops. He kept coming back to the challenge of political organizing in the electronic age. Instead of organizing individuals, he wanted to use television as a shortcut to "educate" the viewing public en masse. He would excite its imagination with bold, flashy images rather than provide dull and didactic information. "The problem with the left," he said, "is that there are ten thousand socialist scholars in this country and not one fuckin' socialist. I mean I talk to guys on the *Guardian* [a left-wing newspaper] and they say yeah, we're working on a serious analysis of the Yippies. I say, that's pretty fuckin' cool, man, that's great. By that time there won't be any Yippies. I mean what the fuck are you analyzin' for, man, get in and do it." [13]

That evening Jerry Rubin introduced Bobby Seale, the chairman of the Black Panther party, who had flown to Chicago from Oakland to make one speech in Lincoln Park. Jerry's first choice had been Eldridge Cleaver, the nationally known author of *Soul on Ice*. Eldridge and Kathleen Cleaver had been scheduled to talk but because of Eldridge's bail restrictions (he was on parole at the time from San Quentin prison), they could not make the trip. Seale, who had had virtually no previous contact with the antiwar movement outside the Bay Area, advocated, in the inflamed language that was characteristic of Panthers, armed self-defense but was carefully obscure about actual violence. "If a pig comes up to us and starts swinging a billy club and you check around and you got your piece—you gotta down that pig in defense of yourself." He also said, "The strongest weapon that we have is all of us. . . . What we gotta do is functionally put ourselves in organizations." For the white radicals in Lincoln Park, Seale's presence validated their sense of revolutionary purpose. The leader of the Black Panthers had flown halfway across the country to talk revolution with *them*. This was proof that the Panthers were willing to take whites seriously, and the whites were determined to uphold their end of the alliance.

Abbie did not hear Seale speak and, in fact, had never met him. He, instead, was at Lyndon Johnson's "un-birthday party," a rally that the Yippies and the Mobe were cosponsoring at the Chicago Coliseum, an old and decrepit auditorium near the Loop. Six thousand people gathered there to hear Dick Gregory, Dave Dellinger, Jean Genet, and William Burroughs. Ed Sanders, the emcee, read a statement from Allen Ginsberg, who was too hoarse to speak. Phil Ochs sang, and Abbie led a chant of "Fuck you, LBJ!"

After the rally a contingent of protesters walking back to Lincoln Park was met by a group of Yippies who had just been driven from Lincoln Park. They united and headed for Grant Park, where they linked up with Mobe supporters and together gained access to an area inside the park directly in front of the Hilton Hotel. The police formed a line between the park and the Hilton, but the demonstrators had no interest in storming the hotel. By driving the Yippies out of Lincoln Park and not blocking access to Grant Park, the police had allowed the Yippies and the Mobe to unite in an ideal situation. Quickly they made a makeshift stage in front of the television cameras and began a teach-in for the delegates in the Hilton. Late at night the National Guard replaced the police in the line separating the demonstrators from the Hilton Hotel.

Abbie's police tails had warned him that he was going to be arrested on Wednesday, the day of the planned march on the convention. That morning at six Abbie, Anita, and Paul Krassner were having breakfast in the Lincoln Hotel. Abbie was wearing a gray cowboy hat, and on his forehead he had written the word *Fuck* in order, he said, to keep his picture out of the papers and so that he could eat breakfast peacefully. According to Abbie, three or four squad cars of policemen plus his and Krassner's tails entered the coffee shop with their guns drawn and arrested him while he was eating eggs and bacon. "The first duty of a revolutionist is to get away with it. The second duty is to eat breakfast. I ain't going," Abbie wrote that he told the arresting officers. They lifted the hat from his head and arrested him for obscenity. For the next thirteen hours he was moved to four different station houses and was worked over by the police in at least some of them. "I laughed hysterically through the beatings, I was so winged-out from not sleeping and all the tension," Abbie recalled in his autobiography.[14]

Anita speculates that Abbie's response to the beatings was a symptom of his manic mood. "He had a strain of antiauthority that

would lead to his loss of control. He'd leap into a role and take it
to the edge and not hold back. He'd be so into his role defying
authority that he'd lose all sense of self-preservation and push the
role as far as he could. He would lose all concern for his own well-
being. Like in Chicago when he wrote 'Fuck' on his forehead. The
cops took him from precinct to precinct and beat him up. Likely
he went into his antiauthority thing and likely taunted the cops—
in other words instead of making it easier for himself he would
refuse to say uncle and by upping the ante infuriate them more."[15]

While Abbie was in police custody, the convention defeated a
peace plank that had been drafted by the leaders of the McCarthy
campaign and the Kennedy forces. The vote was 1,567 to 1,041,
and it ratified the split between the liberal peace wing and the party
regulars taking orders from Lyndon Johnson. Because of his arrest, Abbie also missed the police attack on Wednesday afternoon's
legal rally in Grant Park in which a formation of police chanting,
"Kill! Kill!" charged into the crowd, sending Rennie Davis to the
hospital with a bloodied head as he, his back to the police, organized a line of marshals to absorb the attack and protect the rally.

At the end of this rally Dellinger announced three options for the
demonstrators. They could avoid further confrontation with the
police by going home; or they could take their protest to the convention site, either by joining him on a nonviolent march to the
amphitheater or by breaking into small groups and trying to reach
it on their own. Most of the demonstrators joined Dellinger's
march, an indication that the majority of the movement in Chicago, if not the militant hard core, still preferred nonviolent tactics. (In the aftermath of these events, Dellinger commented
bitterly that nonviolence had failed to meet the test of Chicago.[16]
The failure, however, was less a matter of will than it was a matter
of tactics and organization.) The police, however, refused to allow
this spontaneous march to leave the park, and the marchers got
restless while Dellinger negotiated. Blocked by National Guardsmen and police, the marchers could do nothing except sit and wait
for the outcome of the negotiations. Rather than sit idly, the demonstrators, without prompting, left the line of march and began
running north, still inside the park, in an attempt to outflank the
authorities and get out. Inexplicably, there was a gap in the guardsmen's line at the Jackson Street Bridge, and the demonstrators
rushed over the bridge onto Michigan Avenue, almost directly in
front of the Hilton and the cameras of network television.

Here, on Wednesday night, was the site of the most concentrated violence of convention week, where the pictures were taken which have come to symbolize the Chicago convention. About five thousand demonstrators were assembled in front of the Hilton, chanting slogans like "Dump the Hump!" "Hell no, we won't go!" "Peace now!" and "Ho, Ho, Ho Chi Minh!" In addition to the provocative chants, many protesters were shouting obscenities at the police. The police began to clear the avenue, at first peacefully, with demonstrators quietly accepting arrest. Then, all of a sudden, the police broke ranks and began to attack individual protesters, beating them fiercely. "In a matter of minutes, hundreds of people—some just bystanders, some peaceful protesters, some violent militants— were beaten, bloodied, or Maced."[17] Some of the protesters fought back, which made the police attack with even greater ferocity. People were knocked down and then clubbed as they lay helpless. Police pushed a group through a plate glass window and then rushed through the window to assault the victims. The police arrested anybody they could grab and threw them into paddy wagons, where other cops clubbed them. Photographers were especially singled out for beating. Sidney Peck, a leader of the Mobe, tried to address the crowd in order to calm the situation; he was brutally clubbed and then charged with assaulting a police officer. Klieg lights illuminated the violence, television cameras whirred, and the demonstrators in the rear, who were not being attacked, chanted, "The whole world is watching!" Within half an hour Michigan Avenue was cleared, and the protesters were pushed back into Grant Park, still directly across from the Hilton, now protected by National Guardsmen who rushed to relieve the police.[18] Tear gas blanketed the hotel district and the Loop.

At the convention center presidential nominating speeches were just beginning when the first videotapes from the Hilton were shown on television. Senator Abraham Ribicoff, who was in the middle of a speech nominating George McGovern for president, adlibbed: "With George McGovern we wouldn't have Gestapo tactics on the streets of Chicago."* The television cameras then focused on Mayor Daley, who, off mike, uttered an angry curse which lip readers later translated as "Fuck you, you Jew son of a bitch."[19]

---

* McGovern entered the race when he saw that McCarthy was not willing to lead a fight against Humphrey. Many of the Kennedy delegates supported McGovern.

Late that night Hubert Humphrey was nominated with 1,760¼ votes to 601 for McCarthy and 141½ for McGovern. The antiwar delegates were already enraged by the defeat of the peace plank, the televised scenes of the battle on Michigan Avenue, and Daley's reaction. The inevitability of Humphrey's nomination inspired a desire to link up with the protesters. Returning to the hotel district, they set out on a candlelight march down Michigan Avenue into Grant Park, where the demonstrators had established an all night teach-in.

★   ★   ★

Released from custody, Abbie made it back to Grant Park to witness the movement's triumphant moment. It seemed that the liberals had indeed been radicalized by the policeman's club and that the Democratic party was irrevocably split, with the McCarthy and McGovern forces moving left to join the radical Yippies and the Mobe in holding the park. Throughout the night and into the morning protesters and delegates, liberals and radicals, mingled in Grant Park. Senator J. William Fulbright addressed them through a bullhorn, as did Norman Mailer, Gore Vidal, Julian Bond, and numerous less prominent delegates including Endicott "Chub" Peabody, who in 1966 had run for the U.S. Senate as a hawk against Abbie's candidate, Thomas Boyleston Adams. The movement had withstood and exposed to a national television audience the brutality of the Chicago police and, despite itself, had achieved the long-debated alliance with liberal Democrats. The antiwar movement was momentarily united on the radicals' terms and, in Grant Park, on the radicals' turf. "We should be happy we came here, fought, and survived. If we can survive here, we can survive in any city in the country," Tom Hayden told the crowd after the sun came up. Senator McCarthy also spoke. Addressing the crowd as "the government of the people in exile," he vowed to continue his commitment to ending the war.

After McCarthy spoke, about five hundred protesters, including Abbie, prepared for a march to the convention. Before setting off Abbie gave a short rap, thanking, among others, Ho Chi Minh, Marshall McLuhan, the Chicago police, and Mayor Daley for making the convention week a success, and condemning the Mobe marshals for assuming the role of activist cops and curtailing the demonstrators' revolutionary fervor. Anticipating an analysis that the more radical protesters would make after the convention, Abbie dismissed the prospects of a radical-liberal alliance, denounced McCarthy and other liberal leaders as "false prophets," and urged the protesters to take the revolutionary road. "I was really flying. It was the best," he wrote later of his "rap" and the events that followed.[20]

It would take more than fervor to get to the convention amphitheater, however. A few blocks past the Hilton the march was stopped by fifty policemen backed by a company of guardsmen with fixed bayonets. The marchers turned around and were returning to Grant Park when they were met by a second march of about three thousand demonstrators, organized by the Mobe marshals, heading out of the park at the invitation of Dick Gregory. Gregory lived at the edge of the black ghetto on the route to the convention center. His idea was for the marchers to go to his house not as protesters but as his personal guests "to have a beer." From there they would decide how to get to the amphitheater. Thomas Frazier, a paraplegic delegate from Oklahoma, and several New York delegates—the Reverend Richard Neuhaus, columnist Murray Kempton, former Kennedy adviser Harrison Wofford, and senatorial candidate Paul O'Dwyer—led scores of other delegates in the march. The National Guard and police raced ahead to cut them off at Eighteenth Street, where Michigan Avenue starts to become a black neighborhood.

With the march blocked by police in the front and with National Guardsmen and police moving down parallel streets in order to control the flanks, the marchers were in a tactical cul de sac: the only direction they could move was back into Grant Park. Eric Weinberger, a leader of the marshals, tried to get people to sit down while Gregory and Neuhaus negotiated with the police. What they wanted was for the marchers, or at least the delegates among them, to be allowed to commit civil disobedience by walking through the police line one by one and accepting arrest.

Abbie was enraged at Weinberger for using his authority to halt the demonstration and at Gregory for negotiating what he recalled, a few weeks later, as a "front of the line, easy bust, suffer-jail-we-shall-overcome-fast-bullshit-masochistic theater." Abbie began arguing loudly with Weinberger. To get the attention of the other marchers, he made a great show of lying down in front of an armored personnel carrier (which, in writing of it later, he described

as a tank) and raised his middle finger. Then he began shouting a
demand to see the officer in charge of the police. His idea, apparently, was to engage the ranking officers in negotiations and divert
their attention while the marchers pushed past the police lines.
Without direct orders from their officers, the police would not be
able to respond in time to contain the breakthrough—at least that
was Abbie's thought. It was a cockamamy notion. All week the police had been beating up demonstrators with and without orders
from their commanders. Even if some of the demonstrators broke
through the police line, the authorities had the mobility to race
ahead and contain them a few blocks farther along the route. What
would a breakthrough achieve? Probably, Abbie was hoping to
reach the black ghetto, where a confrontation with the police might
turn into a more explosive situation. Abbie, apparently, thought
that the second American revolution was about to begin right there
on Eighteenth Street. This is one of the few incidents during the
1960s when he was obviously in a manic phase and out of control.

Eric Weinberger bore the brunt of Abbie's rage. Weinberger was
a veteran pacifist, a few years older than Abbie. In 1963 he had
been honored as CORE's "man of the year" for his work organizing
black-run craft cooperatives, similar to the Poor People's Corporation, in Haywood County, Tennessee—a county bordering Mississippi, notorious for its violence against blacks and civil rights
workers. He was not a man to shy from action. At the Pentagon
demonstration he had stationed himself at the foot of the steps
leading to the upper parking lot and directed those activists who
he knew could handle difficult situations up the steps, where the
nonviolent sit-down and the teach-in with the troops would later
materialize. Now, however, Weinberger was determined to protect
the demonstrators, who were surrounded and outnumbered. Ultimately, seventy-nine Democratic convention delegates were arrested—most for the first time—for crossing a police line and
engaging in peaceful acts of civil disobedience. Other marchers
who wanted to follow them through the line were stopped by the
police but not arrested. With the jails full and the courts over-
loaded, the police refused to cooperate with any such massive civil
disobedience effort.

Abbie meanwhile tried to enlist demonstrators in an attempt to
break through the police lines along the side streets, but Weinberger would not give up his bullhorn and his control of the march.

Disgusted, Abbie returned to Grant Park. The remaining marchers, however, were still confronted by police and National Guardsmen; they were unable to move except backward, into the ranks of
other marchers still hoping to move forward. With nowhere to go,
and with no means of communicating to the rear what was happening at the front, the marchers' frustration rose. At one point a
chant was taken up, "Fuck Daley! Fuck Daley!" The police responded with tear gas, and the demonstrators were forced to flee
through a cordon of guardsmen back into Grant Park.

As Dellinger had discovered the previous day, without alternative
plans and a way for the leaders to communicate with their
"troops," and without an agreement among "the troops" to follow
the leadership and adhere to a nonviolent discipline, nonviolence
was not a viable tactic. But Abbie's impulsive plan to lead un-
trained, unarmed, and outnumbered protesters into a running
skirmish would likely have ended in a repeat of the previous night's
violence. The radicals—at least as they were then organized—had
reached the tactical limits of direct action. Most of them, including
Abbie, did not realize this. In *Revolution for the Hell of It*, written
within weeks of Chicago, Abbie was still enraged at Weinberger for
stifling his attempt to break through the police line. "Then the
Chickenshit marshals took over. They are always the ones who
bring the megaphones and should never be trusted. In fact, if I
ever see Eric Weinberger again I'm going to slice not only his mega-
phone but his throat as well."[21] Significantly, ten years later, in his
autobiography, Abbie made no mention of the march to the amphitheater, his disagreement with Weinberger, or anything else that
happened the day in Chicago when he was "really flying."

On Friday, with the confrontation in front of the Hilton winding
down and the Mobe leaders going off to a rural retreat to discuss
their next moves, Abbie flew home to New York with Wolfe Lowenthal. Lowenthal recalls Abbie as deep in thought, uncharacter-
istically tired and quiet. The plane taxied out to the runway and
then stopped. Two men came aboard, obviously some kind of government officials. They walked down the aisle looking at passengers
and stopped where Abbie was sitting. Ascertaining that, yes, Hoffman was leaving Chicago, they left the plane, and it took off
for New York. It was the beginning of a new phase in Abbie's life.
For the next five years he would be under continuous police
surveillance.

CHAPTER

8 | GIVING UP ON AMERICA

1968–1969

Elated by what he considered to be a great movement victory in Chicago, Abbie plunged back into the New York activist scene. He organized a series of Yippie demonstrations protesting the elections, helped members of Newsreel, a movement film collective, produce a movie about the Yippie actions in Chicago, and wrote the chapters on Chicago to complete *Revolution for the Hell of It*, the book that he had started in the Florida Keys the previous winter.* In it he predicted: "Because of our actions in Chicago, Richard Nixon will be elected President. Furthermore, Nixon will end the war in Vietnam. He will not only have a better chance than Humphrey but even than McCarthy of achieving a solution. Nixon will find it easier to deal with the National Liberation Front in Vietnam than to deal with the American Liberation Front here at home."[1]

This prediction was more a result of revolutionary fantasizing than of hard, objective political analysis. Political theater, which Abbie had initially conceived as a tactic to bring young people into the movement, had now become both a metaphor for politics and a strategy for revolution. Abbie was not alone in believing that rev-

---

*Evidently feeling a need to portray himself as a man of action even in writing a book, Abbie boasted that he wrote *Revolution* in one sitting. While he did write the sections on Chicago—about one-third of the text— in one energetic burst, the rest of the book consists mostly of strung-together articles that were previously published in *The Realist*, *WIN*, and other underground journals.

olution was imminent. In September SDS invited an international delegation of student leftists to a conference at Columbia University to discuss the role of students in a worldwide revolutionary movement. (In previous months the Columbia SDS chapter had provoked a student strike that had shut down the university, and students in France, Mexico, and Czechoslovakia had almost toppled their respective governments.) The New Leftists at the conference believed that students, being free of economic and family constraints, were in a position to take exemplary political actions that would inspire rebellion throughout society. Students represented the little motor that would start the big motor that would start the revolution.

Most of the international delegates were well versed in Marxist theory. Whether or not they agreed with it, Marxism was a common reference point that set them apart from the nonideological American participants. The Americans, with a war to stop, had neither the patience nor the intellectual grounding to sit through "more-revolutionary-than-thou shouting matches in a half-dozen different languages."[2] Bored and feeling guilty for being bored, they were a captive but restless audience.

Enter Abbie, uninvited, wearing a full cowboy getup—western boots, shirt, and hat. He rushes to the front of the hall, leaps up on the table that is serving as a podium, and starts doing tricks with a psychedelic yo-yo that lights up in fluorescent colors every time it reaches the end of its string. As he casts out the yo-yo, he begins to talk.

Now, more than twenty years later, the substance of his remarks has been forgotten (as have most other details of the conference); what is recalled is the way Abbie galvanized the audience. As he talked and the yo-yo lit up, the audience was jolted into life. Some thought he was denigrating political theory and, worse, mocking the very idea of rational discourse. Others responded to the magnetism of his physical energy and the chutzpah of his stealing the stage. His message, they understood, was about the liberating power of open-ended experience, being open to and ready to embrace any possibility. By breaking the rules of linear discourse, by being outrageous and doing the unexpected, he was showing them how they could control events and outmaneuver (by blowing the minds of) those who lived by stodgy laws and stifling bureaucratic ways. If only people could break through the repressive constraints of conventional behavior, they would be ready to march into the streets and storm the barricades.[3]

★   ★   ★

Having cast himself in opposition to every form and manifestation of authority, Abbie was not going to reopen for questioning anything that challenged his political theories or his newly created political identity. The street was his stage, and he was possibly the only person in America who could fill the role he had invented. He needed—or thought he needed—Richard Nixon, though, as his foil. A victory by Hubert Humphrey in the November election would undo the Yippie gains: it would harness the momentum for change to the Democratic party. Having forged a mass hippie-youth movement to end the Vietnam War, with no help from liberal Democrats, thank you, Abbie and his radical comrades were not going to step down and allow the Washington insiders to take control of what they had created.

Nixon, on the other hand, offered radicals like Abbie leading roles in a continuing national drama. Nixon would polarize society and drive the liberals further left. Without power in Washington, liberals would have to join the radicals in the streets, where imagination was power. There would be confrontations, tear gas, police brutality, mass arrests, battles in the courts, excitement, drama! Having survived Chicago, Abbie thought that the movement could survive any force the government could muster. Disruptive tactics would create a domestic crisis and force Nixon to end the war, if only because he would need the military to contain the movement and uphold his authority. The counterculture would serve as the energy core of a new society. Rock 'n' roll would get the message into every American home: Individual freedom! Do your own thing! Free love! Psychedelic utopia! As everyday life became more difficult, more and more people would be attracted to the countercultural vision of an alternative society.

In rejecting an alliance with Democratic liberals, Abbie and the radicals dismissed evidence of the historic split in the Democratic party and thus gave up on the last and best opportunity to end the Vietnam War short of another massive and bloody military escalation. The disaffection of President Johnson's "Wise Men," Johnson's stunning decision not to run for reelection, and the resounding victories of the Kennedy and McCarthy primary cam-

paigns indicated that opposition to the war had become the majority sentiment within the Democratic party. Although the convention
had been rigged by the Johnson forces to assure Hubert Humphrey's nomination, Chicago represented the last gasp of the party
bosses. Outside the conservative white South, and with the exception of those craft unions controlled by labor boss George Meany,
the party's most powerful and influential supporters had come
around—however unwillingly—to the antiwar position. To be
sure, there was ample reason to distrust (and detest) Hubert Humphrey. But those who are serious about making revolution are supposed to make difficult choices based on hard realities. Abbie and
his comrades made their choice on the basis of what they wanted
to happen and not what was likely to happen. Hubert Humphrey,
if elected president, would have been compelled to withdraw
American ground forces in Vietnam (as Nixon was forced to do
three years later). With the momentum of that success, the antiwar
movement might also have forced Humphrey to stop the massive
strategic bombing and end all American involvement in Vietnam
(as Nixon was forced to do six years later). Humphrey could have
been pressured more easily than Nixon not because he was a secret dove but because continuing to fight the war would have destroyed the Democratic party.[4] Needing to keep the party together to
secure his own renomination in 1972, Humphrey would have had
to yield to its ascendant peace wing. This would have created a
political climate in which the counterculture could have thrived
as a social experiment relatively free (except in the more conservative parts of the country) from political assaults and police
repression.

Just as Humphrey had to move to the left in order to hold his
party together, Nixon had to run—and rule—as a law and order
hawk in order to capture the vote of racist whites disaffected from
the Democratic party and attracted to George Wallace's third-
party movement, and in order to solidify the support of the Republican party's newly assertive right wing. Despising Humphrey,
when they should have been worrying about Nixon, was an indul-
gence neither radicals (nor liberals) could afford. If Nixon had to
move to the right out of political expediency, his course was all the
more dangerous because of the demagogic tendencies that liberals
and radicals knew were at the core of his personality.

Abbie and his comrades misjudged the 1968 election for the same reason they misinterpreted the events in Chicago. The radical activists' claim of success in Chicago was based on their assertion that "the whole world was watching" and that the public would condemn the visual evidence of police brutality. The whole world *was* watching, but few Americans identified positively with the Mobe and Yippies. To many people, what happened in Chicago was not a confrontation between hawks and doves but a confrontation between those who upheld America's familiar, workaday values and an unruly army of young and irresponsible rebels who had no respect for those values. While opposition to the war was continuing to grow within the broader American public, opposition to the antiwar movement was even more pronounced. Just prior to the convention, polls indicated that a majority of Americans, agreeing with the movement, thought sending troops to Vietnam a mistake. Polls taken after Chicago showed that Americans who opposed the war were even more opposed to the antiwar movement. Abbie read the polls but dismissed their importance. He had wanted to define the confrontation in Chicago on generational and cultural rather than on political terms, and in that he had succeeded. Having anointed the young as a revolutionary vanguard, he no longer cared about communicating with ordinary Americans. A small, dedicated, youthful minority, Abbie hoped, would undermine the old order and be the catalyst of change.

Abbie's belief in the revolutionary potential of the young was not farfetched. A public opinion poll taken of student leaders in October 1968 found that 27 percent considered themselves to be part of the left—a far larger percentage than in the population as a whole. Che Guevara was more popular than any of the candidates for president; two-thirds of the students believed the war a mistake; and draft resistance and civil disobedience were considered by the majority to be legitimate protest tactics. On college campuses, as well as in the East Village and other countercultural bastions, a new generation of radicals was coming to the fore. These activists were too young to have been part of the civil rights movement during its early, nonviolent, community-organizing phase. They had been radicalized almost instantly, it seemed, by the war, and their idea of politics was action in the streets. The Yippie strategy of merging radical politics and radical lifestyles had triumphed. Most youthful radicals did drugs, and many young "freaks" (as the new generation of hippies called themselves) were indeed ready to take to the streets to protest the war.

Rejecting an alliance with liberal doves, Abbie and his Yippie cohorts looked further left for allies among the more militant and self-professed revolutionary groups. Of these the Black Panther party had the most renown. Every white radical wanted the Panthers' blessing. In early October Jerry Rubin and Stew Albert, both of whom had returned to Berkeley after the Chicago demonstrations, signed a "YIPanther" Pact with Eldridge Cleaver, the Black Panther minister of culture who, virtually alone among the Panther leadership, had an interest in hip, white cultural radicalism.[5] Although Abbie endorsed the agreement, it represented Jerry's (more than his own) eagerness to pursue organizational politics. In reality the pact played into the illusions, rather than the real needs, of each signatory. The Panthers did need white allies in order to blunt the attack the government was mounting against them, but the Yippies were more a provocation than a source of protection. And though the Panthers had effective community programs in black neighborhoods, it was their image as gun-toting, cop-baiting street toughs that the Yippies admired. Abbie's support for the Yippie-Panther alliance reflected confusion about the direction of his own politics. He had always insisted that individuals are best motivated to participate in politics through an affirmative identification of their own positive needs. Yet the Panther approach to whites in the movement was often to shame them into feeling guilt. Moreover, the Panthers were a quasi-militaristic, hierarchical organization whose ideology, such as it was, consisted, for the most part, of Maoist sloganeering. Abbie had always rejected that kind of politics. It is thus disconcerting to read (in an interview from this period) Abbie's endorsement of the Panthers' ersatz Maoism and his touting of Mao's "Little Red Book": "I read it continuously."[6*]

* If the comment was said jokingly (and it's hard to imagine Abbie seriously studying Mao's quotations), the irony was lost in print. The irony with which the Panthers initially took up Maoism was also lost in the actuality. According to Panther leader Bobby Seale (interviewed in the film documentary *Berkeley: The Sixties*), the Panthers bought copies of Mao's book in San Francisco's Chinatown wholesale in order to sell them to eager Berkeley students at retail. In this way they were able to raise money to buy a few rifles, which they intended to flourish (as was their legal right) as theatrical props. When the organization expanded faster than expected, the "Little Red Book" provided them with an instant ideology, a shortcut to maintaining some kind of organizational unity.

In the text of the YIPanther Pact, the Yippies proclaimed their plans for the campaign season. "Vote with your feet. . . . Make music and dance at every red light! . . . Let's make 2–300 Chicagos on election day." In New York, Abbie looked forward to an election day victory rally for Pigasus in Times Square and an inaugural day celebration: "We will bring our revolutionary theater to Washington to inaugurate 'Pigasus'—our Pig—the only honest candidate." Abbie expected Pigasus to be an effective symbol of opposition to the 1968 election, and he was buoyed when live pigs were carried in antiwar demonstrations in Montreal and London. In New York on the last weekend in September he organized a "pignic" on a Hudson River pier near Greenwich Village and gave away ham sandwiches along with Yippie buttons and balloons. The turnout was small, however. Yippie humor was becoming predictable—and beside the point. There was an election campaign going on and a war to be stopped. Yippie pranks were no substitute for serious debate. Should the movement support Humphrey, attack Humphrey, or quietly sit the election out? These were questions that the Yippies, even more than other radicals, refused to address. Abbie's position was to ignore the Republican right and attack the liberal Democrats. Anyone who disagreed with this formulation was "part of the problem and not the solution"—another example, like "pigs," of polarizing Black Panther rhetoric that white radicals quickly adopted as their own.

The Democratic candidate for the U.S. Senate in New York was Paul O'Dwyer, an early and outspoken opponent of the Vietnam War and a participant, with Abbie, in the protest march to Dick Gregory's house in Chicago. O'Dwyer had a long record of support for progressive causes; he was the kind of left-wing Democrat around whom a progressive electoral movement could have been forged. But because he was a Democrat, the Yippies in New York heaped him with abuse, disrupting one speaking engagement in order to present him with a pig's head on a platter, and staging a nude-in at an O'Dwyer rally in one of the city's most liberal churches. Abbie was not directly involved in these pranks, but he supported them as he supported any audacious act carried out under the Yippie banner. Significantly, the Yippies who plagued O'Dwyer's campaign were not flower children but members of a coalition of militant anti-imperialist organizations. Their basic position was that the country could not be changed from within. Their hope was that the victories of third-world liberation move-

ments (like the communist-led NLF in Vietnam) would destroy the
American imperialist system, ending its exploitation of third-world
resources and its dominance over international affairs. Losing control of third-world economies would result, the anti-imperialists
believed, in an economic depression at home. This would in turn
create the material conditions for a working-class revolution. Until
those conditions existed, the role of anti-imperialists within the
United States was to help third-world liberation movements by undermining America's use of military power.

Political certainty was not the only attraction of the anti-imperialist position. By identifying with third-world revolutionaries,
the anti-imperialists felt themselves in solidarity with guerrilla war-
riors the world over. The ascetic Gandhi was not their hero; they
fancied themselves, instead, like the dashing, martyred interna-
tionalist Che Guevara. As the movements of political radicals and
cultural rebels coalesced, Abbie found his closest allies not among
the countercultural freaks but among the members of the anti-imperialist left. Never one to embrace hard and fast ideological positions (or concern himself with political contradictions), Abbie
didn't accept the entire anti-imperialist package. He agreed that
the United States could not be changed by traditional political
means but believed that cultural change could open up political
possibilities. Given the cultural ferment within American society,
he saw no reason to give up on the goal of changing the country
from within. Unlike the anti-imperialists, who made a fetish of the
NLF flag, Abbie, though supporting the Vietnamese cause, still
wanted to play capture the American flag. The counterculture, for
Abbie, was a uniquely American and positive phenomenon.

Abbie was hospitalized with hepatitis on election day (contacted,
he claimed, from a blood test administered in a Washington, D.C.,
jail). He missed nothing, because the protest demonstrations called
by the Yippies and other radicals were flops. The biggest, in Boston, drew just two thousand people. Many commentators have
blamed the Yippies for the defeat of Hubert Humphrey. Certainly
the protests in Chicago ignited a cultural backlash for Nixon to
exploit. But conservatism was, and is, an authentic force in America, and it was already gathering steam in resentment over the
interracial civil rights movement and the hedonism of the cultural
revolution. That resentment existed independently of the Yippies'

organizing efforts. True, the Yippie mix of cultural radicalism and antiwar politics invigorated the backlash and gave it a focus. But the reaction was inevitable. The Yippies (and the Mobe) in Chicago derailed the antiwar movement, but Hubert Humphrey was responsible for his own electoral defeat.

Hubert Humphrey was the wrong candidate at the wrong time. He was a man coasting on his liberal credentials from the past, a Washington insider who expressed no appreciation of the anguish that the war was causing throughout society. Unlike Kennedy and McCarthy, who sought out radical leaders in order to understand the antiwar movement, Humphrey had nothing but disdain for the insurgents. Although he was the loudest cheerleader within the Johnson administration on behalf of the war, he could not understand why antiwar activists heckled him at every campaign stop, and would not forgive them. Instead of courting the movement, he attacked it. "There are certain people in the United States who feel that all you have to do is riot and you can get your way. I have no time for that," he proclaimed after Chicago.[7] Instead of courting the disaffected doves within his own party, his initial strategy—to challenge Nixon and Wallace for the hawkish, law and order vote—further alienated them. Refusing to run as a peace candidate, he let Nixon get away with the monstrous lie that he, Nixon, had a secret plan to end the war. Humphrey's strategy backfired. A Gallup poll in late September had Nixon leading Humphrey 43 percent to 28 percent, with Wallace at 21 percent.

In early October Humphrey finally broke with Johnson and promised, if elected, to stop the bombing in exchange for concessions from the NLF. But his transition from hawk to dove came too late. A last-minute effort by Johnson to put Humphrey over the top by negotiating a peace settlement—further evidence that leading Democrats understood that the party could survive only by ending American involvement in Vietnam—was sabotaged when Nixon's campaign secretly persuaded the South Vietnamese government to denounce the plan. The final tally was Nixon 43.4 percent, Humphrey 42.7 percent, and Wallace 13.5 percent. Out of nearly 73 million ballots cast, only 500,000 votes separated Humphrey from Nixon.

★   ★   ★

The Mobe's feeble demonstration at Nixon's inauguration indicated the weakness of the radicals in the post-Chicago period. Although

Abbie was in Washington for the protest, he was recovering from his bout with hepatitis and thus did not play a role in the planning. Davis and Dellinger, the principal organizers, did, however, adopt the Yippie concept of mixing rock 'n' roll with protest politics in order to attract young people to the demonstration. On the evening of the inaugural ball they held a "counterinaugural ball" under a huge circus tent on the banks of the Potomac River. While the freaks danced to rock bands, a group of antiimperialists occupied the Mobe's Washington office, demanding that the Mobe officially endorse disruptive tactics at the inaugural parade. Although Dellinger was able to talk them down, this confrontation highlighted a growing split within the radical movement. While most demonstrators, Abbie included, heckled the president as his motorcade drove along the parade route, small groups of militants skirmished with the police on the side streets of Washington. "If the CIA had set out to produce a savage burlesque of the peace movement," I. F. Stone complained in the aftermath, "it could not have done better."

In fact, the ranks of the movement were filled with police agents. Much of the undercover work, even from the government's standpoint, was a waste of taxpayers' money. One group of military agents, posing as a television news team, filmed what they claimed to their superiors was an exclusive interview with Hoffman.[8] Abbie, of course, would talk to anyone carrying a microphone and a camera.

More effective, from the government point of view, was the work of its *agents provocateurs*. As in Chicago, undercover agents advocated tactics that were meant to embarrass the movement.* But there was never any shortage of willing followers. There were, for example, the anti-imperialist factions, who shared with the government the goal of portraying the antiwar movement as procommunist and anti-American. And there were the anarchist Motherfuckers, the SDS action-factionists, and, in addition, innumerable free-lance militants who came to demonstrations wearing military helmets and body padding, believing that taunting the

---

* One of the most ubiquitous and effective of such agents was Jack Godoy of the New York City police department's "red squad," who, as a member of numerous antiwar organizations in New York, was known for his advocacy of tactics that would provoke the police to violence. Godoy often stationed himself in front of Gem's Spa, a candy store on a busy corner of St. Marks Place near Abbie and Anita's apartment, where he exchanged movement gossip with the activists passing by.

police and creating mayhem in the streets were what defined revolutionary commitment. Thanks in part to Abbie's successful advocacy of do-your-own-thing tactics, the movement could not enforce a discipline on its members. It was a political climate in which agents provocateurs could easily operate. The counterinaugural demonstration was a sign that a small number of activists could fix in the media, and hence in the public mind, the anti-American message that it wanted to get across. As a result of this fiasco the Mobe decided that, as it could not control what Rennie Davis called "guerrilla street activity," it would stop organizing mass demonstrations.[9]

During this period many veteran activists came to a similar conclusion. If the antiwar coalition could not control its constituent organizations or exercise authority over individual activists—and if the movement could not put across a coherent message that expressed their own beliefs—they would stop going to demonstrations. Having dropped out of the straight society to join the antiwar movement, some now dropped out of the antiwar movement to move "back to the land," starting communes in rural areas of Vermont, western Massachusetts, northern California, New Mexico, Oregon, and elsewhere. Abbie's friends from Worcester, Susan and Marty Carey, were among those who left the Lower East Side for the country at this time. They had been with Abbie at the Pentagon but refused to go to Chicago because of the expected violence. Keith Lampe, the Yippie emissary to pacifist activists, also dropped out. Influenced by the poet Gary Snyder, he began a column for the underground press called Earth Read Out that helped to popularize environmental issues. Marshall Bloom and Ray Mungo, the founders of Liberation News Service and the Yippie supporters who had accompanied Abbie to the Lake Villa conference, also left the movement during this period, with Bloom moving his faction of Liberation News Service to a farm in western Massachusetts. "The Movement, like society, has run amok," wrote a despairing Yippie comrade of Abbie's who, after Chicago, helped start a commune in Vermont. "Fighting cops. Killing pigs. Hurray! Our vision for the future. A new age soaked in blood. I'm crying."[10]

That is not to say that most activists gave up on resisting the war. There was a strong argument for using the new tactics of disruption to upset normal business activity and thus raise the domestic cost of prolonging the war. Liberals might argue that disruptive street actions strengthened the power of the conservatives in government. But the radical answer was that nothing else seemed to work, least of all electoral politics and congressional opposition. Trying to chart a middle course, many radicals advocated the disruption of draft boards, government buildings, and corporate offices, such as by breaking in at night to destroy files, so as to not focus hostility on the police and the working people who would be inconvenienced by overtly disruptive street tactics. In practice, however, disciplined disruptions could not be organized. The Yippie ethos of total personal freedom, combined with the militants' determination to create chaos in the streets (and the ease with which government agents moved in the movement), made more thoughtful radical politics impossible.

★   ★   ★

The publication in late 1968 of *Revolution for the Hell of It* elevated Abbie to the role of a nationally known symbol for radical activism. Covering his organizing activities in the East Village and ending with his experience as a Yippie in Chicago (and including the text of *Fuck the System*, a survival handbook Abbie had written in 1967 about living in the East Village as a hippie dropout), the book caught Abbie in his pre-Chicago phase, as the political prankster rather than the militant street warrior. Its success (200,000 copies sold in the first six months) placed him into a celebrity time warp. The politics expressed in the book were far more optimistic than the politics he was espousing at the time it was published. In the mainstream press the book was treated as a titillating report from the hip underground. Some critics were so taken by Abbie's sense of humor that they treated his politics as a harmless confection. Abbie didn't object to *Time* magazine's mistaken description of him as a "nice Jewish boy from the Bronx." But he was angered by *Time*'s characterization of the Yippies as "nonviolent." Writing under the pseudonym Pat McNeil of the Bronx, Abbie penned an angry letter to the editor urging the magazine to "wake up." The book, Abbie insisted, was proof that the Yippies were "willing to use any means necessary to further their revolutionary aims, including violence."[11]

Reviewers on the left were politically more discerning, worrying that Abbie's mixing of cultural radicalism with antiwar politics would exacerbate the right-wing backlash. To *Village Voice* writer

Jack Newfield, *Revolution for the Hell of It* contained "recipes for private amusement and public catastrophe." Dave Dellinger, acknowledging Abbie's comic abilities and political sincerity, charged him with promoting hedonistic values that turned out to be "distressingly like the mirror image of the culture he thought he was rejecting." Dellinger also took him to task for irresponsible rhetoric about guns and violence that could influence "kids who might take him seriously." This charge could have been applied to any militant in the movement, but in Abbie's case it had a special meaning. Abbie's glib celebration of guns and violence, so at odds with the zany brilliance of his political theater, can best be understood as macho role-playing: he was still the hood from Worcester. In using theater as an extended metaphor for political action, Abbie thought he was transforming weapons into props. But the streets were not a stage, and to the police (and most everyone else in society), guns were not props but weapons that killed. When the authorities took the hyperbolic rhetoric of self-proclaimed revolutionaries as an actual threat and responded with armed attacks, the radicals were woefully unprepared to defend themselves, much less fight back.

The movie rights for *Revolution for the Hell of It* were bought by MGM for $25,000, with more money promised as the film moved toward production. Abbie promptly endorsed the check over to the Black Panther bail fund, fully expecting that he might never see the money again. It was a sincere gesture, helping to buy fellow revolutionaries their freedom, and in harmony with movement ethics. (The only critical note came from a few feminists who, knowing Abbie's family situation, suggested that paying child support would have been a more appropriate gesture. But the women's movement was just starting. In Abbie's circle, the Black Panthers were the more worthy cause.) Abbie and Anita were not concerned with saving money or personal security. Other than electronic gadgetry, Abbie had no expensive tastes. He and Anita liked to eat out and travel; Abbie's income as a writer and speaker enabled them to do what they wanted. Whenever Abbie had extra money, he used it to finance his and others' activist projects. According to Anita, the movie script trivialized Abbie and his politics and turned him into "a cutesy Jewish sitcom hero." She and Abbie hated and rejected it. *Revolution for the Hell of It* was never made into a movie, and within a few years Hollywood's enchantment with radical politics would wilt under government pressure—and the movement's own boorish behavior.

★   ★   ★

After Chicago, Abbie secured the services of Gerry Lefcourt, one of a group of young criminal lawyers in New York who had formed a lawyers' commune in order to provide free legal services to activists working for social change. Defending Abbie became almost a full-time job. Two weeks after the Democratic convention Lefcourt accompanied Abbie to Chicago to his trial for writing "Fuck" on his forehead and resisting arrest. Arriving late in the Windy City because of a missed plane connection, Abbie was arrested for jumping bail. When a subsequent body search turned up a penknife in his pocket, he was charged with additional state and federal counts of carrying a concealed weapon. Released on $2,500 bail, he was required to seek court permission to go anywhere outside Manhattan (except Chicago). His return flight was delayed in order for federal marshals to board the plane and issue him a subpoena to appear at a HUAC hearing. In subsequent weeks he was questioned by the FBI on five different occasions, Justice Department officials twice, and the Internal Revenue Service once.

Dellinger, Hayden, Davis, and other Mobe officials, as well as Jerry Rubin, were also subpoenaed by HUAC. The committee was determined to publicize alleged links between the antiwar movement and Hanoi and Moscow.* The Mobe witnesses also had publicity in mind: they wanted to use the hearings to defend the movement by making a reasoned attack on the war. Intellectual publications like the *New York Review of Books* and movement journals like *Liberation* would publish and discuss their testimony, but to Abbie this was talking to the already converted. His concern was making the most of the minute or two that television news would devote to the hearings. Specifically, he did not want the

---

*Both the Johnson and Nixon administrations tried repeatedly to uncover links between the antiwar movement and international communism. A report from CIA director Richard Helms to Johnson in September 1968 pointed out that even the communist parties in Europe were being undermined by "restless youth." The inability of the CIA to document communist ties to the antiwar movement led Nixon to bypass the CIA and create his own intelligence-gathering unit in the White House.

hearings to be presented on HUAC's terms, with the activists on the defensive, trying to prove their patriotism. One sound byte of a witness—whether piteously or stridently—denying allegations of communist connections was all HUAC needed for its propaganda victory.

Abbie was scheduled to testify on the second day of the hearings, October 5, 1968. He came dressed in a store-bought American flag shirt, determined, literally, to wrap himself in the flag and create a visual portrait of antiwar protesters as patriots. He expected that the sensationalism of the shirt would dominate television coverage; if he could provoke the committee to overreact and arrest him, so much the better. Before the hearings were called to order, he stood outside the Capitol doing tricks with his psychedelic yo-yo, acting as a barker for the committee, alerting the press that showtime was near and putting the committee on guard that he was prepared to upstage them. As Abbie hoped, the police went for his bait and, in the process of arresting him, began ripping the shirt. Anita jumped into the fray to protect Abbie, who was struggling to keep his shirt. Both of them were held in jail overnight (which is when Abbie claimed he got hepatitis). Charges against Anita were dropped the next day, but Abbie was indicted for desecrating the flag. The uproar surrounding Abbie's arrest, and the inability of the committee to put the other witnesses on the defensive, led to a temporary suspension of the hearings. They were resumed in December and then abruptly called off. Never again would HUAC successfully organize a public hearing to investigate the left.

Testifying at his flag case in November 1968, Abbie cited Emanuel Leutze's famous painting of Washington crossing the Delaware as evidence that Revolutionary War patriots also wrapped themselves in the flag; expressed his belief that he and those who had protested in Chicago were closer to the tradition of the founding fathers than the members of the House committee; observed that if he was guilty of desecrating the flag by wearing a flag shirt, then so was Uncle Sam; and noted that the comedienne Phyllis Diller had recently appeared on a television show wearing a miniskirt that looked like a flag and was not arrested. Nevertheless, Abbie was found guilty by the trial judge. His sentence of one hundred dollars or thirty days in jail was suspended pending appeal. Ultimately, Lefcourt argued the case on First Amendment grounds, and the law under which Abbie was charged was overturned by the court of appeals.

The HUAC hearings and the flag case were petty stuff, however. Under Richard Nixon the antiwar movement got the repression that Jerry Rubin and others had said they wanted. The FBI through its counterintelligence Cointelpro program, the CIA through its Operation Chaos, various military intelligence units, local red squads, and Nixon's own White House–controlled National Security Agency were all directed to infiltrate, monitor, and harass individual activists and radical organizations. As a result Abbie's phones were tapped, and his office was broken into. More personally unsettling were the untrue rumors that Abbie and Anita were getting rich off the movement.

One of the undercover agents who infiltrated Abbie's circle was George Demmerle. Known in the East Village as Crazy George, Demmerle was active in every militant group. At one point Demmerle offered to supply Abbie with naval explosives in order to make bombs. Abbie wasn't interested, but he ought to have been suspicious. Demmerle, it seems, made similar offers to other radicals and in Sam Melville found a taker. Melville was part of a group that was already setting off bombs in New York; the targets were carefully chosen to symbolize the connection of capitalist institutions to the war economy. When Melville and Demmerle, acting on their own, set out to bomb a Manhattan military armory, the police moved in, and Melville was arrested (as were his friends later).* Demmerle later falsely claimed that he was once a sincere activist but became disillusioned with the movement because of the high living of some radical leaders. There's Abbie, "sitting up in his penthouse, reaping in tons of money," Demmerle said in one press interview. "I don't know how much he's making, but he's making a fortune, he's a capitalist. And he has hoodwinked the whole college campus movement in this country."[12]

In reality, the Hoffmans had moved from their St. Marks apartment to a loft on top of a ten-story commercial building that they jokingly dubbed "the penthouse." The Hoffmans had worked on it,

---

*Imprisoned in Attica, a maximum security prison in New York State, Melville was killed in 1971 when state police invaded the prison to put down a rebellion.

creating a rooftop garden of plants in barrels. Abbie was sensitive to the accusation that he was living in luxury. He once got angry at Anita for telling the press how they were accosted by FBI agents waiting for them in the building's "lobby." Abbie objected to her use of the word *lobby*. It connoted a ritzy high rise rather than the vestibule of a somewhat run-down commercial property.

In the spring of 1969 the police raided Abbie's office, two buildings away from the Ninth Precinct headquarters, and claimed to discover a shopping bag containing three loaded revolvers, blackjacks, and two bags of heroin. Abbie had set up an office in order to write and to do movement work (and also, Anita surmises, to have a place "to get laid"). The office became a center for the movement in the East Village, and an unknown number of people had keys. At any time the police could have raided his office or his apartment (as they did Jerry Rubin's) and found—or claimed to have found—a stash of marijuana or LSD, and they'd have had a credible story. But that Abbie would have heroin, a drug that he and every other cultural radical always condemned (not to mention guns and blackjacks) was unbelievable. Likely, the raid was a form of harassment to get a headline linking Abbie with guns and heroin, and a way, also, of looking at important papers in his desk and files. Whatever its purpose, the police got their desired headline and forced Abbie and Lefcourt to spend time in court before the charges were eventually dropped.

Abbie was not in the office when it was raided because he was in a Chicago courthouse being indicted on federal conspiracy charges for his role in the demonstrations at the Democratic convention. That case would not come to trial until September, but in the meanwhile the police harassment continued. A month after the Chicago indictment Abbie was in a New York courthouse at a hearing pertaining to his Columbia bust. Some New York Black Panthers were on trial in the same courthouse, and their supporters were demonstrating outside.* Taking Abbie to be a demonstrator, the police

* This was the trial of the Panther 23. Members of the New York chapter were accused on a number of charges ranging from murder to a conspiracy to blow up the Statue of Liberty. The trial uncovered the fact that the principal advocate of violence within the chapter was an undercover policemen, and the Panthers were acquitted on all charges. Doubting the possibility of a fair trial, one of the group had already jumped bail, using Abbie's money.

pulled him out of a phone booth in the courthouse and began to beat him up. Abbie went into a rage and was charged with, among other things, felonious assault on police officers. Immediately he contacted Gerry Lefcourt, who arranged a meeting with Barry Gottehrer, Mayor Lindsay's aide. Jokingly, Abbie threatened Gottehrer that he would campaign for Lindsay's reelection in Queens (a conservative borough where Lindsay was already unpopular) if the charges were not dropped. In fact, according to Lefcourt, all of Abbie's legal cases in New York that were still outstanding in 1973 (the year of his cocaine bust) were ultimately wrapped together, and he never did any time.[13]

In June 1969 Abbie heard of a plan to hold a gigantic rock festival in Woodstock, New York, later that summer. Many radicals instantly condemned the idea as an attempt to commercialize music that was still very much an authentic expression of the counterculture.* Abbie's attitude was not to attack the festival but to try to exploit it. He arranged for a delegation of radical activists to meet with the Woodstock promoters. Much to his surprise, they agreed to give him ten thousand dollars to build a Movement City within the festival grounds where radical organizations could distribute literature and conduct workshops. The promoters viewed this as an inexpensive act of co-optation, for they needed the authenticity that the participation of radical leaders would give them.

The Woodstock Music and Art Festival drew half a million people, a hundred times the number of demonstrators that had come to Chicago. No one paid attention to Movement City. The radicals who had come from New York to hand out leaflets and rap about politics had nothing to do. Many of them returned to New York disgusted with the counterculture and dismissive of the idea that rock music had a role to play in the revolution. Abbie stayed, however, and made himself useful. After the first night of rain, with the roads hopelessly clogged with parked cars (concertgoers stuck

---

* The only previous rock festival in the psychedelic era had been at Monterey in 1967—a free festival organized by musicians within the hip community. The Yippie Festival of Life would also have been free. Woodstock thus represented a break with the prevailing ethos. It was the first rock festival ostensibly promoting countercultural values that was organized as a profit-making venture.

in a massive traffic jam had abandoned their cars and walked to
the festival), the event teetered at the brink of a human disaster.
Abbie helped organize a medical station, locating doctors and medical supplies that were flown in by helicopter. The printing press
that the radicals had lugged up to publish manifestos was used to
print survival messages in the manner of Jim Fouratt's Communications Company two years earlier. Despite the unexpectedly huge
crowd—the promoters had planned for seventy thousand—and
the lack of facilities (and because, some might add, most of the
people at the festival were stoned on psychedelic drugs), Woodstock was transformed into an exhilarating, communal experience.

Abbie rightly took credit for helping to organize the volunteer
effort. Typically, however, he could not leave well enough alone and
felt compelled to impress upon the gathering his own political
agenda. Tripping on acid, he walked out on the stage while Peter
Townshend and The Who were getting ready to begin their set.
Planning to make a speech about John Sinclair, the Ann Arbor
White Panther who was then serving ten years in prison for possession of marijuana, Abbie was brusquely pushed aside by an
angry Townshend, who, as he later put it, didn't want any damned
politico interfering with his music. Although almost no one in the
stone audience noticed, understood, or cared about the incident,
it greatly embarrassed Abbie. Throughout his life he insisted that
Townshend had accidentally "bumped into" him. According to Abbie, the incident was blown out of proportion later in the rock
music press as part of the rock establishment's attack on radical
politics. "In the world of hip capitalism," Abbie argued, "the Yippies *were* politics, because we threatened their pretense as rebels
and leaders of the youth culture."[14] Rock 'n' roll, to Abbie, was a
cultural battlefield; his fight was to keep the music as an expression
of the radical counterculture.

Undaunted by his failure to politicize the festival itself, Abbie
returned to New York and in another burst of energy wrote *Woodstock Nation*, an attempt to have the last word, producing an instant history that laid claim to Woodstock as a political happening.* Published in early 1970, the book caught Abbie as he was

---

* Abbie wrote the book at Random House in the office of his editor, Christopher Cerf. Cerf's father was Bennett Cerf, the publisher of Random
House. One time the elder Cerf was escorting a distinguished guest

awaiting the start of the Chicago conspiracy trial. He was in a
defiant mood, frightened by the prospect of a stiff jail sentence,
completely disillusioned with the possibility of changing American
politics, but still willing to believe that cultural ferment could create space for political organizing.

At the start of *Woodstock Nation*, Abbie staked his identity on
being a cultural outlaw:

> When I appear in the Chicago courtroom, I want to
> be tried not because I support the National Liber-
> ation Front—which I do—but because I have long
> hair. Not because I support the Black Liberation
> Movement, but because I smoke dope. Not because
> I am against the capitalist system, but because I
> think property eats shit. Not because I believe in
> student power, but that the schools should be de-
> stroyed. Not because I'm against corporate liberal-
> ism, but because I think people should do whatever
> the fuck they want, and not because I am trying to
> organize the working class, but because I think kids
> should kill their parents.[15]

This was Abbie as his nihilistic extreme, rejecting any moral basis for political action and using inflammatory language for its
shock value. Many of his friends thought that, especially in urging
kids to kill their parents, he was going too far. Paul Krassner took
him to task for urging others to do what he would not do. "You
don't want your kids to kill you," he said. "You're not killing your
parents." But Abbie saw it as a theatrical statement, the theater of
cruelty. He explained that he meant it in the Oedipal sense, that
children have a libidinal need to act out hostility against their parents. He liked the idea that it would shock people and cause them
to take note of the significance of the generational war. But he also
had second thoughts about using the line and stopped using it in
his speaking engagements. Jerry Rubin, however, picked it up and
made it his own.

---

around Random House and stopped in at his son's office. Abbie, who was
sprawled on the floor, shirt off and likely smoking a joint as he wrote the
book on a yellow legal pad, looked up and greeted the visitors, "Hi, Dad."

The nihilism of Abbie's declaration reflected both the state of the counterculture and his own mood at the time. There were two contradictory attitudes within the counterculture in 1969. One was more counter than culture, a rebellious determination to be whatever the mainstream culture said you could not be. Its focus, akin to hippie nationalism, was on unfettered individualism and hedonism, taking the rebellion against middle-class values as far as it could go. The other, an organizers' attitude, came out of the SNCC/Digger/hippie social service ideal: a utopian idea to build a truly alternative society, a "new society within the shell of the old," the Wobbly idea that Gary Snyder popularized in his influential book *Earth Household*. There was, of course, much overlap in these tendencies, but in 1969 the individualistic tendency, much to the despair of the more earnest organizer types, was in the ascendancy. In *Woodstock Nation*, Abbie recognized the importance of the cooperative ethos that he found at Woodstock but argued (correctly, in retrospect) that capitalism can co-opt any form of cultural rebellion, even the efforts of the most socially conscious hippies to construct an alternative society. Abbie thus rejected the organizers' view and embraced personal rebellion. He took the position of an outlaw, advocating a culture built outside and in defiance of the law so that it could not so easily be co-opted. Instead of discussing the standards of ethical behavior needed to establish that community (as in Bob Dylan's dictum from his song "Absolutely Sweet Marie" on the album *Blonde on Blonde* that "to live outside the law you must be honest"), Abbie pushed for the same kind of stoned and nihilistic, no-lines-drawn behavior that he should have known, from his experience going back as far as the Free Store, almost always caused countercultural projects to fail.

Woodstock Nation presented Abbie with all his contradictions showing. He wanted political change but despaired of reforming American politics. He believed in cultural radicalism but understood how easily capitalism absorbs new cultural styles. He looked toward the creation of a new society but refused to deny the irresponsible demand for instant gratification that he knew would destroy it. He refused to acknowledge that people are motivated by moral concerns, stereotyping civic responsibility as the politics of guilt, although everything he did in his life was based not simply on the idea of politics as fun but on his own keen moral sense and passion for justice.

★   ★   ★

The inability of the Mobe to plan mass demonstrations created a leadership vacuum that was filled by young veterans of the McCarthy and Kennedy campaigns. Their first Moratorium against the War, held in October 1969, was successful beyond expectation. Across the country, in cities and towns, in schools and churches, on organized vigils and in office and factory, people stopped to bear witness to their desire to end the war. Millions of Americans who had never before participated in a demonstration wore black armbands to indicate their opposition to the war. The theme of the Moratorium was reconciliation, symbolized best by a newspaper ad that the Moratorium had run showing a very straight-looking father with his arm around his long-haired hippie son and the headline "October 15, Fathers and Sons Together against the War." The Moratorium was attempting to re-create a mass movement by healing the generation gap and by framing the antiwar protest as if the previous two years of frustration and polarization had never occurred. The Moratorium aimed its appeal at the most humane qualities of American society and hoped that ordinary Americans would respond. They did. The Moratorium brought out people like the New England farmer who had inspired Abbie into activism at the beginning of the decade. But by now he was too embittered to see the changes taking place—changes that his own activism had helped to stimulate.

In November the Moratorium made an uneasy alliance with the Mobe and organized the largest and, from the point of view of political theater, the most remarkable demonstration the country had ever seen. For two nights and a day (November 13 and 14) forty thousand opponents of the war, each carrying a placard with the name of an American killed in battle, marched slowly and silently in single file from Arlington Cemetery past the White House, where one by one they read out the name they were carrying, to the steps of the Capitol, where they placed the sign in a casket. The caskets were then carried to the base of the Washington Monument, where, on Saturday afternoon, November 15, more than half a million people gathered to protest the war. The speeches were forgettable, but the music wasn't. Pete Seeger and Mitch Miller led a million voices in John Lennon's mantra-like "Give Peace a Chance," with Dr. Benjamin Spock, shouting between choruses like a WASP Otis

Redding, "Can you hear us, Nixon?" "Are you listening, Congress?" Here were a blacklisted, left-wing folksinger; a best-selling symbol of square, mainstream pop culture; and the most influential pediatrician in postwar America—together leading a song written by a member of the most popular act in entertainment history who was, himself, highly regarded in radical, freak circles. It represented a convergence of social and cultural forces that earlier would have seemed unimaginable. This was a new movement, addressing an America of untapped potential.

But Abbie didn't see it that way. The Moratorium was a "commuter protest," he wrote in a critique of the demonstration. The presence of Mitch Miller was not a positive sign of the movement's growth but an indication that it was selling out to conservative cultural forces. Although Abbie had once jokingly described himself as a McCartney-Lennonist, he dismissed John Lennon's expressive pacifism as a liberal sentiment. The Moratorium, according to Abbie, was merely a front for "McGovernment," preparing the way for George McGovern's presidential candidacy in 1972, and Abbie would have no truck with any attempt to get the movement back into a voting booth. As for theater, the March against Death didn't rate an observation; what galled Abbie was that "Amerikan [*sic*] flags were thrust into the crowd to hide the NLF flags." The demonstration's marshals, according to Abbie, had once again acted as if they were the police.

The high point for Abbie was a march, later that afternoon, on the Justice Department sponsored by the support group for the Chicago Eight, whose trial on charges of conspiring to incite riots in Chicago had begun two months earlier. Abbie and Jerry Rubin, both forbidden to speak at the insistence of the Moratorium leaders, stood next to Dave Dellinger as he announced the march on behalf of the conspiracy defendants. Predictably, Dellinger urged the marchers to act nonviolently. Just as predictably, hundreds of militants (and government agents) taunted and hurled missiles at the police in order to provoke them into attacking the marchers. Again, predictably, they succeeded. The police used tear gas to disperse the crowd; the gas then drifted all over downtown Washington. Watching this turmoil from his office in the Justice Department, Attorney General John Mitchell was reminded of the Russian Revolution, but Mitchell, of course, considered everything that the peace movement did—even the rally on Saturday—as an outgrowth of Soviet communism.

Stunned by the size of the previous month's October Moratorium, the Nixon administration was determined to combat the antiwar movement as if it was, as Mitchell believed, part of an international communist conspiracy. To this end, Nixon had unleashed Vice President Spiro Agnew (and speechwriter William Safire) to bully the press by accusing the movement and those in the media who publicized it of undercutting American troops and aiding and abetting the communist enemy. It was tantamount to a charge of treason. Unwilling to stand up to this assault on the free press, the media blacked out the March against Death and focused its coverage of Saturday's rally on the skirmish at the Justice Department, rather than on the half-million Americans singing along for peace with Mitch Miller at the Washington Monument. Nixon himself claimed to have watched a football game in the White House during the protest and insisted that the antiwar movement would not deter him from pursuing his secret plan to end the war. In reality, the size of the turnout convinced him that the American public would not tolerate another escalation of the war. He therefore decided to conduct all further escalations (e.g., the bombing of Cambodia) in secret and to step up efforts to destroy the antiwar movement—two paths that led directly to Watergate.

Shunned by the media, the Moratorium had no way of measuring its effectiveness. Startled by the initial quick success, its liberal leaders did not know how to build on their momentum. There was talk of community organizing, of trying to re-create Vietnam Summer, but the mood on the campuses, where the community organizers would have had to come for volunteers, was, as Abbie and the radicals knew, for militant action and countercultural living, not organizing. In the space of two months the Moratorium had recapitulated the experience of the antiwar movement during the five previous years. It had petitioned peacefully, cast its objections to the war in considered and patriotic arguments, and sought the support of mainstream politicians. The result was a new mass movement for peace but no indication of any movement toward peace within the government.

Given all this, Abbie had a point: What good was singing "Give Peace a Chance" or of having another peaceful rally in Washington? In his critique of the Moratorium, Abbie wrote, "The movement doesn't understand imagery. From a revolutionary point of view, the only drama is Sex and Violence. Check out the movies. See what people go to view, especially young people. See what they get involved with. Peace equated with nonviolence is boring."[16] This was precisely the argument that Jerry Rubin had used in advocating a confrontational scenario for the Yippies in Chicago. If peaceful demonstrations didn't have a public impact because the media wouldn't cover them, and if violence was the only kind of action that attracted media attention and government reaction, then the radicals were right: the movement had no choice but to provoke a domestic crisis by disrupting the normal activities of everyday life.

CHAPTER 9

THE TRIAL

HOFFMAN VS. HOFFMAN
1969–1970

On March 20, 1969, Abbie Hoffman, Jerry Rubin, Dave Dellinger, Tom Hayden, Rennie Davis, John Froines, Lee Weiner, and Bobby Seale were indicted in a Chicago federal court on various felony charges, including conspiring to cross state lines "with the intent to incite, organize, promote, encourage, participate in, and carry on a riot," and committing, and aiding and abetting others "in inciting, participating in, and carrying out a riot."[1]

By indicting Yippie and Mobe leaders along with a prominent Black Panther, the Nixon administration believed that it could cripple the antiwar movement. Instead of using its resources to protest in the streets, the movement would have to raise hundreds of thousands of dollars to defend itself in the courts, where its conduct could be controlled by judicial authority.[2]* The administration no doubt believed it was in a no-lose situation. In the early twentieth century the government had used the courts to destroy the Wobblies and the Socialist party, which, led by Eugene Debs, was becoming a contending political force in many areas of the country. The history of the 1950s again indicated that if the leaders of a radical political movement could be prosecuted on criminal charges, ordinary people would be frightened into silence. Even if the defendants were ultimately acquitted by a jury or (as had happened with many of the communists) if their convictions were

---

*The defense effort ultimately cost $500,000. Additional hundreds of thousands of dollars in expenses were saved because lawyers and staff all worked for movement wages.

overturned on appeal, the administration could hail this as proof that the system worked; hence there was no need for a protest movement.

The charges against the "Conspiracy" or the Chicago Eight—the two names that the defendants gave themselves—were suspect on a number of levels. The Rap Brown or Stokely Carmichael Act, as the federal antiriot act was called, had been drafted by southern congressmen (and passed during the Johnson administration as an amendment to a fair housing act) to stop the SNCC leaders Brown and Carmichael from touring the country and giving what Congress considered incendiary speeches about black power. The law was the racists' revenge on the civil rights movement; its hypocrisy was blatant. Southerners who defended states' rights in opposition to the federal government's attempts to enforce civil rights and protect civil rights workers now called upon the federal government to prosecute these same civil rights workers on the assumption that local criminal law (i.e., states' rights) was inadequate to deal with racial outbreaks. In blaming the speeches of "outside agitators" for ghetto strife, the proponents of the antiriot act were using the law to cover over the oppressive conditions that actually caused the rebellions.

Aside from this strange history, the indictment was exceptional for legal reasons. The antiriot act required no concrete evidence linking speech to riot. If Abbie spoke at a meeting in New York with the intent to foment a riot in Chicago (as one undercover agent alleged) and a riot did occur in Chicago six months later, then Abbie could be convicted, not for the riot, but for allegedly having had a riot on his mind six months earlier. There was also a question of double jeopardy. The six major defendants (Froines and Weiner were not charged with the full indictment) were accused of committing felonies that they were also accused of conspiring to commit. For example, Abbie could be acquitted of inciting a riot and still be found guilty of conspiring to incite a riot, meaning that he could conceivably be found guilty of crossing state lines with an intent to commit a crime that the jury found him not guilty of committing.[3]

The factual basis of the conspiracy charge was also questionable. A conspiracy implies plotting together. Yet the Mobe (Dellinger, Hayden, and Davis) and the Yippies (Hoffman and Rubin) had rarely worked together; Froines and Weiner were Mobe marshals whom Hoffman and Rubin knew only in passing; and only Jerry Rubin had ever met, much less talked to, Bobby Seale, who had never had a role in planning the Chicago demonstration and had been there only to speak as a last-minute substitute for Eldridge Cleaver.

★   ★   ★

Abbie took the lead in creating a public image of the Conspiracy as a united front of political and cultural radicals against a repressive government. The Nixon administration, Abbie insisted, was out to convict them not only for their politics but for their way of life. Collaborating with satirists Christopher Cerf, Michael O'Donoghue, and George W. S. Trow, he produced a fund-raising program for the trial (the "official pogrom," it was called), portraying the defendants and the prosecutors as opposing baseball teams— the Chicago Conspiracy and the Washington Kangaroos—in the "World Series of Injustice." The idea was to give a positive and nonthreatening connotation to the notion of a conspiracy, and to satirize the prosecution as clumsy and foolish foils for the Yippie imagination.

Still mulling the experience of Woodstock, Abbie wanted to use the trial not just to publicize opposition to the war but to undercut the government's legitimacy and amplify the meaning of the counterculture, which he now called Woodstock Nation. The Chicago Eight would comport themselves in court not as defendants pleading for justice but as they would at any movement activity, thus turning the formal court proceedings into informal be-ins so that young people, watching the news on television, would identify with the Conspiracy by the way they looked and acted, no matter how the media distorted or ignored their actual political positions. Abbie entered the courtroom every morning by doing a handspring; his intention was to create a visual image of his own (and the Conspiracy's) free-spirited philosophy as a contrast to the humorless and rigid authoritarianism of the government prosecutors. "We are out to discredit the court system," Abbie said in an interview early in the trial. "We are going to show that you cannot get justice in the courts."[4]

The weakness of Abbie's strategy was the power of the judge to find disruptive defendants in contempt of court. The Conspiracy assumed from the onset that the judge was in cahoots with the

Nixon administration.* Abbie faced ten years in prison and expected the maximum penalty should he be convicted. For all his
outward display of confidence and bluster, he was frightened by
that prospect. He understood his psychological makeup and
doubted that he could control his need to be rebellious. Paul
Krassner remembers Abbie's nervousness. "He wasn't in control.
He wasn't in charge. There was the possibility he could get caught
here. . . . He was such a free individual and an anarchistic, outgoing, freewheeling guy that prison for him—terrible for anybody—but for him he dreaded it." Thus, however much Abbie and
his codefendants wanted to mount a counterattack and put the government on trial, they were constrained by the power of the court
and the seriousness of the charges.

Ultimately it was Judge Julius Hoffman who was most responsible for transforming the trial into a dramatic and ofttimes comic
legal spectacle such as Abbie, in his wildest imagination, could not
have more effectively stage-directed. The seventy-four-year-old
Eisenhower appointee, documents indicate, was (illegally) hand-
picked by the government to try the case. He had a reputation for
running a strict courtroom, favoring the prosecution, and meting
out harsh sentences. Early in the case it became apparent to the
Conspiracy that they could use legal jujitsu against Judge Hoffman. By encouraging his passion for strict control they could provoke him to overreact to anything unexpected and thus make
judicial errors they could use, if need be, in an appeal.

Judge Hoffman's control of the case began to unravel even before
the jury was selected. Charles Garry, the lawyer for the Black Panthers, was chosen by the defendants as their chief attorney. But he
had to undergo an emergency gallbladder operation and petitioned
the court to postpone the trial six weeks so that he could recuper-
ate. Such a request is routinely accepted, but Judge Hoffman,
inexplicably, rejected it and ordered the trial to commence with
William Kunstler and Leonard Weinglass, the movement lawyers
who had agreed to work as Garry's assistants, as the chief defense
attorneys. Had Garry remained on the case, he likely would have
insisted on determining the defense strategy and controlling the

---

*Their assumption was right. In the aftermath of the case documents
were uncovered indicating collusion between the FBI, the federal prosecutor, and Judge Julius Hoffman.

defendants' courtroom conduct. He had never met Abbie (and, other than Bobby Seale, barely knew the other defendants) and was not sympathetic to Yippie theatrics. Kunstler and Weinglass, on the other hand, knew Abbie, Jerry, and the Mobe leaders, and were sympathetic to the counterculture. They were willing to work collectively with the defendants, allowing them to have an equal say in determining courtroom tactics and the trial strategy. Kunstler, especially, had a gift for flamboyant theatricality. In short, the absence of Garry laid the defense wide open to Abbie's ideas for a theatrical counteroffensive against both the government's case and judicial authority.

By bumping Garry from the case, Judge Hoffman made Bobby Seale the focal point of the trial. Seale had never met Kunstler and Weinglass and was unwilling to have them stand in for Garry, so he requested the court's permission to defend himself. There were ample precedents for allowing Seale to serve as his own counsel. A number of communist leaders in the Smith Act trials of the 1950s had argued their own cases, and the federal court in Chicago had recently allowed draft resisters to defend themselves without lawyers. Nevertheless, Judge Hoffman rejected Seale's motion and ruled that Kunstler and Weinglass would serve as his attorneys.

The trial began in late September 1969, and its early days were marked by Seale's attempts to act as his own attorney. Unable to silence Seale with contempt citations, Judge Hoffman ordered, on October 30, that he be gagged and bound to a chair at the defense table while the trial proceeded. Dave Dellinger, who was sitting closest to Seale, tried to protect Seale by placing himself in front of the marshals so that they could not tie him up. Abbie and Jerry also tried to hinder the marshals (for which they, as well as the other defendants, who vocally protested what was happening, were later given contempt of court citations). Abbie and Jerry wanted to show solidarity with Seale by wearing a gag in court the next day, while Dellinger wanted to boycott the trial (which would likely have led to bail revocation), but they were all dissuaded by Seale, who, on the advice of Garry (consulted by phone in his hospital bed), wanted to keep the focus on the way the court was mistreating him.[5] Indeed, the sight of a black activist bound and gagged in a court of law catapulted the case into the media limelight—not only in the United States but all over the world. A week later, under a hail of criticism from the media and, one presumes, other federal justices,

Hoffman declared a mistrial for Seale and severed his case from that of the seven white defendants (who thereafter became known as the Chicago Seven). At the same time he sentenced Seale to four years in jail for sixteen acts of contempt, each citation representing an attempt by Seale to act as his own attorney or to protest what he considered the judge's racist conduct.

Controversial rulings followed one upon another. Kunstler and Weinglass (whose name the judge continually mispronounced) had hired a team of four lawyers, including Gerry Lefcourt, to assist them in pretrial motions. With their work done, the lawyers sent the court a telegram withdrawing from the case, a common procedure for out-of-state lawyers. Nevertheless, Judge Hoffman issued bench warrants for their arrest because they had not declared their intent to withdraw directly before his court. Protests from the bar, the press, and from other judges eventually forced Judge Hoffman to retreat, but not before Lefcourt and lawyer Michael Tiger were briefly jailed when they rushed to Chicago to explain their position.

During jury selection Judge Hoffman rejected the defense's request to question potential jurors about their social and political attitudes. Abbie had prepared a list of questions in the hope of screening jurors for their sympathy or hostility to the youth culture: If your children are female, do they wear a brassiere all the time? Do you consider marijuana habit-forming? Can you identify Country Joe, Phil Ochs, and the Jefferson Airplane?[26] Judge Hoffman disallowed these and other, more political lines of questioning. Believing that the most they could hope for was a hung jury, the defendants settled for two men and ten women, four of whom were black. Shortly after the jury was seated, Judge Hoffman announced that two of the jurors had received threatening notes from the Black Panthers. One of the jurors, whom he identified, was the youngest woman on the jury. She, in fact, had not seen the note (it was intercepted by her parents and turned over to the court). Informed by the judge that her life was in danger, she accepted his offer to be excused from the jury. The Conspiracy believed that the notes were government ploys to enable the judge to get rid of a juror who seemed sympathetic to them. The notes also served as an excuse for Judge Hoffman to sequester the jury for the duration of the trial, a move that the defendants opposed because it would isolate the jurors from the social and political turmoil that they saw as supporting the arguments in their defense: if social and political unrest existed without the defendants being free to organize it, then the turmoil in Chicago wasn't necessarily caused by any "conspiracy."

The trial continued for four additional months without Bobby Seale. The prosecution's case rested on the testimony of policemen and undercover agents, including the phony biker Robert Pierson, and of the young journalist student who had infiltrated the Mobe at the behest of the Chicago columnist Jack Mabley. The testimony droned on through the autumn and into the winter. Abbie and his fellow defendants occupied themselves at the defense table by reading, writing, and answering their mail. Sometimes they dozed. What drama there was occurred when Kunstler or Weinglass tried to argue against Judge Hoffman's rulings, which, virtually in every instance, went against the defendants. To be sure, in turning the defense table into a desk for movement business, the defendants were breaching customary courtroom etiquette. More provocative was their attempt to bring a birthday cake to the defense table to celebrate Bobby Seale's birthday, and their observance of the October Moratorium by wearing black armbands and having the flags of both the United States and Vietnam's National Liberation Front draped across the table. When Dellinger rose to read the names of Americans killed in action, he was ordered silent by Judge Hoffman. Persisting, he was surrounded by armed guards who forced him back into his chair. When the guards tried to confiscate the flags, Abbie and Jerry grabbed on to them and a tugging match ensued. As Jason Epstein noted in *The Great Conspiracy Trial*, the defendants had succeeded in recapitulating the entire history of the antiwar movement: attempts to speak out and peacefully protest the war in the court as well as in public were quashed by armed guards under government orders.[7]

The prosecution rested in December. Weinglass felt that the government had failed to make a convincing case and wanted to go directly to the jury, but the seven defendants were intent on transforming the trial into a political forum. Abbie arranged for Allen Ginsberg, Norman Mailer, Phil Ochs, Judy Collins, Arlo Guthrie, Pete Seeger, and other cultural figures to testify about the Chicago demonstrations and the cultural and lifestyle issues that Abbie insisted were also on trial. Another group of defense witnesses, including Jesse Jackson, Julian Bond, former Kennedy aide Richard Goodwin, and a number of Democratic party delegates, testified about the political significance of the Chicago demonstrations.

An attempt to have Ramsey Clark testify about the efforts of Abbie and Rennie Davis to get permits from Mayor Daley was crushed by Judge Hoffman, who would not let the former attorney general take the stand. Kunstler tried to question Mayor Daley, but Judge Hoffman, on motions by the prosecution, ruled his questions out of order. The day that Daley took the stand, Abbie walked up to him with his fists raised in a mock fighter's pose and said, "Let's you and me go outside and duke it out." Daley laughed, for once understanding Abbie's bravado.

Abbie and Rennie Davis were selected by the defendants to testify for the defense. Davis represented the Mobe's perspective and, as Abbie put it, "would play the good scout, the kid next door who unselfishly mowed your lawn in the summer." He himself would be the "neighborhood prankster. A minor nuisance whose neck you'd like to wring but not someone you'd send to prison for ten years."[8] Abbie's testimony, according to Dwight Macdonald, was "the crux of the trial, the most extensive and intensive expression of the new-radical style. It's also extremely amusing and penetrating; Abbie combines wit, imagination and shrewdness in a way not so common, and he has mastered his peculiar style so thoroughly that he can play around in and with it like a frisky dolphin. They can't even get him to give his name and address."[9] Abbie's testimony began:

> DEFENSE ATTORNEY WEINGLASS: Will you please identify yourself for the record.
>
> HOFFMAN: My name is Abbie. I am an orphan of America. . . .
>
> WEINGLASS: Where do you reside?
>
> HOFFMAN: I live in Woodstock Nation.
>
> WEINGLASS: Will you tell the Court and jury where it is?
>
> HOFFMAN: Yes. It is a nation of alienated young people. We carry it around with us as a state of mind in the same way the Sioux Indians carried the Sioux nation around with them. It's a nation dedicated to cooperation versus competition, to the idea that people should have better means of exchange than property and money, that there should be some other basis for human interaction, it is a nation dedicated to—

JUDGE HOFFMAN: Just where is it, that is all.

HOFFMAN: It is in my mind and in the minds of my brothers and sisters. It does not consist of property or material but, rather, of ideas and values. . . .

JUDGE HOFFMAN: No, we want the place of residence, if he has one, place of doing business, if you have a business. Nothing about philosophy or India, sir. Just where you live, if you have a place to live. Now, you said Woodstock. In what state is Woodstock?

HOFFMAN: It is the state of mind, in the mind of myself and my brothers and sisters. . . .

WEINGLASS: Can you tell the Court and jury your present age?

HOFFMAN: My age is 33. I am a child of the 60's.

WEINGLASS: When were you born?

HOFFMAN: Psychologically, 1960. . . .

WEINGLASS: Can you tell the Court and jury what is your present occupation?

HOFFMAN: I am a cultural revolutionary. Well, I am really a defendant—full time.[10]

The most lasting image of the Chicago Seven is of Abbie and Jerry heckling and pulling pranks on the judge. But when it came to speaking out in court, it was Dave Dellinger rather than Abbie or Jerry who consistently risked charges of contempt in order to protest judicial rulings or the testimony of dishonest government witnesses. Dellinger was the one defendant who believed that it was sometimes necessary to go to jail for one's principles. He believed in the Quaker principle of speaking truth to power and letting the chips fall where they may. Toward the end of the trial, when Chicago's deputy chief of police James Riordan testified (incorrectly) that Dellinger had led a march of demonstrators carrying the NLF flag, Dellinger muttered, "Oh bullshit" (which the *New York Times* referred to as a "barnyard epithet"). Judge Hoffman reacted by revoking Dellinger's bail. As Dellinger was led off to jail, pandemonium broke out in the court, with the defendants shouting insults at the judge and declaring their support for Dellinger. Abbie, of course, joined in, accusing Judge Hoffman of being "a disgrace to the Jews." In the midst of the commotion, Abbie went over to Dellinger's thirteen-year-old daughter, Michele, who was seated in the courtroom, and put his arm around her. "Your daddy is going to be all right," he assured her.[11]

Abbie and Jerry wanted to force Judge Hoffman to jail them all—in solidarity with Dellinger and so that the testimony would end on a theatrical flourish, with all the defendants in jail. Tom Hayden was especially opposed to the idea. Yippie theater is like pacifist politics, he later explained, showing his distaste for both. It "can expose institutions, but . . . can never prevent repression and punishment."[12] Hayden, who fought with Abbie over tactics throughout the trial, wanted to stay out of jail so as to conclude the defense with an appeal to the jury that could be taken seriously by middle-class America.

Without a consensus among the defendants, the two Yippies decided to act on their own. The next day they each appeared in a black judicial robe over the blue uniform of the Chicago police. Abbie took his robe off in front of the stand and stomped all over it. When the judge didn't react, Abbie unleashed a deliberate verbal attack (possibly unprecedented in the annals of American jurisprudence), the high points of which included:

"Your idea of justice is the only obscenity in the room."

"You schtunk. Vo den? Shanda fur de goyem? Huh?" (which Abbie later translated from the Yiddish for the press as, "What are you, a front man for the WASP power elite?").

"Julie. . . . This ain't the Standard Club" (a reference to an exclusive downtown club for wealthy German-American Jews where the judge regularly took his lunch).

"Oh, tell him to stick it up his bowling ball. . . . How's your war stock, Julie?" (a reference to the stock that the judge's wife held in the Brunswick Corporation, a manufacturer of equipment for both bowling and war).[13]

★   ★   ★

The case went to the jury on February 14, 1970. While the jurors deliberated, Judge Hoffman declared the defendants and their lawyers guilty of 159 instances of contempt of court. The penalties ranged from four years and thirteen days for Kunstler to two months and eighteen days for Weiner. Dellinger, Davis, and Rubin got over two years, while Hayden got one year and thirteen days. Abbie was cited on 24 counts of contempt (only Dellinger, with 32 counts, had more), but for inexplicable reasons he was sentenced to just eight months.*

Had Abbie touched some soft spot in the judge? Whereas Dellinger, as well as Hayden and Davis, fought the judge on political principles, Abbie treated Judge Hoffman with the mocking disdain of a stand-up comedian (someone like Jack E. Leonard or Shecky Green) insulting a boorish loudmouth in a Borscht Belt hotel. Abbie's attacks on his namesake were cutting, personal, and at times very funny. And it wasn't just in the courtroom that Abbie went after Judge Hoffman. Outside, Abbie joked that he was "Julie's son" and would change his first name to "Fuck" in order to identify himself in his courtroom testimony as "Fuck Hoffman." On weekend speaking dates at colleges throughout the country Abbie often led the students in chanting, "Fuck the judge!" One afternoon Gordon Sherman, the founder of the Midas Muffler Company and a supporter of progressive causes, took Kunstler, Dellinger, Jerry, and Abbie to lunch at the Standard Club, where he, too, was a member. The two Yippies had to wear borrowed barbers' jackets to get in because they didn't have jackets of their own. According to Kunstler, they were seated next to where Judge Hoffman was lunching with two U.S. marshals. When the judge moved to a new table to get away from the defendants, Abbie and Jerry moved with him, five times in all, until the judge and his luncheon companions left without eating.[14]

In *The Ordeal of Civility*, a book that Abbie claimed offered the keenest understanding of his conduct at the trial, John Murray Cuddihy noted the "ethnic infighting" that was the subtext to what he called "A Tale of Two Hoffmans." Abbie, in this period of his life, didn't make much of his Jewishness. He was quietly proud of the prominence of Jews in the radical movement and observed that Jews in the movement were often attracted to the hedonism of the Yippies ("Yiddish hippies," he sometimes called them), whereas left-wing Christians seemed more comfortable with what Abbie called "the politics of guilt." (Guilt is a question of nuance, he once explained. Jews don't feel guilty about politics or history, for they have been the victims of both, and they have no concept of original sin. Thus, Jews don't feel guilty about people starving in Africa,

*He got six days for insulting the judge in Yiddish and seven days for wearing judicial robes.

for example, although in identifying with these victims they likely
will want to help. What Jews feel guilty about are personal issues,
like "not being a 'success,'" and interpersonal issues, as when
"parents and children don't get along.")[15] While not religiously
observant, Abbie didn't reject his Jewish roots (as some left-wing
radicals did) and remained interested in the intellectual conflicts
within the secular Jewish community. Moreover, Abbie felt comfortable as a Jew and assured as an American and sensed in Judge
Hoffman a defensiveness about his Jewish background, a vulnera-
bility that he, Abbie, could exploit. Perhaps it was the way the
judge deliberately mispronounced the name "Weinglass" as "Wein-
stein" or "Weinburg" (which might have been taken as a crude
form of anti-Semitism coming from someone else). Or perhaps
Abbie noted Judge Hoffman's hostility toward Arthur Waskow, a
witness for the defense who insisted on wearing his yarmulke on
the stand. As a German Jew and as an assimilationist who had
married into Republican money, Judge Hoffman was an inviting
target in the game of Jewish infighting that Abbie was familiar with
from his youth in Worcester and at Brandeis.

The jury deliberated for four days, with four jurors favoring
acquittal on all counts and the other eight insisting on various convictions, but Judge Hoffman refused to accept a deadlocked jury.
To end their ordeal (they had been sequestered for five months),
the jurors then forged a compromise, acquitting all the defendants
on the conspiracy charge but convicting Hoffman, Rubin, Dellinger, Davis, and Hayden of crossing state lines with intent to riot.
The judge then imposed the maximum sentence of five years in
prison and a fine of five thousand dollars each and immediately
revoked bail despite their stated intention to appeal the verdict.
Abbie's parting shot as he was being escorted to jail was, "When
decorum is repression, the only dignity that free men have is to
speak out."

It was a peculiar line, coming from Abbie—formal, aphoristic,
old-fashioned—and Cuddihy analyzed it closely: "With this declaration in early 1970, Abbie Hoffman had finally surfaced and
articulated the latent issue that had been secretly at work all along
in the civil rights agitation of the two preceding decades. With this
declaration as its manifesto, the civil rights movement came to self-
consciousness: in discovering that it was a counterculture and con-
sequently a counterpolitics, the movement demonstrated . . . the

inherently bourgeois nature of civil liberties, the real meaning of 'bourgeois civil liberties'; decorum was experienced as political repression. What *you* define as public decorum, Abbie Hoffman told Julius Hoffman, *I* define as political repression." [16]

Cuddihy overstates the scope of Abbie's remark, because civil rights activists, in the early days of the movement, strove to present themselves as models of decorum. Committing civil disobedience at lunch counters and on buses, activists wore their best clothes and, in court, abided by judicial rules, believing that the constitutional guarantees embedded in the Bill of Rights would ultimately protect them. But once the civil rights activists and then the antiwar movement began pushing for policy changes that were not mandated by the Constitution, the courts and all the trappings of legal decorum stopped working for them, becoming, as Abbie charged, instruments to uphold the status quo.

Abbie's strategy in court was based on his knowledge of Lenny Bruce's experience. Arrested for using obscene words as part of his nightclub act, Bruce armed himself with constitutional citations about civil liberties and went bravely before the courts convinced that the law would protect his act. Not only was his faith misplaced, but in abiding by the rules of judicial decorum he gave up the source of his own unique strength—his verbal wit. Abbie thus resolved to stake his freedom—and the movement's survival—on the power of the imagination. He and his codefendants, believing that the court was stacked against them, set out to strip it of its decorous veneer. To this end, Abbie Hoffman could not have found a better foil than Judge Julius Hoffman, whose zeal for the prosecution, prodded and provoked by the defendants, yielded judicial mistakes that even the bourgeois legal system would not tolerate.

Within two weeks an appeals court reversed Judge Hoffman on the issue of bail, and the five radicals were released from Cook County Jail. In May 1972 the court of appeals reversed all the contempt citations pending a hearing by a new judge and ruled that Judge Hoffman had made a mistake in not allowing Seale to defend himself. In November 1972 the court of appeals overturned all the convictions on the basis of judicial and prosecution errors. In November 1973 a reduced number of contempt charges were upheld against Hoffman, Dellinger, Rubin, and Kunstler, but the appeal judge, Edward Gignoux of Maine, sentenced them to time already served. Thus, the two weeks in Cook County Jail was the longest

time Abbie ever spent in jail for his political activity. The low point
of his jail experience was having his hair shaved from his head and
later displayed by the Cook County sheriff as a personal trophy.

Abbie credited the courtroom counteroffensive and the power of
street demonstrations for keeping the Conspiracy out of prison. He
refused to acknowledge that the legal system had also come through
for them. As he so often did, Abbie elevated a tactical success to a
strategic guideline. Since direct action had saved the Conspiracy,
more direct action—that is, a continuation of the assault on decorum—would build the movement, end the war, and change the
nation. Just as he would not acknowledge the role that the Bill of
Rights had played in the acquittal, he would not allow the possibility that traditional politics, including finding allies within the system, could play a role in changing the country.

The government succeeded in forcing the radical movement to ex-
pend precious resources on behalf of the Conspiracy. To raise
money and build political support, the defendants would split up
every weekend and fly to speaking engagements around the country. (Tom Hayden estimates that the Chicago Seven plus their lawyers made approximately five hundred campus appearances.) At a
typical fee of one thousand dollars an appearance, the speeches
were the major source of money for the defense. Abbie, especially,
was a popular speaker. Everywhere he went he brought controversy, excitement, and the exhilaration of confrontation. The FBI
dogged him, taping his every word, planting hostile stories in the
local press, encouraging hawkish politicians, wary college administrators, and right-wing vigilantes to try to prevent, or at least
protest, his speaking engagements. By this time, however, Abbie
was a virtuoso in exploiting negative publicity. With civil liberties
lawyers ready to defend his right of free speech and students ready
to take to the streets if his appearance was banned, his speaking
tours became affirmations of the movement's power.

Like any good performer, Abbie had the ability to make every
appearance seem as if it was totally fresh and spontaneous. But in
fact he crafted his speeches, honing every provocation down to the
last shouted obscenity. Before each speaking date he would fa-
miliarize himself with local history and with the issues that were
important to the local activists. He treated his audience not as a

passive and impersonal mass but as fellow-activists making history. Speaking at a 1970 rally on the Boston Common, Abbie began by pointing to the John Hancock insurance company building, a controversial skyscraper casting its shadow over the park, and shouting, "John Hancock was a revolutionary! He wasn't any fuckin' insurance salesman." When the gales of cheers had subsided, Abbie brought the rally down to hometown reality, comparing the demonstrators to other local heroes—Paul Revere and the minutemen—connecting their radical activism to the Boston Tea Party and the battles of Concord, Lexington, and Bunker Hill, and treating the rally as a historic moment in this ongoing American revolutionary tradition. As was his style, he worked the crowd as if he was the headline act in a Las Vegas nightclub: "Pacing, mugging, squatting, pacing again, swearing, jumping, and all the time exhorting people to begin freeing themselves before they talked about freeing others." Ken Hurwitz, a Harvard student who was the rally's organizer, was not sympathetic to Abbie's politics, considering him "a clown" who took people away from "genuine politics." But Abbie's "admittedly grandstanding performance," Hurwitz conceded, "was the closest the afternoon came to capturing the best of the cultural spirit of the anti-war movement. . . . He didn't talk that afternoon about what split us but about what we had in common." [17]

Abbie was believable as a speaker because people saw that he was doing what he advocated, risking imprisonment, provoking the police, making a life out of being an agitator, putting himself on the front line of change. A good part of every speech—during and after the conspiracy trial—was a description of his adventures with the police and the judiciary. Rather than describing the prosecutors, judges, and police as powerful adversaries and symbols of evil, he portrayed them as buffoons, mock villains that anyone with verve could turn into fools. Although he faced years in prison, Abbie always presented himself as having the last laugh at the law.

Abbie delighted in pushing his performances beyond the boundary of acceptable taste and official tolerance. He advocated draft resistance and applauded GIs who "fragged" their officers. He didn't just advocate smoking marijuana, he puffed on a joint on stage, daring campus and local police, state troopers, and FBI special agents who were usually in attendance to arrest him, knowing that they knew such a move would likely touch off a student riot.

Leading a chant of "Fuck the judge," as Abbie often did when talking about the conspiracy trial, was meant to break through the barrier of propriety and thus meld youthful audiences into feeling the power of their generational solidarity. Abbie used obscenity to expose the topsy-turvy moral universe of American society during the Vietnam era. What was evil? What was hypocrisy? The authorities, and many older Americans, were shocked by Abbie's use of obscene language; but many of them supported a policy that involved bombing civilians, torching peasant villages, and napalming children.

After government policy was skewered and scorned, Abbie's basic message was that young people should commit themselves to changing the system. He was a one-man recruiting officer for the revolution, bolstering younger activists (many of whom faced disciplinary actions for their antiwar activity) and showing them by his own experience that it was possible to live a life dedicated to radical politics and that dropping out of the system was a career move that was not only fun but righteous and exciting. As a civil rights worker, Abbie had argued for job opportunities, good wages, and meaningful work. Now, as an advocate for the counterculture, he demanded full *un*employment. His concept of a postaffluent, cybernetic (that is, thoroughly automated) society had special appeal to students who hadn't yet entered the job market and didn't have families to raise, payrolls to make, or ends to meet. "We want a society of leisure, a society of creative artists in which we're free to do whatever we want, in which we enjoy what we're doing. If you enjoy it, it's not work. Work is something you do for money, for the kids—you know, for the boss, for the machines. I'm never gonna work again, ever," Abbie would tell his youthful audiences.[18]

The idea of a postaffluent or postscarcity economy in which machines would do all the drudge labor was commonplace in the counterculture. Murray Bookchin, the intellectual mentor of the Motherfuckers, wrote that technological advances had created the preconditions for an anarchistic utopia. Gary Snyder, Allen Ginsberg, Alan Watts, Buckminster Fuller, Timothy Leary, and other countercultural leaders advanced Digger-like notions of decentralized, cooperative communities where people would be free to pursue higher levels of consciousness and survive without money by producing arts and crafts.

Abbie was neither a utopian thinker nor a radical economist with a detailed plan for postscarcity living. His impact as a speaker was as a motivator. He was a salesman of change, a living inspiration that people could walk away from the demands of mainstream society and invent themselves as anyone they wanted to be. Beyond that, he represented the idea of political activism as the highest calling. Ideally, he wanted people to use their skills to advance the revolution, and he thus admired and considered as his peers the serious doctors, lawyers, creative artists, architects, social workers, engineers, carpenters, and scientists who refused to enlist in the corporate world and, without concern for financial gain, were working in the popular movement.

Yet, speaking to students, he presented a mixed message. With his glib and giggly hedonism, Abbie made working for change sound too easy. There was no hint of the hard work and the lifelong commitment that would be needed to change society. In describing his own organizing efforts, he ignored the planning behind his well-rehearsed spontaneity. His enthusiasm, however, fit the mood of his audience. Young people in the late 1960s and early 1970s had the choice (because in Abbie—and in radicals like him—they had a model) of dropping out of the mainstream and jumping into the effort to create a new society. Abbie made it sound exciting. An instant high! No sacrifice! Instant gratification! Abbie had started out to organize for the antiwar movement within the hippie counterculture. In the balance, the hedonism and utopian grandiosity of countercultural politics disorganized him.

CHAPTER

10 LAST HURRAH

1970–1972

Abbie was now a celebrity, a symbol of the country's polarized culture, loathed by some, extolled by others. He was hot and not just in police terminology. Harassed on the one side by the government, he was courted on the other by businessmen who saw money to be made by promoting America's most mediagenic revolutionary. One company wanted to market a windup Abbie doll, while advertising executives wanted his advice on selling to the youth market. Abbie rejected these and similar offers before they reached the discussion stage. Neither he nor Anita had any interest in making money or doing anything that did not further the goals of the revolution. In this they were typical of most activists of this period. The Hoffmans did, however, meet with an executive from the William Morris theatrical agency who wanted to represent Abbie in his "career" as a media personality. They were amused by the attention but otherwise unimpressed. "It was so Hollywood, such a different world," Anita recalls. "It struck us as sleazy, as out of anything that we could remotely connect to."

Abbie liked being a public personality and was ready with a quick quip and an engaging smile for anyone who recognized him as the famous Yippie. He was as conscious of his role as a "famous person" as he was of his position as a radical leader, and used his status to promote his politics (as other celebrities promoted their latest books and movies) to a mass audience. As a student of the media, he understood that fame is fleeting and that being a celebrity has nothing whatever to do with being a person of substance, accomplishment, or historical importance. But he was also tempted by the ego boost that came from public recognition and from being

able to approach other celebrities on a superficially intimate first-
name basis. Invited to appear on the Dick Cavett and Merv Griffin
shows, he was angered that he was not invited to do the Johnny
Carson show (and also wondered if, as a media performer, he was
ready for America's number one late night show). Although it
would have been a boost for the movement to have Abbie appear
on shows like Johnny Carson's, he began to see his media career as
itself a crucial issue, with the prospects of the movement rising and
falling on the basis of his public appearances. Many activists were
put off by his media-tripping. "By what incredible arrogance did
this pathological ego tripper decide three years ago that he *was* the
movement?" huffed one Boston activist in a letter to *WIN* magazine
in the autumn of 1971.[1]

Abbie had a different relationship with celebrities who were sympathetic to the movement. He got Jimi Hendrix to help pay for the
marijuana that he, Anita, and Marty and Susan Carey rolled into
joints and mailed, along with an explanatory message, as Valentine
gifts to news reporters and one thousand other people whose names
they picked from the telephone book. According to Mayer Vishner,
Abbie treated rock stars and other sympathetic celebrities as if
they of course shared a common goal. "He would argue politics and
smoke dope with them. He would engage them as equals, giving
them the feeling that they were part of the movement, part of a
fellowship of struggle. They would want to help, and he would suggest that they give money to his projects." Among his best friends
in the rock world were Grace Slick and Paul Kantner of the Jefferson Airplane. Abbie had initially criticized the Airplane for doing
television ads for Levi's jeans. But they met and liked one another.
Slick had been a classmate of President Nixon's daughter Tricia at
Finch College and in 1970 was invited to the White House for a
class reunion. Grace asked Abbie to accompany her as her beau.
She planned to hide LSD under her long fake fingernails and mix
it into the punch. The plan was foiled when the *Life* photographer
whom they had alerted to film their surprise tipped off the White
House. Abbie was not allowed into the party, and Grace Slick did
not want to carry out the plan alone.

While enjoying celebrity status, Abbie tried to maintain a distinction between his public image and his private life. In 1971 Jerry
Rubin read that John Lennon and Yoko Ono were living in Greenwich Village. Jerry phoned Apple Records in London to make ar-
rangements to meet them. With Abbie and Anita, Jerry met John

and Yoko one Saturday afternoon under the arch in Washington
Square Park. They drove around in John's limousine and then
went to Abbie and Anita's apartment, smoked pot, and, as Jerry
recalled, talked for hours about "how the Yippies had been apply-
ing Beatle tactics to politics, trying to merge music and life." John
Lennon, who had been friendly with new leftists in Great Britain,
wanted to do something political in the United States. Abbie and
Jerry suggested that he tour with them to raise money to free John
Sinclair and to help pay for other political projects. Afterward,
Jerry pursued a personal relationship with John and Yoko,
whereas Abbie and Anita did not. Stew Albert, who worked on the
concert project, recalls that Abbie would not defer to Lennon's
fame. "He had no time for that." Whereas Jerry looked up to celebrities, Abbie considered them his peers.*

On April 30, 1970, President Nixon announced that American
troops had invaded Cambodia. This touched off the most massive
antiwar demonstrations in the history of the nation. When, on May
4, National Guardsmen fired at two hundred demonstrators at
Kent State University in Ohio, killing four students and wounding
nine others, the demonstrations reached explosive proportions.
Abbie spent the days of the Cambodia and Kent State protests
speaking on college campuses throughout the Northeast, encouraging the student strikes that were spreading from campus to
campus and urging people to join the march on the White House,
an emergency demonstration the Mobe was hurriedly planning for
May 9. Everywhere he went there was tension and conflict. In New
York, Abbie received death threats, and students had to protect
him from right-wing vigilantes armed with baseball bats and other
weapons. Egged on by labor leader Peter Brennan, construction
workers and longshoremen were beating up antiwar protesters. (In
one incident a gang of longshoremen assaulted students at Pace
College with meat hooks.) Brennan was rewarded by the Nixon
administration with the position of secretary of labor.

On May 9 more than 100,000 people gathered in Washington to

---

*According to Anita: "Yoko bragged about her avant-garde connections.
She was so pushy. But John was just a regular, sweet person. His genius
was in his art form. He was easy to be with."

protest the invasion of Cambodia and the Kent State killings. Thousands came ready to commit civil disobedience. Abbie here supported the idea of nonviolent civil disobedience at the White House as potentially "effective and forceful." But the factionalized Mobe was unable to organize a concerted action—and the opportunity was lost. That night a few thousand frustrated protesters trashed the Washington streets. "But there is a time to run, a time to fight, a time to be silent, a time for every tactic the imagination can dream up, I suppose," Abbie wrote in his autobiography. "This, however, was the time to sit down and refuse to move until the war ended." The next day he commiserated with Dave Dellinger; what could have been a powerful nonviolent action had turned out to be "a big picnic."[2]

During this same period the cultural wing of the movement was trying to rally support for Tim Leary, sentenced to ten years on drug charges and facing still more indictments. Abbie was asked to speak at a benefit for Leary at the Village Gate nightclub in Greenwich Village. For Abbie, the evening only highlighted the divisiveness that was tearing apart the movement. To begin with there were "bad vibes in the green room," as Anita Hoffman put it. The speakers were all males, and Anita was depressed by what she felt as their heavy misogyny. Abbie was angered by the antipolitical attitude of the speakers who had preceded him. He responded by taking the position that Leary could be freed only by political change, becoming more politically hard-line as the spiritually oriented cultural nationalists tried to drown him out by militant omming. Afterward, according to Anita, Abbie realized that he had misplayed the situation and that his stridency had prevented the audience from hearing his message. Returning home, the Hoffmans were surprised by a uniformed policeman with a searchlight lurking on their roof. He slunk away without explaining his presence, but Abbie and Anita suspected that he was on a spying mission. Thoroughly demoralized, they talked about going into exile and the next day visited the Cuban Mission to the United Nations to plan for that contingency.[3]

Their despair passed. In May and June more than 80 percent of the country's colleges and universities experienced some kind of strike action in protest over Kent State and Cambodia. In October 1970 Tim Leary climbed over a twelve-foot fence surrounding a minimum security prison in San Luis Obispo, California, and with the help of the Weather Underground—a remnant of SDS's action-faction that had turned to urban terrorism—escaped to freedom. Abbie, who was in contact with the Weather Underground, was one of a number of white radicals who interceded with the Black Panthers and arranged for Leary to take refuge in Algeria with Eldridge Cleaver. Cleaver had jumped bail after a gun battle with Oakland police and had escaped to Algeria, where the left-wing Algerian government had allowed him to set up a quasi-official Black Panther embassy. To the Yippies, this was the fulfillment of a political dream: revolutionary culture and politics united. To most everyone else in the movement it was simply mind-boggling: the guru of the psychedelic counterculture had joined with the Black Panthers and the Weather Underground, the gun-toting self-proclaimed vanguards of the black and white left. In a typically good-natured gesture, the Yippies decided to organize a joint Yippie-Weather delegation to fly to Algeria in order to celebrate Leary's birthday and publicly announce the unity of these three wings of the radical movement. Because bail restrictions prohibited Abbie and Jerry Rubin from traveling to Algeria (their conspiracy convictions were still on appeal), Anita Hoffman was delegated to go with Stew Albert as one of the two Yippie representatives. Abbie meanwhile paid the fare of four other Americans: Marty Kenner, his friend from Berkeley who now headed the Black Panther Defense Fund; Brian Flanagan and Jonah Raskin, both of whom were associated with the Weather organization; and Jennifer Dohrn, the sister of Bernardine Dohrn, who, as a leader of the Weather Underground, had recently made the FBI's "ten most wanted" list.

Anita was reluctant to play the role of Abbie's stand-in and was put off by the Panthers' rigid hierarchical concept of political organization. What she saw in Algiers shocked her. Eldridge Cleaver was on a power trip. Other Panthers who were with him in exile were completely under his orders, as, so it seemed, were Leary and his wife Rosemary. The women in the Panther entourage seemed to Anita to be in an especially oppressive situation. Kathleen Cleaver, who was well known as a dynamic party leader in the United States, seemed to be in a condition of house arrest. Eldridge

Cleaver was having an open affair with a Belgian woman, while his wife was not allowed to spend time alone with Anita or any of the other American women. Worse, none of the other Americans in the delegation thought there was anything strange about this arrangement. "It seemed to me that the other members of our party totally knuckled under to Cleaver, forgetting they were Yippies or Weather representatives, or anything other than obedient Cleaver followers," Anita wrote a couple of years later in an article she did not try to get published. Disobeying Cleaver's orders, Anita spent a day wandering "like any tourist through Algiers' grim and womenless streets," and as a result was ostracized by both the Panthers and the American delegation. "None of the other Americans ever considered for one moment standing up to Cleaver on any issue. Perhaps they were afraid or perhaps they were just better leftists than I," she later recorded in her unpublished article.

Anita Hoffman had been an activist for almost ten years. Other leftists perceived her simply as Abbie's wife—or as his "gun moll," as she and her friends sometimes joked (she and Abbie liked the image of Bonnie and Clyde, the outlaw couple portrayed by Faye Dunaway and Warren Beatty in a popular movie of that time). Yet Anita was never Abbie's obedient follower; nor was she a partyliner. "What had inspired me to enter the movement," she wrote in her article, "was the feeling of equality and love among the brothers and sisters in it who shared a vision of how the world could be better. Fundamental to that vision was a profound respect for the autonomy of the individual. Through all the years of organizing movements and demonstrations, the Yippies had always striven for the minimal degree of structure and authority needed to produce unity. If anything united the counterculture it was a belief in the motivational possibilities of life rather than fear. But it was fear that operated in the exile community in Algeria, for whatever reasons, and I could not support it."

Isolated in the Panther compound, Anita climbed out a window, talked her way through Algerian customs, and boarded a plane for Paris. There, she told Abbie her story, and he believed her. (Still under bail restrictions, Abbie and Jerry were allowed to travel in Europe.) When the other delegates flew to Paris they, joined now by Jerry Rubin, criticized Anita and ostracized both the Hoffmans. Later that year Anita was vindicated when Cleaver imprisoned the

Learys, denounced the Yippies, and was himself denounced by
Huey Newton and the Panther leadership in America.* The Algerian trip was the beginning of Anita's disillusionment with the
movement. But she didn't write up her experience until much later,
and even then didn't try to publish it. She knew that most radicals
would not believe a white, middle-class woman against the word of
Eldridge Cleaver, a black male movement hero.

Anita Hoffman's anger at the sexism she witnessed at the Leary
benefit and in Algiers was heightened by her awareness of the radical women's movement, which in New York was centered in her
and Abbie's Lower East Side political circle. Indeed, the first public manifestation of the new movement, a satirical send-up of the
1968 Miss America pageant in Atlantic City, was an offshoot of the
Yippie plan for Chicago. The principal organizer of this demonstration was Robin Morgan, a member of the Lower East Side
affinity group that included, among others, Abbie and Anita, Paul
Krassner, Ellen Maslow, and Jerry Rubin. At the same time that
she was participating in Yippie, Morgan was attending meetings of
New York Radical Women, the first women's liberation group organized in New York City. The idea of women's liberation had been
percolating among movement women beginning in the mid-1960s as
a critique of the sexist behavior of movement men and the sexist
bias of movement organizing. This led to an analysis of sexism in
the larger culture and, as a result, increasing anger, first at the
disdainful attitude that movement men had toward feminist ideas
and ultimately at how deeply rooted and pervasive sexism was in
male society. Gradually Morgan drifted away from the Yippies and
began to devote her energy to women's liberation. Still, she spent
long hours arguing with the Yippies about the importance of the
new feminism. They were not listening. Their attitude, she remembered, was "'You must be crazy, going to demonstrate against
something so irrelevant as the Miss America Pageant.' The revolution is going to take place in Chicago."[4]

---

* Albert and Kenner later apologized to Anita for their conduct in Algeria
and in interviews with this author acknowledged the accuracy of her version.

Coming out of the same Lower East Side milieu that spawned the Yippies, Morgan and her sisters brought to the women's movement a bohemian perspective similar to that which the Yippies brought to the antiwar movement. Their organization, WITCH, was structured (nonstructured, actually) in the Yippie manner, with "totally autonomous" chapters springing up across the country, all sharing a common Yippie style of "insouciance, theatricality, humor, and activism."[5] WITCH covens, like the Yippie groups, perceived the world through a hip/straight dialectic and targeted straight women as if they were a cause rather than the victims of sexism in society. In addition to protesting Miss America, WITCH activists let mice loose at a New York bridal fair, which not only disrupted the fair but reinforced the sexist stereotype of women becoming hysterical at the sight of a mouse. This kind of activism provoked the same kind of cultural backlash that the Yippies had aroused by their presence in Chicago. But the feminists moved beyond the polarizing Yippie assumptions. Whereas the Yippies existed to exploit the conflict between the hip and the straight, radical feminism eventually opened outward to embrace the totality of women's experience.[6]

Although men held most of the positions of power within the radical movement, women were often the most accomplished community organizers: the ability to sit at a kitchen table and talk about the problems of everyday living would seem to lie at the heart of reaching out to ordinary Americans. But such efforts got very little acclaim in radical circles, especially after 1966, when, because of the urgent need to stop the war, radicals began looking for shortcuts to mobilize the masses. Yet even the *masses* was defined as if it was a masculine noun. The Yippies' idea of utopia had nothing to offer liberated women except a notion of sexual freedom (which liberated men defined as opportunity for sex, not responsibility toward a sexual partner). Radicals like Abbie saw themselves as making real gains only when they recruited men into the movement. The legendary (and illusionary) alliance between bikers and hippies was considered an example of effective outreach. Abbie's ability to deal with men was given more recognition than the work of the few (mostly female) community organizers who were talking to the mothers, girlfriends, sisters, and wives of these men.

Abbie was one of the first radical men—which is to say one of

the first men anywhere—to be challenged by women's liberation.
Many movement men were forced on the defensive, trying to adjust
to the new feminist ideas. Some dismissed feminism as a secondary
issue to ending the war, stopping imperialism, building an alternative society, or legalizing drugs: whatever men thought important
was important. Some men hoped that feminism was a fad that
would quickly pass, while other men attempted to reconstruct
themselves, over and over again, according to ever evolving feminist insights and demands. For his part, Abbie was quick to accept
the rhetoric of women's liberation but was determined to adjust to
the new movement in his own way. Women's liberation, "more than
any other movement to emerge during the last two years, forces us
to examine our style of living," he said in an interview about his
book *Woodstock Nation* during the autumn of 1970. "To enter the
twenty-first century, to have revolution in our lifetime, male supremacy must be smashed (including the chauvinism in my book)."
His support of feminism, at least in the abstract, was not glib op-
portunism. He admired assertive women. He was secure enough in
his own identity that feminist ideas did not threaten him. Being a
Maslovian, he readily grasped one of feminism's basic arguments
(as Betty Friedan, a Maslovian herself, expressed it in *The Feminine Mystique*), that "our culture does not permit women to grow
and fulfill their potentialities as human beings."[7] But having lov-
ingly crafted his own self-identity, he was not going to re-create
himself in order to fit any women's ideal of an antisexist man. Nor
would he be guilt-tripped into personal change. Just as he became
the symbol of a hippie without ever really becoming a hippie, he
would heed the challenge of women's liberation without in any way
compromising his powerful sense of self.

In giving the ideas of women's liberation his own personal fit,
Abbie came up with a position that he called "macho-feminism."
He would confront the challenge of women's liberation from a position of strength. As a leader in the movement he was an inviting
target for women who held leadership aspirations and for women
(and men) who opposed the very idea of leadership or who opposed
Abbie for his politics but found it easier to attack him because he
was a man. On the issue of leadership Abbie refused to back down.
He considered that he had achieved his position on the basis of
merit; his status as a public figure was similarly earned. "Some
qualities like bravery and courage were being put off as macho,"

he told one interviewer, "but they were good qualities and I was trying to look at things in a new way and decide for myself."[8] He would champion the right of women to become fully self-actualized, but not at his expense and not at the point where he would have to withdraw from the limelight. He was big on encouraging Anita to succeed as an organizer, a writer, or anything else that she tried. At times he was harshly critical of her for not fulfilling the role of a superwoman equal to the idea he had of himself as a superman. But he found no reason to adopt a low profile that would enable her to shine. Like a natural force, he abhorred vacuums and rushed to do every task that he felt wasn't getting done. He believed in affirmative action in the abstract, but he was not personally going to make way for women by gracefully stepping back from center stage.

To be sure, Abbie was somewhat insulated from the intensity of the feminists' challenge because he and Anita had a private life that they zealously protected. For days at a time Abbie would disappear from the scene. Friends would call him on the phone, and instead of being enthusiastic and "up," as he usually was, he would be curt in his response, anxious, so it seemed, to get off the phone. In retrospect, some surmise, these were periods of depression that Abbie didn't want to show his friends. More likely, as Anita explains, the two of them were holed up in their nest, watching movies on television, tending their rooftop garden, and doing other domestic chores. Ellen Maslow, on one visit, found them baking pies.[9]

Radical women, in the early 1970s, were struggling to define and strengthen their personal identities, which too often had been defined by their relationships with men. Caring for a man, much less a child, was considered by many to be a diversion from this necessary goal. By projecting themselves as a couple and choosing to have a baby in a milieu where many couples were breaking up, Abbie and Anita further distanced themselves from the intense social experimentation that was riveting most of their friends. Anita was in a difficult position. She understood the validity of feminist issues but sensed that radical women, with leadership ambitions of their own, wanted to draw blood from Abbie in order to score points for themselves. As a proud and macho male leader, he was a sitting duck, representing much that feminists found oppressive in the male-dominated left. Although Anita disagreed with some of

Abbie's political positions, she publicly kept her counsel, register-
ing her disenchantment by withdrawing as an activist. Still, she
believed in the radical movement's idealistic goals and respected
Abbie's abilities as a leader. In the sectarian climate that affected
the women's movement as much as it did the left, she knew that
feminists would use her confidences in order to get at Abbie. Agreeing with much that the radical women were saying, she nevertheless
felt that she had to observe the new movement from a distance.

The feminist idea that the personal is political cut many ways.
On its most obvious level it meant that people who advocated justice in public ought to adhere to a similar standard in their personal life. For Abbie, however, it also meant that his personal
decisions had public meaning and should be transformed from
private experiences into media events. Thus the birth of his and
Anita's son, "america," was treated as a political statement, as an
affirmation of their optimism about the future and their roots in
American culture. (To distinguish the child's name from a jingoistic
sentiment, the couple deliberately spelled his name with a small a.)
On WBAI, Bob Fass heralded the birth with an entire evening of
Kate Smith singing "God Bless America." And with typical Yippie
foresight Abbie and Anita sent a birth announcement to the Nixon
White House so that they could get and show off the personal con-
gratulations of Dick and Pat.

In a similar public way Abbie had a vasectomy after Anita gave
birth. Sympathetic to Anita's gynecological problems with an
embedded Dalkon Shield IUD, Abbie read up on birth control issues and understood how unfair it was to consider birth control to
be the woman's responsibility alone. Always willing to act publicly
on his beliefs, he had a friend, the artist Larry Rivers, film his
vasectomy. He planned to use the film as a public statement about
men's responsibility for birth control.[10]

On this, his third try at fatherhood, Abbie took more responsibility for raising the child. He did most of the cooking and is
recalled by many of their friends as being devoted to child care. It
was rare for men to help with child care at movement activities,
and Abbie had a high profile holding the baby at conferences and
demonstrations. It is easy to be cynical. Taking care of baby america was an easy way of winning brownie points with the feminists
(far easier than acknowledging their criticisms and trying to re-

form), and it was an easy way of getting out of the meetings he hated—at least when his projects weren't on the agenda. But no one would deny that Abbie was there for his children when he *was* in their presence. He was a fun-loving father and, given his psychology background, had an avid interest in child-rearing issues. But organizing the revolution was his priority. The movement came first. He considered radical politics his calling, the way he created meaning in his life and achieved his personal goal of self-actualization.

In late June 1969 the police raided the Stonewall Inn, a gay bar in Greenwich Village. The police often raided gay bars, but this time the patrons fought back. It was the beginning of the gay liberation movement. When the riots broke out, Jim Fouratt phoned Abbie and other of his movement friends asking them to support the gay rebellion. Abbie expressed verbal enthusiasm for what was happening but, like most other heterosexual activists, did not take part in the street demonstrations that followed the riot. As with the women's movement, Abbie readily understood the reasons for gay liberation and adjusted his politics accordingly. Most important, he stopped the fag bashing that had always been a part of his macho style. Typical of this was his appearance on a 1967 New York public television talk show on which he and Jim Fouratt were discussing hippies. Abbie was trying to put on the host, David Silver, by denying that hippies existed and arguing that they were a media invention. Then, to clinch the point that he was no hippie, he added, "Hippies are fags, they don't know how to love." Homophobic statements—and actions—were not untypical of Abbie in the period before Stonewall, and Fouratt often bore the brunt of them, as when he criticized the Yippie plan to focus on Chicago.[11]

According to Fouratt, who considered Abbie his brother and was deeply hurt by these incidents, Abbie was not a conscious homophobe, despite his homophobic language. Everything Abbie believed attested to his tolerance for human diversity and his support for human dignity. Yet he had a blind spot when it came to homosexuality—not a fear or a hatred or a prejudice against it, but an inability to understand the vulnerable position that homosexuals had in society. Determined to sound tough, Abbie was willing to exploit society's homophobia as a weapon in his political arsenal. That he got away with it indicates how vulnerable gays were before Stonewall and gay liberation. In one of Abbie's last interviews he regretted the "childish" homophobia in *Revolution for the Hell of It* but then excused it by saying, "You can't gain enlightenment without being exposed to it," implying that in 1967 and 1968 he had no idea that gay bashing was wrong.[12] But the East Village of that period was not Middle America, and Abbie Hoffman was not an unsophisticated honkie. The shroud that prevented him from seeing the truth was the tough-guy image he had adopted in Worcester, which he never did fully shake. "Homophobia hurt him; it didn't make him a bad person," Fouratt says in retrospect. "It was too bad that Abbie never learned some of the lessons of the women's movement, that women's consciousness raising taught all of us—how we treat people, how we interact, how we treat ourselves." Many men in the movement wanted to become new men and integrate within their character appropriate (for them) insights from the gay movement and feminism. Abbie wanted to change and grow too, but only within the perimeters of his established character.

There was, however, a soft and sentimental side to Abbie that he rarely allowed himself to express in public. He often wrote poetry, which he showed to friends like Father Gilgun but never tried to publish. When Paul Goodman's son Matthew, a draft resister who, like his father, was closer to pacifism than he was to the Yippies, died in a climbing accident in the White Mountains, Abbie, who had no personal relationship with either of the Goodmans, sent Paul this poem:

To Die for Why

Sadness is
  and Sadness was
Tears stream down New Hampshire cheeks
Filling oceans of loneliness
A young man scales the granite cliffs
Searching for the secret
        locked in jagged heights
A young man asks the question why
Why draftboards, Kings and Cops

Why traffic lights, 3 squares a day and
acid indigestion
He died a noble death
Searching for the unknown
why
in shared saddness [*sic*]
Abbie Hoffman

Throughout his life he often wrote words of support and encouragement to people he didn't know—or to strangers who asked him
for help in dealing with the media or with authorities. Whether it
was a letter to help soldiers get out of the army, raising money to
help deserters flee the country, a phone call to journalists to ask
them to look into a stranger's story of injustice, or unsolicited advice to troubled people he heard about in the news, he considered
himself a public resource with a certain area of expertise that could
be put to use by others. He did this quietly, without publicity,
simply as an expression of human solidarity.

After the conspiracy trial Random House wanted Abbie to write a
follow-up to *Woodstock Nation* with a focus on the trial. Instead,
Abbie wrote *Steal This Book*, his magnum opus, which brought
together all the contradictory strands of attitude and politics that
constituted Abbie's sense of himself as a revolutionary and an outlaw, a leader and a prankster, a serious theorist and a tongue-in-
cheek put-on artist. An expanded version of *Fuck the System* (the
little booklet he wrote about living for free in New York), *Steal
This Book* deliberately obliterated the moral distinction between
legal and illegal activity. Side by side with useful advice on how to
legally obtain free food, free furniture, free transportation, and
even free elk were descriptions of various scams that he himself
used for getting free airline tickets and making free long-distance
telephone calls. To shoplift requires a taste for larceny, while to set
up counterinstitutions requires a degree of honesty and responsibility greater than required by law. In *Steal This Book* the distinction between the merely criminal and the truly revolutionary was
blurred. In addition to describing techniques for shoplifting, the
book offered advice on organizing food cooperatives and communal
land trusts, starting underground newspapers, establishing free

medical clinics, organizing demonstrations, creating guerrilla theater, dodging the draft, and living underground as a political fugitive in the United States or living in exile in Sweden and Canada.
A section on knife fighting was right out of Abbie's fantasy of juvenile delinquency, circa the 1950s. Next to a section about using
the Yippie put-on "Lace" to "send any pig twirling into the Never-
Never Land of chromosome damage" were serious instructions for
making Molotov cocktails and pipe bombs. The discussion on
bombing and political violence came with a single caveat: never use
it against people, always direct it at clearly defined political targets.
But what was the put-on and what was serious? *Steal This Book*
was a user's guide to rebellion, revolution, and mayhem with the
problems of political strategy and moral responsibility left to the
discretion of the reader.[13]

Despite Abbie's track record as a popular author, Random
House and thirty or so other publishing houses turned it down—
but not, ostensibly, because the contents were irresponsible. The
title was the principal roadblock. No bookstore would display a
title that invited readers to rip it off. Abbie would neither change
the title nor temper his advocacy of bombings and violence. Instead, against the advice of those of his friends who knew about
book publishing, he decided to publish the book himself. Just before going back to Chicago to serve a thirteen-day jail sentence for
writing *Fuck* on his forehead, he hired Tom Forcade to get the
manuscript edited, typeset, and ready for publication.

Forcade was a business administration dropout who had published an underground newspaper in Arizona and come to New
York to run the underground press syndicate (UPS), a structure-
less organization of underground papers that allowed its members
to reprint material from one another without formal permission or
an exchange of money. More a cultural radical than a political activist, Forcade cultivated a hustler's image, wearing black clothes
with a black wide-brimmed cowboy hat and driving around in an
old black Cadillac. He was rumored to be a heavy drug dealer. Few
people trusted him, and some radicals unfairly suspected him of
being an undercover agent. Abbie, who didn't know him well,
probably felt a kinship with Forcade's hustler pose. More to
the point, Forcade agreed to do what Abbie's friends said could
not be done. Above all else Abbie valued positive, self-motivated

people who, when challenged with a difficult problem, set out to
solve it.[14]

When Abbie got out of jail, Forcade showed him the work he had
done on the manuscript and presented him with a bill for two
weeks of work, amounting to five thousand dollars. Abbie didn't
like either the editing or the bill. He therefore completed the book
on his own, published it himself under the name of Pirate Editions,
and arranged for Grove Press to distribute it. A favorable review
by Dotson Rader in the *New York Times* gave *Steal This Book* its
first publicity, and within four months 100,000 copies were sold,
not stolen.*

Abbie was delighted with the book's success. Around the same
time Anita's novel (written under the pen name Ann Fettamen)
Trashing, a soft-core look at life in the East Village with Abbie as
the model for the romantic and very macho movement hero, was
also published, and both Hoffmans were able to tour the country
promoting their books. But the success of *Steal This Book* was
tarnished by attacks within the movement on Abbie's integrity.
First, Tom Forcade sued Abbie for the money he claimed as his
due. Fortunately, mutual friends interceded and encouraged a
settlement out of court. With the cooperation of both Abbie and
Forcade they put together a "people's court," which they hoped
would serve as an model for settling intramovement disputes.[15] A
panel of three arbitrators was chosen including Mayer Vishner;
journalist Craig Karpel, who had written on alternative economics;
and Dr. Howard Levy, the army doctor who had recently been convicted (and was out on bail) for refusing to train Green Beret medics to serve in Vietnam, an assignment that he felt violated the
ethical standards of the medical profession assumed by his taking
the Hippocratic Oath. Many people in the movement assumed Abbie's guilt. There was a feeling that he had become too egotistical
and that a comedown was in order. In addition, as Karpel wrote,
"When the government accuses somebody in the movement of doing

---

*On November 18, 1990, the *New York Times Book Review* listed *Steal
This Book* as among the ten book titles most stolen from libraries and
bookstores (the Bible was number one). The book is missing from the
Library of Congress and all the local branches of the New York Public
Library. A used paperback copy of the original Pirate Edition is worth
more than fifty dollars.

something, movement people universally assume the accused is innocent; but perversely enough, when the accusation comes from *within* the movement, you're guilty until proven otherwise."

At the hearing Abbie offered to pay five hundred dollars for the work and one thousand dollars in recognition of the misunderstanding between Forcade and himself. Forcade wanted the five thousand dollars that he said he was owed. This fee, he said, was based on what he charged Madison Avenue advertising agencies as a consultant on the youth market. This was the kind of work that Abbie had regularly turned down, and Forcade's frank explanation compromised his position with the arbitrators, who now saw him not as a trusted movement comrade but as someone who had already sold out. As for Abbie, the court felt that "he didn't know his ass from his elbow about publishing, and had expected people to go around picking up after him on what amounted to a speculative basis." As Karpel explained, "If Tom was trying to use his competence to hustle Abbie, Abbie was trying to use his incompetence to hustle Tom."

The arbitrators' settlement of one thousand dollars for Forcade was one-fifth of what Tom had asked for, double what Abbie thought Tom was worth, and two-thirds of what Abbie had said he was prepared to pay. In addition the arbitrators ruled that Abbie should sell Forcade a specified number of books for him to sell at retail, the idea being to set a precedent for movement writers and artists to distribute the profits from their work. At a press conference discussing the agreement Forcade upstaged Abbie by declaring that since the court had ordered Abbie to pay him money, he had won the case and proven Abbie guilty. A headline of Abbie Guilty! was more newsworthy than an explanation of the complexity of the decision, so this was the interpretation that the media—both mainstream and underground—gave the entire story.

Abbie might have admired Forcade's media manipulation if he had not been the one whose reputation was stung. The humiliation was deepened when, during this same period, *Rolling Stone* printed an interview with one Izak Haber charging that he, and not Abbie, had written most of the book and that Abbie had refused to pay him for his work. The interview revived the accusation, first raised by George Demmerle, of high living in the Hoffmans' plush "penthouse" pad. In fact, Haber was a young admirer of Abbie. Thinking that they ought to live more communally, Abbie and Anita had invited him and his girlfriend to share their rooftop apartment. Haber had helped Abbie on some of the research and then gone off to Europe. He was not heard from again until the article appeared (and was not heard of thereafter).

Abbie was hurt by the Forcade dispute and the *Rolling Stone* article. He felt that after all the effort he had put into the movement (when he could easily have sold out for big money) and all the risks he had taken for the revolution, *this* was his reward. He was a celebrity, true, but in his own eyes he had not sought stardom; it had been thrust on him. He had paid his dues and was willing to face up to attacks from the right. But he was thin-skinned when it came to criticism from the counterculture and the left.

Ultimately, it was the issue Abbie had refused to deal with in *Steal This Book* that came back and gave him grief. "Our moral dictionary says no heisting from each other," Abbie advised in the introduction. "To steal from a brother or sister is evil. To *not* steal from the institutions that are the pillars of the Pig Empire is equally immoral."[16] That Abbie had felt a need to write such a warning indicated his awareness that a rip-off mentality had become commonplace within the movement. One person's theft was another person's act of righteous liberation; one person's personal property was another person's bourgeois fetish.

This rip-off mentality, as well as Abbie's problems with the women's movement and gay liberation, and his refusal to alter his concept of leadership, undercut his effort to organize WPAX, an alternative radio station for American troops in Vietnam. Rennie Davis had the idea that the movement should produce radio tapes to be broadcast in Vietnam. This was to be part of a movementwide effort, already underway, to organize against the war within the military. It included establishing movement-run coffeehouses near stateside military bases, publishing underground newspapers written by and directed to Americans in the service, and holding peace demonstrations outside military bases, at which Abbie sometimes spoke.[17] Abbie agreed to direct the WPAX project and went about it in his typical fashion, without formal plans or a detailed budget, simply by using his contacts with celebrities to raise money and his hustling instincts to secure quality radio-recording equipment.

The only way to reach the troops in Vietnam by radio was over

Radio Hanoi. The fact that broadcasting antiwar messages from
Hanoi came very close to the legal definition of treason deterred no
one from the project. Abbie diffused the risk by getting prominent
people, including Dwight Macdonald, to lend their names to a
board of advisers. He also recruited volunteers to produce the programs. A typical broadcast day included rock, comedy, satire,
country-western music, poetry readings, and news. The Weathermen, the gay movement, and antiwar GIs were among the dissident
groups given free time on PAX radio tapes.

Creating the tapes was not a problem; it was internal politics that
destroyed the project. As always, Abbie worked well with other
creative people whom he trusted to get things done with a minimum
of direction. But the women and the gay members of the radio
collective, as well as the representatives of the political factions
producing the various programs, were all competing for power
within the station. Each group wanted its political line to be dominant, or, failing that, each at least wanted recognition for its own
style of politics. As usual, Abbie was goal-oriented, impatient with
group processes, and the obvious target for everyone else's frustration. He compounded his difficulties by being insensitive to both
political factionalization and sexual politics. Mayer Vishner, who
ran the WPAX office, recalls how Abbie ran meetings. "He never
knew how to act at meetings. He thought meetings were where he
told everyone what to do and what was happening. He'd become
impatient because people didn't 'get it.' He liked to argue, but not
at meetings. Meetings were where he issued orders."

Abbie had energized the project, but it fell apart as a result of
internal bickering, a conflict over who owned the equipment, and
a lack of planning and money. To this day no one knows for certain
if the tapes, supposedly carried to Hanoi by way of Paris in diplo-
matic pouches, were ever played on Hanoi radio.[18]

Increasingly, Abbie felt unappreciated and put upon. Though famous, he lacked the support system that made fame worthwhile.
He had no press agents, security guards, or flunkies to do his bid-
ding. When the show was over, he had to go home by subway. In
September 1971 he wrote an article for *WIN* magazine resigning
from the movement. Fed up with the attacks from others, he
threatened to go underground, go Hollywood, or both. "I don't use

the phrase 'brothers and sisters' much anymore, except among real close friends and you'll never hear me use the word 'movement' except in a sarcastic sense," he wrote.[19] To Father Gilgun he complained about the difficulties of fame. He loved it and despised himself for loving it. He didn't know how to handle it for himself or his family. "It just started to overpower us," he wrote Father Gilgun. "Like once we were walking the baby in Central Park and some cops started playing with the kid. Immediately camera buffs started buzzing around and I flashed on seeing the cops playing with my kid in the centerfold of the *Daily News*—so I quickly insulted them and they went off hurt and I was pissed cause how can you be mad at folks who play with your kid and I got sick of all this image crap and I don't hate cops."

In his autobiography, written almost a decade later, he recalled this incident and added, "The public image had been saved, but inside I was shattered. The insults were not real. To protect an image, I was being forced to be something other than human. Anita chased after the police, and out of camera range, she explained it all. No one but another famous person is likely to understand this. We rode home on the subway in silence. We just knew we could hack it no longer."[20]

That winter Abbie, Anita, and america rented a cabin in the Virgin Islands. They went under an assumed name, as much to keep their vacation secret from hostile activists as to prevent government authorities from harassing them. Abbie took up scuba diving and perfected his cooking skills. To visiting friends, he expressed the worry that he would be attacked by other radicals if it were known that he was vacationing on a Caribbean island. Anita was happy to be away from the movement. But the 1972 presidential campaign was getting underway, and Abbie returned for the Yippies' last hurrah.

In February 1972 Abbie, Jerry, Ed Sanders, and Stew Albert announced plans to demonstrate at the Democratic national convention scheduled to be held in Miami Beach that coming summer. It looked like an attempt to re-create the past (ten thousand naked Yippies will march in Miami, they promised) even though the political situation in the country had changed. But the Yippie leaders understood this.

Nixon's secret plan to end the war was to intensify it, spread it from Vietnam to neighboring countries he called "sanctuaries" for communists, and then withdraw demoralized American ground troops, expecting that a massive strategic bombing campaign would destroy the communists' ability to fight. The plan would have succeeded except for the fact that America's South Vietnamese allies would not fight and the communists would not surrender. Yet because of overwhelming American air power, the Vietnamese were taking a terrific beating. Millions of soldiers and civilians were dead, and the area's productive capacity was destroyed.

With no influence in the Nixon administration, the movement once again had to focus its election-year attention on the Democratic party. Hubert Humphrey, Edmund Muskie, and George McGovern were the principal contenders for the Democratic nomination. Humphrey was still hated by the antiwar movement, and his nomination would have split the party. After four years of Nixon even the Yippies felt that such a goal was no longer desirable. The repression of the Nixon years had polarized the country, as they had guessed it would, but without galvanizing the movement. Another Humphrey-Nixon race would further alienate people, driving them not to rebellion but into despair and withdrawal. "We need breathing space, room to move," Jerry and Abbie wrote in *Vote!*, a paperback book about the 1972 presidential campaign that they coauthored with Ed Sanders.[21]* Muskie, a centrist who hoped to unite the party after Humphrey and McGovern had canceled each other out, was considered a political clone of Humphrey and was unacceptable to the radicals as well as to many liberals. McGovern was the antiwar movement's unanimous choice. Unlike McCarthy, who withdrew from a leadership role after the 1968 debacle, McGovern had continued to lead the Democratic doves and had inherited the followers of Robert Kennedy and McCarthy.

In April 1972 the Yippies formally endorsed McGovern for president. They did this without any illusions. Their goal was to stop Nixon and to end the war. They understood that McGovern did not share their positions on other issues and that he would have to tack

---

*The publisher, Warner Brothers, gave the three authors a thirty-three-thousand dollar advance. According to Sanders, half went to Yippie and half was divided among the authors.

to the right in order to get elected. But they considered him a decent man, and they trusted him to end the war. Abbie expected to be demonstrating against him six months after he took office—but to pressure rather than attack him, as the Yippies were attacking Richard Nixon. They understood now what they hadn't understood in 1968, that a liberal who wants to make a serious run for power has to balance the demands of the left with the demands of the conservative elements in the party, especially labor and the moneyed interests who finance Democratic campaigns. The Yippies saw their role as building a movement around McGovern, a grassroots movement with enough popular support to beat back the influence of party conservatives and the special interests.

Many activists enlisted in the McGovern campaign. They had had enough of the strident rhetoric and sectarianism of the radical movement, and McGovern offered them unity and a sense of achievable purpose. Abbie apparently held a vague hope that he could play an official role in the McGovern campaign. But when he thought about it he realized that he was too controversial: if he was perceived as too close to the candidate, Nixon could attack McGovern by attacking him. None of the Yippies wanted to embarrass McGovern. "In the past few years the world has proven to be more complicated than we suspected," Abbie and Jerry confessed in *Vote!*[22] They, the radicals, had tried everything from teach-ins to bombings without ending the war or coming any closer to power. Abbie and the Yippies fully realized that 1972 was not 1968: the wild era of do-your-own-thing demonstrations was over. So they declared victory—and changed the strategy. "The cultural revolution has happened, now is the time to give it direction and put the energies in motion," Abbie told more than two thousand students at Northern Michigan University on a campus speaking tour in which he touted McGovern. He was now having second thoughts about the outlaw mentality that he had boldly espoused in *Woodstock Nation* and *Steal This Book*. There was a "large gray area" of morality that activists needed to talk about, he told the students. In *Vote!* he and Jerry offered an apology for past excesses. "In some way we were responsible for the excesses of the youth culture." Some kids had read their books and thought the revolution was all about "smoking grass or blowing up buildings" and "ripping off everyone in sight." Speaking to students in Michigan just prior to the Michigan primary, Abbie sounded like an organizer for the McCarthy campaign of 1968, urging them "to go out in the streets, ring doorbells and talk to people," and not make "phony divisions" between students and working people. The days of generational conflict were over. "The McGovern campaign offers a chance to encourage people to go home and change their parents' way of thinking. It is the road back from the Quaalude quagmire of despair," Abbie and Jerry wrote.[23]

Abbie and Ed Sanders led an advance party of Yippies to scout out Miami Beach before the summer conventions and discovered that there were no young people there. The population consisted mainly of senior citizens, retired people living on pensions in rooming houses and dingy hotels. Many of them were Jewish and held memories of walking picket lines during the radical 1930s. The first rule of community organizing is to organize where people are at, and the Yippies were astute enough to realize that the senior citizens were the community they had to organize. Ranging out from the Albion, a seedy hotel that they shared with elderly retirees, they learned that despite the reputation of Miami Beach as a citadel of luxury and ostentation, most of the residents were hardpressed on their fixed incomes. The Yippies saw the plight of the old people in Miami as they had seen the plight of young people in Chicago. The disaffection of the young would have been invisible to most Democrats in 1968 had the Yippies not imposed themselves on the city. The elderly would be invisible at the 1972 convention unless the Yippies made their well-being a political issue. Given the Jewish background of many of the Yippies and the Borscht Belt political style of Abbie and Jerry, a Yippie-yenta alliance held more potential than the Yippie-Panther pact that they had signed with Eldridge Cleaver.

The authorities had also learned their lesson from Chicago. The mayor of Miami Beach gave the Yippies and other protesters the use of Flamingo Park, near the convention center, with the full backing of the city's services. Abbie was even invited to address the police department. Despite his jokes ("I guess you wondered why I called this meeting"), he was greeted by a wall of hostility, though later he claimed to have met younger cops who were sympathetic to the Yippies. Whatever their sentiments, the police were on strict orders to contain rather than confront the demonstrators and, above all, not to allow the kind of confrontations that would give the resort area bad publicity.

Using student volunteers to mount a grassroots, door-to-door canvassing effort, McGovern swept the primaries. The only force capable of stopping him at the July convention was an alliance of the neoconservative hawks, the machine Democrats like Daley, and the conservative trade union leaders. In 1968 they had controlled the convention. But reforms within the Democratic party, pressed by McGovern, had greatly altered the power balance. The protesters of 1968 were the delegates in 1972. Women, blacks and other minorities, long-haired men, and the first out-of-the closet gay politicians were a visible presence within the convention hall.

The Yippie role, in this situation, was to prevent anything from happening that might embarrass McGovern. The Yippies in Miami Beach played the role of the Mobe marshals they had loved to hate four years earlier. They performed this task not with armbands and directives but by creating a festival atmosphere that, in effect, diverted protesters from the convention proceedings. The result was wonderful, although irrelevant, political theater. Whereas in Chicago the Yippies instigated dramatic confrontations between protesters and cops, here they promoted a spirit of generational reconciliation.

The central event was a "wedding of the generations," conducted by Allen Ginsberg and catered by the Yippies. Wearing a yarmulke, Ginsberg led the young people in a slow, winding circle dance, inviting the seniors to join in. While Ginsberg chanted shalom (instead of the Buddhist om), everyone toasted one another with orange juice and flowers. Old and young joined hands and did horas. Then Ginsberg led a chant about McGovern, the war, and Nixon, and the afternoon was gently transformed from a wedding party into a protest rally. Ed Sanders read a poem about his father, and Abbie read a statement in Yiddish that he had carefully written with the help of an English-Yiddish dictionary and the advice of senior citizens who helped him with his pronunciation.

> Nixon Genug!
>
> Vos tutzick America?
> Vuh bis der gaein?
> Mit und ganise tacke Nixon
> A vilder chiye tzmachen dem war in Vietnam
> Un tucheslecher mit de ganse gesheft
> Yentzer de urermer und kranke

Vos tutzick America?
Vuh bis der gaein?
Mit un nishgutnick Nixon
Un schlump mit Mantovani records
Ver tzozugen un gansser yuntef in Miami
Uber tzegevden a shtickel white bread (Ech!)

Vos tutzick America?
Vuh bis der gaein?
Drai unzerer kaink kop
Mit dinah luftraizer
Tzebleiden in Key Biscayne
Kibittzin mit Kissinger
Leben a guten tog mit Pat

Nixon Genug! Nixon Genug!
Shvieg! Shvieg! Shvieg!
Cumt November est do kreegen vost comt der.
Shvieg! Shvieg! Shvieg!
Nixon Genug! Nixon Genug![24]*

* Nevertheless the poem, according to translator Aaron Krishtalka, was nearly "incomprehensible" in its arrangement of words. His free translation reads:

What! pipsqueak!
Where have you gone?
With the real guy Nixon
A wild beast to make war in Vietnam
An ass licker of big business
Screwing the poor and the sick.

What! urchin America?
Where have you gone?
With no-goodnik Nixon
A schlump with Mantovani records
Who calls a whole festival in Miami
Over the giving of a piece of white bread. Ech!

What! urchin America?
Where have you gone?
Stop bothering us

In August, Abbie and the Yippies returned to Miami Beach and
the Albion Hotel for the Republican convention. Obtaining floor
credentials to the convention (much to the concern of Nixon officials), Abbie and Jerry spent a good part of the time mugging for
the media by stalking Republican noteworthies and embarrassing
them by greeting them before the television cameras. In one deli-
cious moment Abbie and Jerry threw their arms around the conservative newspaper columnists Rowland Evans and Robert
Novak. The pundit team had long been a conduit for J. Edgar
Hoover's smear attacks on the civil rights and antiwar movements.
But all this was small compensation for the failure of the antiwar
movement to mount an effective protest.

Among the few thousands who came to protest at the Republican
convention and camp in Flamingo Park were the Zippies, a group
led by Tom Forcade and other of Abbie's East Village rivals bent
on recreating the Chicago riots and seizing the mantle of outrageous militancy from the middle-aged Yippies. The Vietnam
Veterans against the War, by contrast, had come to assume the
movement's moral authority. Much of Abbie's energy in the park
was spent, with the vets, in trying to neutralize the Zippies' impact.
One episode particularly rankled Abbie. The Zippies had staged a
"Free Arthur Bremer" rally to declare their support for the would-
be assassin who had shot and crippled George Wallace. "No matter
how distasteful Wallace's politics, once paralyzed he was somewhat
off-limits," Abbie judged. "A middle-aged man slipping on a ba-
nana peel is funny. A woman is less funny. A child even less. If it
happens to a handicapped person, any ridicule is simply cruelty.
The Zippies failed on several occasions to understand these subtle-
ties. Their act got heavy-handed. They made an enemy of anyone

With your flights of fancy
To stay in Key Biscayne
Kibitzing with Kissinger
Having a good time with Pat.

Enough Nixon! Enough Nixon!
Shut up! Shut up! Shut up!
Come November you'll get what's coming to you.
Shut up! Shut up! Shut up!
Enough Nixon! Enough Nixon!

(including me) who did not see things their way."[25] But it was all a matter of maturing politics and changing sensibilities. Abbie's criticism of the Zippies reflected the criticism others had made about the pig-calling Yippies at the previous Democratic convention.

Abbie was thirty-five years old and committed to a political campaign that had no room for him. He was a man with a career as a radical but without a movement to support that career. Jerry Rubin was already losing interest in politics, throwing himself into the human potential movement and declaring with the same self-centered enthusiasm he had devoted to the Yippies that *this* was the road to revolution. It was Abbie alone who remained committed to a life as an organizer, if not for the revolution then at least for George McGovern. Despite McGovern's shift to the right on issues such as abortion rights and gay rights that were important to Abbie and other radicals, Abbie continued to campaign for him, hoping to the last that the Watergate break-in, which Abbie believed was the tip of an iceberg of illegal campaign activity, would destroy the Nixon candidacy. But expecting the worst, he tried to look beyond the election. "If McGovern loses in November, don't be discouraged. McGovern is only the beginning. Trust yourself—not McGovern!" he and Jerry wrote in *Vote!*[26]

Two weeks before the election Henry Kissinger announced that "peace is at hand." The terms of the settlement he claimed to have sealed with the North Vietnamese were exactly what the communists had been offering since 1965: complete U.S. withdrawal, leaving the Vietnamese to sort out their differences without foreign interference. It was essentially the same agreement that Lyndon Johnson had negotiated with the communists before the 1968 election, an agreement the South Vietnamese government had sabotaged with the connivance of the Nixon campaign. But immediately after Nixon's reelection the Kissinger settlement came unraveled. A week before Christmas the United States began the most intensive strategic bombing attack in world history, targeting Hanoi and other centers of civilian population. One hundred thousand tons of bombs—the equivalent of five Hiroshima-size nuclear bombs— were dropped on the first five days alone. Then, on January 27, 1973, an agreement was signed for U.S. withdrawal on essentially the same terms that had been possible in 1965, in 1968, and before the 1972 Christmas bombing, giving American forces sixty days to vacate the country. The United States had lost the war, but the antiwar movement had not been able to stop the U.S. military from destroying Vietnam.

11 REBEL WITHOUT A CAUSE

1973–1980

Abbie had played by the rules and had nothing to show for it. He was in a quandary. His reputation sprang from his being on the cutting edge, from his being the rebel who broke all the barriers and crossed all the lines. But he had lost his credibility with the most rebellious elements in the movement. The controversies with Haber and Forcade, the rumors of his plush penthouse living, the criticism from the women's movement, the bickering within WPAX, and now the attacks by the Zippies, his political progeny, demoralized him. Confronted with personal attacks from within the movement, his sense of humor deserted him; he lost his resiliency. Frustrated and embittered, he withdrew. After Miami, Ed Sanders recalls, "He was harassed, hated, getting ready to retire. He was very unhappy. He had lost his strength, and he understood that. He was thunderstruck by the criticism of him within the culture he had helped to create. He felt it was unfair. He felt unappreciated. There was no way for him to get credit for all the work he did pro bono. He drowned his sorrow with pleasure."

Many of Abbie's political allies, at least those who did not drop out into rural living, were beginning to cast about for straight careers: in academia, in the media, in social work. Abbie's strength of character, which gave authenticity to his identity as a rebel, inhibited him from changing as, many of his friends realized, the times demanded. Careers were open to him. But advertising would have violated every principle he stood for; it would have forced him to recast his entire self-identity. Had he believed in electoral politics and the two-party system—and had he not been persona non grata in the Democratic party—he would have made a brilliant political consultant. Certainly, his understanding of the importance of condensing political information into exciting visual advertising and inflammatory photo opportunities predated the prominence of Roger Ailes and the other Republican media manipulators of the Reagan-Bush era. Strangely, a career in theater or as a comedian or performance artist held no interest for him. He could not divorce politics from performance. Art for art's sake didn't inspire him, nor did entertainment as an end in itself. He needed issues to get his creative juices flowing. He could not be creative without a political motivation.[1]

Having lost his anchor in the movement, Abbie indulged his outlaw fantasies. He began working on a sequel to *Steal This Book*. It would be a guide to the criminal underworld that he planned to call "Book of the Month Club Selection." The inspiration for the project came from contacts he had made as a result of *Steal This Book*. Scam artists from all over the country were telling him ways that they were ripping off the system. Young electronic wizards, the predecessors of today's computer hackers, sought him out. Self-proclaimed "video freeks" had taught themselves how to pirate cable television signals, while teenage "telephone freeks" had broken intricate telephone company codes and were building sophisticated "black box" gizmos to make free long-distance telephone calls. As a kid in Worcester, Abbie had known how to glue a piece of string to a nickel in order to make free local calls from a telephone booth, but this was inventive, high-tech larceny. Supportive, as always, to dropouts with skills and talent, Abbie helped these young rebels—often engineering or science students—to network among themselves to the point of establishing phone freek conventions and a newsletter.

The philosophic niceties of ripping off the phone company or robbing banks didn't interest Abbie. The new book was going to be a compendium of criminal activity, and Abbie was looking to interview every kind of criminal from dope dealers and con artists to bank robbers and second-story men. During this period Abbie took up the cause of Tommy Trantino, a young Italian who had become a writer and an artist while serving a life sentence in New Jersey for murdering a policeman. Trantino, along with Reuben "Hurricane" Carter, the boxer who was in prison on a bum murder charge (and whose cause was taken up by Bob Dylan, among others), had become a spokesman for prisoners demanding prison reform. Abbie was part of a diverse group of intellectuals who supported Trantino, but where the others wanted to help Trantino, Abbie wanted to learn from him.

Anita, meanwhile, was fed up with being known only as Abbie's wife and having his enthusiasms take up all her time. In the autumn of 1972 she left New York and, using her maiden name of Kushner, moved with america to a small house her mother owned in Springs, a community near the eastern tip of Long Island populated by artists, writers, and other intellectuals. She spent the winter of 1972 and 1973 out there, making her own friends, creating a new life. Abbie and Anita were not officially separated or estranged (bourgeois concepts that had little application in their social circle), but they were pursuing separate lives without any clear idea of where their paths would lead, alone or together. Abbie came out on weekends and spent most of the spring and summer of 1973 there. He played in the ritual weekend baseball game with the artists and writers, went duck hunting with a neighbor, and argued politics with Dwight and Gloria Macdonald, who brought the Hoffmans into their circle of New York intellectuals. Abbie liked the social scene, was proud of the tomatoes he grew in the garden, and liked to cook for his friends who came out from the city. But it was also during this period that Abbie, according to Anita, began hanging out in a misogynist scene of "spoiled rich kids who had no values and were drifting along for the color of the moment, not for the politics." It was in this circle that Abbie began to use cocaine.

For the first time in his movement life, money was becoming an issue. His demand as a speaker depended on his standing in the movement or his celebrity as an author. Lancer Books, the only publisher willing to consider "Book of the Month Club Selection," went out of business before Abbie received any money. Suddenly, Abbie didn't have an obvious source of future income. He had given away his one big stake—the twenty-five thousand dollars he got for the movie rights to *Revolution for the Hell of It*—and had continually dipped into his own pocket to support political projects. He was bitter that he had made those sacrifices and yet was now under attack for profiting from the movement. With a group of artist friends he made plans to buy land and start a commune in Zihuatanejo, Mexico. It would be a place to escape the pressures of being a radical in America. Out of this bitterness and despair, his fascination with the underworld, and the need for money to move to Mexico emerged the idea of doing a coke deal and making a big score.

Cocaine had a bad reputation in the movement. It was not that it was considered dangerous or addictive. People knew that Freud had used it and also that it was in vogue among decadent jet-setters and in Hollywood circles. That was the reason for its poor reputation. It was considered a rich person's drug, and the movement was contemptuous of affluence. Movement drugs of preference—marijuana, hashish, and any of the psychedelics—were consciousness-expanding "soft" drugs, whereas cocaine, like alcohol, was disdained as a body drug, a drug that encouraged individualism, greed, and the thrill of personal power.

There was also the issue of dealing. Dealing soft drugs was acceptable in terms of movement ethics; many activists did it, and Abbie himself often served as a broker who funneled drug money into movement projects. But cocaine was distributed outside the network of friendly, freaky, long-haired dope dealers whom people like Abbie considered part of their revolutionary family. While no one in the early 1970s knew exactly who the drug lords were, it was assumed that, as with heroin, cocaine was controlled by organized crime. The line between dealing soft drugs and dealing coke was clearly delineated, and Abbie knew it. On the other hand, he and most of his friends lived in a world where soft drugs were ubiquitous; the police didn't have the resources to chase after all the dealers and users. There was a generalized feeling, especially strong in Abbie, of individual invincibility, a feeling that by taking simple precautions one could use drugs and not get caught. There was also a generalized sense of existential fatalism that, oddly enough, complemented the feeling of invincibility. Since the whole society was at the brink of self-destruction anyway, getting caught would not be such an extraordinarily horrible fate; taking personal risks was OK. Once, flying home from a conference about drugs at the University of Buffalo, Abbie got in a spat with a stewardess and, in a rage of mindless antiauthoritarianism, refused to fasten his seat belt as the plane was taking off. He was stoned on marijuana at the time and holding a stash, but that didn't faze him. The crew radioed ahead, and in Albany Abbie was taken off the plane for questioning. (Before he was searched, however, he was able to get rid of the dope.) Given the opportunity, Abbie knew how to charm police officers, and after a few hours he was released without being charged. It was typical of him to take the risk of causing trouble while holding drugs; indeed, by movement standards, the risk was not exceptional. "We all felt that we were living a charmed existence," Paul McIsaac, a friend who worked with Newsreel and who was on the plane with Abbie, remembers.

There was Abbie's role in the movement also to be considered. First of all, it made secrecy difficult. He knew that he was a target for surveillance and that it was very likely his phone was tapped. More important, if someone in Abbie's high-profile political position were to get arrested for dealing cocaine, it would reflect negatively on the entire movement. But Abbie now held ambivalent feelings about the movement. As much as he considered himself to be the center of it, he understood how much he was a prisoner of that conceit. The need to set an example for others constrained his freedom as an individual. Thus the idea of endangering the movement was double-edged. He knew his responsibility but also wanted to break free of that responsibility. Unwilling to curb his egotism, he lashed out at the movement. The restraint of acceptable movement behavior became another barrier for Abbie to break.

Abbie made no secret of his plan to do a cocaine deal. McIsaac and other friends tried to dissuade him, but he was ecstatic about the challenge. Absorbed in the research for his book and without the movement as ethical ballast, his tough-guy persona was coming to the fore. A rebel to the core, he was now rebelling against his identity as a sixties person; dealing *cocaine* was a way of reclaiming a connection with his fantasized past, his 1950s world of low-life hustlers and hoods. It was a world that, for all his bluster, he knew very little about. Everything about the deal was amateurish. He was playing out a romantic fantasy and was probably going through a particularly manic phase. It was a rule of thumb in the drug counterculture never to "deal weight" (quantity) to strangers. If this was true for soft drugs, it was even more so for cocaine.

The man who was going to broker the deal by providing buyers for the cocaine Abbie had bought—where he had gotten the coke has never been established—was John Rinaldi, a friend of Carole Ramer, Abbie's secretary. Rinaldi had no apparent politics and likely was unaware that Ramer's boss was anyone special. At any rate Abbie barely knew him. To Abbie, he was simply an Italian off the streets of Brooklyn, but this only made the idea of the deal more enticing. "Man, these guys are Mafia!" McIsaac recalls Abbie saying, with a look on his face and a glee in his voice that made it obvious that there was no way he was going to be talked out of it. Further, Abbie planned to cut the cocaine with sugar and, in so doing, rip off the Mafia, an act that, had the buyers really been Mafia, could have landed Abbie in the East River tied to a cement block. The increased risk made the deal more exciting; the idea of stiffing the crooks made it philosophically more appealing.

Anita had been on a month-long jaunt on her own to Mexico and California during the period when Abbie was planning the deal. He had spent most of that time on Long Island, with Anita's mother sitting for america during his forays into New York. He was in an ecstatic mood. In a letter to Joan Crawford, a Quaker peace activist in whose home he and Anita had stayed during the Chicago trial, he was bursting with plans to finish "Book of the Month Club Selection" and begin working on a book about "SEX, childrearing, love, marriage, etc. friendship, getting old and other funny things." He was also enthusiastic about his garden, the videotape of his vasectomy, betting on Secretariat in the Belmont stakes two months earlier, and future prospects: diving at the Great Barrier Reef, speaking tours, and the commune in Mexico.[2]

Three days after Anita returned, Abbie went to New York and met the buyers at Ramer's apartment, giving them a taste of the cocaine. They were to meet at 6:45 the next evening in a room at the Hotel Diplomat to complete the transaction: 2½ pounds of cocaine for thirty thousand dollars cash. Abbie had a date for that evening with Diane Peterson, a woman he had just met, and he took her along to the Diplomat "to meet some friends." Obviously, Abbie didn't feel that he was in any danger. Accompanying him and Peterson to the Diplomat were Carole Ramer and a young journalist friend named Michael Drosnan, who was researching an article on cocaine for *Harper's*. Rinaldi was not there, since he had completed his duties as broker. Yet he was apparently as naive as Abbie, for he spread the word in his Brooklyn neighborhood that he had coke for sale and had landed two undercover narcotics agents as prospective buyers. After the deal was completed, six policemen burst into the room and joined the two narcs in making the arrests. The undercover agents have always claimed that they had no idea that their pigeon was Abbie Hoffman.

Here the truth gets murky. Abbie's lawyers tried unsuccessfully in a pretrial hearing to get the charges dropped on the basis of illegal entrapment. In pretrial testimony the superintendent of the building in which Anita's mother had lived while in New York identified one of the narcs as a person he had seen in the building several months before the arrest. He withdrew a second allegation, made earlier in an affidavit for the defense, that on other occasions he had given this officer a key to Mrs. Kushner's apartment. The superintendent was a Hungarian immigrant trying to fulfill his citizenship requirements and, the defense surmised, had been intimidated by the police to retract his story. Abbie had often stayed at his mother-in-law's apartment when he was in New York and she was on Long Island and had once interviewed a dope dealer in the kitchen. While staying there, he had received death threats and crank phone calls from the Zippies, whom he later surmised were police checking to see if he was in the apartment. A second defense witness at the pretrial hearing identified the second narc as a "telephone repairman" who had requested, and gotten, entry to Carole Ramer's apartment.

This much seems certain: in the months preceding the arrest, before the plans for a deal were set but when Abbie was researching drug dealing, the police were keeping tabs on him. For what reason? To set him up for a drug bust? Or as a form of political harassment? During this period Abbie had joined a suit against New York City's red squad, demanding that the police turn over their files and enjoining them from further surveillance of political protesters. This alone would have made Abbie a target for a police frame-up. The fact remains, however, that he was caught selling cocaine. Anita, who was on Long Island the night Abbie was busted, says: "I now feel he was not cautious. He was careless. He was never good at detail. I think he was in a manic state in this period. And he had an exaggerated sense of his own toughness and street wisdom. He felt invincible. I was pissed."[3]

Bail was initially set at fifty thousand dollars and then lowered to ten thousand dollars, which the Abbie Hoffman and Friends Defense Committee, organized by Anita, Mayer Vishner, and other of Abbie's friends, was able to raise. The defense committee also tried to perform damage control on Abbie's political reputation. Making the case for entrapment was the only way to win political support. It was also believable. The police had tried to snare Abbie years earlier with guns and heroin, and as a radical leader he was always vulnerable. But many who came forward in his defense also considered the possibility, knowing Abbie, that the bust was legitimate. A support letter in WIN signed by, among others, Julian Beck, Phil Berrigan, Barbara Deming, Allen Ginsberg, David McReynolds, and Norma Becker acknowledged a "legitimate political question" raised by their rallying to Abbie's defense. "Is dealing cocaine a political crime?" they asked. "And, even if it is, is it as important as other political crimes? Should we spend money on this particular defense when so many other people and projects need our time and money?" The letter offered no answers to these questions but quoted approvingly what Mayer Vishner had said at Abbie's arraignment: that were the court to turn him over to his friends in the movement, "we'd not treat him lightly."[4]

Abbie, Carole, and John Rinaldi (who was arrested later) were charged with a class A felony that carried a sentence of fifteen years to life imprisonment. Diane Peterson was charged with the lesser crime of being an accessory, while charges against Michael Drosnan were dropped after he proved to a grand jury that he was actually on a journalistic assignment from *Harper's*. The prosecutors were no doubt happy to release Drosnan so as to make Abbie the focus of their case. Abbie might have tried to produce a similar letter from a publisher, but that would have undercut Drosnan's position, for if both he and Drosnan claimed to be researching drug dealing and Ramer was working for Abbie and Peterson was an innocent friend, who then was behind the deal that they were supposedly researching?

Gerry Lefcourt planned three lines of defense. First, he would call expert medical witnesses to testify that cocaine was erroneously categorized as a narcotic; hence possession should not be illegal. In the early 1970s there was a considerable body of medical opinion supporting such a position. Second, Lefcourt would challenge the law regarding aggregate weight. Abbie was charged with selling 2½ pounds of cocaine, but possibly as much as 85 percent of it was white sugar. Abbie should thus have been charged with selling only a few ounces, a significant distinction in terms of the charge. Finally, Lefcourt would argue entrapment. He hired a private investigator who uncovered the information about local police surveillance. He also intended to press for disclosure of surveillance by federal agencies. But he knew his case was still weak. Abbie himself was the weakest part. His published writings were full of

passages defending drugs and criminal activity. Moreover, if convicted, Abbie faced a stiff sentence and, given his record, could not
expect any favors from the prosecutor or the judge.

★   ★   ★

Jumping bail and going underground held attractions. Abbie no
longer had a leading role in the movement, and this impinged on
his future as a speaker and a writer. Going underground might
solve what was tantamount to a mid-thirties' career crisis. It would
also revive his reputation for derring-do and so enhance his legend.
In *Steal This Book* Abbie had written about using safe houses and
mail drops and forging identification papers. Going underground
would enable him to put his research to use. It would be an adventure, a new challenge.*

Abbie's inspiration for going underground was the Weather Underground. He had been critical of Weather tactics from the time
the Weathermen had formed as an SDS faction in 1969, but he
respected many of its leaders and had helped its aboveground support network raise money and deal with the media. Taking the anti-
imperialist analysis to an extreme, the Weathermen had set out to
support the Vietnamese by waging war on American society. Considering themselves the vanguard of a white revolutionary army,
the Weathermen dismissed all other white activists as cowardly,
liberal, and hence ineffectual. On his campus speaking tours Abbie
had noted the chilling effect the Weathermen were having on student activism. Many student activists believed that Weather tactics
were the only moral and practical response to the death and destruction the United States was causing in Vietnam. Unwilling,
however, to make so total and dangerous a commitment to revolutionary struggle, they simply withdrew from political action.

---

*His going underground would also help his codefendants. With him gone
it would no longer be a politically charged case. Ultimately, Peterson
pleaded guilty and was sentenced to the time she had served while bail
was being raised, then placed on six months' probation. Ramer jumped
bail on her own and, caught in Canada, was sentenced to three years.
Rinaldi was not included in the Hoffman and Friends defense effort. Suspected (erroneously) of being the undercover agent, he was left to get his
own lawyer. He had a previous record for dealing drugs, plead guilty, and
was sentenced to five years.

Although Abbie shared the Weathermen's support of third-world struggles, he was critical of their sectarianism, their arrogance, and their contempt for other white Americans. He also noted that the idea for the Weathermen's initial action in October 1969—the "Days of Rage," a frontal assault on the Chicago police that Abbie and many radicals thought suicidal—originated in the same moral absolutism as the nonviolent actions of the radical pacifists. "Gandhian violence," Abbie called it. The war had to be stopped, and the political system that caused it had to be changed—that much was certain. If elections and nonviolent civil disobedience didn't work, then there was a moral compulsion to turn to violence. But here Abbie parted with the Weathermen's ideas. The motive for both violent and nonviolent direct action was, according to Abbie, "purging guilt through bearing witness." By contrast, Abbie asserted, the Yippies acted not out of guilt but out of positive, self-actualizing feelings. They committed "spontaneous violence" by mounting "symbolic attacks on sanctuaries of power." Direct action ought to be disruptive rather than violent; the political goal should not be destruction but communication, to grab attention.[5]

After the death of three Weathermen in a New York town house when antipersonnel bombs they were arming exploded, the Weather Underground adopted a more careful strategy. Without giving up bombs as their principal weapon, they were moving closer to Abbie's position, attacking symbolic targets, taking care that no one would be hurt in the explosions. More impressive, as far as Abbie was concerned, was their success in setting up an effective underground that the government was unable to penetrate. Despite his criticism of their tactics, Abbie wanted to join the Weather Underground. He arranged to meet Jeff Jones, the Weather leader who was closest to his political views, to discuss his becoming a member of the organization's Central Committee. They met in a darkened movie theater. *The Way We Were* was playing, and the people seated near them kept demanding that they stop talking. Abbie's application was rejected, however. There was little support within leadership circles for his kind of cultural politics. He was also considered too egotistical and too undisciplined for the collective way the underground movement was living. There was no room for Abbie's media politics in a group that had given up on the politics of persuasion; indeed, his talent for attracting attention was likely to put the underground in jeopardy.[6]

Rejected by the Weather Underground, Abbie decided to go it alone. Some of his friends agreed to act as part of his support network; others said no, they didn't want to be involved in subterfuge. Anita refused to go with him. America was two years old, and it wasn't safe. She also felt that "psychologically it wouldn't work out between us." Underground, Abbie would have to create a new identity, but Anita's challenge was to reclaim her own. She was, she recalls, going through what all politicians' wives go through. "Even if it was the counterculture, it was the same thing." Being the wife of a fugitive was certain to exacerbate her problems; their freedom would depend on her attention to his needs, giving up on the progress she had already made toward building a new life. Their separation was no secret to friends, although as part of the effort to raise money for Abbie's defense Anita and Abbie fostered a public image of a happy couple, living quietly on Long Island and trying, as indeed they were, to work out new sexual and parental roles, "trying," as Anita told Hendrick Hertzberg, then a reporter for the *New Yorker* who wrote sympathetically of Abbie, "to raise america without stifling him."[7]

Late in February 1974 Abbie had a speaking date in Atlanta, Georgia. He planned to give the talk and then disappear. His next court appearance was scheduled for April, so this would give him more than a month to test his ability to live underground before the courts officially declared him a fugitive. He was excited to get on with the adventure, but his friends feared that he was "too exuberant, too gregarious, and too distinctive of face and voice to make a successful fugitive."[8] On the day of the talk Abbie and Anita dropped america off at day care, had lunch in Greenwich Village, and then, after fixing a flat tire on their Volkswagen, drove to Newark Airport, where Abbie flew off to Atlanta and a new life.

When Abbie failed to appear for the April hearing, his defense committee held a press conference to announce that he had jumped bail. "Our little family has been broken up by the exigencies of this nightmare situation," Anita mourned, after detailing the evidence of police surveillance and harassment and arguing that the arrest was political, a case of entrapment, and that the stakes were too high to risk going to trial. Abbie would have been delighted by the way they staged the announcement. The media were served coffee and bagels with the emphasis on the bagels, because, as Anita pointed out, there were no bagels where Abbie was going. With the family theme established, it was easy to get the press to photograph Anita holding america, who was eating a bagel—a human interest angle that would make a greater impression than the details about Abbie's cocaine bust and his skipping out on his trial.[9]

As well as this played in the press, many of Anita's feminist friends thought that she was sacrificing her life in behalf of her no-good husband. When Anita later took america to visit Abbie underground, Andrea Dworkin, a feminist theorist, advised her not to write from the place where Abbie was hiding. "I'll protect you but not Abbie," Dworkin warned her. If the cops came for the letter, she would hand it over.[10] This was, in part, an indication of the degree to which radical women's opposition to the male left had hardened. But it was also a signal of the growing individualism that would characterize the transition from the radical 1960s to the "me decade" of the 1970s. In the more selfless spirit of the 1960s what Anita did for Abbie was no more than what any activist would have done for a political comrade. In the new ethos of the 1970s it was considered self-destructive of Anita to put herself at risk even for her husband. That they were coparents, friends, and sometimes lovers, and that they had a past together, shared values, and, despite Anita's disillusionment, were comrades in a historic struggle, was of no consequence.

Most of the people who had put up money for Abbie's bail accepted the loss, as Allen Ginsberg put it, as "an investment in one person's freedom." But there were some who were bitter. According to Mayer Vishner, who had to inform people that they had lost their money, "It was a time of budding yuppification. The movement was tearing itself apart. It had peaked. But people couldn't break with it because Nixon was so awful. So this allowed them to feel ripped off by the movement and get on with their private lives."

Despite Abbie's enthusiasm for the adventure, his journey underground began with "haunting nightmares of doors being kicked in, of police, and more, of jealousies," as he wrote Anita after a month in hiding. "Missing you terribly, missing the kid each time I see one his age bouncing in the park on his father's shoulders."[11] His first stop was Los Angeles for corrective surgery on his nose, which had been broken in an antiwar demonstration in Washington, D.C., on May Day 1971. Altering his physical appearance was the least of his problems, however. Even for such a performing artist, creating a new voice and new speech patterns, new speaking lines, a new gait, and new body gestures was an artistic challenge. More difficult for Abbie was maintaining his psychological strength. "My biggest human fault is not knowing how to live with myself alone," he wrote Anita in December 1974. From the beginning he experienced great mood swings. During his low times he wanted Anita to join him. But in his good moods he warned her, "Don't ever come, even for a peek! I'm living life to its fullest. I'm determined to make a good thing out of this and grow in loads of ways. I fight boredom and mundane living with a manic ferocity that must be sick. I don't give a fuck. I want to die like I live, HIGH!"[12]

His support network struggled to keep up with his demands. He would call people from public phones with a list of errands that he would constantly alter as he went along. Mayer Vishner felt like Abbie's gofer. In addition to funneling messages and manuscripts to designated people, he was charged with such tasks as notifying Abbie's mother that he had received the sweater she had sent him. Anita, who had begun a project organizing welfare women, was also, of course, pressed into service. After one exhausting list of errands that included sending him his tennis shoes and underwear, she chastised him, "You take up whole days which I cannot afford."[13]

The authorities were more troublesome to Anita than they were to Abbie. She was hard-pressed as a single mother, especially after the IRS insisted that she pay back taxes on the earnings Abbie had given to the Black Panther bail fund as well as on money raised for his own defense in the conspiracy trial. FBI agents sometimes visited her and one time dropped a hint about Abbie's having a Swiss girlfriend. When John Hoffman, Abbie's father, died from a heart attack shortly after Abbie went underground, there was a heavy police presence at the funeral. As for Abbie, he was careful at first to stay clear of movement and countercultural circles, relishing the opportunity to reacquaint himself with the culture of Middle America that as a Yippie he had so defiantly rejected. Despite bouts of paranoia, he understood that although the FBI was keeping tabs on his family and would be present at events like his father's funeral, they were not mounting an intensive, full-time search for him. Abbie's problem living underground was not that he might be caught in a manhunt but that his state of mind might lead him to make mistakes that would give his identity away. "The essence of underground life is more a mental struggle and has less to do with the FBI, phony IDs, roadblocks, and tapped phones. It's the agony that comes from being forced to pretend you're somebody you're not. Living daily in a state of controlled schizophrenia," he wrote of his experience.[14]

In the summer of 1974 Abbie went to Mexico. He supported himself by teaching English at a girl's school in Guadalajara and then got a kitchen job in Mexico City. It was there that he met and fell in love with Johanna Lawrenson. Her background made her his perfect partner. Her father, Jack Lawrenson, was a left-wing union organizer for the U.S. National Maritime Union. Her mother, Helen Lawrenson, was a writer for publications as varied as *Vanity Fair, Esquire, Look, Cosmopolitan,* and *Vogue.* Johanna had put in her time as a bohemian rebel in Greenwich Village and, during the 1960s, had been a fashion model in Paris. Like her parents, she could move comfortably in the disparate worlds of left-wing bohemia and international society. In his letters to Anita, Abbie was frank and honest about his love for Johanna. In 1975 Anita and america visited Abbie and Johanna in Mexico. Later they all lived communally with another couple in Santa Fe, where Abbie got a cooking job at the LaFonda Hotel, the most prominent building in the city's center square. Abbie and Johanna and the other couple then went on their own to Florida. America visited them, and Abbie took him to Disney World. To prevent word getting out through his playmates in day care that he had visited his father in Florida, america was told that he was going to Disneyland in California.

Uninvolved in political activism, and believing that there must be more of a purpose to life than eluding the police, Abbie compensated by indulging his revolutionary fantasies. He thought about dying a revolutionary; it was a "macho attitude," he admitted, but he believed in it. *Morality* (and Abbie underlined the word) had reemerged for him as "that old standby." He was thinking of how his father had died, as he had lived, schmoozing with his friends in the steam bath of the Worcester Y. Abbie wanted to die in a way that was consistent with the way *he* lived. "I can think of no better reason to give one's life to the earth than to try and make the world a better place to live in," he wrote Anita.[15] He added, a few weeks later, that he was thinking about linking up with a revolutionary organization. "I blow hot and cold on the idea but am laying the groundwork with study." Such an act was "a form of suicide. Yet I'm not sure. I wonder about what people should do with their lives."[16]

He began studying Marxism-Leninism, declaring himself to Anita to be "more a communist than an anarchist." Always a subjective reader who took only what he needed from a text and distorted it to fit the immediate needs of his life, his interest in communism focused on the Leninist ideas of political discipline and organization. His politics, during the first two years underground, veered back and forth from dramatic notions of revolutionary action to the more orthodox communist position of building a strong organization. Yet in the middle of this revolutionary bluster he was capable of the kind of honest insights that would always keep him from becoming a party-liner. Discussing the need of building a communist movement, he wrote Anita, "I realize the people that do it will be the worst of us, in the sense that they'll be the least creative, the tyrants of groupthink. That's the way the ballgame works."[17]

The fact was that he felt politically isolated and was desperate to get back into the activist thicket. Whenever he found himself in sympathetic circles, he found it difficult to maintain his cover. He didn't like being "a major leaguer playing in the sandlots." For his own self-protection he had to disguise his knowledge of the left and control his instinct to dominate a discussion. Sometimes the subject of Abbie Hoffman would come up. It was tempting to tell other radicals who he was. Describing to Anita a discussion he had with newfound friends in December 1974, he wrote, "I laid out ideas and was so buzzing I almost told them the secret to teach a point but I didn't. . . . The conversation got very intellectual and I was so sharp. . . . They already think I'm a cross between Aldous Huxley and Tarzan."[18]

He was always thinking up schemes of what he would do if he were not in hiding. Anticipating in December 1974 another Arab-Israeli war, he fantasized going to Israel and debating Rabbi Meir Kahane, the Brooklyn-born leader of Israel's extremist anti-Palestinian right-wing Kach party. Abbie figured that he would be tossed out of Israel because of his support of Palestinian self-determination. The ensuing publicity would serve as political credentials. He would then travel in the Arab countries and, armed with facts, return to the United States to argue the Palestinian cause. Abbie's position on the Palestinian issue was typical of the position of many Jews on the American left (and of Israeli leftists as well). Not hostile to Israel's existence but critical of the Israeli government, he believed that the Palestinians should also have a state. He also romanticized the Palestine Liberation Organization, the way he did all third-world liberation movements. Anita took him to task for ignoring the sexism of Arab society. At one point Abbie thought about emigrating to Israel. Feelers were put out to ascertain Israel's reaction. Under the Israeli law of return all Jews are entitled, in principle, to Israeli citizenship. But Abbie was informed that if he went to Israel he would be considered a fugitive from American justice and returned to the United States.[19]

Abbie's desire to get back into political organizing was of a piece with his need to reassert his identity. Late in 1974 he felt sufficiently secure to contact Top Value Television (TVTV), an alternative video documentary group that had helped him with the sections on electronics in *Steal This Book*. For three thousand dollars in cash and a video playback unit worth eight hundred dollars he agreed to sit for a videotaped interview, provided that Ron Rosenbaum, the journalist who would conduct the interview and write about it for *New Times* (a now defunct magazine with a format and audience similar to that of *Mother Jones*), and Michael Shamberg, who would produce the videotape, adhered to the security provisions of the support network that would take them to his hideaway. In March 1975 Shamberg and Rosenbaum were flown to Sacramento, California, with tickets bearing the names A. Bremer and J. E. Ray, after Arthur Bremer and James Earl Ray, the would-be assassin of George Wallace and the assassin of Martin Luther King. In Sacramento they were led to a van, blindfolded, and with exaggerated cloak and dagger theatrics taken to a country house where Abbie greeted them in a room decorated with posters of Ho Chi Minh, Mao Tse-tung, Lenin, Che, Geronimo, and Patty Hearst holding a gun. Abbie's purpose in granting the interview, aside from tweaking the authorities and dropping false leads about his whereabouts, was to assert his revolutionary credentials by declaring himself a communist. He also hinted that he was part of a "family of revolutionary fugitives," which he obviously wanted the audience to believe was the Weather Underground. (Stew Albert, watching the video on television, noted that buying tickets in the name of Bremer and Ray was a Yippie prank, not the kind of a risk the Weather organization would take for the sake of a laugh.) Abbie also wanted to get his name in the media to promote interest in *To america with Love*, a book of Abbie and Anita's letters that Anita had edited for Stonehill Press.

"In Hiding" was premiered on public television on May 19, 1975. Kay Gardella, the television critic for the *New York Daily News*, compared the video to a "bad B movie with Hoffman acting like a cross between Jesse James and John Dillinger," while in the *New York Times* critic John J. O'Connor worried that television was being exploited "for the purposes of self-styled fugitives." Stew Albert, writing in *WIN*, found Abbie's political analysis shallow but concluded that "he is doing what he does better than anyone else, creating hopeful myths for Americans who live outside the narrow ideological confines of the left, but who want to believe they can change their lives and that revolution is possible. He helps maintain our faith in outlaws."[20]

Abbie's hints of an association with the Weather Underground were not entirely false. He communicated with Jeff Jones and other Weather leaders after he went underground, and some members of their aboveground support network assisted Abbie as well. Living, as he was, cut off from the movement, Abbie was naturally attracted to the Weather Underground; it remained his model of an effective revolutionary organization. In the autumn of 1974 he received a copy of *Prairie Fire*, the Weather Underground's manual for revolution. "I'm a big fan of the Weatherpeople," he wrote Anita. "I can't find any real disagreement with their ideas, their actions, their structure or whatever." In his television interview he praised *Prairie Fire* as "the most valuable theoretical contribution ever to come out of the left in the United States."

In the summer of 1975, during the heat of an American League pennant race, the Prairie Fire collectives met in Boston to plan their revolutionary strategy. Abbie sent them a taped message— which they refused to play—that was later published in underground newspapers. The Weathermen and their Prairie Fire supporters always brought out the most contradictory aspects of Abbie's thinking, and on the tape he alternately praised and lampooned their politics. As a Yippie, Abbie had tried to create a synthesis between politics and culture so that the changes wrought by one would feed on the other. Now, supposedly as an advocate of Weather politics, he argued that culture was secondary to politics and that the cause of building a communist movement led by the Weathermen took precedence over every other concern of the movement. There can be "no cultural revolution without a genuine political revolution," he proclaimed in his tape to Prairie Fire. "There can be no peace movement, no women's movement, no black movement, no ecology movement, no Indian movement, no student movement, no worker movement, no consumer movement, no gay movement, no children's movement, no senior citizen's movement, no spiritual movement, no *nice* movement . . . without a Communist movement."

That said, Abbie was not sure whether he himself wanted to be a serious communist leader, with all the discipline such work entailed, or whether he wanted instead to concoct a parody of sectarian Marxism, making Prairie Fire's pretensions the butt of a humorous riff. First, Abbie suggested that the Prairie Fire manual—"that valuable red book"—be made available to all Americans. Yet, because he was aware that the left spoke a language most Americans didn't understand, he wanted to translate the manual into "a hundred languages and dialects," including the "American spoken in the streets, in the comic books, in the movies, in the hallways, in the factories and on the roads," complete, he pressed the point, with "a glossary of terms." Becoming more critical of Prairie Fire as his speech unfolded, and making the point that activists had to be comfortable in the culture in which they were organizing (and ignoring the fact that Prairie Fire and the Weather movement had given up on organizing), he demanded to know who was in first place in the American League pennant race.

"Come on, radicals, who's in first place in the American League today? Forget Tet . . . and bourgeois feminism and syndicalist anarchism and that whole elitist fancy talk for a moment. Who's in first place in the American League tonight?

"*Boston is*, God damn it, and the people in this room are the only ones within miles that don't know."[21]

In *Major Motion Picture*, which Abbie was writing and revising during the late 1970s, he says nothing of his infatuation with communism or his support of the Weather/Prairie Fire perspective. He acknowledges their success in setting up an underground network and carrying out "guerrilla strikes" that, after the town house explosion, did no harm to anybody, but consigns them to the dustbin of history. "The Weatherpeople guessed wrong about the course of the war and the antiwar movement," he concluded. "Had history taken another turn they might have led us down another more militant road. Today, it is fairly easy to write them off as some romantic footnote to a chaotic period in history."[22]

★   ★   ★

The Weather Underground attracted attention to its existence with explosives. Abbie got attention for his politics by giving interviews, writing articles, and staging media events. Late in 1975 Abbie arranged an interview with journalist Ken Kelly, who had once been active in the White Panthers. With Abbie's encouragement Kelly sold the interview to *Playboy*. As the May 1976 publication date approached, Abbie went into a severe manic episode. It was the second such episode since he had gone underground. A year earlier, after the police had found his car in Boston, he had fled cross-country hoping to find safety in the anonymity of Las Vegas, only to freak out in a hotel room, shouting at the walls that he was Abbie Hoffman. Johanna Lawrenson had had to call in friends to help calm him down.

The excitement of appearing in *Playboy* touched off another bout of manic paranoia. Reading advance proofs of the interview, he was convinced that Kelly had betrayed his underground identity. Fearing capture, he left Lawrenson and took refuge in a Montreal hotel, where he ran up a huge bill making frantic telephone calls to his network of supporters. Marty Carey had to rush to Montreal with his son's bar mitzvah money in order to pay the bill and get Abbie out of there. Carey took him back to his home in Woodstock, New York, but neither he nor Susan could handle him. Ed Sanders and Stew Albert, who lived nearby, were called in to help, but there was no calming Abbie. He claimed to have a plan to market Cuban cigars in America; Fidel Castro, he said, had given him the concession (a fantasy that likely had something to do with his need to reconcile his life and the death of his father, an avid cigar smoker). He planned to call them Angel Cigars: Angel was the underground name he used for Johanna. Abbie had written an advertising jingle that he wanted Eric Anderson and other folk musicians in the Woodstock area to record. Ed Sanders recalls: "That's when I knew something was wrong. Everyone knew who he was, but he wouldn't let them call him Abbie. He was totally manic and paranoid, running around with a hunting knife. No one was looking for him, no one cared. But he'd hear a noise and run out the door."

Phil Ochs had just committed suicide, and Abbie, still in his manic state, surprised his friends by showing up in New York for the memorial service. The *Playboy* interview was about to come out, and desperate to inform people that *he* was the subject of the interview, Abbie was recklessly endangering himself. Johanna hustled him out of the city, and ultimately he made his way to a lakeside cabin in Ste. Adèle, Quebec, about forty miles northwest of Montreal. His landlord believed that he was a draft dodger and that this explained his stressful behavior. In the meantime the interview came out. Abbie hung a picture of the May playmate on the cabin wall and came up with the line that the *Playboy* interviewee gets to sleep with the playmate. But he couldn't tell it to anyone. Hysterical telephone calls alerted Mayer Vishner that Abbie was in serious trouble. Vishner figured that Abbie needed to talk to a father figure with movement credibility who could make him feel that he was still important. Dave Dellinger was an obvious choice, but Abbie had often trashed Dellinger's pacifist politics and Vishner was not confident that Dellinger, who was still busy with political activities, would want to take the time. Vishner recalls: "I went to Dave on a personal level. 'I need help. I have this nut on my hand who I can't handle. Will you help me?' I was hesitant about going to Dave. I knew their political differences. Dave was still organizing. Abbie had compromised his credibility in the movement with the coke bust. But Dave understood what was needed immediately. He said, 'Abbie has made an enormous contribution and has enormous potential; anything I can do to help, I will.' He was quite clear, direct and unequivocal. Dave and I had the same sense of Abbie's needs; let him talk it out. His problem, we felt, was identity. You can't know who you are if you can't be who you are."

Abbie was obsessed by two contradictory ideas. On the one hand he believed that the police were closing in and were going to kill him. On the other hand he wanted to use the *Playboy* interview as a manifesto around which to build a new radical movement. Dellinger and Vishner met Abbie at his cabin in Ste. Adèle. "We let Abbie talk that out," Vishner recalls. "We confirmed to him that yes, identity was his problem, and that was why he was acting crazy. Dellinger was great with Abbie, a perfect psychiatric social worker. Unobtrusive but responsive. He also wanted to talk to Abbie about the movement: What next? Dellinger wanted Abbie's political input. Because of the interview his juices were flowing. He had all kinds of plans. He wanted to turn his defense committee into a political organization. I told him no way. People on the committee either wish you well or feel you ripped them off. There is no basis to start a political organization."[23]

After Dellinger and Vishner left St. Adèle, Abbie returned to Montreal. He was still in a precarious state. Wandering around the student ghetto near McGill University looking for a room to rent, he met a hippie-looking medical student named Jack Siemiatychi, who was about to move in with his girlfriend and had an apartment to sublet. They went to the apartment, where Abbie, who seemed troubled and agitated, declared that he needed to talk. As Siemiatychi recalls: "He was babbling, going on not about politics but about living in the country and feeling isolated. After a while he went to my bookshelf and took out Steal This Book and said, 'I need to stay here for a while because this is me.'"

Siemiatychi didn't believe he was Abbie Hoffman. Gary, the name Abbie was using, didn't look like the picture of Abbie in the book, but Siemiatychi was willing to give him the benefit of the doubt. "He had to unburden himself, so we just sat there and talked," Siemiatychi remembers. "He wouldn't give out details of where he'd been, but he made a reference to Sam Melville, who had been killed at Attica, and said, 'If they catch me, I'll end up like Sam.'" That night Siemiatychi took Abbie to meet his girlfriend, Leslie Richardson. She had been in Great Britain the previous four years, involved in Trotskyist and feminist circles, and so was not impressed that Abbie claimed to be the well-known Yippie. Richardson had not been familiar with Abbie's media persona, but when she looked at the picture in Steal This Book, she recognized immediately that this man called Gary was indeed Abbie Hoffman. His teeth, she says, gave him away.

Abbie stayed at Jack Siemiatychi's vacated apartment but spent a lot of time with Jack at Leslie's house. Abbie was still in bad shape and recognized that he needed help. Siemiatychi introduced him to Dr. Joel Kreps, a friend who had had psychiatric training and who had worked with Jack organizing antiwar demonstrations in Canada. Kreps found Abbie verbose, not obviously depressed, but agitated, exhibiting perhaps a mixture of mania and depression. To Kreps, Abbie talked about what Jerry Rubin and other former Yippies were now doing. He described his drug bust as a political frame-up and explained how he'd had to change his identity a number of times and that he didn't know who he was anymore. He also said that he had fallen in love with the woman of his dreams and felt that his psychological state—and his need to be underground and to change identities—was undermining his relationship with her. He further related an incident that had happened while he was scuba diving off the coast of Mexico. His air was running out and he knew it was time to surface, yet he felt a compulsion to go down even deeper. This frightened him. He understood his proclivity for taking risks, but this seemed to him a suicidal impulse. He feared that he might commit suicide if he went into a psychotic state.

At this time Kreps was antipsychiatry. He had his M.D. and a year of psychiatric training, but he was then working as a general practitioner and was not keen on either psychiatric diagnosis or medication. Kreps decided that the best approach was to find a way for Abbie to assert his true identity as Abbie Hoffman. One way to do this, he suggested, was to talk politics with Leslie Richardson, an articulate feminist who could discuss issues on Abbie's level. Kreps thought that this would be a grounding for Abbie; he would be acting out of his strength. Richardson, who didn't know that she was an instrument in Abbie's therapy, recalls her arguments with Abbie as filled with hostility. He was in a very male chauvinist phase and did not do any cooking or wash dishes when he ate at her house, which was often. His arrogance, she says "was a throwback to early SDS nonsense, a source of conflict with me. We fought over feminist and political issues, the relationship of the struggles at the time to socialism." Coming from a vigorous European Marxist background, Richardson was not impressed with Abbie's arguments. She considered his politics "very sloppy . . . without much in the way of solid ideas about conjunctions of movements or the changing of consciousness or of strategies or tactics; it was lots of ideological bullshit and slogans that had nothing to do with the political situation of the time."

Abbie was unsure of his next move. He spent a lot of time at public phone booths and writing letters that he would send in intricate packages, envelopes hidden inside other envelopes. He was frequently on the phone to Johanna Lawrenson, and he was thinking of going to Cuba. Through friends who had contacts with the Quebec Liberation Front, Abbie hoped to get a Canadian passport. But the Québécois activists were wary of him. They knew who he was but considered him flaky and unreliable. Ultimately, Johanna drove to Montreal and got Abbie. Shortly thereafter, in the late summer of 1976, they settled in Fineview, New York, a tiny community on Wellesley Island, one of the Thousand Islands, in a summer house that had belonged to Johanna's grandmother and that looked directly out to the St. Lawrence Seaway.[24]

In Fineview, Abbie took the name Barry Freed and passed himself off as a free-lance writer. Johanna was part of a group of young people who spent summers in the Thousand Islands. They called themselves "river rats" and got around by motorboat, visiting each other on the scattered islands or motoring to Clayton and other river towns to dance and party. Abbie was quickly accepted as a river rat—no questions asked. He put his politics aside, bought a 17½-foot Cobalt speedboat—the fastest boat in river rat circles— and outfitted it with a tape deck and all the latest electronic gadgets: "Barry's pimp-boat," his friends liked to call it. He took up fishing, did repairs on the house, and lived quietly. In this easygoing atmosphere no one cared about Abbie's past, and he felt sufficiently secure to invite his children and his movement friends for visits. He'd take them in his boat for a tour of the islands and then cook them fabulous dinners.[25] He also used the time to complete his autobiography and sell it to a publisher. Through his contacts in Hollywood he sold the movie rights to Universal Studios, splitting the money between Johanna, Anita, and Sheila.

In the autumn, when the seaway froze and most people left the islands, Abbie and Johanna traveled: to Mexico; to Los Angeles, where Anita was living; and to Europe, where, taking a page out of *Steal This Book*, they posed as restaurant critics and got free meals at five-star restaurants, sometimes actually publishing reviews. Abbie also did articles for *Oui* and other publications: he wrote about attending Jimmy Carter's inauguration in January 1977 and recounted his tour of FBI headquarters in Washington, while the FBI was presumably hunting for him. For Abbie, risking freedom was a form of self-therapy. He needed both to express his identity and, when possible, to bait the authorities. He showed up in November 1979 at the opening of the Kennedy Library at Harvard and gave interviews to the Boston media. He visited Worcester after a Holy Cross–Boston College football game and led Holy Cross football cheers in a prominent local restaurant. Walking around San Francisco with Paul Krassner, he took the bell from a sidewalk Santa Claus and began to hustle passersby for Christmas contributions. He seemed congenitally unable to keep a low profile. Passing a strip joint, he assumed the role of a barker, calling out, "You want ladies with stretch marks? We got 'em here!"[26]

Abbie's most audacious act was a birthday party that, with the help of his support network, he threw for himself at the Felt Forum at Madison Square Garden in 1977. The theme was "Bring Abbie Home," and the idea was to raise money for legal fees if and when he gave himself up. According to William Kunstler, Abbie was willing to surrender and even plead guilty as long as he did not have to spend time in jail. Tickets for the event sold for ten dollars at Ticketron, and Abbie's brother Jack, in Worcester, filled two buses at twenty-five dollars a head. Twenty-seven winners of an Abbie Hoffman look-alike contest came for free, and many of the guests wore masks that made them look like Abbie Hoffman. The police were present in force but, concerned about crowd control, acknowledged that they would not attempt an arrest. A prankish gesture to Abbie's unabashed egotism, the party was taken by many survivors of the sixties as proof that the Yippie spirit had not entirely been quashed. But for all intents and purposes the radical movement had disappeared. Members of the Weather Underground were giving themselves up, and Prairie Fire had petered out—a vanguard of disillusionment. Of the Chicago Eight only Dave Dellinger was still a radical organizer, but now, with the end of the Vietnam war, the antiwar movement had little influence. Jerry Rubin had become a yuppie businessman, Rennie Davis a follower of a teenage Indian guru, and Tom Hayden a liberal Democrat. Almost on his own Abbie kept up the image of a sixties free spirit.

He was still experiencing frightening mood swings, however. While in Los Angeles early in 1980 to talk to the movie moguls and to visit Anita and america, he was examined by a psychiatrist, Dr. Oscar Janiger, who was Allen Ginsberg's cousin. Janiger diagnosed

Abbie as suffering from manic depression, a mental illness that is also called bipolar mental disorder. Abbie found it a relief to have a name and an explanation for his psychotic episodes. He was prescribed lithium, which leveled his mood swings. And, as Barry Freed, he had seemingly discovered a way to get on with his life. He could earn a living selling articles. His occasional public surfacing as Abbie Hoffman kept his name in the news and satisfied his ego—and there was a book and movie in the works. He and Johanna could travel a good part of each year and spend time in the Thousand Islands, where his friends and children could visit. It was in an area and a community that he was growing to love.

CHAPTER

12

CAPTURE THE FLAG

1978–1983

In July 1978 one of the river rats, a friend named Steve Taylor, boated up to where Barry Freed was putting down the decking on a new dock (a smaller, floating dock that he had built the previous year had been carried away by the river's current). Taylor gave Barry a report issued by the New York Department of Environmental Conservation detailing the impact on the Thousand Islands of a plan by the Army Corps of Engineers to open the St. Lawrence Seaway for winter navigation. Read this, Taylor said. If this goes through, it will destroy the river.

The St. Lawrence Seaway, a series of locks and deep water channels, had been opened in 1954 to allow oceangoing vessels to ply between the Great Lakes and the Atlantic Ocean. Because of ice conditions between the Thousand Islands, where the water passes funnel-like from Lake Ontario into the St. Lawrence River, and Montreal, a hundred miles downriver, the seaway has to be closed for four months every winter. In the part of the seaway visible from Johanna Lawrenson's house, the thick winter ice often breaks apart and damages the shoreline. By dredging deeper channels and using untested mechanical means to break up the ice cover, the Corps intended to open the seaway for year-round oceangoing traffic and had budgeted $25 million for a feasibility study. Beyond this, the Corps hoped to deepen and widen the seaway in order to open the route to supertankers. The cost for this was estimated at $10 billion.

In their report New York State's environmental experts warned of flooding, the erosion of shorelines, the destruction of wetlands,

aquatic life, and bird populations, and toxic pollution (as toxic
industrial chemicals embedded in the sediment were stirred up and
carried downriver). Oil spills were another danger. There had been
spills in the open water of the Thousand Islands section of the seaway in 1974 and 1976, but there were no technological means of
cleaning up an oil spill in icy, winter conditions. If allowed to happen, winter navigation would forever change the St. Lawrence
River and the Thousand Islands.

That night Barry and Johanna decided that winter navigation
had to be stopped and that Abbie Hoffman, even in his disguise as
Barry Freed, was the only person in the area who had the organizing skills to effectively challenge the Army Corps of Engineers.
Leading such a fight would put him at risk, but walking away from
it would be a denial of everything that he was and wanted to be. "I
knew we could beat the Corps," he would later recall. "I also knew
I had fixed my fate, that I would be caught as soon as I got active."[1]

The next day a group of river rats gathered at Johanna's house,
and Save the River was born. Barry suggested the name of the
organization. Names beginning with "the committee to . . ." are
dull and too bureaucratic, he told them, while "St. Lawrence" in
the name would be too obvious and cumbersome. An organization's
name should be snappy and grammatically active. "Better for
a name to raise a question than give an answer," he explained. It
was his understanding of blank space again. Incite people's imagination, and they would figure out what Save the River was about.
"Questions encourage involvement, and involvement is what makes
a citizen action group," he said.[2]

When the Corps moves into a community, it brings an aura of
can-do patriotism and military authority. Corps officers are as
skilled at public relations as they are at dredging harbors and
building dams. Bulldozing local opposition is for them as routine
as moving mountains. The Corps scheduled its first local hearing
on the project for the first week of August. Save the River had less
than a month to get ready. Through leaflets, an article that Barry
wrote in a local weekly newspaper, the *Thousand Islands Sun*, and
a petition drive, the new organization got more than five hundred
people to fill the high school auditorium. Many in the audience,
prompted by Save the River, had done a quick study of the issue
and were ready with questions. Barry had contacted Dr. James
Geiss, an environmental scientist at the College of Environmental

Sciences and Forestry at Syracuse University, and he challenged the Corps on issues of environmental impact. At a second public hearing in Ogdensburg the Corps tried to dilute the opposition by dividing the audience into small workshops. Barry was quick to object to that tactic, demanding that the audience be allowed to stay together in order to hear the testimony as one group. After a discussion a vote was taken, and his motion carried. The Corps control of the meeting was broken. Word spread through the river towns that Save the River was a force to be reckoned with.

In September eighty-five people turned out for Save the River's first public meeting. Seventeen different working committees were established and officers elected. As with the NAACP in Worcester, Barry gave himself the title of publicity director. For the first few months Save the River was in the news virtually every day. "Every organization needs a fanatic," Barry told one of the members, "and I'm Save the River's fanatic." None of the river rats then knew that Barry Freed was Abbie Hoffman. According to Rick Spencer, the one river rat other than Johanna with any movement experience, Barry was responsible for all the initiatives that got Save the River going. Because he needed to keep in the background, his organizational model was closer to that of SNCC than that of Yippie. What he had to do was teach others his organizing skills and encourage them to lead the battle. "None of us had ever asked another person for a dollar," Spencer recalls. "We knew nothing of fund-raising and were frightened of dealing with the media and speaking in public. We used to rehearse at his house how to speak. He tried to push us, he tried to get other people besides himself to do the talking. He tried to instill confidence in us, show us his tricks." Since many of the arguments against winter navigation were couched in scientific language, Barry set up study groups in which members would go over reports line by line until they mastered the language and understood the technical, economic, and ecological arguments. "The first few months of Save the River was a textbook operation," Spencer said. Barry taught that "the hardest part of organizing is getting people to believe in themselves, that they can make a difference. If you can do that, the rest is easy." That is what Barry Freed succeeded in doing that first summer and autumn. By the time Barry and Johanna left Fineview in the winter of 1978–79, Save the River had established itself as a powerful local presence.[3]

The fight against winter navigation was one that Save the River could easily win—and just as easily lose. The seaway had not, as promised, brought boom times to the river communities, and few people in the area believed that there would be economic benefits from winter navigation. New York State was already on record as opposed to the project, and there was little enthusiasm for the idea in Canada. The Great Lakes steel industry was the major interest supporting seaway expansion. The trucking and railroad industries were opposed, as were environmental organizations. The environmental movement was led by Washington insiders, accustomed to lobbying within the system. They had no experience in community organizing. Their idea of grassroots activity was using direct mail to raise money for their lobbying efforts. But the Army Corps of Engineers had political clout. Its leaders knew how to get pork barrel legislation through Congress and how to cater to the appetite of local politicians for federally funded public works. Environmentalists had successfully blocked Corps projects with expensive, drawn-out lawsuits, but no grassroots organization had ever challenged a Corps project on a local level and won.

Understanding that few people in the Thousand Islands region favored winter navigation, Barry Freed planned a strategy of coalition building rather than confrontation. The full-time residents were overwhelmingly Republican and very conservative, the kind of rural working people who supposedly hated everything that Abbie Hoffman had represented during the 1960s. And then there was the summer crowd. Among the people who owned summer houses there was a lot of "old" money. Uniting the permanent residents with the more affluent summer people would be no easy task. The local people had no experience in fighting political battles, while the summer people were often more comfortable wielding power than fighting for it. Most of them were WASPs, "appreciative of good manners and highly respectful of institutions," Barry noted.[4] "A bunch of the organizing was trying to convince people that abrasiveness, which is their code word for Jews, was a necessary ingredient. You just couldn't sit down with the Army Corps of Engineers and . . . have those people do anything but roll right over you. They didn't know that this kind of Anglo-Saxon politeness wouldn't work because they don't see themselves as oppressed."[5]

Barry viewed everyone in the islands as a potential ally; his vision of Save the River was expansive, with something for everybody. This was different from the countercultural strategy that Abbie had been famous for in the 1960s, and it was different from the way other former sixties activists were organizing around environmental issues during the seventies and eighties. In 1978, for example, when Save the River was starting, the no-nukes movement was also introducing grassroots organizing into the environmental movement. The Clamshell Alliance (started by, among other sixties veterans, members of what was once the Liberation News Service's communal farm) was organized to stop construction of two nuclear power plants in Seabrook, New Hampshire. The alliance followed a dual strategy: like Save the River, it involved local people in the communities around the proposed plant, but it also recruited activists (especially students) to use civil disobedience to block construction at the building site. Drawing a lesson from the failure of the do-your-own-thing Yippies, Clamshell developed an intricate group process that substituted consensus decision making for spontaneous and individual initiative. Although the Clams' civil disobedience at Seabrook put the no-nuke movement on the map (and stopped construction of one of two proposed Seabrook reactors), its alternative cultural style grated against mainstream tastes. (If you liked fast foods rather than granola, liked hunting and watched the Superbowl, you were not going to feel comfortable in the Clamshell Alliance regardless of your opposition to nuclear power.) The challenge of stopping winter navigation was not nearly as intimidating as stopping nuclear power, but Barry Freed could have gone the easy route of organizing a movement around student activists from nearby colleges. Instead, he encouraged Save the River to focus its efforts on winning support in the communities up and down the St. Lawrence River, using culture not as a polarizing issue, as Abbie had done in his Yippie days, but as a social glue that brought people together.

Within thirty-two towns along a fifty-mile stretch on both the American and Canadian sides of the St. Lawrence, Save the River courted service clubs, veterans' groups, and business organizations. As a Yippie, Abbie had adopted a rabble-rousing speaking style that would appeal to rebellious students. With Save the River, Barry collected local expressions on index cards and used them whenever he talked in public. Barry Freed was also a much better listener than Abbie Hoffman. Visiting the islands, Gerry Lefcourt was astonished as Barry went into local stores and *asked* the merchants what *they* thought needed to be done as the next step in stopping winter navigation.

Barry was keenly aware of how cultural differences could fracture an organizing effort. Acknowledging the suspicions that local sportsmen held toward liberal environmentalists, he was quick to state that "many river-savers consider themselves sportsmen and sportswomen. I, myself, hunt and fish with the worst of them," before describing how "river pollution" would hurt sportfishing and the tourist industry, principal concerns of the local people. At a meeting at an American Legion Hall he worked the audience by cracking jokes about fishing and the weather. Noticing that one veteran seemed particularly unsympathetic to his efforts, Barry humorously challenged him to admit that being confronted by an outsider with a beard was the reason for his hostility. Identifying a source of antagonism in a lighthearted manner became his way of defusing cultural tensions. People in the audience appreciated Barry's honesty and were thus more willing to hear him out on winter navigation. "Breaking bread" with the local community, accepting people in the way that they saw themselves, was the key to successful community organizing, Barry Freed insisted. Bold actions and leaflets with ringing words were necessary, but first you had to build the trust that encouraged people to take you seriously.

Other tactics, though, were typical of Abbie. Barry instilled in Save the River an organizing style that made political protest fun. To raise money they rented a tour boat and held "booze cruises" on the river. Save the River encouraged people to participate and organize their own events. There was something for every sensibility and taste: champagne breakfasts, benefit dinners, cocktail parties at local restaurants, and rowdy dances at local bars. In 1979 Save the River declared July 28 "River Appreciation Day," and it became an annual event with picnics, games, dances, a concert (the first year with Pete Seeger), and candlelight ceremonies along the riverbank. Festivities like these kept Save the River in the news, made it an important part of the local social scene. Politics, for Barry as for Abbie, was never distinct from pleasure. He, Johanna, and their friends would cruise the local bars dancing, playing pool, and always talking about Save the River. The organization even had its own coed softball team. Barry played shortstop against teams organized by the different towns, by local merchants, and even by the U.S. Customs Service stationed at a nearby border crossing. According to one customs official, interviewed after Barry's identity became known, Barry was "right in the middle of the arguments" over foul balls and ground rule doubles. "After the game we would have a couple of beers, and Abbie would join us. He was just one of the guys."

Barry's strategy for stopping winter navigation collapsed the distinctions (which had been so important to the antiwar movement) between liberal and radical and between working inside and outside the system. In the immediate area he encouraged people to put pressure on local government and community organizations. One of his first initiatives was to contact the office of New York's governor, Hugh Carey, and pester the staff until he obtained the governor's endorsement for the efforts of Save the River. A telegram from Carey, which Barry read at a public hearing, punctured the idea that the Corps alone had government backing and greatly enhanced Save the River's credibility. Carey's endorsement also served as an entry for Save the River to testify against winter navigation at meetings of the county board of supervisors and other grassroots government bodies. Through his new state contacts Barry prompted the state to finance economic impact studies and popularized the findings in speeches and articles. Thus, working up through its allies in government, Save the River was invited to testify at a congressional hearing of the Water Resources Subcommittee of the House Public Works Committee. Barry, Johanna, and Rick Spencer went to Washington, D.C., on behalf of the organization. Spencer read a prepared statement and was answering questions from members of the committee when Congressman Mike McCormack, a Democrat from the state of Washington, impatiently moved to terminate the hearing. Barry wanted the last word and interrupted. Describing Save the River as representing property holders along the river whose land would be threatened by ice-breakers, he cited the horror of Love Canal, a chemical dump site then in the news, that was so polluted that residents living around it had been forced to abandon their homes. Winter navigation on the St. Lawrence would stir up toxic chemicals like mirex and mercury that had been dumped into the seaway system, he said, and like Love Canal the contaminated water would endanger the health of the river communities.

The local politician with the most clout on the issue of winter navigation was New York's Democratic Senator Daniel Patrick Moynihan, a member of the Senate Committee on the Environment and Public Works. At Barry's behest, Moynihan came to the Thousand Islands in August 1979 to hold a hearing on the project. Save the River went all out for the senator's visit, taking him on an evening tour of the islands in an antique paddle wheel boat. More than eight hundred people showed up for the formal hearing, and local politicians as well as representatives of the state, the railroad industry, and environmental groups all testified. The St. Lawrence Seaway Development Corporation and the Corps of Engineers declined to send witnesses, however, telling a Senate aide that "they don't want to walk into a lion's den." Members of Save the River, introduced by Barry, also testified. After Barry's presentation, Moynihan congratulated Save the River for helping to promote the hearings and then, turning to Barry, said, "Now I know where the sixties have gone. Everyone owes Barry Freed a debt of gratitude for his organizing ability."

In the spring of 1980 Congress voted to delete money for winter navigation from the next fiscal year budget. It was a victory for Save the River but one that Barry predicted would be short-lived. The Corps, he knew, would continue to lobby in Congress for funding, and Save the River would always have to be ready to block it.

Moynihan's acknowledgment of Barry Freed's organizing ability wasn't the first time that Barry feared he was going to be uncovered as Abbie Hoffman. The actress Viva, a longtime friend of Johanna's, summered with her family a few miles from Fineview. She had known Abbie in New York City and quickly caught on that he was Johanna's new boyfriend, Barry. A number of other people who met Barry in the course of his work with Save the River also dropped hints that they knew his identity, and Barry hurriedly left the area at least once on the assumption that his secret was out and the police would soon be coming.

Fear of being exposed added to Abbie's inner turmoil and fueled a growing desire to give himself up. Contrary to his earlier fantasies, his life as an outlaw had made him more respectable. His work with Save the River and the public endorsements of Governor Carey, Senator Moynihan, and other notable figures could be used in a plea for leniency. He could go before the court as a man who had proven himself, even while a fugitive, an asset to the community. Many of Abbie's activist friends from the Yippie period were also advising that the time was ripe to give himself up. Members of the Weather Underground were turning themselves in and, because of uncovered evidence of illegal government surveillance (similar to what Abbie had experienced before he went underground), were getting off with minimal jail terms or having charges against them dropped. Johanna, however, was not enthusiastic about the prospect of Abbie's surrendering. As Barry Freed, taking lithium to balance his manic-depressive mood swings, he was a calmer man than the fugitive she had first run with. As Barry Freed he was effective doing the political work that he needed to do in order to feel self-fulfilled. Becoming Abbie Hoffman might disrupt this stability. She did not know Abbie Hoffman, the Yippie celebrity. She and Barry had a good life together.

At a rally, during the summer of 1980, to protest the construction of a riverside amusement park (Save the River wanted it to be built away from the shore), a local customs agent who knew Barry asked him what he was going to do when people found out he was Abbie Hoffman. Barry didn't know if he was kidding, but the surprising remark seemed to underscore the impossibility of forever maintaining his disguise. Besides, there were positive reasons for Abbie to come out of hiding. His autobiography was due to be published that fall, and a movie script was in the works. It would be far more difficult—psychologically as well as logistically—for Abbie to maintain Barry's anonymity once the book hit the stores. The temptation to bask in attention would be hard to resist, and the inevitable speculation about Abbie's whereabouts could conceivably bring about his arrest even if he tried to avoid it. Just as important was his pride in Save the River, his "best organizing work ever!" as he told Rick Spencer. It wouldn't be enough for Barry Freed to be a local hero, especially when the story of Abbie Hoffman would be in the news again. He very much wanted Abbie—his true self—to get credit for Barry's achievement. It would give integrity to the Abbie legend, provide added meaning to Barry's accomplishment, and close the circle between his life as an organizer in the 1980s and 1960s.

Once the decision was made, Barry/Abbie went to work transforming his surrender into a media event that would highlight his work in the Thousand Islands. His closest friends from Save the River were told his identity, and with Abbie's New York support network they coordinated his reemergence. Barbara Walters of the ABC News show "20/20" was secretly approached and given exclusive rights to the story. Her "20/20" show was chosen over CBS's "60 Minutes" because it had done a piece in 1979 opposing winter navigation in the seaway. Besides, Walters was likely to be a more sympathetic interviewer for Abbie than CBS's Mike Wallace. In an arrangement with ABC News, Abbie's friends rented a Lear jet (billed to ABC at twelve hundred dollars an hour when in the air) to fly Walters and her news team to what for them was a secret destination. Once in the Thousand Islands she was given clippings and photos of Barry at work with Save the River, including a picture of him with Senator Moynihan at the previous year's public hearing. She also, like Moynihan, received the grand boat tour with Abbie acting as tour guide. The trip finished at the dock that Barry Freed had built, which represented the beginning of Save the River's story. With the St. Lawrence in the background Abbie sat for an interview. It was September 3, 1980. On that evening's national news Walters broke the story. Her opening could not have suited Abbie's purpose better:

> The Thousand Islands have a thousand places a fugitive could hide, but Abbie Hoffman chose none of them. In an amazing double life he became one of the area's most visible and most respected citizens, praised by nationally known politicians, serving on a federal commission, honored and esteemed as a man named Barry Freed.[6]

That night Abbie flew to New York. The next morning, September 4, he surrendered to the authorities, pleading guilty to a lesser charge with a five-year maximum sentence instead of the life imprisonment he would have risked by contesting the original cocaine-dealing charge. Sentencing was postponed to the following April.

Abbie Hoffman's second life had begun. Or was he now Barry Freed? In New York City, Abbie was quick to find out that Barry Freed had no cachet outside the Thousand Islands. It was Abbie Hoffman the media wanted to interview, and it was Abbie Hoffman who was in demand as a speaker on the college circuit. On a visit back to the Thousand Islands a few weeks after the arraignment he told a news reporter, "I am Barry Freed. I relate to Abbie Hoffman as a close friend of mine who I am proud to know and who will go into action at a moment's notice if I call him up."[7]

No sooner was he free on bail than he was off on a ten-campus speaking tour—his first as Abbie Hoffman since 1973—in the South, North, and Midwest. His appearance at Syracuse University exemplified the opportunity for Abbie Hoffman and the dilemma of his remaining Barry Freed. Syracuse was a two-hour drive from the Thousand Islands; Barry Freed had spoken there as a representative of Save the River to a handful of environmental activists. Now, as Abbie Hoffman, he was able to pack a thirteen-hundred-seat auditorium and command a speaker's fee of almost three thousand dollars. In his presentations, which, with questions afterward, often lasted two or more hours, Abbie pressed his politics as part of a disjointed and funny narrative that covered the Chicago trial, his harassment by the FBI and the Nixon administration, his life as a fugitive, and his work organizing Save the River. He denounced the growing influence of multinational corporations over both the American economy and American government and stressed the power of the media to determine (and distort) what is news and how it is presented. He offered tips on effective organizing, urging students to press the issues that were important to them in both their schools and their home communities. "Democracy begins and ends with kids in school," Abbie asserted. "Kids must be taught disrespect for authority."[8]

There was an aggressive edge to these and later speeches that hadn't existed in his earlier career. Abbie was impatient with questions about the 1960s, wanting to talk not about protesting the war in Vietnam but about stopping American involvement in El Salvador. ("El Salvador is the way you spell Vietnam in Spanish" was one of his standard lines.) But he also felt a need to take credit for past efforts, as if in making up for lost time he had to assert that yes, he was the notorious Yippie of Judge Hoffman's courtroom and Mayor Daley's city.

Abbie spent that winter preparing for his sentencing. He had thousands of pages of FBI documents detailing government surveillance, including illegal burglaries and wiretaps, but there was no way of connecting the drug bust to that political harassment. On another front Rick Spencer had come to New York to coordinate a committee, headed by Norman Mailer, to solicit letters urging that Abbie be granted clemency. Hundreds of letters of support came in from intellectuals, Hollywood stars, and ordinary citizens. The conservative columnist William Buckley argued, in his syndicated column, that Abbie was an asset to society and should not have to spend time in jail. Despite this show of support, the success of his speaking tours, and his belief that the war in El Salvador was awakening the college campuses, there were times of uncertainty when Abbie wondered whether he had done the right thing in giving himself up.

On April 8, 1981, Abbie was sentenced to three years in prison. With "good time" and parole he served a little less than a year in custody. The first two months were spent in maximum security; then he was let out on a ten-month work-release program for Veritas, a New York City drug rehabilitation center focused on heroin addiction. In his brief two-month prison stay Abbie taught English to Spanish-speaking inmates, went on a brief hunger strike to express solidarity with an Irish Republican Army hunger striker, Bobby Sands, and paid close attention to the running of the prison system. As usual he took it upon himself to distill his observations into pro bono recommendations. To Jean Harris, a white middle-class woman serving a life sentence for murdering her lover (The Scarsdale Diet doctor, Herman Tarnower), who, according to the media, was having a difficult time adjusting to prison, he wrote an unsolicited letter advising her not to distance herself from her sister inmates but to use her education to help them. This would make her time in prison more bearable and also more rewarding. Noting the total failure of the prison system to rehabilitate its inmates, Abbie wrote a memo to the New York State Commissioner of Prisons recommending a program of positive reinforcement to ease the transition from prison to nonprison life. Instead of rewarding antisocial behavior patterns (like informing, passivity, and keeping to oneself) for the sake of prison control, Abbie suggested that the prison offer rewards for conduct that was appropriate in nonprison society. Inmates would be rewarded for initiatives regarding self-improvement, cooperation, and other qualities they could use when they got out of prison. Abbie's essay on prison life, "The Crime of Punishment," is in Square Dancing in the Ice Age and The Best of Abbie Hoffman. It is one of his best pieces of writing, a keen and unsparing look at prisoners and prisons, an indictment of a criminal justice system that reinforces antisocial behavior and encourages further crime.

At Veritas, Abbie worked as a drug counselor and a fund-raiser, using his show business contacts to make up the $100,000 that had been lost to President Reagan's budget cuts. Abbie saw no contradiction between his advocating the legalization of drugs and his opposing the use of heroin. Like many advocates of the psychedelic experience, he saw heroin as a debilitating drug. But prohibition led only to profits for the distributors and criminal records for the victims. His idea of decriminalization included antiheroin educational programs and rehabilitation centers for the addicts who were the drug's victims.

While working for Veritas, Abbie attempted to set up CLARO (the Central Latin America Relief Organization) to funnel medical aid—one million dollars, Abbie promised—to popular organizations in Latin America. The idea was to byass corrupt government officials, who often stole aid supplies and then sold them for personal profit (as Abbie had observed while underground doing earthquake relief work in Guatemala). CLARO was one of a number of projects that Abbie announced with much fanfare during the 1980s. The pattern of these initiatives was that he would come up with an idea, recruit friends to help get it off the ground (while paying their salaries and expenses), and use his contacts with celebrities to stage a benefit at which he would recoup the money already spent. He was still organizing as he had during the 1960s, with a telephone and an idea. But the movement was no longer run on such an ad hoc basis. An organizer with a project now drew up a formal grant proposal and applied to the small group of foundations that funded progressive causes. Abbie, however, could always raise money on his own and spend it. He had no patience for detailed budgets or formal presentations that foundation grants required.

Abbie was paroled on March 26, 1982, despite his telling the parole board that he would not rule out civil disobedience "if they stick a nuclear plant in New York City or send troops to El Salvador." His plan was to mix college speaking tours with living in Fineview and working with Save the River. He was also talking of starting a school for organizers in the Thousand Islands. He was still having difficulty distinguishing Barry Freed from Abbie Hoffman, signing letters to Anita "A and/or B." Away from the Thousand Islands he usually called himself Abbie; yet he maintained all his papers for Barry Freed. Although he enjoyed being recognized by strangers, he hated it when ex-hippies approached him and asked, as they often did, "Hey Abbie, how's Jerry?" Worse were those who lied to him about their having been Yippies in the streets of Chicago.[9]

In the Thousand Islands, however, it was Abbie Hoffman who

was the stranger. Barry Freed had not had a reputation as a 1960s
radical to live up to (or live down). He had been quieter and more
diffident, *nicer*, people said, more relaxed and easier to be around,
a person you could talk to. But now the right-wing *Watertown
Daily Times*, the principal newspaper in the region, made sure to
remind local people that Barry Freed was Abbie Hoffman. One of
the only conspicuous boosters for winter navigation, the Watertown newspaper used Abbie to get at Save the River, forever
reminding readers that its founder was an opponent of the Vietnam
War, a Chicago Seven defendant, and a convicted cocaine dealer.

Largely as a result of Barry's good organizing work, Save the River
had become a powerful environmental watchdog organization for
the region. Although a perfect vehicle for the ambitions of Barry
Freed, it was still too small and isolated to absorb the energy of
Abbie Hoffman. He returned to the river with plans of transforming Save the River into a community advocacy organization willing
to take on such issues as utility rate hikes and to promote fuel oil
co-ops for the poor. Abbie now shunned the environmentalist label
because, he said, it leaves "humans out of the whole scene. We're
fighting to preserve a section of paradise. But it is also a section
with very high and chronic unemployment rates. We talk to people
about the nuclear waste issue and they tell us their problems. We
have to look at the economic issues as well. We have to be people-
oriented."[10]

But any proposal beyond river-connected environmental issues
split the organization. There was no constituency for a multi-issue
radical organization in the Thousand Islands region. To give himself a role in Save the River and still allow it to function without
his often overbearing presence, Abbie invented the position of national spokesman and vowed to stop talking to the local media so
that other leaders of the organization could "learn the cat and
mouse game of dealing with the press."[11] As long as Rick Spencer,
Johanna Lawrenson, and other allies were leading the organization, up until 1987, Abbie continued to play an informal but
influential role. In 1983, when the Army Corps of Engineers again
tried to push a bill for winter navigation, Abbie alerted the Thousand Islands region to the danger by publicly threatening to chain
himself to the door of Congressman Richard Roe if Roe, who was

steering a public works bill through Congress, didn't delete the winter navigation provision. Public pressure from Save the River and allied groups ultimately caused winter navigation to be withdrawn.

Always looking for an opportunity to organize in a wider area, Abbie became one of the key people behind the idea of Great Lakes United, an attempt to build a coalition of community and environmental groups to protect the Great Lakes. Abbie was brought in on the planning by Wayne Schmidt, the staff ecologist of the Michigan United Conservation Clubs, a community-based group of Michigan sportsmen that was 100,000 members strong. Schmidt considered Save the River a model for mobilizing community sentiment behind environmental battles, and he hoped that Great Lakes United would give Abbie's strategy of local organizing more scope to spread. Michigan United, Save the River, and the United Automobile Workers joined forces behind the idea of a strong regional organization. Abbie had high—perhaps grandiose—hopes of making the organization an important political bloc, and he saw it, of course, as a vehicle through which *he* could gain a larger audience.

In May 1982 sixty delegates from eight states and Quebec and Ontario gathered on Mackinac Island, Michigan, to plan the organizing convention. Introduced to the delegates by Schmidt as "the best organizer I know," Abbie quickly became the issue on which the conference ostensibly foundered. Although Barry Freed was known for his success at stopping winter navigation, many delegates balked at the prospect of letting Abbie Hoffman—the notorious Yippie and convicted coke dealer—ride in on Barry's coattails. When questioned by the press, representatives of the Sierra Club, the National Wildlife Federation, the Audubon Society, and the League of Women Voters all professed shock and wondered how they would explain Abbie Hoffman to their members. "Hoffman's name and reputation won't play in Peoria," one delegate said. "A lot of people who came here in good faith to work for a common cause are going to have to explain Abbie Hoffman to the folks back home. It's not going to wash."[12]

This hostility to Abbie's reputation was indicative of the difficulty he would always have finding work within mainstream organizations. But it was a phony issue. Abbie was being scapegoated to disguise the deeper conflict between hunters and bird-watchers, sportsmen and environmentalists. In addition, many participants

wanted an excuse to back out. The Canadian delegates didn't want
to be drawn into American politics, while the national environmental groups were opposed to a strong regional organization that
would detract from their own support networks. Moreover, environmental leaders were generally wary of free-lance community
organizers, like Abbie *or* Barry, who were more interested in
agitating on the grassroots level than in supporting respectable,
"inside the Beltway" lobbying efforts. Instead of becoming a potentially powerful political organization, Great Lakes United
remained a loose network of regional environmental groups. Although Abbie himself lost interest in the coalition, he encouraged
Save the River to maintain a representative on its board of direc-
tors, and Great Lakes United supported Save the River in muster-
ing political force for the final defeat of winter navigation.

In December 1982, a few weeks after the Great Lakes United fiasco, Abbie was invited—on the instigation of Robert Sugarman,
a lawyer from Philadelphia who had assisted Great Lakes United—
to Bucks County, Pennsylvania, to advise a citizens' group called
Del-AWARE in its fight to stop construction of the Point Pleasant
pumping station.[13] A project of the Philadelphia Electric Company
(PECO), the pumping station would divert 95 million gallons of
water per day fifty miles from the Delaware River to cool the proposed Limerick nuclear power plant near Pottstown, Pennsylvania. It would also provide water to foster commercial and residen-
tial development in the Pottstown region. The opponents of the
pumping station had their backs against the wall when Abbie got
the call. All legal attempts to block the project had been defeated,
and a ground-breaking ceremony (with a silver shovel, PECO
promised) was scheduled for January 3, 1983, with construction to
begin on January 7.

On Christmas Eve, 1982, Abbie, who was living in New York City
apart from Johanna, phoned a young friend, Al Giordano, and
insisted that Al join him at once and go down with him to Bucks
County, to a place near the site where, he said, George Washington
had crossed the Delaware, where a utility company was now going
to build a pumping station that would destroy the Delaware River.
Del-AWARE was a great group, Abbie added, made up of all Republicans. Giordano remonstrated that it was Christmas Eve and

he was going to spend the holiday with his family. Couldn't Abbie wait? Abbie responded, "So? Where would we be if George Washington had taken the night off on Christmas Eve?"

The next day, Christmas, they both took the Amtrak train to Pennsylvania. Del-AWARE did have a lot of Republicans in leadership positions, and not everyone was enthusiastic about hiring Abbie. But they were desperate and didn't know what else to do. According to Giordano, support for and opposition to Abbie didn't break down on liberal/conservative, Democratic/Republican lines; it never did. "It would be between the people with personality and the people who wanted a rigid program. There were Republicans who wanted to keep him there and there were Republicans who wanted to keep him out. People with strong self-identities, who were not intimidated by him and who could speak their mind, generally got along with Abbie, no matter what their views." One conservative Vietnam veteran told Abbie right off that they had absolutely nothing in common except their opposition to the pump, and Abbie laughed and said, "That's great, that's your attitude and that's what it should be from now on." The two men continued to disagree but worked together. "I respected him and he respected me," the veteran said.[14]

Before agreeing to help Del-AWARE, Abbie wanted to be sure that the group had the popular support it claimed it had. Pulling out a hundred-dollar bill as if to make a wager, he said he would phone a number at random and ask if the person could tell him what Del-AWARE was. The person who picked up the phone identified the organization, and Abbie accepted a position, on his terms, as a dollar-a-year consultant provided the group would also hire Giordano at $250 a week for two weeks.

As a teenager, Al Giordano had been one of the youngest organizers in the Clamshell Alliance. He had then gone on to run referendum campaigns against nuclear power in Maine and Massachusetts. As a direct actionist in the antinuclear movement, he had often felt constrained by the group process, where every individual initiative had to get unanimous approval. He also had a chip on his shoulder about the sixties generation. He resented the power that veterans of the antiwar movement wielded, and he was uncomfortable with their ambivalence (or outright hostility) toward patriotism and the mainstream culture. Giordano wore an American flag pin on his lapel, and this had often caused arguments with

Clamshell activists. It was Giordano's view that if you wanted to organize people for political change, you had to accept and become part of their culture.

Giordano had read and liked Abbie's books, but when Abbie resurfaced, Giordano was wary of the attention he was getting as the famous sixties hero. Reluctantly, he went to hear Abbie speak at a movement conference center in Rowe, Massachusetts, in April 1981 and was, as he expected, put off by the focus on the good old days. Abbie, too, was disgusted by the exercise in nostalgia and blurted out his frustration. "I didn't come here to talk about the sixties. I wanna talk about the eighties, and how you organize, how you do it." Giordano was won over, and they became friends. He was invited to visit Abbie and Johanna at the Thousand Islands, with Abbie no doubt seeing in Al a younger version of himself.

Del-AWARE needed publicity if it was going to attract support for its final showdown with the Philadelphia Electric Company. On December 28 Abbie held a press conference in Philadelphia in which he promised a thousand-dollar reward to anyone who stole PECO's silver shovel. As expected, Abbie's presence in the pump station fight and his reputation as a prankster attracted the media. But time was running out. Shortly after the new year a New Jersey–based construction company brought in woodchippers and bulldozers to clear the ceremonial site. While Abbie, Al, and the leaders of Del-AWARE were discussing how to respond, they received a phone call that a spontaneous protest had begun at the site and that the construction workers had been chased away.

Abbie responded by urging caution. Yes, the demonstrators should hold the site, but they needed a plan that went beyond the mere fact of their physical presence, which might not last. He and Al decided to visit the Washington Crossing Historical Park, farther down the Delaware River, in order to discuss the situation. They were standing on the bank throwing rocks into the river when Al said, "It's too bad that this site isn't close to Valley Forge, because if it were we could call the occupation a winter encampment." Abbie lit up. "People don't know geography. It's in Pennsylvania. It's close enough." They went into the park store and, on Barry Freed's credit card, bought up the thirteen-star American flags, the Don't Tread on Me banners, and all the patriotic souvenirs the concession was selling. They rushed back to the construction site and handed out the flags and banners. Abbie got some poster paper and began scrawling out patriotic messages. He told people to get red, white, and blue ink and make copies. A banner was raised: Valley Forge II, Dump the Pump. A big holly tree was dubbed the "liberty tree." PECO and its contractors became the "Hessians,'" paid mercenaries brought in to destroy the community's way of life.

By appropriating patriotic symbols and placing the protesters' occupation of the construction site within the American historic tradition, Abbie and Al rallied the community. It was "the American conscience bubbling up," Giordano recalls. The patriotic theme captured everyone's enthusiasm. The protest turned into a permanent encampment. The ground-breaking ceremony was canceled, and at six o'clock on the morning that construction was to begin all access roads to the site were blocked by people and cars. That day all work stopped.

In the next two weeks the battle over the pumping station was turned around. It was Abbie at his most creative and inspiring best. He didn't have to tell people what to do. Having come up with the unifying theme, he encouraged everyone to use their own imagination to express it. Someone suggested the idea of a pump with the international slash/ban symbol covering it, and Abbie responded, "Yeah! Go ahead, print a thousand." The next day the posters were stapled up all over Bucks County. Always the media manipulator, Abbie would gather the press around him and lead them to where something visual was happening, so that however he was quoted the message in the background would be clear and powerful. And just as in the Thousand Islands, Abbie found ways to include everyone. There was a group of young men who hung out at Applejack, a local bar. They were against the pump but unwilling to commit to the nonviolent discipline that Del-AWARE and Abbie insisted was a tactical necessity. Instead of keeping them out of the protest, Abbie found the perfect role for them to play. Dubbing Applejack "security headquarters," he outfitted them with walkie-talkies and assigned them to use their pickup trucks to establish checkpoints where they could monitor the approach of construction equipment and police. It was a lesson that Abbie recalled from the *sereno* episode in Tompkins Square Park some fifteen years earlier. When people feel they have an important role that appeals to their self-esteem, they are usually willing to abide by the rules of a popular movement. But in order to get their cooperation, they also have to feel that the goals of the movement are their own.

Ultimately, hundreds were arrested as state police were called in to clear the site. But that didn't stop the protest. To Abbie, civil disobedience was not an end in itself; holding the construction site was merely a tactic that would lead to another level of struggle. After the construction site was cleared, the demonstrators occupied the county courthouse in Doylestown, allowing the court to operate but insisting that they would remain in the building until a referendum on the pumping station was allowed. Again, the tactic was explained in patriotic terms. The Revolutionary War had been fought so that people could vote on the decisions that affected their lives. To keep the momentum going and to support the courthouse occupation, Del-AWARE started a petition campaign to demand a referendum. Al Giordano was put in charge to run it.

All this happened—Valley Forge II, the arrests, the occupation of the courthouse, the decision to demand a referendum, and the beginning of the petition drive—within a two-week span, and the excitement was getting to Abbie. He had stopped taking his lithium before the new year, and without Johanna there was no one to monitor his moods. He had not told anyone, not even Al Giordano, about his being manic-depressive, and his new friends in Bucks County were confounded by his sudden and inexplicable bouts of irritable, hostile, and sometimes paranoid behavior. During the occupation of the courthouse Abbie went from the focused and high-energy phase of hypomania to the more psychotic states of bipolar disorder. At one point he took a magic marker and, in a manic burst of tasteless egotism, wrote his name on the marble wall beneath the engraved names of past county commissioners. On another day he failed to persuade Johanna to join him in Bucks County and kicked in the locked door of the house in which he was staying. When Giordano tried to calm him, Abbie accused Al of trying to get rid of him so that he could take credit for the effort.

Giordano called Johanna to ask what he should do. She got in touch with the Careys and other old friends, who came down to Bucks County. They wanted Abbie to leave the area in the hope that this would calm him down, but however out of control he was, he was loving the action and would not go. But his behavior was becoming politically self-destructive. He criticized the affluent antipump activists who had blockaded the pump site with their Mercedes Benzes and BMWs, attacked Congressman Peter Kostmayer, a liberal Democrat who was one of Del-AWARE's most important supporters, and denounced the leaders of Del-AWARE for not paying his expenses, for being too rich, for telling the local media that "I'm too mercurial, that I'm nuts." In a huff he resigned from Del-AWARE and also, by long-distance phone, from Save the River, although he continued to work for both with the title of national spokesman and was in almost daily contact with Giordano advising about tactics for the referendum campaign.

In New York, Abbie planned and promoted the "River Rats Ball," which raised thousands of dollars for Del-AWARE, Save the River, and Pete Seeger's "Clearwater" campaign to clean up the Hudson River. The event took place January 31 at Club 54, New York's "in" disco for "beautiful people." Still estranged from Johanna, Abbie showed up acting weird and paranoid. "He was riding an elevator to the sixth floor in a building that only had five floors," Giordano remembers.

In April the wave of manic behavior crested, and Abbie crashed into a debilitating depression. He attempted suicide by taking seventy-five Restorils. Had he taken the pills with a chaser of alcohol, the dosage would likely have been fatal. The suicide attempt was hushed up by Abbie's friends, but in a letter to Anita from Bellevue Hospital Abbie wrote frankly that he had stopped taking his lithium, "cause I was in the manic phase & felt 'well.' No one likes to accept the fact they have a long-term disability especially a 'mental' illness so not taking the drug & getting along is 'proof' to yourself and others that you're not 'ill.'"

Abbie interpreted his suicide attempt as a warning—a "jolt" to remind him of the seriousness of his disorder. Now he was going to use this experience to do some good in the broader society. "Organizer, organize thyself," he wrote Anita. He planned to attend the American Psychiatric Association convention for its symposium on depression. He planned to check out a self-help manic-depressive support network that he had heard about, and he asked Anita to clip items on manic depression for a book he was planning to write that he would title "Attacking Madness." He vowed to limit his movement work and take it easy for a while, but he had commitments for eight speeches in late April and early May, and there was the referendum in Bucks County coming up, and other causes, including Save the River, that needed his aid.

After this suicide attempt Abbie took his prescribed lithium for two years. But he craved the high of functional hypomania and disliked the stomach ailments that were one of lithium's principal side effects. In 1985 he stopped taking lithium and began a program of self-medication, using valium to neutralize his manic energy and supplementing this with various antidepressants when he felt himself sliding. For the next couple of years he was subject to constant mood swings as the elation of his hypomania often escalated into the more aggressive and irritable symptoms of manic behavior. But there were no full-blown psychotic episodes such as he had experienced in Bucks County and, until 1988, no debilitating bouts of extreme depression.

Abbie was out of Bucks County for the May 1983 referendum campaign. PECO outspent Del-AWARE $1.2 million to $64,000 and focused its campaign strategy on tarnishing Del-AWARE's cause with Abbie Hoffman's notoriety. A flier that the company distributed all over the county transformed Del-AWARE's slash/ban-the-pump symbol to slash/ban Abbie. But Del-AWARE had the volunteers to canvass the county, and the attack on Abbie backfired because many people felt that the utility was insulting their intelligence by personalizing the issue. Abbie had fired the movement up, and opposition to the pump had continued to grow after he had gone. Del-AWARE won the referendum 64,179 to 50,729. In the November election antipump Democrats took control of the county commissioner's office, the first time Democrats had been in charge in thirty years. The propump members of the public authority overseeing the project, the Neshaminy Water Resources Authority, were also voted out of office, and the new antipump commissioners appointed Tracy Carluccio, a leader of Del-AWARE, as executive secretary.

Abbie had come to Bucks County only a week before the construction of the pumping station was to begin, yet within two weeks the grassroots protest had gained unstoppable momentum. He had given the movement an organizing theme, which Giordano called "capture the flag," that had prevented the utility company from attacking the motives or patriotism of the antipump demonstrators and had stoked the courage and enthusiasm of the people in the area. According to Colleen Wells, one of the Republicans who was a leader of Del-AWARE, "Right before Abbie arrived we took a poll to find out how many people knew about the pump. Fifteen percent said they did. Two weeks later we took another poll and 97 percent knew about it. He had absolutely turned it around." In the short time he was in Bucks County he had developed a stepping-stone strategy that went from nonviolent occupation of the construction site and the courthouse to door-to-door canvassing to victory in an election campaign, with each step of the strategy based on the success of the previous step. Most of all he had brought excitement to the protest movement and encouraged the local activists to be courageous, use their imagination, and trust their political instincts and their creative selves. "I was all dressed up in white wool and pink chiffon, and here was Abbie Hoffman telling me I had to lie down in front of bulldozers," Wells remembers.[15] In the winter of 1983 construction of the Point Pleasant pumping station was canceled.

CHAPTER

13 | FINAL BATTLES

1984–1989

Abbie Hoffman spent the latter half of the 1980s in the same way he spent the last years of the 1960s: trying to foment a youth rebellion. Between 1984 and 1988 he averaged approximately sixty speeches a year. His attitude toward American students changed with his mood and with the kind of reception he received on a particular campus. In low periods he would denounce the students for their political apathy and their materialistic, yuppie values. He often denounced young people to his friends from the sixties. Much of this was a result of frustration, the failure of the young to lead the opposition against Reagan-era politics. But in more objective moods he understood that young people coming of age in the eighties did not have the economic cushion that had made it easy for sixties radicals to become full-time activists; nor was there one overwhelming moral issue—like civil rights or the Vietnam War—to galvanize the public.

Part of Abbie's disillusion with the students was also a result of the nature of his touring. He was often billed as the famous Yippie activist or Chicago Seven defendant, and there were always students who wanted him to talk about hippies, drugs, rock 'n' roll—everything, it seemed, except the issues and the politics of the era in which they were living. Sometimes he was booked along with Timothy Leary to talk about the sixties. Abbie hated these gigs. Nostalgia, he said, was a disease of middle age. He liked to talk about the past only as an inspiration to activism in the eighties. Central America, the war on drugs, the environment, Iran-Contra, progressive politics—these were his issues. He also talked a lot about nuts and bolts organizing: how to build an opposition movement, both on campus and in one's home community. Abbie was one of the few veterans of sixties radicalism who was talking to college students about the sixties as a positive experience. Many other radicals of the period felt confusion and guilt over the breakup of the movement in the early seventies and passed on their bitterness to the young people who wanted to revive the activist spirit. But Abbie could call up the good feelings of the civil rights movement and the antiwar movement at its peak. He would discuss the mistakes, but he also wanted to celebrate the successes.[1]

Touring the campuses with Jerry Rubin was a natural, however. It was the great Yippie/yuppie debate: the idealism of the sixties versus the challenge of the eighties. There were more than forty debates in 1985 and 1986 with an occasional rematch thereafter. Abbie and Jerry each received as much as twenty-five hundred dollars an appearance, and wherever they spoke they attracted crowds of students and sixties veterans. After going through est and the gamut of other New Age therapies, Jerry had emerged as a born-again capitalist and self-proclaimed spokesman for the yuppies. Clean-shaven and dressed in a business suit, as if posing for an American Express ad, he argued that by working within the system and becoming rich and powerful the baby boomers of the sixties would take control of the country and do everything that the sixties radicals had wanted to do: end the arms race, eliminate poverty, improve relations with the third world, and even cure the "illness of aging."[2] Abbie respected Jerry's accomplishment from the sixties and had residual warm feelings for him from their Yippie days together. But the tour, for Abbie, became an ideological vendetta. What bothered Abbie wasn't so much that Jerry had become a capitalist. Abbie was never a doctrinaire socialist, and gambler that he was, he occasionally took a stock market plunge. What he resented was Jerry's promoting the yuppie lifestyle in the same way that he, Jerry, had previously promoted the Yippie style, as the hope and wave of the future.

Abbie always found it difficult to hate people. If he couldn't talk to a person about politics, he would talk about movies, sports, or fishing—whatever it took to connect. But in time he came to hate going on tour with Jerry. He refused to stay in the same hotel with

him or eat at the same restaurant. Outside the actual public en-
counter they rarely talked. To Abbie, the debate wasn't just political; it was a fight for the souls of the students. Over a packet of
promotional material for Rubin's business, "The Jerry Rubin Business Networking Salon," which Abbie mailed to Anita, he scrawled,
"Here's Jerry Rubin's idiot rip-off. A pimp! I've decided to go after
him. The gloves are off."

To Abbie, Jerry's rags-to-riches scenario about young people
becoming rich and powerful represented a selfish delusion. Few
people ever get rich, and few of those who do are willing to put
themselves at risk to fight the system, Abbie argued. If Jerry were
organizing his fellow yuppies to oppose Ronald Reagan, "I would
be the first to say yippie to the yuppies," he declared. But Jerry
was not networking, not organizing, not doing anything to fight
"union busting, monopolies, or a tax structure that provides welfare for the rich." Jerry was apologizing for the system rather than
fighting it; he had "no strategy for change," Abbie charged. Gaining personal power would not be enough. "You need agitators; you
need people to stir things up on the grassroots level," Abbie insisted. "In the American experience there is no such thing as inside
or outside the system. You fight injustice with every tool you can
find." Become community organizers, not corporate executives,
Abbie challenged. "Go into your local community to fight poverty,
to work on environmental issues."[3]

Reports of these debates invariably noted that Abbie got most of
the applause and most of the attention when the event was over.
But it was also true, as many reporters noted, that Jerry's appeal
was to the head, while Abbie's was to the heart. Once the students
had to make career decisions, most would likely follow Jerry along
the path toward affluence. Abbie conceded that this was true but,
citing the small minority of colonial Americans who had actively
supported the War for Independence, commented that it doesn't
take a majority to make a revolution, "it only takes enough."[4] On
his campus speaking tours Abbie always had an eye out for future
organizers. The most important part of his campus visits—and the
part that he enjoyed the most—was the time spent talking to the
small group of activists that he would find on almost every campus.
In his mind was the idea of bringing them together and creating a
national student organization, an SDS for the eighties.

★   ★   ★

Abbie was always looking for a role to play in progressive politics. He was enthusiastic about the idea of a "rainbow coalition" but wary of its leader, Jesse Jackson. Being a libertine when it came to drugs, he was opposed to Jackson's antidrug crusade. He was also upset by Jackson's off-the-record remark about New York City being "Hymie town." Jackson was campaigning in New York during the 1984 presidential primary as an opponent of Reaganomics and an advocate of the poor. But the media, taking its cue from the city's large and politically active Jewish population, kept pressing Jackson about his position on Israel, so that Israel rather than Reaganomics became the most important issue in the New York Democratic primary, much to Jackson's frustration. Progressive friends who spoke with Abbie during this time tried to get him back on the Jackson bandwagon by explaining Jackson's dilemma in New York and emphasizing the need for progressive whites to rally behind the black candidate. They succeeded. Abbie began talking about starting an organization: Jews for Jackson. The Jackson campaign was wary of Abbie being officially or publicly associated with Jesse. On his own, however, Abbie stumped for Jackson. Phoning Julius Lester, his black friend from SNCC who had since converted to Judaism, he offered to debate, on college campuses, the issues creating friction between Jews and blacks. "*You* speak for the Jews," Abbie suggested. "I'll speak for the blacks."[5]

During this period Abbie was working with a young writer named Jonathan Silvers on a book about the Reagan administration's war on drugs. Because of the notoriety of Abbie's coke bust, many of his friends warned him against speaking out on the drug hysteria, but he felt that he had to speak out. *Steal This Urine Test*, published in 1986, argued that the war on drugs represented the government's overreaction to and misunderstanding of the problem of drug abuse and warned that, in any case, the strategy of prohibition backed by law enforcement and interdiction would never work. The book also denounced mandatory drug testing as a violation of civil liberties and a potential means for big government and business to control working people. The war on drugs, as Abbie saw it, had "nothing to do with drug abuse and a lot to do with controlling citizens." The book was well received as a thoroughly researched critique, even by such mainstream papers as the *Chicago Tribune* and *New York Times*. But it did not make a dent against the government drug war propaganda and the media's supportive hype.

In the winter of 1983 and 1984 Abbie made the first of five trips to Nicaragua. With Johanna doing most of the organizing work, he conducted two-week tours to that embattled country that featured briefings from Sandinista officials. Recalling the efforts of American leftists in the 1930s who volunteered to fight against the Spanish fascists, Abbie referred to Nicaragua as "my Spanish Civil War." If he were younger, he said, he would be in the mountains fighting against the Contras.[6]

In supporting the Sandinistas, Abbie saw himself fighting against American political and military intervention in Nicaragua's internal affairs. On that basis he would not criticize the Sandinistas in public, although in private he sometimes complained, as he wrote Anita, that the midlevel "bureaucratic leftists" in the Sandinista movement were rigid and power-hungry.[7] (One incident that galled Abbie was the denial by a Sandinista tour guide that marijuana was available in revolutionary Nicaragua. Abbie could smell people smoking it as the two argued the point.) Although always a rebel, Abbie was not going to let lesser issues like bureaucratic stupidity compromise his enthusiasm for what the Sandinistas were attempting. Part of their repressiveness, he believed, came from the fear of a U.S. invasion. He himself doubted that it would be forthcoming. He credited the "legacy of the sixties" and the precedent of massive domestic disorders with preventing a Vietnam-like invasion.[8]

In order to help the Nicaraguans survive the U.S. economic boycott, Abbie proposed a People's Peace Corps that would raise $1.25 million to organize "Nicaragua Summer, 1985."[9] There were other American groups already funneling aid and volunteers to Nicaragua, and though Abbie's idea was the catchiest in conception, it was also redundant before it got off the ground. Like CLARO, it was ultimately forgotten. However, stopping American aggression against Nicaragua remained for Abbie an important issue.

★   ★   ★

In November 1986 Abbie was invited to speak at a rally at the University of Massachusetts at Amherst. The rally was called to support eleven students who had been arrested a few weeks earlier while protesting the university's sponsoring of CIA recruiters on campus. Those protesters wanted the university to prohibit the CIA from recruiting on campus on the grounds that the CIA violated international and U.S. laws. But they didn't want the university simply to bow to student pressure; they also demanded that the university discuss the *morality* of having CIA recruiters on campus. Chancellor Joseph Duffey (who had been a McCarthy delegate at the 1968 Democratic convention) refused to meet with them, and eleven protesters were arrested while occupying an office next door to Duffey's, where they were waiting to see him.

The support rally, held November 24, drew activists from campuses throughout the Northeast, including former President Carter's daughter, Amy, from Brown University, as well as Abbie. Abbie did not get a warm reception. After a group of right-wing students announced plans to make a citizens' arrest, he had to be surrounded by student bodyguards. But many of the protesting students also opposed his presence; he was considered a relic from another era. His speech, however—a detailed account of the illegal and undemocratic role that the CIA had played in international affairs—won them over. Abbie then accompanied the students on their march to the administration building, where, again, they hoped to see Duffey. The administration building was closed, so they entered an adjacent building with no plans except to discuss the next step. No one, least of all Abbie, had figured on being arrested, but at that moment state police rushed in to surround the building. The students were ordered to leave, but about fifty, plus Abbie, refused. The brutal way in which the police handled them stirred another group of students, including Amy Carter, to sit down in front of the buses that were carrying them to jail. She and eight others were arrested.

While they were all waiting at the courthouse to be arraigned on charges of disorderly conduct and criminal trespass, Abbie beckoned to Betty Tomlinson, a local activist lawyer who had quickly been called in to handle the arraignments. With himself and Amy Carter as codefendants, Abbie knew that the case could easily attract the national media, and he wanted to make the most of it. Already he was plotting the defense: he suggested to Tomlinson that they go for a jury trial and use the "necessity" defense, which is based on the proposition that the defendants had to commit their

crime in order to stop a greater crime from being committed. Tomlinson had had experience using that form of defense and knew
how difficult it was to get a judge to agree to allow it. "I thought he
was jumping the gun because we hadn't even gotten people out on
bail," she later recalled, "but he was so definite and positive. Abbie had a vision about the trial from the onset, and his vision
carried us on."[10]

In this case the protesters would argue that the CIA's illegal actions against Nicaragua were leading the American people into a
war with Nicaragua, and this was a more serious crime than disorderly conduct or trespass. In other words the defendants would
concede their crime and put the CIA on trial. The judge allowed
the defendants to use that defense, and with Abbie doing much of
the fund-raising, expert witnesses were brought to testify about the
CIA. Ralph McGeehee, a twenty-five-year veteran of the CIA, testified how the CIA's Operation Phoenix had organized the assassination of twenty thousand Vietnamese political officials. A former
leader of the Nicaraguan Contras, Edgar Chamarro, told how the
CIA was training the Contras to assassinate respected Nicaraguans
and blame the killings on the Sandinistas. Ramsey Clark, the former U.S. attorney general who had not been allowed to testify at
the Chicago Seven trial, described the CIA "as totally uninhibited
by law." Other witnesses spoke from their own experience about
Contra attacks in Nicaragua, describing how the Contras destroyed
Sandinista-built health clinics and carried out assassination campaigns against doctors and citizens. Boston University historian
Howard Zinn testified about the important role of civil disobedience in the fight for American independence and its continuing
importance for preserving democracy. Daniel Ellsberg, a former
Pentagon official, told how the civil disobedience of Vietnam-era
draft resisters had inspired him to release the Pentagon Papers,
which documented government deceptions early in the war.

Abbie, who represented himself at the trial, was determined to
portray the defendants as acting within the American democratic
tradition. In his summation to the jury he talked about how his
father had taken him to town meetings around Worcester to see
how democracy worked. "I grew up with the idea that democracy
is not something you believe in, or a place you hang your hat, but
it's something you do. You participate. If you stop doing it, democracy crumbles and falls apart." He quoted Tom Paine: "Every age

and generation must be free to act for itself, in all cases, as the ages and generations which preceded it." And he concluded by saying that "a verdict of not guilty will say what Thomas Paine said: Young people don't give up hope. If you participate, the future is yours."[11]

The jury, which was composed primarily of white, middle-class senior citizens, acquitted the defendants. In effect they ruled that the CIA was guilty of the crimes that the defense witnesses had charged. The victory was especially sweet for Abbie. He wanted to prove that he could beat the system at its own game. "Abbie did not want it to be like Chicago," Tomlinson says of his role in the trial. "He wanted it to be respectful. People didn't expect this of him. He showed up in a suit and a tie and didn't do cartwheels. He wanted to prove that he could use the legal system and play by the rules and still win."

Abbie also used the trial to promote his idea of a national student organization, alerting his student friends about a meeting that had been planned for Amherst at the time of the trial. In fact, it was Abbie alone who singlehandedly engineered the meeting. Not only would it assure a turnout of supporters for the trial, but it would get them together to talk about his idea for a national movement. The seventy or eighty students who came to Amherst were strangers to each other and had no clue why they were gathered except that Abbie had invited them. One of the first things they did when they figured out that it was he who had instigated the meeting was to ban him from speaking. The students had mixed sentiments toward Abbie. On the one hand they felt manipulated; on the other hand they welcomed the chance to talk with fellow activists. But Abbie was one step ahead of them. He had already established close ties with a group from Rutgers University who shared his enthusiasm for a national organization. He advised them that they could now make it happen by taking the initiative and volunteering to do all the follow-up tasks that the meeting came up with.

One of the activists from Rutgers was a graduate student named Christine Kelly, who, like Al Giordano, became another of Abbie's organizer protégés. Kelly had grown up in a liberal Catholic family active in the peace and civil rights movement; nevertheless Abbie, during the sixties, was "a figure my mother hated." As a student, Kelly read the transcripts of the Chicago Seven trial, and "Abbie became a mythic figure for me." She had been a student activist for three years when Abbie spoke at Rutgers. When she introduced herself to him, he barked back, "Don't call me Mr. Hoffman. My name is Abbie!" Seeing that Kelly and her Rutgers group were serious about their politics, Abbie made them the vehicle for his idea of a national student movement. "He was a great teacher," Kelly recalls, "not in the sense of being patient and slow but in getting the information out. If you were quick enough to get it, you could learn a lot."

Kelly, like a number of young activists during this time, became family to Abbie and Johanna. In a torrent of letters and phone calls, and in the process of spending time together, Abbie taught them what he knew about organizing, everything from opening bank accounts and raising money to running a meeting and planning civil disobedience. Once a proponent of structurelessness, Abbie now taught the necessity of parliamentary procedure, the necessity of accountable leadership, and the importance of democratic process. He railed against what he called "the curse of consensus," which referred to a decision-making process in which unanimous approval is needed to pass a proposal. Under consensus decision making, one stubborn individual can block a decision agreed to by everyone else. Under majority rule, the merits of an issue are debated and then voted up or down. But under consensus, debate is often mistaken for contentiousness; the point is to forge a harmonious feeling rather than a workable decision. In order to get unanimous approval it often becomes necessary to strip a proposal of its controversial—and most meaningful—aspects. Abbie thus opted for majority rule, and he advised his protégés on how to achieve it. To forge a majority is a form of organizing, he pointed out. You have to persuade people about the merits of your argument. Most important of all, thought Kelly, Abbie taught that "you cannot build a movement based on any other principle but hope, not nihilism or guilt. And hope is not an illusion but a possibility."

Abbie was not easy to work with. Men were wary because they resented his charisma and saw him as competition; women saw him as a domineering, egotistical heterosexual male. Off lithium he was given to pronounced mood swings: he'd be charming and funny one minute; hostile, impatient, and irritable the next. You had to recognize these difficulties and work around them, Kelly explained. Students, however, are in the process of developing their own personality and are wary of older activists like Abbie who can't help but impose their own. Yet, she explained, "there were rewards, and if you could learn how to deal with him you could learn about organizing from a master." The young were not alone in being confused and put off by his behavior. He was sometimes inexplicably rude to older comrades, too, berating them for holding jobs and raising families.[12] At other times he himself felt vulnerable and defensive about his choice to continue organizing. "I serve an important role in my country and that's my life," he wrote in a June 1987 letter to Anita, apologizing for not being more concerned with his family's life. "Sometimes I have to actually smother certain feelings because if I followed them I would drop out. It's very hard for others to understand this & I am always lonely and isolated. . . . I just want to do what has to be done so much. I'll never understand why everyone else doesn't feel this way."

In February 1988 more than seven hundred student activists from 130 campuses met at Rutgers to discuss forming a mass-based democratic student organization. Abbie had promoted the conference during his campus travels and helped to fund it. The turnout was larger than expected, and Abbie had great hopes. He wanted a full-blown movement to come out of the conference with ringing principles, a new Port Huron Statement. But the handful of SDS activists who had gathered in 1962 at Port Huron were inventing a New Left. The students at Rutgers carried with them the sectarian baggage of the New Left's self-destruction. Many of them had come not to start a new movement but to protect their own organizations. Many came with ironclad positions that they were not about to give up. A minority of vocal anarchists were determined to oppose any attempt to create a cohesive national organization. Sensitive to the diversity of the delegates, Kelly and the group that organized the conference rejected many of Abbie's ideas. For all his advocacy of parliamentary democracy, he wanted to manipulate the process to assure that a national organization would emerge. He also wanted to give the keynote address, but the organizers recognized that he was too controversial. Instead, he appeared on a panel discussion on the "Three Ms" of organizing: media, music, and modems.

Abbie thought the conference a failure when the organization he wanted didn't emerge. But at a follow-up "Unity Meeting" at

Chapel Hill that summer the Student Action Union was born. Abbie promoted the group on his campus tours and advised those in the leadership, like Kelly, who were willing to listen. Although there were more campus demonstrations and more people committing civil disobedience than at any other time since the sixties, there was no galvanizing issue around which students could be organized. Student activism did not have the cachet that it had had in the sixties. It wasn't resonating in the culture of the eighties. But it did represent a crack in the Reagan hegemony, and this was the reason that Abbie, even in his impatience, was still hopeful. "Rome wasn't destroyed in a day," as Abbie reminded two student activists who asked his opinion of how they were doing.

In the summer of 1987 Abbie returned to Bucks County; the fight against the pumping station was on again. After the project was canceled in 1983, the contractors sued for breach of contract and asked the court to order construction to resume according to the contract. Judge Isaac Garb, who had been on the case from the beginning, ruled in favor of the project. Over the objection of many Del-AWARE leaders Abbie was once again asked to lead the community in what was to be its final battle against the pump.

Still intent on playing "capture the flag," Abbie used patriotic symbols to rally the community. "Bring your cannon," he urged a group of Revolutionary War reenactors who wanted to come in costume to an antipump demonstration. He also put out a call for a "Democracy Summer," hoping to attract student activists to the area, but the turnout was a disappointment. Abbie's battle plan was a series of civil disobedience demonstrations at the Bradford Reservoir construction site. When arrested and put on trial, the protesters would use the necessity defense so that Del-AWARE could muster all its arguments against the pump in a well-publicized local jury trial. But the "c.d." actions, organized around themes (Veterans Day, ladies' day, New Jersey day, etc.), were neutralized by Judge Garb and the county's propump prosecutor, who chose not to prosecute demonstrators on criminal charges but to arrest them for contempt of court, setting up hearings to which jury trials did not apply. Abbie himself was arrested three times (once with his son america, now a teenager) in an effort to force a jury trial. The cause seemed hopeless, and Abbie started hinting in the media that it was time to abandon nonviolence and adopt more aggressive tactics. Because he was not taking lithium, his behavior was often erratic. In a repeat of 1983 he began fighting with some of Del-AWARE's leaders and resigned as a consultant. The fight had gone out of the pump opponents. "It's not enough for one personality to get arrested over and over again. It's their turn now," Abbie told the *Philadelphia Inquirer*.[13]

The pumping station defeat was a great disappointment. Abbie had played all the nonviolent and patriotic cards and won battle after battle. The people had voted against the pump and had elected antipump politicians to office. Democracy seemed to have worked. Yet in the end the pump got built.

In November 1987 Abbie had sent in an absentee ballot for the election of selectmen in New Hope, the town in Bucks County where Del-AWARE had its office. The election turned out a tie, and the Republicans challenged Abbie's right to vote. Acting as his own lawyer before Judge Garb, Abbie argued, "No right is more precious in a free country than that of having a voice in the election of those who make the laws under which, as good citizens, we must live. . . . Our Constitution leaves no room for classification of people in a way that unnecessarily abridges this right." Judge Garb denied the validity of Abbie's vote, and the Republican candidate for county commissioner won the election.

Still, Abbie stayed in Bucks County, moving into a small apartment in a converted chicken coop in Solebury Township. Johanna remained in New York, trying to establish a life of her own. They saw each other on weekends and occasionally spent time together in Fineview. But Abbie was Barry in the Thousand Islands, and he was no longer happy in that more subdued role. Bucks County had become his base, a more central location from which he went off on his campus tours. He and Jonathan Silvers were also investigating rumors that in October 1980 the Reagan campaign had struck a clandestine deal with Iran: the Iranians had agreed not to release the American hostages they were holding until after the November election, in order to make the Carter administration look weak and ineffective and thus help Reagan defeat Carter for the presidency.

On June 16, 1988, Abbie was driving from his home in Bucks County to Newark Airport, en route to Chicago to hand in an article that he and Silvers had written for *Playboy* about the so-called October Surprise. Driving stick shift with an ice-cream cone in one hand, Abbie drifted into the oncoming lane and was hit by a truck. His car plunged over a guardrail and turned onto its side.

Abbie was knocked unconscious. When he came to, police and an ambulance had arrived. They wanted him to go to the hospital, but he refused to get into the ambulance, proclaiming that he wasn't hurt and that they couldn't make him go, because he knew his rights. Pulling out a wad of bills, Abbie announced that he'd pay a hundred dollars to anyone who would drive him to the airport by four o'clock. A youth stepped forward, they drove off together, and he made his plane.

Abbie was desperate to get to Chicago because he believed that the article would cost George Bush the 1988 election and turn the country around. He and Silvers were the first journalists to track down the rumors and add substance to the speculation that the Republican party had stolen the 1980 election. What they knew of the case was that President Carter had thought he had a deal with the Iranian government to free the hostages before the election. At the time Carter and Reagan were running even in the polls; if Carter could get the hostages out of Iran, he would likely win re-election. But the Iranians had inexplicably backed out of the deal with Carter. They continued to hold the hostages through the campaign season, releasing them on the very day of Reagan's inauguration. Thereafter, Israel began shipping arms to Iran. There was evidence but no "smoking gun" to prove that Reagan's campaign staff had struck a deal with the Iranians and that Israel shipped the arms as payment not for Iran's releasing the hostages (as many thought) but for Iran's *holding* them until Reagan was elected president. Abbie had tried to get Democratic candidate Michael Dukakis to use these findings, which implicated Vice President Bush, but Dukakis's campaign staff was not interested. In Abbie's egocentric view, the outcome of the 1988 election was riding on the *Playboy* article.

The meeting with the *Playboy* editors didn't go well. The magazine would publish only those parts of the article that were fully documented.[14] Abbie was angry and in great pain from the accident, coughing and pissing blood. When the meeting broke up, he checked himself into a Chicago hospital. The doctors wanted to hold him overnight, but he got painkillers and flew back to New York. The next day, limping and still in pain, he flew to Northampton, Massachusetts, for a "sixties revival," a fund-raising benefit for an anti–nuclear power referendum that Al Giordano had helped organize. Giordano was shocked by Abbie's appearance. "He looked like a ghost; he was defeated, paranoid, drawing crazy people to him." Collapsing on his return to New York, Abbie was hospitalized with a broken leg, a broken rib, a punctured kidney, and two broken fingers.

The injuries healed slowly, and Abbie had trouble working. He found it difficult to accept that his body had broken down and that he could not keep up the hypomanic pace that for him was normal. For the first time since his underground days he began thinking and talking about his own mortality. He wanted to die with his boots on, he told writer Mark Hertsgaard. To die in order to change history was an honor, and he was "absolutely convinced I'll be fighting until I die."[15] It took all his strength to keep up his schedule. He continued to research the October Surprise and, with a cast on his leg that he called his "Quayle kicker," pursued a new career as a stand-up comic. As an activist, Abbie was a wonderful comic. But "as a professional comic," one critic noted, he "is an effective activist."[16] What he did was take the funnier observations from his speaking engagements in order to persuade his nightclub audience that they had to become political activists. On top of all this he was still in demand as a campus speaker and was putting a lot of effort into helping Christine Kelly and her friends organize their national Student Action Union, even listing himself, in a brochure he used to get speaking dates on campus, as the chief adviser. But the crash "took the steam out of him," Kelly recalls. "It was a trauma to his psyche and to his body. It induced the end of a long 'up' cycle."

In mid-November Abbie wrote Anita that he was still having trouble holding a pen and that doctors had told him that his leg would continue to give him pain for eighteen months to two years. "I'm starting to feel old and weary," he wrote, and then added, "You'd hear me speak and you'd never guess. It's sort of a professional talent I have." Although he didn't discuss his mental illness with his younger friends, this too was very much on his mind. Writing Allen Ginsberg in December 1988, he asked about the health of Ginsberg's friend Peter Orlovsky, a fellow sufferer of bipolar disorder. "You can definitely life [sic] a long productive happy life with this illness," he wrote Ginsberg. Always ready to help others no matter how helpless he himself felt, he suggested that Orlovsky get in touch with manic-depressive support groups in New York City, noting, "they have meetings, a newsletter, speakers, etc. It's very good therapy to know you are not alone. . . . Don't give up."[17]

But he himself was falling deeper into a depressed state, the first

serious depression since his attempted suicide six years before.
Still, he was looking forward to more campus speaking tours and a
possible college teaching job the next fall. He was also excited
about the opening of the movie *Born on the 4th of July*. Abbie
knew Ron Kovics, on whose life the movie was based, from the 1972
demonstrations against the war during the national party conventions in Miami. Kovics had been a leader of Vietnam Veterans
against the War, and in the movie Abbie played a radical student
leader in the antiwar movement. He was also working on a project
to design computer software for betting on National Football
League games, and he was in continual contact with his brother
Jack, with whom he placed bets and talked sports. During this
period he was also looking for an apartment in New York so that
he could spend more time with Johanna, but he could not afford
Manhattan rents.

In February 1989 he started to feel that he was losing control of
his mental equilibrium; his depression was deepening. He was prescribed Prozac, a new "wonder drug" that was supposed to treat
bipolar disorder without the side effects associated with lithium.
Prozac can take up to four to six weeks to begin working. There is
also evidence (disputed by its manufacturer, the Eli Lilly Company,
as well as many doctors) that a statistically significant percentage
of patients—estimated by one team of researchers at 1.9 to 7.7
percent—may become dangerously violent or obsessed with suicide
as a result of taking Prozac.[18] According to other medical researchers, patients suffering from bipolar disorder are more prone to
attempting suicide than any other patients classified as having an
affective mental disorder. On or off Prozac, Abbie was vulnerable
to suicidal depressions.

On April 7, 1989, Abbie wrote Anita, "I've been in an acute de-
pressive episode for almost two months. This is the most I've
written and I don't read. I'm scared to cross the street without
Johanna and am on lots of medication." To people he saw or spoke
to, he attributed the depression to his mother's having cancer. But
he also began to withdraw, not phoning his brother to bet on the
NCAA basketball play-offs that he had always intensely followed.
On April 12 Johanna, as well as other friends, began calling him
and got his answering machine. Worried, Johanna called his landlord, Michael Waldron, who found him around seven that evening
in bed, fully clothed and under the covers, his hands folded be-

neath his cheek, seemingly relaxed and at peace. It was called a suicide, but there was no note. The coroner's report said he had swallowed 150 phenobarbitals—more than enough to kill anybody—and washed them down with alcohol. Abbie wasn't a big drinker, but he knew his drugs. His first suicide attempt had probably failed because he hadn't drunk any alcohol. This time he had taken no chances.

Media commentators who knew nothing of Abbie's life in the eighties made the case that his suicide was a political statement. At long last, they were once again declaring, the sixties were over. Some activists, including Dave Dellinger, tried to elevate Abbie to radical martyrdom. Taking their script from the Karen Silkwood case, they insisted that his auto accident had been a set-up in which he was run off the road so that government agents could steal his documents on the October Surprise (a possibility that, according to Anita, Abbie had considered but then dismissed), and that he was killed because of what he had discovered about Reagan's stealing the 1980 election.

Those close to Abbie, who knew his suffering, were not surprised by the suicide. William Styron, a novelist who has suffered and written about bipolar disorder, composed a taped statement that was played at a memorial service for Abbie in New York: "He put himself to sleep not out of any failure of courage, nor out of any moral dereliction, but because the pain of his suffering was simply more than he could bear. . . . Suicide in such an instance . . . arises out of blind necessity."

Abbie's suicide was the result of a downward spiral through a black hole of depression that likely seemed for him to have no bottom. It was a private act, one of the very few of his adult life. The press was not alerted in order that they might cover his death; there was no political message that he wanted to get out. Abbie's death was not a statement. Or to put that in another way, by the silence of his death he made us look at the meaning of his life.

There are many practical political lessons to be drawn from Abbie's life, from both his failures and his organizing successes. In the 1980s, as Abbie matured, he began to integrate his theatrical creativity with his understanding of nuts and bolts community organizing. Although he was often too manic—and too egotistical—to

work effectively with other organizers, wherever he went he offered
commonsense advice. "Isms are *was*isms," Abbie taught. Don't get
sidetracked by ideological battles; don't isolate yourself by taking
dogmatic and sectarian stands. Pick your goal and move toward it;
don't pick fights on issues you cannot win; keep your eye on the
prize; winning is what counts even if it means accepting temporary
detours and setbacks. Celebrate your victories, learn from your
defeats. Do the unexpected, keep the authorities guessing, maintain a sense of humor, and keep an open mind. There's no conflict
between working inside and outside the system; keep a foot in
both. "Activism during the 1960s encompassed electoral politics,
lobbying, door to door canvassing, teach-ins, forums, as well as
demonstrations, guerrilla theater, civil disobedience, and militant
resistance," he wrote. Demonstrations in the street create movement within the political system; movement in political institutions
creates opportunities to organize in the street. There is no dichot-
omy between national and grassroots organizing. Local issues need
outside support; national movements need local groups to do grassroots organizing. Don't waste time attacking the press. Learn how
to use the media. Don't attack leaders, but insist that they be accountable. Impatience is a virtue, but you also have to be responsible and businesslike: show up on time for meetings, do what you
say you are going to do. Politics should be fun, but people *are* also
moved by moral persuasion.[19]

The movement in the 1960s was confronted with a youth rebellion that Abbie tried to channel in a political direction. It was a
bold initiative. Everywhere, or so it seemed, people were shedding
their past and declaring themselves to be new persons. Once, during the Yippie period, Abbie appeared on stage at the Fillmore
East, New York's major venue for rock 'n' roll concerts, dressed in
a suit, white shirt, and tie, and with his long hair tied back and
hidden beneath the collar of his jacket. As he interwove verbal riffs
about his life as a salesman in Worcester and how he had dropped
out of that career to become a full-time political activist, he began
to disrobe, stripping off the cloaking of straight, middle-class respectability until he was down to the colorful and tattered clothes
of a long-haired freak—a political striptease that had many in the
audience wanting to strip off their own layers of conformity and
fear.

But that was Abbie as a showman, transforming rabble-rousing into performance art, mythologizing his life in order to give people the idea that change is easy—all too easy, it would seem in retrospect. In the brilliance of Abbie's *theater* lay a personal dilemma and, in addition, the seeds of the sixties movement's spectacular failure. It was easy to play at becoming a new person, harder to be that person over the long haul. Abbie devoted his life to fomenting social, cultural, and political change, yet he himself remained, throughout the seventies and eighties, identified (and in the end one might say trapped) by a public image created for the sixties. Yet as Abbie himself so often insisted, he never wanted to break the mold of the fifties rebel he had so carefully crafted back in Worcester and at Brandeis. If the avatar of change found change so difficult, what does it say about a politics that was premised on the necessity of almost instantaneous personal transformation?

In a pluralistic society, radical lifestyles don't necessarily lead to political change. Building a revolution around the demands of youth not only alienates older people, but when young people grow up, *they* become the older people. Abbie's Yippie experiment exemplified (indeed exacerbated!) a problem that has always plagued the American left: the politics of hedonism and transcendence have always grated against the less spectacular, even dull, coalition-building priorities of the programmatic left (with its more workaday, reformist agenda). His and other efforts do not suggest that the two styles of organizing can easily be meshed, but they do call attention to the need to be conscious of both.

Abbie played the youth revolt like a maestro, pitting the hip counterculture against the straight mainstream culture with spectacular effect. But cultural issues, reflecting as they do the way people live, are always explosive. Abbie's Yippie years are a warning against fighting political battles on cultural turf. Learning the lessons of Yippie, he came to appreciate that the challenge of cultural politics is not to divide people but to find in the American mix a common ground where all the people of a community can "break bread," as he put it, and can, whether or not they share one another's lifestyles or tastes, walk arm in arm toward a shared political goal. He was impatient with "political correctness," the constant judgments, common among leftists, on other leftists' lifestyles and tastes. "What people are they are," he wrote in a 1985 symposium on the peace movement's organizing tactics, "and they should be proud of it." But "it simply is *not* correct that sex, sexual

preference, race, age or what people eat or smoke make them better than someone else," he warned. "We should stop demanding
that we all become instant saints and be more tolerant of our comrades, especially if they are active."[20]

Abbie died certain of his accomplishments and those of his generation: "In the sixties apartheid was driven out of America. Legal
segregation—Jim Crow—ended," he said at his last public speaking engagement at Vanderbilt University. "We didn't end racism,
but we ended legal segregation. We ended the idea that you can
send a million soldiers ten thousand miles away to fight in a war
that people do not support. We ended the idea that women are
second-class citizens. . . . We were young, we were reckless, arro-
gant, silly, and headstrong—and we were right."

To the student activists at Rutgers he explained, "In the sixties
we were so fed up we wanted to destroy everything. But you have
to save America, not destroy it." To the end, Abbie refused to accept limits on the tactics that he considered open to activists. In
one of his last written statements, composed just before he went
into his final depression, Abbie responded to an article written by
the former Weatherman leader Mark Rudd at the behest of Christine Kelly and others in the Student Action Network. Rudd warned
the new generation of student activists against romanticizing the
Weathermen as revolutionaries; he condemned all forms of political violence, no matter what the cause, and blamed the violent
tactics of the Weathermen for destroying the antiwar movement at
the height of the Vietnam War. Abbie responded by reiterating his
opposition to politics motivated by guilt, but instead of attacking
pacifism, as he would have done in the past, he sought to bridge
the differences between advocates of nonviolence and those who
believed in "more militant behavior" including armed struggle.
True revolutionaries respect nonviolence, Abbie stated. "Revolutionaries are born to love, they are not born to kill. If the choices
in this world were between war and peace, only the mentally de-
ranged would choose war, but life and global politics are not that
easy. The choice has always been between justice and injustice,
oppression and resistance. There are scores of tactics and combi-
nations thereof. Good tacticians will be those who best respond to
the objective and potential conditions in which they find themselves."[21]

Yet Abbie believed that the American left, even in its most militant acts of protest and resistance, had to communicate a positive message. And he understood that patriotic feelings could be used to create the common ground he saw as essential for a successful political fight. Patriotism is not necessarily a right-wing or divisive force in the United States, and he believed that jingoistic flag-wavers could be challenged and beaten at their own patriotic game. A rebellious spirit runs deep in the American psyche. A belief in democracy, equality, tolerance, fair play, and justice can always be tapped, if only American radicals would believe in their own polit-ical heritage. Wave the flag, Abbie was saying. Democracy is not an abstract principle to believe in or support; it's something to *do*, and it can be done. "All you need is a little nerve and a willingness to be considered an embarrassment. Then you just keep pushing," Abbie wrote in his autobiography.[22]

And that is what Abbie did. Sometimes rudely and often too fast, but aways with courage, spirit, humor, and an underlying optimism that people possess the power and imagination to change their world, Abbie Hoffman kept on pushing until he could push no more.

Notes

The place and date of unpublished interviews referred to in these notes are as follows: Stew Albert, by phone, September 6, 1990; Joan Crawford Ashley, White River Junction, Vt., December 21, 1989; Carol Brightman, Walpole, Maine, April 14, 1990; Marty and Susan Carey, Willow, N.Y., November 6, 1989; Hank Chaiklin, Goose Rocks, Maine, June 30, 1990; Jim Fouratt, New York City, December 21, 1989; Herb Gamberg, by phone, October 25, 1990; Father Bernard Gilgun, Worcester, Mass., October 5, 1990; Allen Ginsberg (interview with Larry Smolen), New York City, January 15, 1990; Al Giordano, Huntington, Mass., October 20, 1990; John Giorno, New York City, December 20, 1989; Bob Greenblatt, Brooklyn, N.Y., December 20, 1990; Abbie Hoffman, New York City, December 12, 1983, and (interviews with Stuart Hutchison) Bucks County, Pa., December–January 1989; Anita Hoffman, Los Angeles, January 30 and February 1, 1990; Jack Hoffman, Worcester, Mass., October 19, 1989; Christine Kelly, New Brunswick, N.J., April 26, 1990; Marty Kenner, New York City, April 28, 1990; Paul Krassner, Los Angeles, January 30, 1990; Dr. Joel Kreps, Montreal, March 26, 1991; Gerry Lefcourt, New York City, April 27, 1990; Julius Lester, Amherst, Mass., November 6, 1989; Wolfe Lowenthal, New York City, April 29, 1990; Ellen Maslow, Boulder, Colo., January 28, 1990; Paul McIsaac, New York City, November 9, 1989; Gus Reichbach, New York City, April 25, 1990; Leslie Richardson and Jack Siemiatychi, Montreal, April 3, 1990; Ed Sanders, Woodstock, N.Y., November 12, 1989; Danny Schechter, New York City, December 19, 1989; Manny Schreiber, by phone, July 24, 1990; Rick Spencer, Thousand Islands, N.Y., May 27 and 28, 1990; Rich Torkelson, Mt. Pleasant, Pa., June 6, 1991; Mayer Vishner, New York City, November 9, 1989, and December 19, 1989.

INTRODUCTION

1. Ronald R. Fieve, M.D., *Moodswing* (New York: Bantam Books, 1975), 22.

ONE. "I NEVER LEFT WORCESTER"

1. Abbie and Anita Hoffman, *To america with Love: Letters from the Underground* (New York: Stonehill Press, 1976), 206.

2. Both *Revolution for the Hell of It* and *Woodstock Nation* are out of print (and seem to have been stolen from many library collections). They have, however, been reprinted in *The Best of Abbie Hoffman* (New York: Four Walls, Eight Windows, 1990). When quoting either of these books, I refer to page numbers in *The Best of Abbie Hoffman*.

3. Abbie Hoffman, interview with Harvey Wasserman, *New Age* (March 1983), 33.

4. Abbie Hoffman, interview with author.

5. James Yaffe, *The American Jews: Portrait of a Split Personality* (New York: Random House, 1968), 6–19. Although generous in their philanthropic aid to the eastern European Jewish immigrants, the German Jews considered them socially inferior. It was German Jews who coined the word *kike*, for example, as an expression of their disdain for the newcomers. Having themselves successfully assimilated into American life, they feared that the greenhorn immigrants would refocus attention on their own Jewishness.

6. Fred A. Bernstein, *The Jewish Mothers' Hall of Fame* (New York: Doubleday, 1986), 60–62.

7. Information about the Hoffman family in this chapter comes from my interview with Jack Hoffman.

8. Abbie Hoffman, *Soon to Be a Major Motion Picture* (New York: Perigee Books, G. P. Putnam's Sons, 1980), 2–10; James A. Gourgouras, "Heartache Real for Hoffmans," *Worcester Gazette*, October 8, 1968, 1; Abbie Hoffman, "I Remember Papa," *Boston Globe*, June 28, 1976, 19.

9. Jack Hoffman, interview with author.

10. Abbie Hoffman, interview with Stuart Hutchison.

11. Abbie Hoffman, *Major Motion Picture*, 13.

12. Abbie Hoffman, "I Remember Papa."

13. Leslie Richardson and Jack Siemiatychi, interview with author.

14. Abbie Hoffman, "I Remember Papa."

15. Abbie Hoffman, *Revolution*, in *Best of Abbie Hoffman*, 87: "I was always better at games than working. I was a Duncan Yo-Yo champion (remember the Filipino that came around with all the fancy tricks. He would carve initials in your yo-yo if you were good)." And, almost a dec-

ade later, from *Major Motion Picture*, 6: "I was a bowling maniac. I was a Duncan yo-yo champ at eleven. Could do a one-and-a-half somersault off a diving board and scramble like a rabbit on the basketball court."

16. Pauline Kael, capsule review of *Broken Arrow* in *The New Yorker*, August 6, 1990.

17. Abbie Hoffman, interview with Stuart Hutchison.

18. Abbie Hoffman, interview with Stuart Hutchison.

19. Bernstein, *Jewish Mothers' Hall of Fame*, 61.

20. Herb Gamberg, interview with author.

21. Abbott Hoffman, FBI file #176–6, dated 9/12/68.

22. Abbie Hoffman, *Revolution*, in *Best of Abbie Hoffman*, 88.

23. Mayer Vishner, interview with author.

24. Abbie Hoffman, *Major Motion Picture*, 20–21.

25. Jack Hoffman, interview with author; Abbie Hoffman, *Major Motion Picture*, 19.

26. Abbie Hoffman, interview with Stuart Hutchison; *Major Motion Picture*, 22–23.

TWO. BRANDEIS TO BERKELEY

1. Abbie Hoffman, interview with Stuart Hutchison; *Major Motion Picture*, 24.

2. Herb Gamberg, interview with author.

3. The quote is from Abbie Hoffman, *Major Motion Picture*, 26. Maslow's distaste for the politics Abbie represented is a frequent theme in his journals during the period from 1967 through 1970. See *The Journals of A. H. Maslow*, ed. Richard J. Lowry (Monterey, Calif.: Brooks/Cole Publishing, 1973). See the entries for 8/19/66 (pp. 748–749), 7/30/67 (p. 811), 9/6/67 (p. 825), 3/1/69 (p. 948), 5/25/69 (p. 964), and, e.g., 2/22/70 (p. 998): "The Chicago trial & its aftermaths, *big* riots in favor of these clowns, murderers, & rioters."

4. Edward Hoffman, *The Right to Be Human: A Biography of Abraham Maslow* (Los Angeles: Jeremy P. Tarcher, 1988), 207.

5. Abraham Maslow, quoted in Edward Hoffman, *The Right to Be Human*, 204.

6. Edward Hoffman, *The Right to Be Human*, 155.

7. Abbie Hoffman, interview with Stuart Hutchison.

8. Edward Hoffman, *The Right to Be Human*, 226. See also *Journals of A. H. Maslow*, 55–61.

9. Abbie Hoffman, interview with Stuart Hutchison; *Major Motion Picture*, 27.

10. Allen Wheelis, *The Quest for Identity* (New York: W. W. Norton, 1958), 91. Abbie first read the book at either Brandeis or Berkeley. In his

interview with Stuart Hutchison and in an interview with Harvey Blum (summer of 1988, transcript given to the author by Mark Rudd), he talks about the impact of the book on his thinking. My treatment of identity is drawn from Wheelis and thus parallels Abbie's own understanding of the subject.

11. Herb Gamberg, Ellen Maslow, and Manny Schreiber, interviews with author.

12. Irving Howe, "The Age of Conformity," in *Steady Work: Essays in the Politics of Democratic Radicalism 1953–1966* (New York: Harcourt, Brace & World, 1954, 1966), 317–318.

13. Abbie Hoffman, interview with author. Abbie made essentially the same point in "The Political Fallout of the Beat Generation," a speech delivered at the Naropa Institute, Boulder, Colo., August 1982.

14. Abbie Hoffman, interview with author.

15. Norman Mailer, "The White Negro," *Advertisements for Myself* (New York: Putnam, 1959), 337–358.

16. Marty Jezer, *The Dark Ages: Life in the United States, 1945–1960* (Boston: South End Press, 1982), 255.

17. Abbie Hoffman, interview with author.

18. Jack Hoffman, interview with author.

19. Abbie Hoffman, interview with author.

20. Ellen Maslow and Manny Schreiber, interviews with author.

21. Benny Avni, "An Interview with Abbie Hoffman," *Tikkun*, vol. 4, no. 4, 18.

22. Abbie Hoffman, interview with Stuart Hutchison.

23. Edward Hoffman, *The Right to Be Human*, 209–210, 212. See also Colin Wilson, *New Pathways in Psychology: Maslow and the Post-Freudian Revolution* (London: Victor Gollancz Ltd., 1972), 180–189. It can be argued that the Maslovian hierarchy of needs better explains the democratic upheavals in eastern Europe and the Soviet Union than does the Marxist theory of class struggle. Once people have their material needs assured, they want self-esteem (cultural identity) and self-actualization (democracy). The premises of that argument are outlined in the pages cited in Wilson above.

24. For discussion of SLATE and radical politics at Berkeley, see Michael Rossman, *The Wedding within the War* (New York: Doubleday/Anchor, 1971); Hal Draper, *Berkeley: The New Student Revolt* (New York, Grove Press, 1965); C. Michael Otten, *University Authority and the Student: The Berkeley Experience* (Berkeley: University of California Press, 1970); Max Heirich, *The Beginning: Berkeley 1964* (New York: Columbia University Press, 1968, 1970); and Milton Viorst, *Fire in the Street: America in the 1960's* (New York: Simon and Schuster, 1979).

25. Marty Kenner, interview with author; Abbie Hoffman, interview with author; *Major Motion Picture*, 37.

26. Rossman, *Wedding within the War*, 41. As a writer and activist, Rossman is a key figure in the history of Berkeley radicalism from 1960 to the present.

27. Rossman, *Wedding within the War*, 60–61.

28. Rossman, letter to author, August 18, 1990.

29. Abbie Hoffman, interview with Stuart Hutchison.

THREE. CIVIL RIGHTS WORKER

1. Abbie Hoffman, *Major Motion Picture*, 38–44. Sheila Hoffman declined to be interviewed for this book. The one published interview she has given about her life with Abbie is by Amy Zuckerman, "The Political Roots of Abbie Hoffman," *Worcester Magazine*, June 1989.

2. Abbie Hoffman, *Major Motion Picture*, 46–47.

3. Walter Goodman, *The Committee: The Extraordinary Career of the House Committee on Un-American Activities* (New York: Farrar, Straus and Giroux, 1968), 431.

4. Abbie Hoffman, *Major Motion Picture*, 48–49.

5. Jack Tubert, "Like Goddard, Hoffman Was Part of a New Frontier," *Worcester Telegram*, April 16, 1989.

6. Abbie Hoffman, *Major Motion Picture*, 56–57. According to Anita Hoffman, Abbie liked to tell this story about himself.

7. William D. Miller, *A Harsh and Dreadful Love: Dorothy Day and the Catholic Worker Movement* (New York: Liveright, 1973).

8. The letter was found, apparently unanswered, in the Abbie Hoffman folder, Allen Ginsberg papers, Butler Library, Columbia University.

9. Sheena Levy, letter to author, March 9, 1991.

10. Zuckerman, "Political Roots," 9.

11. Hank Chaiklin, interview with author; Chris Pope, "Recalling Hoffman, Idealist in Action," *Worcester Telegram*. April 14, 1989.

12. Zuckerman, "Political Roots." Father Gilgun confirms that Abbie devoted most of his working time to movement causes.

13. Abbie Hoffman, interview with Stuart Hutchison.

14. My discussion of SNCC is drawn primarily from Clayborne Carson, *In Struggle: SNCC and the Black Awakening* (Cambridge, Mass.: Harvard University Press, 1981); Doug McAdam, *Freedom Summer* (New York: Oxford University Press, 1988); Emily Stoper, *The Student Nonviolent Coordinating Committee: The Growth of Radicalism in a Civil Rights Organization* (Brooklyn, N.Y.: Carson Publishing, 1989); and Howard Zinn, *SNCC: The New Abolitionists* (Boston: Beacon Press, 1965).

15. Stoper, *Student Nonviolent Coordinating Committee*, 38–42. For Hoover's racism see Richard Gid Powers, *Secrecy and Power: The Life of J. Edgar Hoover* (New York: The Free Press, 1987), 367–373; and

David J. Garnow, *The F.B.I. and Martin Luther King, Jr.* (New York: W. W. Norton, 1981), 164–165.

16. Abbie Hoffman, *Major Motion Picture*, 66.

17. Rustin amplified his position in "From Protest to Politics: The Future of the Civil Rights Movement," *Commentary*, February 1965.

18. The account of the MFDP is drawn from Stoper, *Student Nonviolent Coordinating Committee*, 48–52; Carson, *In Struggle*, 123–128; and McAdam, *Freedom Summer*, 118–120, 130.

19. Stoper, *Student Nonviolent Coordinating Committee*, 277.

20. Abbie Hoffman, "The Press of Freedom," *Village Voice*, December 22, 1966.

21. The details of the Hoffmans' 1965 trip south are from Abbie's interview with Stuart Hutchison.

22. Ellen Maslow, interview with author.

23. Todd Gitlin, *The Sixties: Years of Hope, Days of Rage* (New York: Bantam Books, 1987), 168.

24. Abbie Hoffman, *The Drum*, April-May 1965, Civil Rights Collection, Worcester Public Library.

25. Abbie Hoffman, "The Press of Freedom," *Village Voice*, December 15 and 22, 1966.

26. Marty and Susan Carey, Anita Hoffman, and Danny Schecter, interviews with author. Dr. Howard Zinn, letter to author, April 17, 1992.

27. Nick Peck, interview with author.

28. Marty and Susan Carey, interview with author.

29. Martin A. Lee and Bruce Shlain, *Acid Dreams: The CIA, LSD, and the Sixties Rebellion* (New York: Grove Press, 1985).

30. Manny Schreiber, interview with author; Abbie Hoffman, *Major Motion Picture*, 72–75.

31. Marty and Susan Carey, interview with author; Abbie Hoffman, *Major Motion Picture*, 81.

FOUR. THE EAST VILLAGE

1. Anita Hoffman, interview with author.

2. Ellen Maslow, interview with author. See also *Journals of A. H. Maslow*, entry for June 6, 1966: "Economic arguments with her [Ellen Maslow] and Abby [sic] Hoffman, one of the SNCC boys." See also entries for July 30, 1967, and October 20, 1967.

3. For a fuller discussion of the sexism in the bohemian lifestyle see my essay "Patriarchy, the Great Underground Subculture and I," in *Men Against Sexism* (Albion, Calif.: Times Change Press, 1976); and Barbara Ehrenreich, *The Hearts of Men: American Dreams and the Flight from Commitment* (Garden City, N.Y.: Doubleday/Anchor, 1984).

4. Abbie Hoffman, *Major Motion Picture*, 91–92.

5. Abbie Hoffman, "Liberty House/Poor People's Corporation," *Liberation*, April 1967, 21.

6. James Dempsey, "A Punchy History of the 1960s," *Worcester Gazette*, March 12, 1985.

7. Anita Hoffman, interview with author.

8. Naomi Feigelson, *The Underground Revolution: Hippies, Yippies and Others* (New York: Funk & Wagnalls, 1970), 180–181; Abbie Hoffman, *Major Motion Picture*, 102.

9. Abbie Hoffman, "Read Any Good Books Lately?" *WIN*, June 1, 1968, 17.

10. Marshall Berman, Letter to the Editor, *Village Voice*, October 26, 1967.

11. Don McNeill, *Moving through Here* (New York: Knopf, 1970), 7–11.

12. McNeill, *Moving*, 99.

13. Howard Smith, "Scenes," *Village Voice*, June 15 and July 13, 1967.

14. Abbie Hoffman, interview with author.

15. Marty Carey, interview with author.

16. The most complete account of these actions is in the *Village Voice*. See Don McNeill, "Youthquake," June 8, 1967; "Scenes," June 15, August 10, and August 17, 1967; and "Love: A Groovy Idea While He Lasted," October 17, 1967.

17. Abbie Hoffman, *Major Motion Picture*, 97.

18. Feigelson, *Underground Revolution*, 11, 95–96; Abbie Hoffman, *Major Motion Picture*, 97; Jim Fouratt, interview with author.

19. Abbie Hoffman, *Major Motion Picture*, 95; Ed Sanders and Anita Hoffman, interviews with author.

20. Abbie Hoffman, *Major Motion Picture*, 99.

21. McNeill, *Moving*, 101; Al Giordano, interview with author.

22. Marlene Nadle, "Hippies in Newark: Loving a Ghetto," *Village Voice*, July 27, 1967, is a critical account of this action. Ann Douglas defended the Diggers in a letter to the *Village Voice*, August 3, 1967.

23. Abbie Hoffman, *Revolution*, in *Best of Abbie Hoffman*, 12; Anita Hoffman and Paul Krassner, interviews with author.

24. Abbie Hoffman, "Diggery is Niggery," *WIN*, September 15, 1967, 8–9.

FIVE. PROTESTING THE WAR

1. The delegation included Kay Boyle, Paul Goodman, Nat Hentoff, Dwight Macdonald, David McReynolds, William H. Meyer, and Harvey Swados. See Thomas Powers, *The War at Home* (New York: Grossman, 1973), 52.

2. Nancy Zaroulis and Gerald Sullivan, *Who Spoke Up? American*

Protest Against the War in Vietnam (Garden City, N.Y.: Doubleday, 1984), 78–79.

3. Powers, *War at Home*, 158.

4. For a history of the underground press see Abe Peck, *Uncovering the Sixties* (New York: Pantheon, 1985); and Robert J. Glessing, *The Underground Press in America* (Bloomington: Indiana University Press, 1970).

5. Abbie Hoffman, *Major Motion Picture*, 107–108. In this account Abbie confused the November 5, 1966, demonstration with the later and larger April 15, 1967, Spring Mobilization demonstration, which he also attended but which did not include a separate march of East Village hippies and bohemians.

6. Todd Gitlin, *The Whole World Is Watching: Mass Media in the Making and Unmaking of the New Left* (Berkeley: University of California Press, 1980), 113, 131.

7. Allen Ginsberg, "Berkeley Vietnam Days," *Liberation*, January 1966, 42–47.

8. Abbie Hoffman, *Major Motion Picture*, 90–91; David McReynolds, "An Open Letter to Richard Alpert," *WIN*, July 1967.

9. Zaroulis and Sullivan, *Who Spoke Up?* 114–116.

10. Anita Hoffman and Jim Fouratt, interviews with author; Joe Flaherty, "The Hawks in May," *Village Voice*, May 18, 1967. Abbie's account was carried by *WIN*, June 16, 1967, and reprinted in *Revolution*, in *Best of Abbie Hoffman*, 16. See also Abbie Hoffman, *Major Motion Picture*, 108.

11. Paul Krassner, interview with author.

12. Abbie Hoffman, *Major Motion Picture*, 83.

13. Julius Lester, interview with author.

14. Abbie Hoffman, "Elections, 1968," *WIN*, March 15, 1968, 5. See also Abbie Hoffman, *Major Motion Picture*, 242–250, an analysis written approximately ten years later.

15. Dale Lewis, "Digging the Diggers: The New Left at Bay," *Village Voice*, July 6, 1967. This is the most immediate account of the conference and describes Abbie's participation in the workshop on the hippies and the New Left. *The Best of Abbie Hoffman*, 22–25, contains Abbie's version; part of *Revolution for the Hell of It*, it was likely written six months later. Gitlin, in *The Sixties*, 225–231, gives a more comprehensive view of the conference and suggests that Abbie, in his account, exaggerated Grogan's violence. Abbie says nothing of this conference in *Major Motion Picture*. Likely, he was embarrassed by his enthusiastic response to Grogan's homophobia. See also Kirk Sale, *SDS* (New York: Random House, 1973), 347ff.

16. My account, "$$$," written under the name "George Washington," is in *WIN*, September 15, 1967, 9–10.

17. Details of Rubin's background are taken from J. Anthony Lukas, *Don't Shoot—We Are Your Children* (New York: Random House, 1971); and Jerry Rubin, *Growing (Up) at Thirty-Seven* (New York: M. Evans and Company, 1976).

18. Hillary Mills, *Mailer* (New York: Empire Books, 1982), 290–291; Abbie Hoffman, *Major Motion Picture*, 84.

19. Abbie Hoffman, *Major Motion Picture*, 128.

20. Jerry Rubin, *Do It!* (New York: Simon and Schuster, 1970), 66.

21. Quote from *Fuck You*, cited in entry for Ed Sanders, *Contemporary Authors*, new revision series, 13:448; Peck, *Uncovering the Sixties*, 15.

22. Allen Ginsberg, *Howl, Original Draft Facsimile . . .* , ed. Barry Miles (New York: Harper & Row, 1956, 1986), 128, 129.

23. Ed Sanders, interview with author; Allen Ginsberg, interview with Larry Smolen.

24. Powers, *War at Home*, 235; Fred Halstead; *Out Now! A Participant's Account of the American Movement against the Vietnam War* (New York: Monad Press, 1978), 315–316.

25. Marty Carey, interview with author.

26. Marty and Susan Carey, Anita Hoffman, Paul Krassner, interviews with author.

27. Abbie Hoffman, *Major Motion Picture*, 126; Halstead, *Out Now*, 314; Stew Albert and Bob Greenblatt, interviews with author.

28. The discussion of the Pentagon demonstration is drawn primarily from "The American Resistance" issue of *Liberation*, November 1967, which I helped edit and which includes my own article "Pentagon Confrontation." For Abbie's activities that weekend see Abbie Hoffman, *Major Motion Picture*, 129–136; and *Revolution*, in *Best of Abbie Hoffman*, 28–33. Also Marty and Susan Carey, Anita Hoffman, and Wolfe Lowenthal, interviews with author. I was at the Pentagon demonstration, was arrested during the wedge, and was with Abbie in prison.

29. James Reston, "Everyone Is a Loser," *New York Times*, October 23, 1967, 1, 32; Ben A. Franklin, "Foes of Pentagon Insist on Prison," *New York Times*, October 24, 1967, 8.

SIX. THE ROAD TO CHICAGO

1. Abbie Hoffman, *Revolution*, in *Best of Abbie Hoffman*, 5–6, 54. Paul Krassner, interview with author.

2. The story of the Key West trip is from Ellen Sander, *Trips* (New York: Charles Scribner's Sons, 1973), 124–128. Also Anita Hoffman and Paul Krassner, interviews with author.

3. The two most objective accounts of the beginning and evolution of Yippie are found in David Farber, *Chicago '68* (Chicago: The University

of Chicago Press, 1988); and Daniel Walker, *Rights in Conflict* (New York: Dutton, 1968).

4. Ed Sanders, interview with author.

5. Jason Epstein, *The Great Conspiracy Trial* (New York: Random House, 1970), 337.

6. Walker, *Rights in Conflict*, 87.

7. Jerry Rubin, "I Am the Walrus," *WIN*, February 15, 1968.

8. Abbie Hoffman, "Elections, 1968," 5.

9. Sally Kempton, "Yippies Anti-Organize a Groovy Revolution," *Village Voice*, March 21, 1968, 5ff.

10. Wolfe Lowenthal, interview with author.

11. David Dellinger et al., *The Conspiracy Trial*, transcript ed. Judy Clavir and John Spitzer (New York: Bobbs-Merrill, 1970), 295.

12. Rossman, *Wedding within the War*, 262–270.

13. Yip-in leaflet, in possession of author.

14. Marty Jezer, "Yip!" *WIN*, April 15, 1968, 2.

15. Abbie Hoffman, *Major Motion Picture*, 123.

16. Michael Stern, "Political Action New Hippie 'Thing,' " *New York Times*, March 24, 1968, 1, 72.

17. Abbie Hoffman, *Revolution*, in *Best of Abbie Hoffman*, 57. See also McNeill, *Moving*, 224–230; Feigelson, *Underground Revolution*, 163–168; and Farber, *Chicago '68*, 30–32.

18. The Lake Villa Conference is described in Farber, *Chicago '68*, 34–35, 87–92; Viorst, *Fire in the Street*, 446–447; and Zaroulis and Sullivan, *Who Spoke Up?* 176–177.

19. Farber, *Chicago '68*, 90.

20. Farber, *Chicago '68*, 89.

21. Bob Greenblatt, interview with author. In the winter of 1990 and 1991 the lack of public toilets became an issue in New York. Homeless people had no place to go to the bathroom, and many people were decrying that the city was beginning to smell like a urinal.

22. Farber, *Chicago '68*, 35.

23. Abbie Hoffman, *Revolution*, in *Best of Abbie Hoffman*, 56.

24. Powers, *War at Home*, 285.

25. Abbie Hoffman, "Elections, 1968," 4–5.

26. Charles Kaiser, *1968 in America: Music, Politics, Chaos, Counterculture, and the Shaping of a Generation* (New York: Weidenfeld & Nicolson, 1988), 122–126; Stanley Karnow, *Vietnam: A History* (New York: Penguin, 1984), 561–564; Gitlin, *The Sixties*, 303–304.

27. Clark Clifford, "Annals of Government," *New Yorker*, May 13, 1991, 70.

28. Farber, *Chicago '68*, 94.

29. Clifford, "Annals of Government," 78.

30. Kaiser, *1968 in America*, 83–84, 85.

31. Theodore H. White, *The Making of the President 1968* (New York: Antheneum, 1969), 263. White, who from Nixon to Humphrey to Lyndon Johnson to Chou En-lai never met a powerful political figure he did not like, neither liked nor understood popular movements that challenged established authority. His account distorts the antiwar movement's purpose and presence in Chicago.

32. Farber, *Chicago '68*, 95.

33. Peck, *Uncovering the Sixties*, 106–107.

34. Abbie Hoffman, *Major Motion Picture*, 140; Tom Hayden, *Reunion: A Memoir* (New York: Random House, 1988), 276.

35. Editorial in *Fortune*, June 1968, cited by Sale, *SDS*, 443.

36. Farber, *Chicago '68*, 48–49.

SEVEN. CHICAGO

1. Lewis Chester, Godfrey Hodgson, and Bruce Page, *An American Melodrama: The Presidential Campaign of 1988* (New York: Viking, 1969), 517.

2. Farber, *Chicago '68*, 170.

3. Farber, *Chicago '68*, 257.

4. David Lewis Stein, *Living the Revolution: The Yippies in Chicago* (New York: Bobbs-Merrill, 1969), 38.

5. Farber, *Chicago '68*, 166.

6. Dellinger et al., *Conspiracy Trial*, 374; Also, recall Abbie's comments in chapter four at note 19. But for examples of his saying "pig" at Chicago see *Revolution*, in *Best of Abbie Hoffman*, 69.

7. Barry Miles, *Ginsberg: A Biography* (New York: Simon & Schuster, 1989), 414–415.

8. Farber, *Chicago '68*, 173–174; Stein, *Living the Revolution*, 60.

9. Farber, *Chicago '68*, 175; Stein, *Living the Revolution*, 63.

10. Dellinger et al., *Conspiracy Trial*, 360–361.

11. Farber, *Chicago '68*, 187.

12. Farber, *Chicago '68*, 188.

13. Abbie's "rap" was taped and played on WBAI. It was transcribed and published in *The Movement toward a New America* (Knopf and Pilgrim Press, 1970), an anthology of movement writings edited by Mitchell Goodman, and in Stein's *Living the Revolution*.

14. The account of his arrest and beating is drawn from Stein, *Living the Revolution*, 123; Abbie Hoffman, *Revolution*, in *Best of Abbie Hoffman*, 66–68; *Major Motion Picture*, 159–160; and from Paul Krassner and Anita Hoffman.

15. Anita Hoffman, interview with author.

16. Zaroulis and Sullivan, *Who Spoke Up?* 199.

17. Farber, *Chicago '68*, 200.

18. Farber, *Chicago '68*, 199–201.

19. Viorst, *Fire in the Street*, 459.

20. Abbie Hoffman, *Revolution*, in *Best of Abbie Hoffman*, 68.

21. Abbie Hoffman, *Revolution*, in *Best of Abbie Hoffman*, 66–70. The author was in this aborted march.

EIGHT. GIVING UP ON AMERICA

1. Abbie Hoffman, *Revolution*, in *Best of Abbie Hoffman*, 82–83.

2. Sale, *SDS*, 489.

3. Carol Brightman and Julius Lester, interviews with author; phone conversation with Lewis Cole, May 1990; letter to author from Mark Rudd, January 15, 1990.

4. This analysis is drawn from Paul Joseph, *Cracks in the Empire* (Boston: South End Press, 1982).

5. "YIPanther Pact," *Rat*, October 18–31, 1968.

6. Abbie Hoffman, interview, in *Our Time: An Anthology of Interviews from the East Village Other*, ed. Allen Katzman (New York: Dial, 1969).

7. Farber, *Chicago '68*, 206.

8. Frank Donner, *The Age of Surveillance* (New York: Knopf, 1980), 313. The Stone quote is from *I. F. Stone Weekly*, January 27, 1969.

9. Charles DeBenedetti, *An American Ordeal: The Antiwar Movement of the Vietnam Era* (Syracuse: Syracuse University Press, 1990), 244.

10. Martin Jezer in *WIN*, November 15, 1968, 4. Cited in DeBenedetti, 230.

11. Al Giordano and Anita Hoffman, interviews with author; Pat McNeil (Abbie Hoffman), Letters, *Time*, January 3, 1969.

12. George Demmerle, press interview, *Rat*, June 5–19, 1970.

13. Gerry Lefcourt, interview with author.

14. Abbie Hoffman, *Major Motion Picture*, 183–184.

15. Abbie Hoffman, *Woodstock Nation*, in *Best of Abbie Hoffman*, 100.

16. Abbie Hoffman, *The Rat*, undated, late 1969. The author was at this demonstration.

NINE. THE TRIAL

1. Dellinger et al., *Conspiracy Trial*, 602.

2. Dave Dellinger, *More Power Than We Know* (Garden City, N.Y.: Doubleday, 1975), 277.

3. Epstein, *Great Conspiracy Trial*, 86.

4. Eleanor Lester, "Is Abbie Hoffman the Will Shakespeare of the 1970s?" *New York Times*, October 11, 1970, D3.

5. Epstein, *Great Conspiracy Trial*, 256.

6. Epstein, *Great Conspiracy Trial*, 146.

7. Epstein, *Great Conspiracy Trial*, 215.

8. Abbie Hoffman, *Major Motion Picture*, 199.

9. Dwight Macdonald, *The Tales of Hoffman* (New York: Bantam Books, 1970), xxiii-xxiv.

10. Dellinger et al., *Conspiracy Trial*, 344.

11. Dellinger, et al., *Conspiracy Trial*, 529; Dellinger, letter to author, August 9, 1991.

12. Epstein, *Great Conspiracy Trial*, 400.

13. Hayden, *Reunion*, 396–397.

14. William Kunstler, "What Abbie Taught Us," speech at the Learning Alliance, New York, June 1, 1990.

15. Abbie Hoffman, interview with Stuart Hutchison.

16. John Murray Cuddihy, *The Ordeal of Civility: Freud, Marx, Levi-Strauss, and the Jewish Struggle with Modernity* (New York: Basic Books, 1974), 190.

17. Ken Hurwitz, *Marching Nowhere* (New York: W. W. Norton, 1971), 191–197.

18. Abbie Hoffman, "Freedom and License," in *Conspiracy*, ed. Peter and Deborah Babcock and Bob Abel (New York: Dell, 1969), 43–44.

TEN. LAST HURRAH

1. John Kyper, Letter to *WIN*, October 15, 1971, 32.

2. Dellinger, *More Power Than We Know*, 142; Zaroulis and Sullivan, *Who Spoke Up?* 323–328; Abbie Hoffman, *Major Motion Picture*, 251–252.

3. Marty and Susan Carey and Anita Hoffman, interviews with author.

4. Peck, *Uncovering the Sixties*, 209.

5. Robin Morgan, *Sisterhood Is Powerful* (New York: Vintage Books, 1970), 538.

6. Judith Hole and Ellen Levine, *Rebirth of Feminism* (New York: Quadrangle Books, 1971), 123–124.

7. Betty Freidan, *The Feminine Mystique* (New York: W. W. Norton, 1963), 69.

8. Jeff Nightbyrd, "Love and Pain in the Underground," *Austin Sun*, December 11, 1973.

9. Anita Hoffman, Paul McIsaac, and Ellen Maslow, interviews with author.

10. Abbie Hoffman, *Major Motion Picture*, 280–281.

11. "The Sixties," PBS television documentary. For another blatant example see Abbie Hoffman, *Revolution*, in *Best of Abbie Hoffman*, 22–24.

12. Abbie Hoffman, interview with Stuart Hutchison.

13. Abbie Hoffman, *Steal This Book*, reissue edition (Worcester, Mass.: Contemporary Classics, 1972). Much of the text is reprinted in *Best of Abbie Hoffman*.

14. Peck, *Uncovering the Sixties*, 186. Abe Peck's description of Forcade meshes with my own recollection of him.

15. Craig Karpel, "Steal This Court," *WIN*, November 11, 1971.

16. Abbie Hoffman, *Steal This Book*, reissue edition, xviii.

17. For an example see David Cortright, *The American Military Today* (Garden City, N.Y.: Doubleday/Anchor 1975), 67–68.

18. John Giorno and Mayer Vishner, interviews with author.

19. Abbie Hoffman, "I Quit," *WIN*, September 1, 1971.

20. Abbie Hoffman, *Major Motion Picture*, 270.

21. Abbie Hoffman, Jerry Rubin, and Ed Sanders, *Vote!* (New York: Warner Paperback Library, 1972), 43.

22. Hoffman, Rubin, and Sanders, *Vote!*, 57.

23. Hoffman, Rubin, and Sanders, *Vote!*, 150–151.

24. Hoffman, Rubin, and Sanders, *Vote!*, 37–38. See also Nora Sayre, *Sixties Going on Seventies* (New York: Arbor House, 1973), 373–410.

25. Abbie Hoffman, *Major Motion Picture*, 278.

26. Hoffman, Rubin, and Sanders, *Vote!*, 60.

ELEVEN. REBEL WITHOUT A CAUSE

1. Marty and Susan Carey, interview with author.

2. Letter from Abbie Hoffman to Joan Crawford, August 25, 1973.

3. My account of Abbie's coke bust is based on interviews with Anita Hoffman, Gerry Lefcourt, Paul McIsaac, Gus Reichbach, and Mayer Vishner.

4. "Letter," *WIN*, September 13, 1973. The author, then an editor of *WIN*, drafted the letter and was one of its signers.

5. Abbie Hoffman, *The Rat*, undated (late December 1969).

6. Jeff Jones, interview with author.

7. "Talk of the Town," *New Yorker*, May 6, 1974.

8. "Talk of the Town," *New Yorker*, May 6, 1974.

9. Anita Hoffman and Mayer Vishner, interviews with author.

10. Anita Hoffman, interview with author.

11. Abbie and Anita Hoffman, *To america with Love*, 1.

12. Abbie and Anita Hoffman, *To america with Love*, 32.

13. Abbie and Anita Hoffman, *To america with Love*, 29.

14. Abbie Hoffman, *Square Dancing in the Ice Age* (Boston: South End Press, 1982), 184–185.

15. Abbie and Anita Hoffman, *To america with Love*, 13–14.

16. Abbie and Anita Hoffman, *To america with Love*, 31.

17. Abbie and Anita Hoffman, *To america with Love*, 200.

18. Abbie and Anita Hoffman, *To america with Love*, 176–177.

19. Abbie and Anita Hoffman, *To america with Love*, 166–167, 188.

20. Kay Gardella, review of "In Hiding" in *New York Daily News*, May 19, 1975; John J. O'Connor, review of "In Hiding" in *New York Times*, May 19, 1975; Stew Albert, review of "In Hiding" in *WIN*, June 19, 1975.

21. Abbie Hoffman, "Breaking Control and Getting In Tune," taped speech intended for a conference of the Prairie Fire Organizing Committee, late summer 1975, printed in *Berkeley Barb*, December 19–25, 1975, 5.

22. Abbie Hoffman, *Major Motion Picture*, 250.

23. Mayer Vishner, interview with author.

24. My account of Abbie in Montreal is drawn from my interviews with Dr. Joel Kreps, Leslie Richardson, and Jack Siemiatychi.

25. Marty Kenner, Rick Spencer, and Mayer Vishner, interviews with author.

26. Jack Tubert, "Say, Dear, Wasn't that Abbie Hoffman," *Worcester Telegram*, November 11, 1979; Paul Krassner, interview with author; Paul Krassner, "Abbie," *The Nation*, May 8, 1989, 617–618.

TWELVE. CAPTURE THE FLAG

1. Abbie Hoffman, "My Life as a Fugitive," *Parade*, December 14, 1980, quoted in *Watertown Daily Times*, December 15, 1980, 10.

2. Abbie Hoffman, "The Great St. Lawrence River War," in *Best of Abbie Hoffman*, 350; originally published in *Square Dancing in the Ice Age*.

3. Rick Spencer, interview with author, and Rick Spencer, "What Abbie Taught Us," speech at the Learning Alliance, New York, June 1, 1990.

4. Abbie Hoffman, "St. Lawrence River War," in *Best of Abbie Hoffman*, 352.

5. Richard Kleiner and Lawrence Wechsler, "Going for Broke," interview with Abbie Hoffman, *L.A. Weekly*, September 26–October 2, 1980, 7.

6. The full account of Abbie's surrender is in the *Watertown Daily Times*, September 3 and 4, 1980. The Walters quote is in Marsha J. Davis, "Walters Story on Hoffman 'Shrinks' Wellesley Island," *Watertown Daily Times*, September 4, 1980.

7. "Hoffman Announces School," *Watertown Daily Times*, September 25, 1980.

8. Thomas J. Martello, "1,300 Cheer Abbie Hoffman in Syracuse," *Watertown Daily Times*, October 9, 1980.

9. Abbie Hoffman, interview with Stuart Hutchison.

10. Thomas J. Martello, "Can Save River Survive Rift," *Watertown Daily Times*, July 20, 1982, 9.

11. Thomas J. Martello, "Hoffman Bows Out of North Spotlight," *Watertown Daily Times*, August 10, 1982.

12. Paul MacClennan, "Hiring of Ex-Yippie Throws Parley on Great Lakes into an Uproar, *Buffalo Evening News*, May 24, 1982.

13. My description of the pump station battle is drawn from John Seabrook, "Abbie Hoffman's Last Stand," *7 Days*, May 17, 1989, 22ff.; from my interviews with Al Giordano and Rich Torkelson; from Fred Duke and Tracy Carluccio, "What Abbie Taught Us," speeches at the Learning Alliance, New York, June 1, 1990; and from *Citizens Voice*, Del-AWARE's newspaper.

14. *Bucks County Courier Times*, April 14, 1989, A9.

15. Seabrook, "Abbie Hoffman's Last Stand," 25.

THIRTEEN. FINAL BATTLES

1. Christine Kelly, interview with author.

2. David Corn, "The Abbie & Jerry Show," *Mother Jones*, February/March 1985, 16.

3. Linda Allnock, "Yippie vs. Yuppie," *Watertown Daily Times*, January 30, 1985; Corn, "The Abbie & Jerry Show," 16–17.

4. Avni, "Interview with Abbie Hoffman," 18.

5. Julius Lester, interview with the author.

6. Avni, "Interview with Abbie Hoffman," 17.

7. Abbie Hoffman, letter to Anita Hoffman, postmarked August 27, 1985.

8. Abbie Hoffman, "The Young Have to Be There" (1986), in *Best of Abbie Hoffman*, 380–382. A similar sentiment is in his letter to Anita Hoffman, postmarked August 27, 1985.

9. Michael D. Klemens, "Hoffman's Recruiting Thousand," *Watertown Daily Times*, January 28, 1985.

10. Betty Tomlinson, "What Abbie Taught Us," speech at the Learning Alliance, New York, June 1, 1990.

11. Abbie Hoffman, "Closing Argument," reprinted in *The Nation*, May 2, 1987; *Harper's Magazine*, July 1987; *Best of Abbie Hoffman*, 384–387.

12. Ellen Maslow, interview with author.

13. Seabrook, "Abbie Hoffman's Last Stand," 27.

14. Abbie Hoffman and Jonathan Silvers, "An Election Held Hostage," *Playboy*, October 1988.

15. Mark Hertgaard, "Steal This Decade," *Mother Jones*, June 1990, 34.

16. Paula Span, "Abbie Hoffman Takes Jabs to Comedy Stage," *Washington Post News Service*, September 4, 1988.

17. Abbie Hoffman, letter to Allen Ginsberg, December 1988, Ginsberg papers.

18. Natalie Angier, "Eli Lilly Facing Million-Dollar Suits on Its Antidepressant Prozac," *New York Times*, August 16, 1990, B13.

19. Abbie Hoffman, "Where Do We Go from Here," in *Best of Abbie Hoffman*, 375–379; Abbie Hoffman, interview with Stuart Hutchison; Betty Tomlinson, "What Abbie Taught Us"; Al Giordano, Christine Kelly, and Rich Torkelson, interviews with author.

20. Abbie Hoffman, "Where Do We Go from Here," in *Best of Abbie Hoffman*, 339.

21. Mark Rudd, "Sixties' Lesson: Guilt-motivated Militancy Can Be Dangerous," *The Guardian*, January 18, 1989, 19; Abbie Hoffman, "Hoffman to Rudd: Don't Apologize," *The Guardian*, February 22, 1989, 19.

22. Abbie Hoffman, *Major Motion Picture*, 105.

Index

Baez, Joan, 27, 76
Bailey, D'Army, 51–52
Ball, George, 95, 138
ban the bomb movement, 34, 35, 37,
    44, 46, 49, 64, 83
Bay of Pigs, 48
beat generation, 28–30, 36, 74
Beatles, The, 79, 215; "Revolver," 73;
    "Sergeant Pepper," 97; "Yellow
    Submarine," 97, 99
beatniks, 14, 75, 97, 114, 150. *See
    also* beat generation
Beck, Julian, 249
Becker, Norma, 249
be-ins, 81–83, 85, 86, 87, 102, 123,
    131
Berg, Peter, 86, 109–110
Berkeley: The Sixties (documentary
    film), 177n
Berkeley, University of California at,
    13, 35–37
Berkeley Vietnam Day Commitee
    (VDC), 98–99, 113, 150
Berman, Marshall, 82
Berrigan, Philip, 249
Bible, The (film), 122
black Americans, 18–19, 30, 92, 137,
    140. *See also* Negroes
black liberation movement, 191
black music, 18–19, 27, 29, 76, 78
black nationalism, 66–67
Black Panther party, 123–124, 154–
    155, 164, 177–178, 184, 200, 202,
    218–220, 254
black power, 52n, 78, 109
Bloom, Marshall, 133
blues, 27
bohemianism, 14, 25, 30, 37, 45, 73,
    75, 76; in America, 27–28; at Bran-
    deis, 26–28, 31; in Europe, 26–27;
    hip underground, 74–75, 79, 135–
    136, 183; Irving Howe on, 28–29; in
    New York, 74–75, 83, 183; and po-
    litical left, 75; sexism of, 73. *See
    also* beat generation; countercul-
    ture; hippies

Bond, Julian, 59, 168, 203
Bookchin, Murray (Lewis Herber),
    128n, 212
Born on the 4th of July (film), 304
Borscht Belt, 5–6, 30, 207
Boston Celtics, 10
Boston College, 10, 50
Boston Red Sox, 6, 10, 44, 122, 259
Brandeis University, 8, 13, 16, 19,
    20–21, 25, 49, 62; faculty, 21; his-
    tory, 20–21; Abbie Hoffman at, 20,
    21–26, 31, 32, 34, 45, 206; politics
    at, 33–34, 35
Brando, Marlon, 14
Bread and Puppet Theater, 83, 97, 99
Bremer, Arthur, 239, 257–258
Brennan, Peter, 216
Bridges, Harry, 39, 41
Broken Arrow (film), 11, 18
Bronstein, Leo, 21
Brooke, Senator Edward, 68
Broonzy, Big Bill, 27
Brown, Governor Edmund (Pat), 38
Brown, H. Rap, 115, 198
Brown, James, 62
Bruce, Lenny, 30–31, 36, 209
Buckley, William, 73, 277
Burlage, Rob, 48
Burroughs, William, 165
Bush, George, 302

capital punishment, 35, 37–38
Carey, Governor Hugh, 273, 274
Carey, Marty, 68–69, 87, 88, 116–
    117, 215, 260, 286
Carey, Susan, 68–70, 88, 215, 286
Carluccio, Terry, 288
Carmichael, Stokely, 198
Carson, Johnny, 215
Carson, Rachel, 128n
Carter, Amy, 295
Carter, Jimmy, 264, 301–302
Carter, Reuben "Hurricane," 243
Castro, Fidel, 48, 122, 261
Catholic Worker movement, 34, 49,
    64, 72, 83

Hog Farm, 153–154
Holy Cross College, 10, 49, 52, 67, 265
homophobia, 110, 128, 160, 225–226
homosexuality, 30, 128. *See also* gay liberation movement
Hoods, The (Harry Grey), 15
Hoover, J. Edgar, 115, 239; and civil rights movement, 55, 57; and Kennedy administration, 55
Horney, Karen, 25
House Committee on Un-American Activities (HUAC), 27, 38–41, 43–44, 102; and Abbie Hoffman, xiii, 40, 185–187; and Jerry Rubin, 113, 126, 185; San Francisco hearings (1960), 38–41, 43–44; Yippies and Mobe (1968), 185–187
House, Linn, 85, 106
Howe, Irving, 21, 28–29, 33
HUAC, *see* House Committee on Un-American Activities
Hughes, Supreme Court Justice Charles Evans, 46
Hughes, H. Stuart, 46–48, 68, 109
humanist psychology, 22, 25
human potential movement, 240
Humphrey, Hubert: and anti-Vietnam War movement, 175, 180; Democratic national convention, 1964, 57–60; election of 1968, 143, 144, 146, 149, 167n, 168, 172, 174–175, 178, 179–180; election of 1972, 234; and Vietnam War, 95
Hurwitz, Ken, 211
Huxley, Aldous, 256
hypomania, *see* Hoffman, Abbie, bipolar disorder

identity, discussion of, 25–26, 75
I Hear America Talking (Stuart Berg Flexner), 124n
Internal Revenue Service (IRS), 184, 185, 243
Iran, 12. *See also* October Surprise
Iran-Contra, 290

Irish Republican Army, 278
Israel, 256–257

Jackson, Senator Henry "Scoop," 138
Jackson, James Lee, 60
Jackson, Jesse, 203, 293
Jade Companion Bail Fund, 83, 100
Janiger, Dr. Oscar, 265
jazz, 27, 75
Jefferson Airplane, 76, 81, 202, 215
Jim and Jean (folksingers), 160
John XXIII, pope, 49
John Birch Society, 53
Johnson, Dean, 152–153
Johnson, Lyndon Baines, 6, 113, 164–166, 198; and anti-Vietnam War movement, 114, 144, 185n; 1964 election, 57–58, 60; 1968 election, 123, 136–139, 174–175; Vietnam policy, 68, 93–95, 101, 102, 121, 138, 140, 146, 180, 240
Jones, Jeff, 251, 258
Joplin, Janis, 129
Journal of Humanistic Psychology, 25
Judaism, 15, 41; anti-Semitism, 6–8, 20, 21, 49, 167, 208; assimilation, issue of, 6–9; and blacks, 293; and conspiracy trial, 205–208; German Jews, 3, 208, 312n5; in New York, 5–6; philanthropy of, 8–9, 20–21; quotas, 6–7, 20; Russian Jews, 2; in Worcester, 5–7, 51; Yiddish language, 7, 237–238; and Yippies, 236–238
juvenile delinquency, 13, 15, 29

Kael, Pauline, 11
Kahane, Rabbi Meir, 256
Kantner, Paul, 215
Karpel, Craig, 229–230
Kelly, Christine, 297–300, 303, 308
Kelly, Ken, 260
Kempton, Murray, 169
Kempton, Sally, 127
Kennedy, Senator Edward "Ted," 46–48